Available!

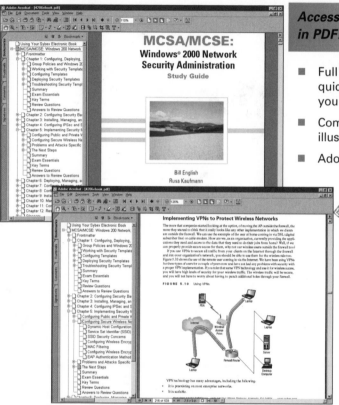

Access the entire book in PDF!

- Full search capabilities let you quickly find the information you need.

- Complete with tables and illustrations.

- Adobe Acrobat Reader included.

Reinforce understanding of key topics with flashcards for your PC, Pocket PC, or Palm handheld!

- Contains over 150 flashcard questions.

- Runs on multiple platforms for usability and portability.

- Quiz yourself anytime, anywhere!

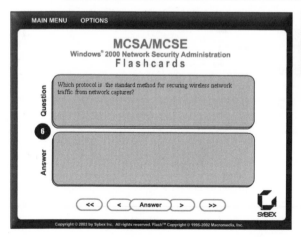

SYBEX

MCSA/MCSE: Windows® 2000 Network Security Administration Study Guide

SYBEX

Exam 70-214

OBJECTIVE	CHAPTER

Exam objectives are subject to change at any time without prior notice and at Microsoft's sole discretion. Please visit Microsoft's website (www.microsoft.com/traincert) for the most current listing of exam objectives.

SYBEX

MCSA/MCSE:
Windows 2000 Network Security Administration
Study Guide

MCSA/MCSE:
Windows® 2000 Network Security Administration
Study Guide

Bill English

Russ Kaufmann

San Francisco • London

Associate Publisher: Neil Edde
Acquisitions Editor: Jeff Kellum
Developmental Editor: Colleen Wheeler Strand
Production Editor: Dennis Fitzgerald
Technical Editors: Andy Barkl, Goga Kukrika
Copyeditor: Pat Coleman
Compositor: Interactive Composition Corporation
Graphic Illustrator: Interactive Composition Corporation
CD Coordinator: Dan Mummert
CD Technician: Kevin Ly
Proofreaders: Emily Hsuan, Darcey Maurer, Nancy Riddiough, Monique van den Berg
Indexer: Nancy Guenther
Book Designer: Bill Gibson
Cover Designer: Archer Design
Cover Illustrator/Photographer: Georgette, Douwma, FPG Int'l

Library of Congress Card Number: 2003100046

ISBN: 0-7821-4206-0

SYBEX

To Our Valued Readers:

Thank you for looking to Sybex for your Microsoft certification exam prep needs. We at Sybex are proud of the reputation we've established for providing certification candidates with the practical knowledge and skills needed to succeed in the highly competitive IT marketplace.

Sybex is proud to have helped thousands of MCSA and MCSE certification candidates prepare for their exams over the years, and we are excited about the opportunity to continue to provide computer and networking professionals with the skills they'll need to succeed in today's highly competitive IT industry.

The Sybex team of authors, editors, and technical reviewers have worked hard to ensure that this Study Guide is comprehensive, in-depth, and pedagogically sound. We're confident that this book, along with the collection of cutting-edge software study tools included on the CD, will meet and exceed the demanding standards of the certification marketplace and help you, the Microsoft certification exam candidate, succeed in your endeavors.

Good luck in pursuit of your Microsoft certification!

Neil Edde
Associate Publisher—Certification
Sybex, Inc.

Software License Agreement: Terms and Conditions

Acknowledgments

As with every book I've worked on, there are many more people whose efforts are reflected in these pages but whose names are not on the cover. Without their help, this book would not be in your hands. At Sybex, I'd like to thank Jeff Kellum and Colleen Strand for their work and patience in seeing this book through to its completion. Both were flexible and yet focused on getting this book done on time. Dennis Fitzgerald worked hard to ensure the production portion of this book went well. In addition, Colleen offered timely advice and assistance when it was needed. Our technical editors, Andy Barkl and Goga Kukrika ensured this manuscript was free of technical errors. Of course, any mistakes in the book belong to Russ or I, not to Andy, Goga, or any of the editors.

I'd also like to thank my co-author, Russ Kaufmann, who came into this project after it started and did a bang-up job with his chapters even though he experienced several setbacks that were out of his control. Russ, thanks for writing this book with me and for being such a good friend. I would be honored to work with you again.

Neil Salkind, my agent from StudioB, did his usual great job in pulling together the contractual elements that enabled me to co-author this book. Thanks, Neil, for being such an outstanding agent.

As always, my wife Kathy supported me in this project. Thanks Kathy, for your love and friendship.

Finally, I'd like to thank Jesus Christ, who gave me the talent and opportunity to write this book and without whom I'd be lost forever.

Bill English
Nowthen, Minnesota
February 2003

Fire, flood, and blood. It seems like anything that could have gone wrong did go wrong while working with Bill to write this book. Yet, somehow, with Bill's guidance, and the great work of the editing team, it all came out well. I want to thank everyone on the team for pulling together to make it all happen. This was definitely a team effort! Everyone on the team deserves a few cheers of gratitude: Bill English, Jeff Kellum, Colleen Strand, Dennis Fitzgerald, Pat Coleman, Andy Barkl, and Goga Kukrika.

Although I have been a technical editor for several books over the last few years, this is my first book as a named author. It is definitely a different experience, and it is incredibly challenging. Without Bill English being involved, I would have never taken this on. I owe a very special thanks to Bill. I really hope that I have the opportunity to work with him again in the future. Not only is he a colleague that I admire, he is a friend that I can depend on again and again.

Ben Smith and David Lowe were extremely helpful during this process. Whenever I was not exactly sure what they were looking for with the test objectives, they each took the time to help out. Ben was extremely helpful during the process. David, while not directly involved in answering my questions, was a great conduit to information. Without his help, I would have had to spend several hours hunting down some answers.

Another person that deserves his own paragraph in the acknowledgments is Brian Komar. You should recognize Brian from his many contributions to our community: TechNet articles, Microsoft Official Courseware contributions, MEC and TechEd speeches, and several books. Brian was extremely helpful. I definitely owe him a favor; however, I think I am repaying that favor right now with another project that is in progress. Actually, Brian, I think you owe me one now!

There are others that deserve acknowledgment for this project even through they did not do any of the work. My family helped in so many ways that I cannot name them all. My special thanks go to my wife of almost 20 years, Annabelle, and my two children, David and Eric. Without their support, I would never have completed my part of this project.

This book has been a great experience for me, and I have to thank everyone involved for its success. I hope to have a chance to work with all of you again in the future.

Russ Kaufmann
Westminster, Colorado
February 2003

Contents at a Glance

Contents

Table of Exercises

Introduction

The Microsoft Certified Systems Associate (MCSA) and Microsoft Certified Systems Engineer (MCSE) tracks for Windows 2000 are the premier certification for computer industry professionals. Covering the core technologies around which Microsoft's future will be built, the MCSE program is a powerful credential for career advancement.

This book has been developed to give you the critical skills and knowledge you need to prepare for one of the elective requirements of the MCSE certification program: *Implementing and Administering Security in a Microsoft Windows 2000 Network* (Exam 70-214).

As security becomes more and more important in today's network infrastructure, our abilities to design and implement security using Microsoft's operating systems grow in importance as well. In the future, it may very well be that significant career advancement will be tethered to how well you understand security issues.

The Microsoft Certified Professional Program

Since the inception of its certification program, Microsoft has certified almost 1.5 million people. As the computer network industry grows in both size and complexity, this number is sure to grow—and the need for *proven* ability will also increase. Companies rely on certifications to verify the skills of prospective employees and contractors.

Microsoft has developed its Microsoft Certified Professional (MCP) program to give you credentials that verify your ability to work with Microsoft products effectively and professionally. Obtaining your MCP certification requires that you pass any one Microsoft certification exam. Several levels of certification are available based on specific suites of exams. Depending on your areas of interest or experience, you can obtain any of the following MCP credentials:

Microsoft Certified System Administrator (MCSA)   The MCSA certification is the latest certification track from Microsoft. This certification targets system and network administrators with roughly 6 to 12 months of desktop and network administration experience. The MCSA can be considered the entry-level certification. You must take and pass a total of four exams to obtain your MCSA.

Microsoft Certified Systems Engineer (MCSE) on Windows 2000   This certification track is designed for network and systems administrators, network and systems analysts, and technical consultants who work with Microsoft Windows 2000 Professional and Server and/or Windows XP Professional. You must take and pass seven exams to obtain your MCSE.

Microsoft Certified Application Developer (MCAD)   This track is designed for application developers and technical consultants who primarily use Microsoft development tools. Currently, you can take exams on Visual Basic .NET or Visual C# .NET. You must take and pass three exams to obtain your MCAD.

Microsoft Certified Solution Developer (MCSD)   This track is designed for software engineers and developers and technical consultants who primarily use Microsoft development tools. Currently, you can take exams on Visual Basic .NET and Visual C# .NET. You must take and pass five exams to obtain your MCSD.

Microsoft Certified Database Administrator (MCDBA)   This track is designed for database administrators, developers, and analysts who work with Microsoft SQL Server. As of this printing, you can take exams on either SQL Server 7 or SQL Server 2000. You must take and pass four exams to achieve MCDBA status.

Microsoft Certified Trainer (MCT)   The MCT track is designed for any IT professional who develops and teaches Microsoft-approved courses. To become an MCT, you must first obtain your MCSE, MCSD, or MCDBA; then you must take a class at one of the Certified Technical Training Centers. You will also be required to prove your instructional ability. You can do this in various ways: by taking a skills-building or train-the-trainer class, by achieving certification as a trainer from any of several vendors, or by becoming a Certified Technical Trainer through CompTIA. Last of all, you will need to complete an MCT application.

How Do You Become an MCSA or MCSE on Windows 2000?

Attaining any MCP certification has always been a challenge. In the past, students have been able to acquire detailed exam information—even most of the exam questions—from online "brain dumps" and third-party "cram" books or software products. For the new Microsoft exams, this is simply not the case.

Microsoft has taken strong steps to protect the security and integrity of the MCSA and MCSE tracks. Now, prospective students must complete a course of study that develops detailed knowledge about a wide range of topics. It supplies them with the true skills needed, derived from working with Windows 2000 and XP and related software products.

The Windows 2000 MCSA and MCSE programs are heavily weighted toward hands-on skills and experience. Microsoft has stated that "nearly half of the core required exams' content demands that the candidate have troubleshooting skills acquired through hands-on experience and working knowledge."

Fortunately, if you are willing to dedicate the time and effort to learn Windows 2000 and XP, you can prepare yourself well for the exams by using the proper tools. By working through this book, you can successfully meet the exam requirements to pass the Windows 2000 Security Administration exam.

This book is part of a complete series of MCSE Study Guides, published by Sybex Inc., that together cover the core MCSE as well as numerous elective exams. Study Guide titles include the following:

- *MCSE: Windows 2000 Professional Study Guide*, Second Edition, by Lisa Donald with James Chellis (Sybex, 2001)

- *MCSE: Windows 2000 Server Study Guide*, Second Edition, by Lisa Donald with James Chellis (Sybex, 2001)

- *MCSE: Windows 2000 Network Infrastructure Administration Study Guide*, Second Edition, by Paul Robichaux with James Chellis (Sybex, 2001)

- *MCSE: Windows 2000 Directory Services Administration Study Guide*, Second Edition, by Anil Desai with James Chellis (Sybex, 2001)

- *MCSE: Windows XP Professional Study Guide*, Second Edition, by Lisa Donald with James Chellis (Sybex 2003)

- *MCSE: Windows 2000 Network Security Design Study Guide*, by Gary Govanus and Robert King (Sybex, 2000)

- *MCSE: Windows 2000 Network Infrastructure Design Study Guide*, by Bill Heldman (Sybex, 2000)

- *MCSE: Windows 2000 Directory Services Design Study Guide*, by Robert King and Gary Govanus (Sybex, 2000)

MCSA Exam Requirements

Candidates for MCSA certification on Windows 2000 must pass four exams, including one client operating system exam, two networking system exams, and one elective, as seen in the following graphic.

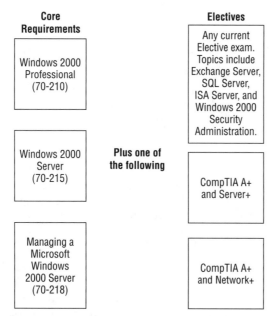

MCSE Exam Requirements

Candidates for MCSE certification on Windows 2000 must pass seven exams, including four core operating system exams, one design exam, and two electives, as seen in following graphic.

**Core
Requirements**

Windows 2000
Professional
(70-210)

Windows 2000
Server
(70-215)

**Plus one of
the following**

Windows 2000
Network
Infrastructure
Administration
(70-216)

Windows 2000
Directory
Services
Administration
(70-217)

**Design
Requirement**

Designing a
Windows 2000
Directory
Services
Infrastructure
(70-219)

Designing
Security for
Windows 2000
Network
(70-220)

Designing a
Windows 2000
Network
Infrastructure
(70-221)

Designing Web
Solutions with
Windows 2000
Server
Technologies
(70-226)

**Plus two of
the following**

Electives

Any of the
Design exams
not taken for
the Design
requirement

Any current
Elective exam.
Topics include
Exchange Server,
SQL Server,
ISA Server, and
Windows 2000
Security
Administration.

For a more detailed description of the Microsoft certification programs, including a list of current and future MCSA and MCSE electives, check Microsoft's Training and Certification website at www.microsoft.com/traincert.

MCSE versus MCSA

In an effort to provide those just starting off in the IT world a chance to prove their skills, Microsoft recently announced its Microsoft Certified System Administrator (MCSA) program.

Targeted at those with less than a year's experience, the MCSA program focuses primarily on the administration portion of an IT professional's duties. Therefore, the Windows 2000 and XP Professional exams and the Windows 2000 Server exam can be used for both the MCSA and MCSE programs.

Of course, it should be any MCSA's goal to eventually obtain theirr MCSE. However, don't assume that, because the MCSA has to take two exams that also satisfy an MCSE requirement, the two programs are similar. An MCSE must also know how to design a network. Beyond these two exams, the remaining MCSE required exams require the candidate to have much more hands-on experience.

The Implementing and Administering Security in a Microsoft Windows 2000 Network exam covers concepts and skills related to installing, configuring, and managing security in a Windows 2000 environment. It emphasizes the following:

- Understanding concepts related to baseline security

- Implementing and staying current on service packs and hotfixes from Microsoft

- Troubleshooting secure communication channels

- Working with remote authentication and remote access security

- Implementing and managing a PKI and EFS infrastructure

- Responding to security events if or when they occur

Although you won't see it in the exam objectives, this exam is heavily weighted toward using Group Policies to implement many of these concepts. A good understanding of Group Policies from your Windows 2000 training will go a long way toward helping you pass this exam.

Microsoft provides exam objectives to give you a general overview of possible areas of coverage on the exams. For your convenience, this Study Guide includes objective listings at the beginning of each chapter in which specific Microsoft exam objectives are discussed. Keep in mind, however, that exam objectives are subject to change at any time without prior notice and at Microsoft's sole discretion. Please visit Microsoft's Training and Certification website (www.microsoft.com/traincert) for the most current listing of exam objectives.

Types of Exam Questions

In an effort to both refine the testing process and protect the quality of its certifications, Microsoft has focused its Windows 2000 and XP exams on real experience and hands-on proficiency. There is a greater emphasis on your past working environments and responsibilities and less emphasis on how well you can memorize. In fact, Microsoft says an MCSE candidate should have at least one year of hands-on experience.

Microsoft will accomplish its goal of protecting the exams' integrity by regularly adding and removing exam questions, limiting the number of questions that any individual sees in a beta exam, limiting the number of questions delivered to an individual by using adaptive testing, and adding new exam elements.

Exam questions may be in a variety of formats. Depending on which exam you take, you'll see multiple-choice questions, as well as select-and-place and prioritize-a-list questions. Simulations and case study–based formats are included as well. You may also find yourself taking what's called an *adaptive format exam*. Let's take a look at the types of exam questions and examine the adaptive testing technique, so you'll be prepared for all the possibilities.

With the release of Windows 2000, Microsoft has stopped providing a detailed score breakdown. This is primarily because of the various and complex question formats. Previously, each question focused on one objective. The Windows 2000 and XP exams, however, contain questions that may be tied to one or more objectives from one or more objective sets. Therefore, grading by objective is almost impossible. Also, Microsoft no longer offers a score. Now you will only be told if you pass or fail.

For more information on the various exam question types, go to www.microsoft.com/traincert/mcpexams/policies/innovations.asp.

MULTIPLE-CHOICE QUESTIONS

Multiple-choice questions come in two main forms. One is a straightforward question followed by several possible answers, of which one or more is correct. The other type of multiple-choice question is more complex and based on a specific scenario. The scenario may focus on several areas or objectives.

SELECT-AND-PLACE QUESTIONS

Select-and-place exam questions involve graphical elements that you must manipulate to successfully answer the question. For example, you might see a diagram of a computer network, as shown in the following graphic taken from the select-and-place demo downloaded from Microsoft's website.

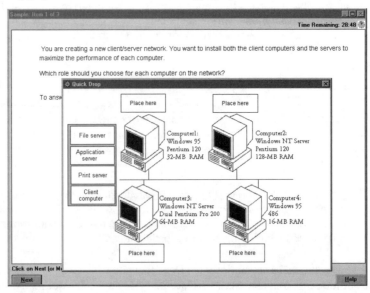

A typical diagram will show computers and other components next to boxes that contain the text "Place here." The labels for the boxes represent various computer roles on a network, such as a print server and a file server. Based on information given for each computer, you are asked to select each label and place it in the correct box. You need to place *all* the labels correctly. No credit is given for the question if you correctly label only some of the boxes.

In another select-and-place problem you might be asked to put a series of steps in order, by dragging items from boxes on the left to boxes on the right and placing them in the correct order. One other type requires that you drag an item from the left and place it under an item in a column on the right.

SIMULATIONS

Simulations are the kinds of questions that most closely represent actual situations and test the skills you use while working with Microsoft software interfaces. These exam questions include a mock interface on which you are asked to perform certain actions according to a given scenario. The simulated interfaces look nearly identical to what you see in the actual product, as shown in this example:

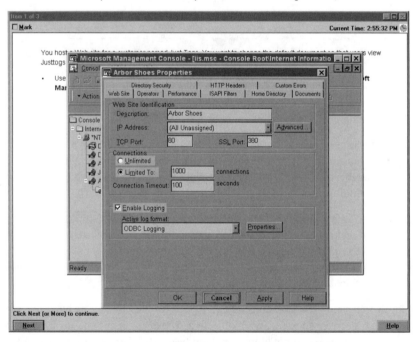

Because of the number of possible errors that can be made on simulations, be sure to consider the following recommendations from Microsoft:

- Do not change any simulation settings that don't pertain to the solution directly.

- When related information has not been provided, assume that the default settings are used.

- Make sure that your entries are spelled correctly.

- Close all the simulation application windows after completing the set of tasks in the simulation.

The best way to prepare for simulation questions is to spend time working with the graphical interface of the product on which you will be tested.

CASE STUDY–BASED QUESTIONS

Case study–based questions first appeared in the MCSD program. These questions present a scenario with a range of requirements. Based on the information provided, you answer a series of multiple-choice and select-and-place questions. The interface for case study–based questions has a number of tabs, each of which contains information about the scenario.

At present, this type of question appears only in most of the Design exams.

Microsoft will regularly add and remove questions from the exams. This is called *item seeding*. It is part of the effort to make it more difficult for individuals to merely memorize exam questions that were passed along by previous test-takers.

Exam Question Development

Microsoft follows an exam-development process consisting of eight mandatory phases. The process takes an average of seven months and involves more than 150 specific steps. The MCP exam development consists of the following phases:

Phase 1: Job Analysis Phase 1 is an analysis of all the tasks that make up a specific job function, based on tasks performed by people who are currently performing that job function. This phase also identifies the knowledge, skills, and abilities that relate specifically to the performance area being certified.

Phase 2: Objective Domain Definition The results of the job analysis phase provide the framework used to develop objectives. Development of objectives involves translating the job-function tasks into a comprehensive package of specific and measurable knowledge, skills, and abilities. The resulting list of objectives—the *objective domain*—is the basis for the development of both the certification exams and the training materials.

Phase 3: Blueprint Survey The final objective domain is transformed into a blueprint survey in which contributors are asked to rate each objective. These contributors may be MCP candidates, appropriately skilled exam-development volunteers, or Microsoft employees. Based on the contributors' input, the objectives are prioritized and weighted. The actual exam items are written according to the prioritized objectives. Contributors are queried about how they spend their time on the job. If a contributor doesn't spend an adequate amount of time actually performing the specified job function, their data is eliminated from the analysis. The blueprint survey phase helps determine which objectives to measure, as well as the appropriate number and types of items to include on the exam.

Phase 4: Item Development   A pool of items is developed to measure the blueprinted objective domain. The number and types of items to be written are based on the results of the blueprint survey.

Phase 5: Alpha Review and Item Revision   During this phase, a panel of technical and job-function experts reviews each item for technical accuracy. The panel then answers each item and reaches a consensus on all technical issues. Once the items have been verified as being technically accurate, they are edited to ensure that they are expressed in the clearest language possible.

Phase 6: Beta Exam   The reviewed and edited items are collected into beta exams. Based on the responses of all beta participants, Microsoft performs a statistical analysis to verify the validity of the exam items and to determine which items will be used in the certification exam. Once the analysis has been completed, the items are distributed into multiple parallel forms, or *versions*, of the final certification exam.

Phase 7: Item Selection and Cut-Score Setting   The results of the beta exams are analyzed to determine which items will be included in the certification exam. This determination is based on many factors, including item difficulty and relevance. During this phase, a panel of job-function experts determines the *cut score* (minimum passing score) for the exams. The cut score differs from exam to exam because it is based on an item-by-item determination of the percentage of candidates who answered the item correctly and who would be expected to answer the item correctly.

Phase 8: Live Exam   In the final phase, the exams are given to candidates. MCP exams are administered by Prometric and Virtual University Enterprises (VUE).

Tips for Taking the Windows 2000 Security Administration Exam

Here are some general tips for achieving success on your certification exam:

- Arrive early at the exam center so that you can relax and review your study materials. During this final review, you can look over tables and lists of exam-related information.

- Read the questions carefully. Don't be tempted to jump to an early conclusion. Make sure you know *exactly* what the question is asking.

- Answer all questions. Remember that the adaptive format does *not* allow you to return to a question. Be very careful before entering your answer. Because your exam may be shortened by correct answers (and lengthened by incorrect answers), there is no advantage to rushing through questions.

- On simulations, do not change settings that are not directly related to the question. Also, assume default settings if the question does not specify or imply which settings are used.

- For questions you're not sure about, use a process of elimination to get rid of the obviously incorrect answers first. This improves your odds of selecting the correct answer when you need to make an educated guess.

Exam Registration

You can take the Microsoft exams at any of more than 1000 Authorized Prometric Testing Centers (APTCs) and VUE Testing Centers around the world. For the location of a testing center near you, call Prometric at 800-755-EXAM (755-3926), or call VUE at 888-837-8616. Outside the United States and Canada, contact your local Prometric or VUE registration center.

Find out the number of the exam you want to take, and then register with the Prometric or VUE registration center nearest you. At this point, you will be asked for advance payment for the exam. The exams are $125 each, and you must take them within one year of payment. You can schedule exams up to six weeks in advance or as late as one working day prior to the date of the exam. You can cancel or reschedule your exam if you contact the center at least two working days prior to the exam. Same-day registration is available in some locations, subject to space availability. If same-day registration is available, you must register a minimum of two hours before test time.

You can also register for your exams online at www.prometric.com or www.vue.com.

When you schedule the exam, you will be provided with instructions regarding appointment and cancellation procedures, ID requirements, and information about the testing center location. In addition, you will receive a registration and payment confirmation letter from Prometric or VUE.

Microsoft requires certification candidates to accept the terms of a Non-Disclosure Agreement before taking certification exams.

Is This Book for You?

If you want to acquire a solid foundation in administering security for a Windows 2000 network, and your goal is to prepare for the exam by learning how to use and manage this operating system, this book is for you. You'll find clear explanations of the fundamental concepts you need to grasp and plenty of help to achieve the high level of professional competency you need to succeed in your chosen field.

If you want to become certified as an MCSE or MCSA, this book is definitely for you. However, if you just want to attempt to pass the exam without really understanding how to administer security for a Windows 2000 network, this Study Guide is *not* for you. It is written for people who want to acquire hands-on skills and in-depth knowledge of this topic.

How to Use This Book

What makes a Sybex Study Guide the book of choice for more than 100,000 MCSEs? We took into account not only what you need to know to pass the exam, but what you need to know to take what you've learned and apply it in the real world. Each book contains the following:

Objective-by-objective coverage of the topics you need to know   Each chapter lists the objectives covered in that chapter, followed by detailed discussion of each objective.

Assessment Test   Directly following this introduction is an Assessment Test that you should take. It is designed to help you determine how much you already know. Each question is tied to a topic discussed in the book. Using the results of the Assessment Test, you can figure out the areas where you need to focus your study. Of course, we do recommend you read the entire book.

Exam Essentials   To highlight what you learn, you'll find a list of Exam Essentials at the end of each chapter. The Exam Essentials section briefly highlights the topics that need your particular attention as you prepare for the exam.

Key terms and Glossary   Throughout each chapter, you will be introduced to important terms and concepts that you will need to know for the exam. These terms appear in italic within the chapters, and a list of the key terms appears just after the Exam Essentials. At the end of the book, a detailed Glossary gives definitions for these terms, as well as other general terms you should know.

Review questions, complete with detailed explanations   Each chapter is followed by a set of Review Questions that test what you learned in the chapter. The questions are written with the exam in mind, meaning that they are designed to have the same look and feel as what you'll see on the exam. Question types are just like the exam, including multiple choice.

Hands-on exercises   In each chapter, you'll find exercises designed to give you the important hands-on experience that is critical for your exam preparation. The exercises support the topics of the chapter, and they walk you through the steps necessary to perform a particular function.

Real World Scenarios   Because reading a book isn't enough for you to learn how to apply these topics in your everyday duties, we have provided Real World Scenarios in special sidebars. These explain when and why a particular solution would make sense, in a working environment you'd actually encounter.

The topics covered in this Study Guide map directly to Microsoft's official exam objectives. Each exam objective is covered completely.

What's on the CD?

With this new member of our best-selling MCSE Study Guide series, we are including an array of training resources. The CD includes numerous simulations, bonus exams, and flashcards to help you study for the exam. We have also included the complete contents of the Study Guide in electronic form. The CD's resources are described here:

The Sybex Ebook for Windows 2000 Network Security Administration   Many people like the convenience of being able to carry their whole Study Guide on a CD. They also like being able to search the text via computer to find specific information quickly and easily. For these reasons, the entire contents of this Study Guide are supplied on the CD, in PDF. We've also included Adobe Acrobat Reader, which provides the interface for the PDF contents as well as the search capabilities.

The Sybex Test Engine   These are a collection of multiple-choice questions that will help you prepare for your exam. There are four sets of questions:

- Two bonus exams designed to simulate the actual live exam.
- All the questions from the Study Guide, presented in a test engine for your review. You can review questions by chapter or by objective, or you can take a random test.
- The Assessment Test.

Here is a sample screen from the Sybex MCSE test engine:

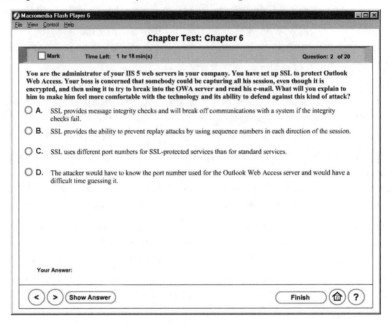

Sybex MCSE Flashcards for PCs and Handheld Devices   The "flashcard" style of question is an effective way to quickly and efficiently test your understanding of the fundamental concepts covered in the exam. The Sybex MCSE Flashcards set consists of more than 100 questions presented in a special engine developed specifically for this Study Guide series. Here's what the Sybex MCSE Flashcards interface looks like:

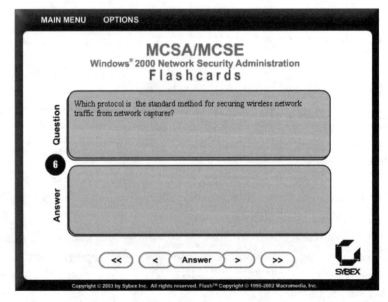

Because of the high demand for a product that will run on handheld devices, we have also developed, in conjunction with Land-J Technologies, a version of the flashcard questions that you can take with you on your Palm OS PDA (including the Palm handheld and Handspring's Visor).

How Do You Use This Book?

This book provides a solid foundation for the serious effort of preparing for the exam. To best benefit from this book, you might want to use the following study method:

1. Take the Assessment Test to identify your weak areas.

2. Study each chapter carefully. Do your best to fully understand the information.

3. Complete all the hands-on exercises in the chapter, referring to the text as necessary so that you understand each step.

4. Read over the Real World Scenarios to improve your understanding of how to use what you learn in the book.

5. Study the Exam Essentials and key terms to make sure you are familiar with the areas you need to focus on.

6. Answer the review questions at the end of each chapter. If you prefer to answer the questions in a timed and graded format, install the test engine from the book's CD and answer the chapter questions there instead of in the book.

7. Take note of the questions you did not understand, and study the corresponding sections of the book again.

8. Go back over the Exam Essentials and key terms.

9. Go through the Study Guide's other training resources, which are included on the book's CD. These include electronic flashcards, the electronic version of the chapter review questions (try taking them by objective), and the two bonus exams.

To learn all the material covered in this book, you will need to study regularly and with discipline. Try to set aside the same time every day to study, and select a comfortable and quiet place in which to do it. If you work hard, you will be surprised at how quickly you learn this material. Good luck!

Contacts and Resources

To find out more about Microsoft Education and Certification materials and programs, to register with Prometric or VUE, or to obtain other useful certification information and additional study resources, check the following resources:

Microsoft Training and Certification Home Page

www.microsoft.com/traincert

This website provides information about the MCP program and exams. You can also order the latest Microsoft Roadmap to Education and Certification.

Microsoft TechNet Technical Information Network

www.microsoft.com/technet

800-344-2121

Use this website or phone number to contact support professionals and system administrators. Outside the United States and Canada, contact your local Microsoft subsidiary for information.

Prometric

www.prometric.com

800-755-3936

Contact Prometric to register to take an MCP exam at any of more than 800 Prometric Testing Centers around the world.

Virtual University Enterprises (VUE)

www.vue.com

888-837-8616

Contact the VUE registration center to register to take an MCP exam at one of the VUE Testing Centers.

MCP Magazine Online

www.mcpmag.com

Microsoft Certified Professional Magazine is a well-respected publication that focuses on Windows certification. This site hosts chats and discussion forums and tracks news related to the MCSE program. Some of the services cost a fee, but they are well worth it.

Windows & .NET Magazine

www.windows2000mag.com

You can subscribe to this magazine or read free articles at the website. The study resource provides general information on Windows 2000, XP, and .NET Server.

Cramsession on Brainbuzz.com

cramsession.brainbuzz.com

Cramsession is an online community focusing on all IT certification programs. In addition to discussion boards and job locators, you can download one of several free cram sessions, which are nice supplements to any study approach you take.

Assessment Test

1. A security template is _____.

   A. A method of applying security settings to a group policy

   B. A way to discover the current security settings

   C. A set of guidelines published by Microsoft for securing a server

   D. A physical layout of the server room's security system

2. A Group Policy contains which of the two following configuration settings?

   A. Network

   B. System

   C. User

   D. Computer

3. A limitation of L2TP/IPSec is _____.

   A. It is unable to traverse NAT implementations.

   B. It isn't as secure as PPTP.

   C. It only works with Windows XP Professional clients.

   D. It requires that Active Directory be in native mode.

4. Which of the following are EFS features in Windows XP Professional? (Choose all that apply.)

   A. Sharing EFS files with multiple users

   B. Encrypting offline files

   C. Using web folders for encrypted files

   D. Encryption without an enterprise certificate authority

5. Which of the following terms describes the process of tracking noteworthy events on your network?

   A. Process tracking

   B. Auditing

   C. Resource recovery

   D. Countermeasure

6. Which of the following is a popular Microsoft tool designed to secure an Internet Information Services website?

   A. URLScan

   B. IISLockDown

   C. Security Toolbox

   D. Snort

7. When you have confidence that a message could only have been sent by the person claiming to be the sender, you have _____.

    A. Nonrepudiation

    B. Integrity

    C. Confidentiality

    D. Anti-Replay

8. Your coworker states that he is still able to successfully use a certificate that was revoked yesterday. What is the most likely reason?

    A. A new CRL with the information for his certificate has not been published yet.

    B. The CRL Distribution Point is offline.

    C. The revocation must still be in the pending requests folder on the CA.

    D. The CA's chain must be broken.

9. When you have confidence that a message has not been altered in transit, you have _____.

    A. Nonrepudiation

    B. Integrity

    C. Confidentiality

    D. Anti-Replay

10. The server software used to authenticate wireless users to your Active Directory is called _____.

    A. Kerberos Server

    B. Key Distribution Center

    C. RADIUS Server

    D. Internet Authentication Server

11. Which of the following operating systems support Kerberos v5? (Choose all that apply.)

    A. Windows 9x

    B. Windows 9x with the Directory Services client

    C. Windows NT 4 Workstation

    D. Windows 2000 Professional

12. The graphical tool used to determine which service packs and hotfixes are missing from a Windows 2000 computer is called _____.

    A. HFNetChk

    B. EventComb

    C. MBSA

    D. Server Monitor

13. The method of incorporating service pack updates into the base set of installation files is called _____.

    A. Service Pack Installation

    B. Hotfix Installation

    C. Windows Updates

    D. Slipstreaming

14. The method of ensuring that the latest service packs and hotfixes are automatically updated on all your Windows 2000 computers is called _____.

    A. Service Pack Installation

    B. Hotfix Installation

    C. Slipstreaming

    D. Software Update Service

15. The process of inserting a digital signature into each packet is called _____.

    A. Slipstreaming

    B. Digital signatures

    C. SMB signing

    D. Encryption

16. When a person sends a message as if they are another person, this process is called _____.

    A. Eavesdropping

    B. Impersonation

    C. Nonrepudiation

    D. Confidentiality

17. When a hacker uses a tool such as LoftCrack to crack a user's password, this process is called _____.

    A. Password attack

    B. Network intrusion

    C. Compromised-key attack

    D. Nonrepudiation

18. Which of the following authentication methods can Windows 2000 clients use? (Choose all that apply.)

    A. CHAP

    B. MS-CHAP

    C. MS-CHAPv2

    D. EAP

19. When the computer portion of a Group Policy is applied last, this process is called
_____.

   A. Reverse Policy Assignment

   B. Loopback

   C. Missing Policy Assignment

   D. Impersonation

20. Before data can be securely exchanged between two computers, what must be accomplished?

   A. Negotiation of a common dialect

   B. Negotiation of a session key

   C. Negotiation of the window size

   D. Negotiation of a Security Association

21. A limitation of PPTP is _____.

   A. It is Microsoft specific.

   B. It isn't as secure as L2TP/IPSec.

   C. It only works with Windows XP Professional clients.

   D. It requires server and client certificates.

22. When an encrypted packet is sent to a tunnel endpoint, it is said to be in _____.

   A. Tunnel mode

   B. Transport mode

   C. Mixed mode

   D. Native mode

23. Which of the following are two methods to test an IPSec policy assignment?

   A. Net View

   B. PING

   C. Telnet

   D. IPSec Monitor

   E. Network Monitor

   F. MBSA

24. A warning message in the System log indicates that _____.

   A. An event of no importance has occurred. You can safely ignore the message.

   B. An event of importance has occurred. You should investigate.

   C. A serious catastrophe has occurred. You should shut down the servers and plan on being fired.

   D. Without knowing a warning message's contents, you cannot discern if it is important or not.

25. SSL can be used with which of the following technologies? (Choose all that apply.)

  A. SMTP

  B. HTTP

  C. FTP

  D. IMAP4

26. A certificate contains which of the following information? (Choose all that apply.)

  A. Expiration date

  B. Issuing certificate authority name

  C. Length of the key

  D. CRL publication interval

27. If you want to audit access to objects that exist in the configuration partition, you should enable _____.

  A. Directory Services auditing

  B. Object Access auditing

  C. Process auditing

  D. Logon auditing

28. To view the packets that have passed between two computers, you use which of the following tools?

  A. Systems Management Server

  B. Microsoft Security Baseline Analyzer

  C. Network Monitor

  D. IPSec Monitor

29. To summarize a group of Application logs across multiple Windows 2000-based computers, you use which of the following tools?

  A. MSBA

  B. Network Monitor

  C. IPSec Monitor

  D. EventComb

30. Self-contained code that replicates itself across a TCP/IP network is called a _____.

  A. Trojan

  B. Worm

  C. Virus

  D. Natural disaster

31. Which of the following are user certificate types? (Choose all that apply.)

 A. EFS

 B. S/MIME

 C. Computer

 D. IPSEC

32. Code that embeds itself inside a legitimate program and is executed when the program is executed is called a _____.

 A. Trojan

 B. Worm

 C. Virus

 D. Natural disaster

33. Your network has just experienced an attack. You begin to gather the evidence of this attack by printing the pertinent logs. In which of the following activities are you engaging?

 A. Preserving the chain of custody

 B. Preserving the chain of evidence

 C. Analyzing the response effort

 D. Analyzing the evidence

34. Public key cryptography uses which kind of key(s)?

 A. Symmetric

 B. Asymmetric

 C. Shared secret

 D. Pairs of shared secret

35. Your network has just experienced an attack. After printing the logs, you place the hard copies of the logs in a special file. You record the date and time the logs were placed in the file. In which activity are you engaging?

 A. Preserving the chain of custody

 B. Preserving the chain of evidence

 C. Analyzing the response effort

 D. Analyzing the evidence

Answers to Assessment Test

1. A. You can think of a template as that which has predetermined settings which can be applied to multiple objects either at the same time or at different times. You can use a template to build a Group Policy. Only answer A matches the purpose and use of a template. For more information, see Chapter 1.

2. C, D. When you take a long step back from Windows 2000 Server, you'll find that there are really two parts to a GPO: a Windows part and a user part. A GPO really has two settings: one for the computer and the other for the logged-on user. For more information, see Chapter 1.

3. A. L2TP is unable to work through NAT. For more information, see Chapter 8.

4. A, B, C. Windows XP Professional offers some improvements on EFS from Windows 2000, including sharing EFS-encrypted files, encrypting offline files cached on a laptop, using web folders for storing encrypted files, using 3DES, and the ability to reset passwords without breaking EFS by using a special reset disk. For more information, see Chapter 10.

5. B. Auditing is the process by which you define the kinds of events you want to display in the Security log. Process tracking is one type of event that can be audited. For more information, see Chapter 11.

6. B. You use the IISLockDown tool to configure IIS to work with only some types of requests based on the type of web you want to lock down. This tool is rather useful and is popular too. URLScan runs as part of IISLockDown. For more information, see Chapter 2.

7. A. Nonrepudiation describes the assurance that the person who claims they sent the message is the same person who actually sent the message. Although similar, the terms in the other answers really have different foci. For more information, see Chapter 2.

8. A. If the CRL does not list his certificate as being revoked, the certificate is assumed to be good. The next time the CRL is published, the certificate will be on it, and it will no longer work. For more information, see Chapter 9.

9. B. Unlike nonrepudiation, which assures that the sender really sent the message, integrity assures that the message itself has not been altered in transit. It is important to have integrity so that you know that the message received was the same as the message sent. For more information, see Chapter 2.

10. D. IAS works with your wireless users to ensure that they can be authenticated to Active Directory. Although your server may use Kerberos as the authentication protocol, the point that wireless users interact with is the IAS. For more information, see Chapter 2.

11. D. Only Windows 2000 and later support Kerberos authentication. For more information, see Chapter 7.

12. C. Microsoft Baseline Security Analyzer is the graphical equivalent to HFNetChk. It is a rather nice tool. For more information, see Chapter 3.

13. D.   None of the other answers deal with service pack file incorporation into the source install files. Slipstreaming is a method for ensuring that the latest version of each file is installed the first time, and it eliminates the need to install a service pack after the initial operating system installation. For more information, see Chapter 3.

14. D.   This free software—Software Update Service—is designed to ensure that your servers and workstations are kept up-to-date with the latest hotfix installations. Employing this tool will help you close known vulnerabilities quickly. For more information, see Chapter 3.

15. C.   Although digital signatures can sign an entire message as a single package, SMB signing signs each packet while it is in transit between two points. This type of signature gives added security and assures nonrepudiation. For more information, see Chapter 4.

16. B.   Impersonation is the process of acting and looking like another person on the network. Successful impersonation damages nonrepudiation. For more information, see Chapter 2.

17. A.   This is a rather straightforward answer. Cracking a password is considered a password attack. For more information, see Chapter 2.

18. A, B, C, D.   Windows 2000 supports all of these authentication methods. For more information, see Chapter 7.

19. B.   Loopback is the process of ensuring that the computer portion of a GPO that would not have been assigned based on the user's logged-in security context is still assigned. This usually happens in the context of having multiple GPOs assigned or inherited by a given object in the folder. For more information, see Chapter 1.

20. D.   A Security Association (SA) is the term used to describe the process of two computers negotiating all the aspects of security so that they can talk to each other. The other three answers are all part of the SA negotiations. For more information, see Chapter 4.

21. B.   L2TP is more secure than PPTP. For more information, see Chapter 8.

22. A.   You'll see these two terms, *tunnel mode* and *transport mode*, on the exam. Just remember that in tunnel mode the packet is encrypted all the way to its final destination endpoint. In transport mode, this is not the case. For more information, see Chapter 4.

23. B, D.   How do you know that an IPSec policy assignment is really working? Well, you can either user PING (Packet Internet Groper), or you can use IPSec Monitor. For more information, see Chapter 4.

24. B.   Check event logs every day. Warning messages can be especially problematic if they are difficult to troubleshoot. Although you can skim past the blue information icons, be sure to stop and read the warning and error messages. For more information, see Chapter 11.

25. A, B, D.   SSL can be used with SMTP, HTTP, and IMAP4 to secure these protocols. For more information, see Chapter 6.

26. A, B, C.   Certificates do not list the CRL publication interval because it can be changed on the CA well after certificates have been issued. For more information, see Chapter 9.

27. A. This type of auditing will audit events related to objects in Active Directory. Object Access auditing can refer to objects outside AD, such as a printer. For more information, see Chapter 11.

28. C. Network Monitor is Microsoft's sniffer. It can capture packets that flow on the network line for later analysis. For more information, see Chapter 11.

29. D. EventComb is the tool used to coalesce multiple log entries. For more information, see Chapter 11.

30. B. Knowing the difference between a Trojan, a worm, and a virus is helpful in passing the exam. In this book, we'll spend good page space explaining the differences. For more information, see Chapter 2.

31. A, B. EFS and S/MIME are user certificate templates and are stored in the user profile. For more information, see Chapter 10.

32. A. A Trojan looks like a legitimate program but really has malicious code in it that will harm your computer system. For more information, see Chapter 2.

33. B. There are a chain of custody and a chain of evidence. The chain of custody refers to *who* had the evidence, when, and for what purpose. The chain of evidence refers to *what* events and verifiable data can be gathered about the attack. For more information, see Chapter 12.

34. A. Public/private keys use asymmetric keys. When one key is used to encrypt, the other key is used to decrypt. For example, if you send an e-mail to somebody encrypted with their public key, they use their private key (the matching one of the pair) to decrypt the e-mail. For more information, see Chapter 6.

35. A. What you're doing here is recording when the evidence was placed in the vault, not what data is contained in the evidence. This is an example of preserving the chain of custody.

Chapter

1

Configuring, Deploying, and Troubleshooting Security Templates

MICROSOFT EXAM OBJECTIVES COVERED IN THIS CHAPTER:

✓ **Configure security templates.**

- Configure registry and file system permissions.
- Configure account policies.
- Configure audit policies.
- Configure user rights assignment.
- Configure security options.
- Configure system services.
- Configure restricted groups.
- Configure event logs.

✓ **Deploy security templates. Deployment methods include using Group Policy and scripting.**

✓ **Troubleshoot security template problems. Considerations include Group Policy, upgraded operating systems, and mixed client-computer operating systems.**

Windows 2000 Server provides a rich set of security features that enable administrators to secure information and activity on their Windows 2000–based networks. Through the use of Group Policy Objects (GPOs), you can push configurations out to each Windows-based machine on the network to help ensure network-wide security. You can quickly create GPOs to perform this task by applying a template. A template is a pre-configured set of values that can be used to create a GPO. Security templates are text-based `.inf` files that allow the administrator to create security configurations once and then apply those configurations to multiple servers. Templates also reduce the amount of administrative effort required to secure a group of Windows 2000 workstations and servers. These templates are administered through the Microsoft Management Console (MMC) and are applied to multiple servers using one or more Group Policies.

Because this exam emphasizes the use of GPOs, we are going to spend some time going over how GPOs work and how you can deploy them effectively. We understand that this may be review for many of you. If you are comfortable and confident in your GPO skills and depth of understanding, you can skip this section and start with the "Working with Security Templates" section.

This book jumps right in with the specific information you will need to pass the exam. If you need to get up to speed with the basics, try *Network Security JumpStart* by Matt Strebe (Sybex, 2002). For more on general networking theory and concepts, try *Mastering Network Security*, 2nd Edition by Chris Brenton and Cameron Hunt, (Sybex, 2002).

However, if you feel you need a refresher on Group Policies, read this section. You will need this information to do well on the exam and to better understand how to implement security in a Windows 2000 environment.

Group Policies and Windows 2000 Server

Policies are not new to Microsoft products. Since the release of Windows 95, policies have been a way to ensure that Registry settings are configured correctly across multiple computers with a single administrative act.

You can use GPOs to define a user's work environment and then implement changes to that environment without the user needing to reboot their workstation. User and computer settings are defined once in a GPO and then the object is used to push those settings out to the computers and user accounts you designate. Windows 2000 continually enforces the settings in the GPO, and as updates to the settings in the GPO are configured, these updates are pushed out to the Windows 2000 and XP computers on your network.

 In addition to handling security concerns, you can use Group Policies to reduce lost productivity—which is often due to user error—by removing unnecessary programs and abilities that ship standard with the Windows 2000 platform. This also can lower the overall total cost of ownership (TCO).

GPOs are linked to a site, a domain, or an organizational unit (OU) container. When linked to a site or a domain container, GPOs allow you to centralize settings for an entire organization. When GPOs are linked to an OU container, you can apply different settings to different sets of user and/or computer accounts.

GPOs also ensure that users have the desktop environment necessary to perform their job effectively. You can configure settings to ensure that certain shortcuts, drive mappings, and other configurations exist whenever the user is logged on. Furthermore, you can automate software installations, negating the need to send a technician to the desktop to install or update software packages.

Corporate security and business policies can also be enforced through the use of GPOs. For example, you can ensure that security requirements for all users match the security required by corporate policy.

Configuring Group Policies

When a GPO is first opened, you'll find several types of settings that you can configure:

Administrative Templates These are Registry-based settings for configuring application and user desktop environments.

Security Your choices here are local computer, domain, and network settings. These settings control user access to the network, account and audit policies, and user rights.

Software Installation These settings centralize software management and deployment. Applications can be either published or assigned.

Scripts These settings specify when Windows 2000 runs a specific script.

Remote Installation Services These settings control the options available to users when running the Client Installation Wizard by Remote Installation Services (RIS).

Internet Explorer Maintenance These settings let you administrate and customize Internet Explorer configurations on Windows 2000 and XP computers.

Folder Redirection These settings store specific user profile information and take a shared folder on a server and make it look like a local folder on the desktop of the computer.

Now, a GPO comprises two elements: the *Group Policy Container (GPC)* and the *Group Policy Template (GPT)*. The GPC is located in *Active Directory (AD)* and provides version information used by the domain controllers to discern which GPO is the most recent version. If a domain controller (DC) does not have the most recent version, it relies on replication with other DCs to obtain the latest GPO and thereby update its own GPC.

The GPT is a folder hierarchy in the shared `sysvol` folder on domain controllers. The GPT contains the settings that are applied to the computers on your network. Computers connect to the `sysvol` folder on the DC to read the settings in the GPT before applying them to their local Registry. The GPT is named after the Globally Unique Identifier (GUID) of the GPO. When the GPO is created, it is assigned a new GUID, and the GPT name is the GUID of the GPO.

Each GPO has two sets of configuration settings: one for computers and the other for users. This basic architecture has not changed since Windows 95, in which we used `user.dat` and `system.dat` as the basis for forming the policy file. This was also the case in Windows 98, but many additional configuration settings are available in Windows 2000.

The configuration settings for computers specify the following:

- Operating system behavior

- Desktop behavior

- Security settings

- Computer startup and shutdown scripts

- Application assignments, options, and settings

The configuration settings for users specify the following:

- Operating system behavior

- User-specific desktop settings

- User-specific security settings

- Assigned and published applications

- Folder redirection options

- User logon and logoff scripts

When a GPO is linked to a site, a domain, or an OU container, the user and computer accounts hosted in that object are affected by the policy. GPOs can be linked to more than one container such that the following statements are true:

- You can link one GPO to multiple sites, domains, and/or OUs.

- Linking at the site or domain level gives you centralized administrative abilities.

- Linking at the OU level decentralizes your administration, yet maintains uniformity for those objects affected by the GPO.

- You can link multiple GPOs to a single site, domain, and/or OU.

- Creating multiple GPOs allows you to easily administer each group of settings you want to apply.

- Link inheritance is maintained in AD: lower-level objects inherit the upper-level settings from a GPO. For example, all OUs in a domain inherit the settings of a GPO linked to the domain object.

- You cannot link GPOs to default AD containers including the Users, Computers, and Builtin containers.

After a GPO is created, it is not required to be linked to an object. GPOs can simply be created and then linked later to the desired object when the GPO's settings are needed. In addition, when you work on GPOs from a domain controller, by default, you work in the memory space of the domain controller that has been assigned the Flexible Single Master Operations (FSMO) role of primary domain controller (PDC) emulator. The PDC Emulator looks and feels like a PDC to Windows NT Backup Domain Controllers (BDC) and Windows NT workstations. The FSMO role of PDC Emulator is implemented for legacy compatibility purposes. You will use *Active Directory Users and Computers (ADUC)* to link a GPO to a domain or an OU. You will use *Active Directory Sites and Services (ADSS)* to link a GPO to a site. You must be a member of the Enterprise Admins security group to link a GPO to a site object.

 If you would like to learn more about the PDC and BDC roles in Windows NT 4.0, please consult *Mastering Windows NT Server 4*, 7th Edition (Sybex, 2000).

Applying Group Policies

To be successful on the exam, you'll need to understand how GPOs are applied in AD. GPO inheritance constitutes the order in which policies are applied. GPOs are first applied to the site container, then to the domain container, and then to the OU container. As policies are applied, they override the previous policy, meaning that a policy setting at the OU level overrides the policy setting at the domain level and policy settings at the domain level override policy settings at the Site level. In other words, the most recently applied policy, the one that is applied last, has the greatest priority in setting the final configurations for objects hosting in the linked container.

However, bear in mind that inheritance is at work too. An OU could be inheriting multiple policies that have been linked to the site, domain, and upper-level OU objects. The policies are applied, even though no policy has been directly linked to the OU.

You'll also need to understand how GPOs are processed, which is different from how they are inherited or linked. When we talk about policies being processed, we are talking about the order in which policies are applied when multiple policies are linked to the same container. And because there are two parts to every GPO, it is important to understand which part of the GPO is processed first.

The computer settings of a GPO are processed and applied before the user settings. When Windows 2000 processes computer settings, the startup scripts run. When a user logs on, the logon scripts are processed, and the reverse happens when a user cleanly shuts down a workstation. Logoff scripts run first, and then shutdown scripts run.

If multiple polices are linked to the same container, the default setting is to process all policies synchronously. You can change the processing of a GPO to asynchronous by using a group policy setting for both computers and users. In asynchronous processing, all policies are processed simultaneously using multiple threads. In synchronous processing, one policy must finish processing before the next policy can begin processing. Also in synchronous processing, the desktop for the user does not appear until all policies are processed and applied. If you decide to use asynchronous processing, you might possibly sacrifice reliability in each policy being enforced correctly system-wide. Best practice is to leave policy processing at the default of synchronous.

Windows 2000 clients refresh their policies every 90 minutes with an additional, randomized offset of 30 minutes to ensure that the domain controller doesn't become overloaded with policy calls from clients. Domain controllers refresh every 5 minutes. Thus, new policy settings are applied more quickly to domain controllers than to workstations.

When multiple policies are applied to a single container, they are applied in the order listed in the Group Policy tab of the object's properties, from bottom to top. The GPO at the top of the list is applied last and thus can overwrite earlier settings and it has top priority in the application of the settings to the workstation or server. An exception occurs to the application priority when the most recent setting processed conflicts between user and computer settings. In this case, the computer setting overrides the user settings.

As long as there are no conflicts or overwrites during the application of multiple policies, the settings in all policies linked to a given container are cumulative for all objects that reside in that container.

Modifying Group Policy Inheritance

Policy inheritance is not absolute, however. Inheritance can be blocked and modified. You can prevent a child container from inheriting any GPOs from the parent containers by enabling Block Inheritance on the child container. Enabling Block Inheritance lets you set new policies for the child container. However, you need to bear the following in mind:

- You cannot selectively choose which GPOs to block. It is an all-or-nothing proposition.

- GPOs can be configured with the No Override setting, which means that the GPO is applied even if inheritance is blocked. You can use this setting to push down necessary settings even if an OU administrator doesn't like the settings. GPOs that represent critical, corporate-wide rules should have the No Override option enabled.

- The No Override option is really set on the link, not on the GPO itself. Thus, if you have a GPO that is linked to multiple containers, you can configure the No Override option on each container and gain administrative flexibility to decide to which containers the GPO will always be applied.

If you want to block some GPOs on a child container but apply others, best practice is to block inheritance and then create new links on the child container to the desired GPOs.

You can also link a GPO to a container and then filter the application of the GPO to certain objects within the container. By default, for any given container, the GPO settings are applied to all objects within the container. However, you might not want this. You might want certain objects not to inherit the settings. Well, you can control or filter the application of those settings by using the *Discretionary Access Control List (DACL)* in the properties of the objects you want to filter.

By default, the DACL contains two *Access Control Entries (ACEs)*:

Authenticated users   Allow Read and Allow Apply Group Policy

Domain Admins, Enterprise Admins, and SYSTEM   Allow Read, Allow Write, Allow Create All Child Objects, Allow Delete All Child Objects

You can modify these permissions in two ways. You can explicitly deny the Apply Group Policy permission for the group that contains the user or computer account for whom you want to filter. Or you can remove Authenticated Users from the ACL. When you do so, Authenticated Users have no explicit permission on the GPO. However, if you remove Authenticated Users, you will need to create a security group for the other accounts in the container to whom the GPO should apply and then use that group account in place of the Authenticated Users security group account.

You can also set a Loopback processing mode, which essentially ensures that the computer GPO is applied last rather than the user GPO. This setting might be useful if applications that are assigned to a user should not be automatically available on a server. Hence, you use the Loopback processing mode to ensure that the computer portion of the GPO is applied last.

Now that we've reviewed GPOs, we'll look at security administrative templates for much of the rest of this chapter. Templates are a collection of settings that modify the Registry on the target computer. You use administrative templates to configure user and computer Registry-based settings that control the user's desktop environment. Specifically, the template settings modify the HKEY_LOCAL_MACHINE and HKEY_CURRENT_USER registry trees.

Microsoft provides a number of preconfigured templates for security purposes that we will discuss in detail. It is important to understand what these templates do and their purposes since they will be a focus on this exam.

Working with Security Templates

You create and modify *security templates* using the Security Template snap-in of the MMC. The way to access the templates is to create a new MMC and add the security template to the new MMC. Follow these steps:

1. Choose Start ➢ Run to open the Run dialog box, and in the Open box, enter **mmc.exe** to run a new MMC.

2. Choose Console ➢ Add/Remove Snap-In to open the Add/Remove Snap-In dialog box.

3. Click the Add button to open the Add Standalone Snap-In dialog box, shown in Figure 1.1, and select Security Templates from the list of snap-ins.

4. Click Add to add the snap-in to the MMC, and then click Close to close the Add Standalone Snap-In dialog box.

5. Click OK in the Add/Remove Snap-In dialog box to add Security Templates to the new MMC, as shown in Figure 1.2.

FIGURE 1.1 The Add Standalone Snap-In dialog box

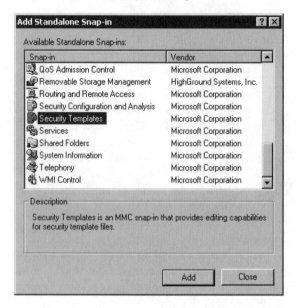

FIGURE 1.2 The Security Templates snap-in added to a new MMC

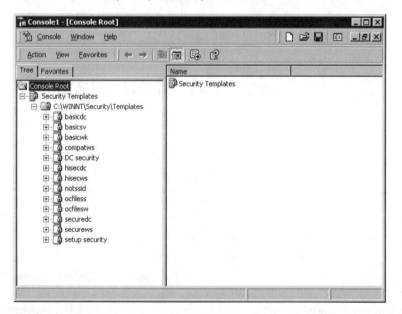

You'll notice in the Security Templates MMC that the templates reside (by default) in the C:\WINNT\Security\Templates folder. If you were to look at this folder, you'd see a listing

of `.inf` files that you can easily open in any text editor. What the Security Templates snap-in really does is provide a graphic front-end to what would be a taxing task of modifying these `.inf` files.

If you select any template in the left pane of the MMC, you'll see seven objects in the right pane, as shown in Figure 1.3.

FIGURE 1.3   The seven objects that can be secured in a Windows 2000 security template

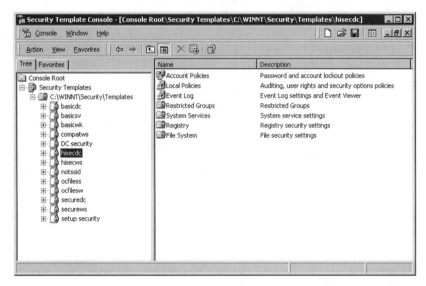

Here is an explanation of each of these objects:

Account Policies   This area covers a cluster of policies that pertain to user accounts. Even account policies are specified at the domain level, domain controllers receive their account policies settings from the domain controller OU. Account policies include the following three individual policies:

Password policy   With this policy, you can set restrictions on password length, age, uniqueness, and complexity.

Account lockout policy   With this policy, you set the rules for account lockout, including duration and method of releasing the account.

Kerberos policy   This policy governs such settings as the ticket lifetime.

Local Policies   This object includes a cluster of policies that focus on auditing local and/or network access to the server. *How* events are audited is also included in this policy. This template includes the following three policies:

Audit policy   This policy specifies which events are recorded for later reference.

User rights policy   With this object, you specify rights for user accounts and security groups.

Security options policy   This policy holds a wide-ranging set of configurable values, including the logon banner and SMB (Server Message Block) signing.

Event Log   This object contains configurable options on how the application, security, and system event logs behave.

Restricted Groups   This setting allows the administrator to define membership in the built-in security groups or other administrative-defined security groups that are given elevated privileges.

System Services   This policy lets you specify security attributes of all system services, including file, print, network, and telephone.

Registry   This object contains security settings for your Registry keys and lets you set auditing values and access permissions.

File System   This object allows for the configuration of access permissions and the auditing of specific folders and files on the local server.

Two items should be noted at this point. First, these templates will not work on a FAT (File Allocation Table) partition, so ensure that you are running NTFS (New Technology File System) on all partitions on the server that you want to secure. Second, never deploy these templates on production systems without first testing them in a lab environment. Unintended access or denials can occur if you don't first test these templates on an offline server to observe their effects.

The names of the .inf files might appear confusing at first, but after you work with them for a while, they'll make more sense. Let's now take a look at each template type and the .inf files that are included in each type.

Default Security Templates

Microsoft has some predefined templates that you can use as is or customize to meet your specific needs. Some of these templates only modify existing templates, and others install an entire set of values on the computer.

The default security templates provide basic Windows 2000 settings for workstations, servers, and domain controllers. You can use these templates to reverse unwanted behavior that is a result of a customized template being applied. You can also use these templates to apply an initial set of security values to any computer that has been upgraded to Windows 2000 from Windows NT. These templates contain default settings for the following:

- Account policies
- Local policies
- Event log maintenance
- Basic permissions for system services
- Access permissions for files

These policies do not include configuration values for user rights assignments so that these policies will not overwrite any assignments made by an installed application. Because the members of the Windows 2000 Users group have stricter permissions than members of the Windows NT Users group, Windows NT applications that are not certified for Windows 2000 may not run under the security context of the Windows 2000 Users group. You can fix this by doing one of the following:

- Add all user accounts to the Power Users group (not recommended for most security environments due to the added permissions enjoyed by the Power Users group).

- Apply the compatible security template (`compatws.inf`).

- Upgrade the application to be Windows 2000 certified.

The `ocfiles` templates contain default settings for all optional components that may or may not exist on a given system. If the file doesn't exist, a warning message is generated in the event logs, and this indicates that a file was not present on which to set security.

The files and their purposes are as follows:

basicdc   For Windows 2000 domain controllers

basicsv   For Windows 2000 Server computers

basicwk   For Windows 2000 Professional computers

ocfiless   For stand-alone or member servers

ocfilesw   For Windows 2000 Professional computers

Incremental Templates

Windows 2000 Server ships with several templates that only modify existing security settings. When working with these templates, you'll need to first have a default template applied. These templates include only modifications. They do not include the default settings, and they elevate security settings from the default settings found in the default templates.

No Terminal Server SID Template (notssid)   The `notssid` template removes the Terminal Server (TS) security identifier (SID) from all file systems and Registry objects. Once applied, TS users' permissions are defined through membership in the Power Users or Users group.

You can use this template in a couple of different situations. First, you can use it to remove older applications' rights that ran under elevated privileges once the application is upgraded to run under Windows 2000 Server. Second, you can use it to control where users can go during a TS session. In either scenario, this template is used to restrict user and application access to resources using the TS SID.

Secure Templates   Two templates fall into this area: `securews` (workstations and servers) and `securedc` (domain controllers). These templates provide increased security for the operating system. Resources secured by permissions are not covered in these templates. These templates do remove members of the Power Users group from the DACL on resources.

High Security Templates   The `hisecws` (workstation and server) and `hisecdc` (domain controller) templates increase security for parameters that affect network protocols, such as SMB Signing. Use this template only in pure Windows 2000 environments; applying this template will likely degrade performance of your servers. Moreover, this template removes the TS SID from your system and removes members from the Power Users group and gives them permissions similar to that for the Users group.

Compatible Template   This template (`compatws`) is for workstations and servers. Because the permissions for the Users group in Windows 2000 were tightened, you might need to "loosen" them just a bit to allow older applications to run on your servers and workstations. This template makes these applications "compatible" with the Windows 2000 operating system so that these older applications can run as they did under older operating systems.

Other Templates   You might run across a few other templates that provide a specific function. First, the `setup security` template resets all values to default, which means that you'll be taking your server or workstation back to the state it was in when first installed. The `rootsec` template is used to secure the system root on a Windows 2000 Professional computer. The `DC security` template is used to reset all values to default on domain controllers.

Configuring Templates

You can select numerous options in each section to increase security on your systems. However, since it would be of little value to discuss each and every one in detail, we'll discuss at a high level how you configure each area.

Account Policies

To modify any of the account policies settings, expand the Account Policies settings node inside the Group Policy you want to configure. Beneath this node, you'll see three policies that you can configure: password, account lockout, and Kerberos. When you select a policy, the actual settings appear in the right pane (see Figure 1.4).

FIGURE 1.4   Individual security policy settings under the Account Policies node

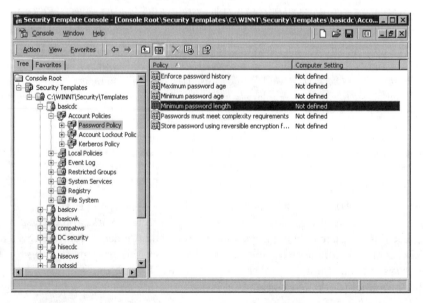

To configure an individual setting, double-click it in the right pane to open a dialog box that is specific to that setting. However, you'll also be given the choice to either enable or disable the setting by selecting or clearing the Define This Policy Setting In The Template check box. In Figure 1.5, you can see that we've selected to enforce a minimum password length of seven characters.

FIGURE 1.5   The individual policy setting dialog box for setting a minimum password length

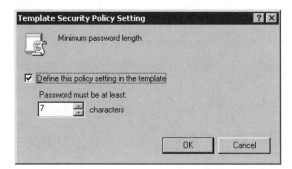

Once you define the setting and click OK, the MMC displays the new configuration in the Computer Setting column in the right pane (see Figure 1.6).

FIGURE 1.6   The results of the new minimum password setting displayed in the Computer Setting column in the Security Templates MMC

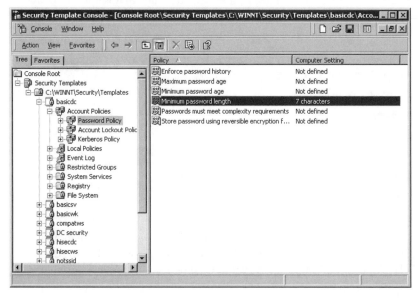

In Exercise 1.1, you will configure an account policy.

EXERCISE 1.1

Configuring an Account Policy

1. Open the Active Directory Users and Computers MMC.

2. Open the properties of the Domain or OU you wish to apply the account policy against.

3. Click the Group Policy tab.

4. Click Edit to open the Group Policy dialog box.

5. Navigate to the Account Policies section of the Group Policy.

6. Make your configuration changes in either the Password or Account Lockout policy or both.

7. Close the Group Policy dialog box.

8. Click OK to close the Properties dialog box.

Audit Policies

Auditing is both a proactive and reactive security measure: it informs administrators of events that might be potentially dangerous and leaves a trail of accountability that can be referenced in the future. By default, all auditing is turned off; so if you want to use this feature, you'll need to turn it on. The easiest way to do this is through a security template that is applied to all your servers.

Before you can configure a template for auditing, you must first plan your audit policy. The following categories are available for auditing:

- Account logon events
- Account management
- Directory service access
- Logon events
- Object access
- Policy change
- Privilege use
- Process tracking
- System events

On nondomain controller computers, you'll use Computer Management to enable auditing on the local machine. On a domain controller, you'll use a Group Policy to edit the audit policy.

When developing your audit policy, you'll need to account for three elements:

- Who will be audited
- Whether to audit failed events, successful events, or both
- What type of object access will be audited

When you want to audit an individual resource, such as a folder or printer, you'll need to enable object access auditing on the server or domain controller, and then you'll need to go to the resource's Properties dialog box and enable auditing there as well. Hence, when auditing for object access, there is always a two-step process that doesn't exist with other event categories.

The results of your auditing policy are displayed in the Security Event Log. This log displays detailed information about the chosen events.

In the "Event Logs" section of this chapter, we'll discuss how to use security templates to configure the behavior of all logs on your Windows 2000–based servers and workstations.

The auditing options are as follows:

Audit account logon events Tracks events related to user logon and logoff activity system-wide. Events are recorded on the domain controllers in your domain even if they occur on member servers or workstations.

Audit account management Tracks account management actions in Active Directory Users and Computers. Any time a user, a computer, or a group account is created, modified, or deleted, an event can be generated and placed in the log file.

Audit directory service access Tracks access to Active Directory by users or computers. You will need to configure the object's properties to audit either success or failed events.

Audit logon events This is the same as Windows NT's Logon and Logoff audit category. User logon and logoff activities are recorded in the local server's logs. This policy records only activity for the local server to which the policy is applied.

Audit object access Tracks access to objects on nondomain controllers. You will need to configure the object's properties to audit either success or failed events.

Audit policy change Tracks changes to user rights, auditing, and trust relationships.

Audit privilege use Tracks the use of user rights and privileges, such as when a user shuts down a server.

The Audit privilege use policy does not track the following user rights: bypass traverse checking, debug programs, create a token object, replace process level token, generate security audits, back up files and folders, and restore files and folders. If you want to track backup and restore activities, you'll need to override this default behavior by enabling Audit Use Of Backup and Restore Privilege under the Security node nested inside the Local Policies node.

Audit process tracking Tracks each process running on the server and the resources it uses.

Audit system events Tracks system events such as startup, shutdown, and restart. It also tracks actions that affect system security or changes to the security log.

To turn on auditing, navigate to the desired template, drill down to the Audit Policy node as shown in Figure 1.7, and make your selections.

FIGURE 1.7   Audit log selections for a security template

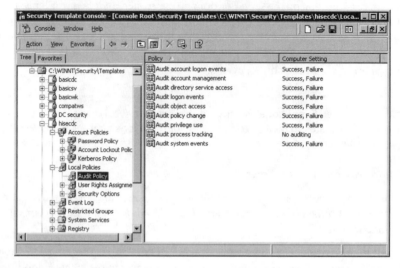

To enable auditing for object access, you'll need to access the folder or file properties directly and enable it. To do so, follow these steps:

1. Open the object's Properties dialog box.
2. Click the Security tab.
3. Click the Advanced button to open the object's Access Control Settings dialog box, as shown in Figure 1.8.

FIGURE 1.8   The Access Control Settings dialog box, open at the Auditing tab

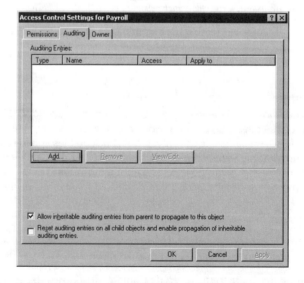

4. Click the Auditing tab, click Add, select the accounts you want to audit, and then click OK.

In the Auditing Entry For *name_of_object* dialog box (see Figure 1.9), you can select exactly which actions you want to audit and how to apply your selections. The information in the Auditing Entry dialog box will depend on the object, because the auditing options are different for folders, files, and printers.

FIGURE 1.9   Selecting auditing options for a folder

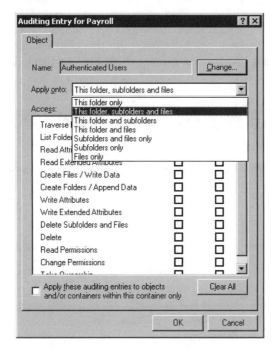

You have two other options that you can use to specify the objects to which your auditing policy should be applied. At the bottom of the Auditing Entry dialog box, you'll see an Apply These Auditing Entries To Objects And/Or Containers Within This Container Only check box. Select this check box to specify that the auditing policy you are implementing be applied only to objects that reside within the target container (or folder).

At the bottom of the Auditing tab in the Access Control Settings dialog box, you can push down the auditing configurations you've selected to all child objects of the target object you are configuring by selecting the Reset Auditing Entries On All Child Objects And Enable Propagation Of Inheritable Auditing Entries check box.

Selecting this check box does not override settings on individual child folders after the values have been applied. For example, if you have a parent folder named Payroll and a subfolder named ShopWorkers, you can set auditing on both folders by making your configuration choices on the Payroll folder and then selecting the Reset Auditing Entries On All Child Objects And Enable Propagation Of Inheritable Auditing Entries check box. Thereafter, if you make further selections on the ShopWorkers folder, you'll find that those choices will be added to the settings being pushed down from the Payroll folder.

You can also block auditing inheritance from parent objects by clearing the Allow Inheritable Auditing Entries From Parent To Propagate To This Object check box. This allows you to either copy or remove the current auditing policies and create a new set of policies for an individual folder or for a new hierarchy of folders. However, this can be overridden by selecting the Reset Auditing Entries On All Child Objects And Enable Propagation Of Inheritable Auditing Entries check box on a parent folder.

To enable auditing for an Active Directory object, you'll need to access the object in Active Directory Users and Computers and open the object's Properties dialog box. From there, create a new Group Policy and create your audit policy for that object. If necessary, you can block policy inheritance so that you can create a new, fresh policy on an individual AD object.

In Exercise 1.2, you will configure an audit policy.

EXERCISE 1.2

Configuring an Audit Policy

1.   Select a target container upon which to configure the audit policy, such as an OU.

2.   Open the container's Properties dialog box.

3.   Click the Group Policy tab.

4.   Highlight the group policy you want to use and click Edit to open the group policy.

5.   Navigate to the Audit Policy node under the Local Policies node.

6.   Double-click an individual policy setting.

7.   Click the Define These Policy Settings check box.

8.   Make your configuration choices.

9.   Click OK to close the policy setting dialog box.

10. Close the Group Policy dialog box by selecting Close from the Group Policy menu.

11. Click OK to close the container's Properties dialog box.

User Rights Assignment

You use the User Rights Agreement node to assign users and/or groups rights to perform activities on the network (see Figure 1.10). To configure user rights, select the User Rights Assignment node, and then double-click the right you want to configure in the right pane. Select the Define The Policy Settings In The Template check box, and then add the users and/or groups to the setting. Click OK to display the new settings next to the right in the Computer Setting column in the right pane.

FIGURE 1.10   The User Rights Assignment node and settings in the Security Templates console

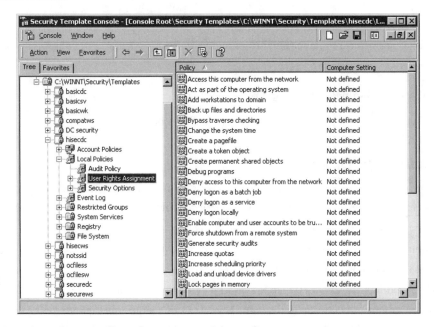

In Exercise 1.3, you will configure a user rights policy.

EXERCISE 1.3

Configuring a User Rights Policy

1.   Select a target container upon which to configure the user rights, such as an OU.

2.   Open the container's Properties dialog box.

3.   Click the Group Policy tab.

4.   Select the Group Policy you want to use and click Edit. This will open the group policy.

5.   Navigate to the User Rights Assignments node under the Local Policies node.

6.   Double-click an individual policy setting.

7.   Click the Define These Policy Settings check box.

8.   Click Add to open the Add user or group input box. Select the user and/or group accounts you want to apply this policy setting to by clicking the Browse button. This will open the Select Users or Groups box.

EXERCISE 1.3 *(continued)*

9. Click OK to close the Select Users or Groups box after making your selection.

10. Click OK to close the User and group names box.

11. Click OK to close the policy setting.

12. Close the Group Policy dialog box by selecting Close from the Group Policy menu.

13. Click OK to close the container's Properties dialog box.

Security Options

The Security Options node provides many options to strengthen security on your network. The options are too numerous to list here, but some of the highlights include the following:

- Do Not Display Last Username In Logon Screen
- Automatically Logoff Users When Logon Time Expires
- Message Text For Users Attempting To Logon
- Force Communications Between Servers To Be Digitally Signed

You set options in this node in the same way that you assign user rights.

In Exercise 1.4, you will configure the last logged-on username so that it does not appear in the Logon dialog box.

EXERCISE 1.4

Configuring the Last Logged-On Username So That It Doesn't Appear in the Logon Dialog Box

1. Select a target container upon which to configure the account policy. In this example, we'll select the domain object.

2. Open the container's Properties dialog box.

3. Click the Group Policy tab.

4. Select the group policy you want to use and click Edit to open the group policy.

5. Navigate to the Security Options node under the Local Policies node.

6. Double-click Do Not Display Last Logged On Username In Logon Screen policy setting to open this policy setting.

7. Select the Define This Policy Setting check box.

8. Make your desired configuration choices.

9. Click OK to close the policy setting.

10. Close the Group Policy dialog box by selecting Close from the Group Policy menu.

11. Click OK to close the container's Properties dialog box.

System Services

You use the System Services node to configure the startup and access control settings for each of the system services, such as the Server service, Workstation server, DHCP (Dynamic Host Configuration Protocol) server, and so forth.

Setting a system service policy can be both useful and destructive. Ensure that the services configured in your template don't conflict with any of the roles your servers or workstations are performing.

To configure a system service setting, select the System Services node in the left pane (see Figure 1.11). Double-click the target service in the right pane. Click the Define This Policy In The Template check box to open the security dialog box for this service. Edit the security as needed, and then select the startup mode for the service. Click OK to configure a policy for a system service.

FIGURE 1.11   The System Services node in the Security Template console

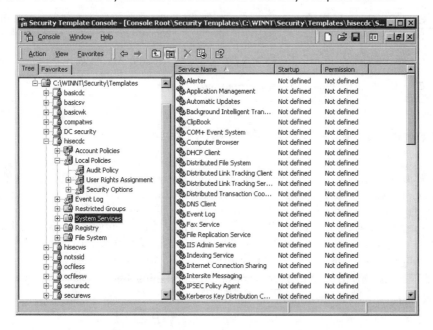

In Exercise 1.5, you will configure a policy for a system service.

Configuring a System Service Security and Startup Policy

1. Select a target container upon which to configure the account policy, such as an OU.

2. Open the container's Properties dialog box.

3. Click the Group Policy tab.

4. Select the group policy you want to use and click Edit to open the group policy.

5. Navigate to the System Services node under the Security Settings node.

6. Double-click an individual security policy setting.

7. Select the Define These Policy Settings check box. The Security tab for this setting will automatically appear.

8. Make your configurations by clicking the Browse button to add user and/or group accounts from the Select Users, Groups or Computers dialog box. If you are happy with the Everyone Group as the only choice, then you need not click the Add or Remove buttons. Once you've made your selections, they will appear on the Security tab of the service. Click OK to close the Security tab.

9. Select the Service Startup Mode you need for this service, and click OK to close the policy setting.

10. Close the Group Policy dialog box by selecting Close from the Group Policy menu.

11. Click OK to close the container's Properties dialog box.

Registry and File System Permissions

You use the Registry node to configure both access control and auditing values for specific Registry keys. To modify the Registry settings, first select the Registry node in the left pane. Some templates may not display anything in the right pane, but those that can modify the Registry entries will display a list of Registry settings in the right pane (see Figure 1.12).

In the right pane, double-click the Registry setting you'd like to configure to open the Template Security Policy Setting dialog box for that Registry key (see Figure 1.13). From here, you can configure the key and then do the following:

- Add permissions to existing permissions on the key and subkeys.

- Replace existing permissions on all subkeys.

FIGURE 1.12   The Registry node in the Security Templates console

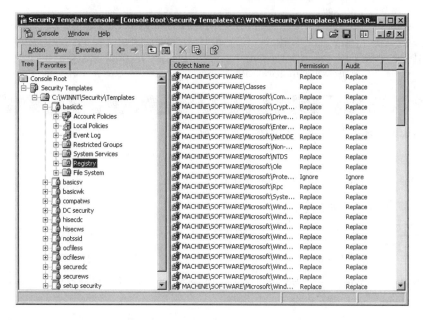

FIGURE 1.13   The Template Security Policy Setting dialog box

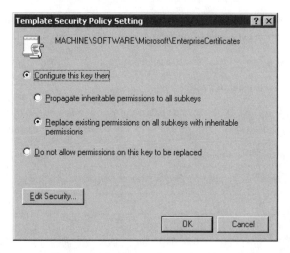

You can also select to not allow permissions to be replaced on this key. This selection is most helpful *after* the desired permissions have been applied to the key or if you want to essentially block permission inheritance on a particular key.

To change the permissions on the key, click the Edit Security button and make your selection.

If you right-click the Registry node, you can add a key and then configure permissions on that individual key. By designating individual keys, you can set and then block permissions for an individual key in the Registry and ensure that those permissions will persist after other settings have been applied.

File system permissions work exactly the same way as described for the Registry permission settings except that you will be working on file and folder hierarchies and not on Registry keys. The look and feel of the dialog boxes is the same under the File System node as it is for the Registry node.

In Exercise 1.6, you will configure a Registry setting for a security policy.

EXERCISE 1.6

Configuring a Registry Setting Policy

1. Select a target container upon which to configure the Registry setting, such as a domain.

2. Open the container's Properties dialog box.

3. Click the Group Policy tab.

4. Select the group policy you want to use and click Edit to open the group policy.

5. Navigate to the Registry Settings node under the Security Settings node.

6. Right-click the Registry Settings node and select Add Key from the context menu. This will open the Select Registry Key box.

7. Select a key from the list to be entered into the policy. The Security tab for this key's properties will automatically appear.

8. Make your security choices for this key by clicking the Browse button on the Security tab to select user and/or group accounts from the Add Users, Groups or Computers dialog box.

9. Select the type of permission(s) you want the account to enjoy for this key.

10. Click OK to close the security tab.

11. Configure how you want permissions to be applied to the key in the Template Security Policy Setting dialog box, and then click OK to close the dialog box.

12. Close the Group Policy dialog box by selecting Close from the Group Policy menu.

13. Click OK to close the container's Properties dialog box.

 Real World Scenario

Using Security Policies to Configure Settings for DNS Dynamic Updates

You have decided that you want to prevent your Windows 2000 Professional workstations from registering an A (host) and PTR (pointer) record with your DNS (domain name server) server. You'd like to rely on your DHCP server to perform the registrations for your workstations. How would you go about this?

Well, the way to do this is to configure the following Registry key on each workstation:

NKLM\System\CurrentControlSet\Services\Tcpip\Parameters\DisableDynamicUpdate

How would you configure this Registry key network wide? Create a GPO and apply it to the OU that hosts your workstations. Modify the GPO to include this registry key. Wait 2 hours to ensure the registry key has been applied to all your workstations. Thereafter, when the workstations reboot, the DHCP server will register their DNS settings.

Restricted Groups

You use the Restricted Groups node to define who should and should not belong to a specific group. When a template with a restricted groups policy is applied to a system, the Security Configuration Tool Set adds and deletes members from specified groups to ensure that the actual group membership coincides with the settings defined in the template.

For example, you might want to add the Enterprise Admins to all Domain Admins security groups or to add the Domain Admins group to all Local Administrators groups on your workstations and servers.

To create a restricted Group Policy, right-click the Restricted Groups node and choose Add Group from the shortcut menu. Select the group you want to modify by either entering the group's name or browsing to find and select the group. Then click OK.

You'll see the group in the right pane. Right-click the group and select Security from the shortcut menu to open the Configure Membership dialog box, as shown in Figure 1.14. You can configure the membership of this group or configure the groups of which this group will be a member. Make your choices about membership, and then click OK. The group membership policy will now be set.

FIGURE 1.14   The Configure Membership dialog box

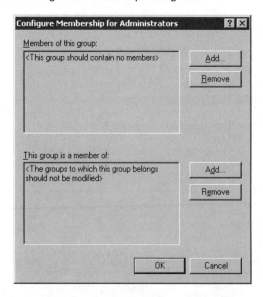

In Exercise 1.7, you will add the Domain Administrators Global Security group to a new security group you have created. For this exercise to work properly, you'll first need to create a new security group.

EXERCISE 1.7

Adding the Domain Administrators Global Security Group to a New Security Group That You Have Created.

1. Select a target container upon which to configure the account policy, usually a domain container.

2. Open the container's Properties dialog box.

3. Click the Group Policy tab.

4. Select the group policy you want to use and click Edit to open the group policy.

5. Navigate to the Restricted Groups node.

6. Right-click the Restricted Groups node and choose Add Group from the shortcut menu to open the Add Group box. Click the Browse button to open the Select Groups box and select the Domain Administrators Security Global Group.

7. Click OK to close the Select Groups box.

8. Click OK to close the Add Group box.

9. Right-click the Domain Administrators group in the right pane of the group policy and select Security from the context menu to open the Configure Membership for Guests dialog box.

10. In the This Group Is A Member Of section, click Add to display the Group Membership box. If you don't know the name of the group you wish to use, click Browse to display the Select Group selection box and select the group from this box.

11. Click OK to close the Select Groups box.

12. Click OK to close the Group membership box.

13. Click OK to close the Configure Membership box.

14. Close the Group Policy dialog box by selecting Close from the Group Policy menu.

15. Click OK to close the container's Properties dialog box.

Event Logs

The settings for the event logs are configured under a common policy, regardless of the log type. As you can see in Figure 1.15, you can set the log size, guest access, the log retention period, and other options unique to log files in Windows 2000 Server. To change the configurations on these settings, simply double-click the setting in the right pane and make your configuration choices. Changing these settings works the same as it does for account and local polices, which we described earlier in this chapter.

FIGURE 1.15 Event log settings in the Security Template console

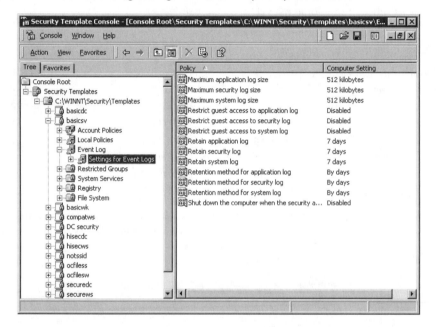

Deploying Security Templates

After you configure your security templates to your requirements, you'll need to deploy them. We'll describe two ways to do so, using group polices and using scripts.

Using Group Policies to Deploy Templates

The best way to deploy security templates is to use a GPO. As we mentioned earlier in the chapter, a GPO is a collection of policy settings that is applied in a uniform manner across a set of objects. You can import security templates into a GPO and then apply that GPO to a site, a domain, or an OU.

If you need to apply security settings to one or more Windows 2000 computers in a workgroup setting, the only way to do so is to use a local policy template and apply it to the local system directly. Use this method when you are in a workgroup environment, when your Windows 2000 server is on a non-Microsoft network, or when no Active Directory is present.

The effective policy applied to a Windows 2000 computer is really the culmination of several policies applied in a particular order. The policies on a Windows 2000 computer are processed in the following order:

1. Local policy of the computer
2. Policies applied at the site level
3. Policies applied at the domain level
4. Policies applied at the parent OU level
5. Policies applied at the child OU level

The policy applied last takes precedence. Hence, policies processed at the local OU level override any policy settings defined at other levels. The only exception to this is domain controllers, whose account policy settings defined in the default domain policy override any account policy setting from other GPOs. Hence, domain controllers use the account policies defined in the default domain policy regardless of the account policies set on the domain controller OU.

To assign a GPO to a container in Active Directory, follow these steps:

1. Navigate to the container and open its Properties dialog box.
2. Click the Group Policy tab then click Edit to open the group policy.
3. Navigate to the Security Settings node, then right-click on the node and select Import Policy from the shortcut menu to open the Import Policy From selection box. (Figure 1.16).

FIGURE 1.16   Import Policy From selection box.

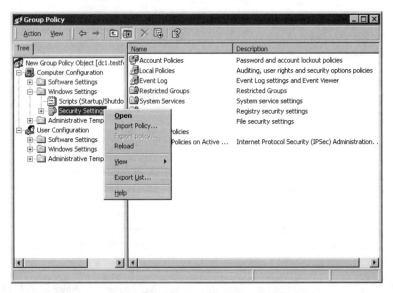

4. Select the template you wish to import and click Open. You will be returned to the group policy focused on the Security Settings node.
5. Select Close from the Group Policy menu. You've just applied a template to multiple computers using a GPO.

Remember that domain controllers update their GPO assignments every 5 minutes whereas servers and workstations update ever 90 minutes with a random offset of 30 minutes.

To import a policy template for an individual server, use the Local Security Policy console on the Administrative Tools menu.

Using Scripts to Deploy Templates

You can also use the command-line version of the *Security Configuration and Analysis tool (secedit.exe)* to deploy security templates. Specifically, you use `secedit /configure` to apply a stored template to one or more computers. Here are the switches and what they mean:

/db *filename* Use this switch, which is required, to specify the location of the database file you want to use. The database referred to here is one that is created using the Security Configuration and Analysis tool (SCA). We'll discuss how to do this shortly.

/cfg *filename* This switch can only be used in conjunction with the /db switch. Use this switch to import a template into an existing database.

/overwrite This switch can only be used when the /cfg switch is used. This switch specifies whether the template in the /cfg switch should be appended to current settings or whether the template should overwrite current settings in the selected database. If you don't use this switch, the template settings are appended to the current settings.

/areas *area1, area2* Use this switch to specify which security areas should be applied with this command. If you don't use this switch, you apply all the areas of the template. Separate area designations using a single space. Here are the area names and their meanings:

SECURITYPOLICY Apply the local and domain policies.

GROUP_MGMT Apply Restricted Group settings.

USER_RIGHTS Apply User Logon Rights settings.

REGKEYS Apply Registry settings.

FILESTORE Apply File System settings.

SERVICES Apply System Services settings.

/logpath Use this switch to specify the path and name of the log file in which you want to record the results of this command.

/verbose Use this switch if you want to know everything there is to know about the progress of your command and how it is working or not working.

/Quiet This switch suppresses both screen and log file output.

If this is the first time you're applying the template to one or more computers, your database is named *basic*.sdb, and the path to the database is x:\securitydbs, use this syntax:

```
Secedit /configure /db x:\securitydbs\basic.sdb
```

If this is not the first time you're applying the template to one or more computers, and you want to use a new template to overwrite the existing configurations in *basic*.sdb, and the new template file is named highsecurity.inf, use this syntax:

```
Secedit /configure /db x:\securitydbs\basic.sdb /cfg
f:\templates\highsecurity.inf /overwrite
```

To create a new database in the SCA tool, follow these steps:

1. Create a new MMC with the SCA snap-in.

2. Open the snap-in.

3. Right-click Security Configuration and Analysis, and choose Open Database from the shortcut menu to open the Open Database dialog box.

4. In the File Name box, enter a name for the database. In this example, we named the new database HighSecurity (Figure 1.17).

FIGURE 1.17   The Open Database dialog box

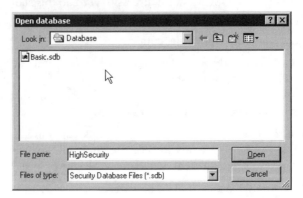

5. Click Open to open the Import Template dialog box, as shown in Figure 1.18.

FIGURE 1.18   Associating the hisecdc template with the HighSecurity database

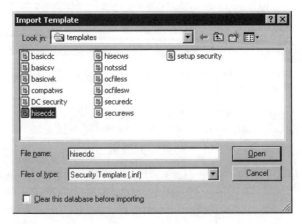

6. Select the template to apply to the database (in our example, we selected the `hisecdc` template) and then click Open again.

7. By default, the database is saved in the `My Documents\security` folder of the user account under which you are logged on when the database is created. You can, of course, move the database to another location for easier path administration when using the `secedit` command.

Troubleshooting Security Templates

When troubleshooting security settings, you need to understand which GPO has been applied and at what level that GPO resides. You can determine where a GPO has been applied in the overall folder structure in two ways: look at each site, domain, and OU container or use the `gpresult` resource kit utility. Let's look at each one briefly.

If you want to know which objects a particular GPO has been assigned to, open the Properties dialog box of the GPO in either Active Directory Users And Computers or Active Directory Sites And Services. This dialog box has three tabs: General, Links, and Security. On the Links tab, click Find Now to find all the objects to which this GPO has been explicitly applied. Containers that are inheriting the GPO will not appear on this list.

The gpresult resource kit is a command-line tool that quickly runs through Active Directory and displays the results for your currently logged on user account as well as the computer at which you are logged on. For our purposes, you can look to the end of this report and find all the GPOs that have been applied to this computer and user and what areas were affected (see Figure 1.19). Use this information to direct your efforts when troubleshooting the deployment of *security templates*.

FIGURE 1.19   The results of running the gpresult utility at the command prompt

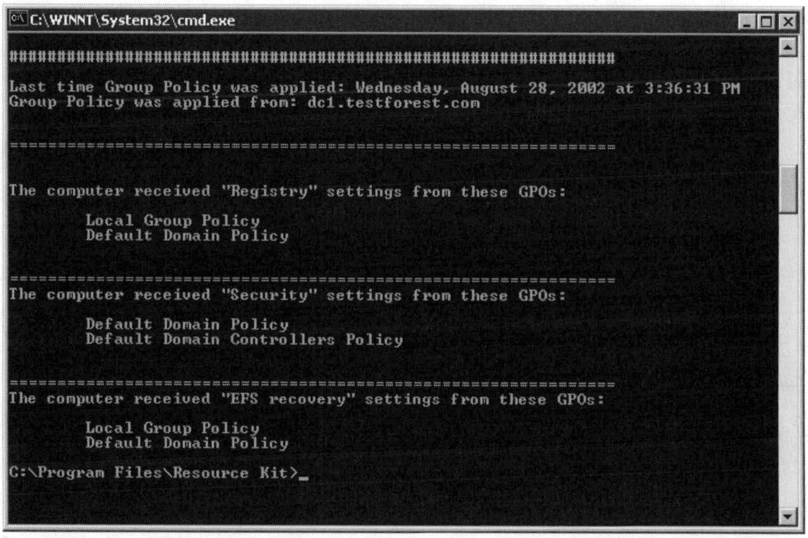

One of the most common scenarios when troubleshooting templates is that once applied, they don't do what you thought they would do. If this happens, bear in mind the following:

- Deleting the Group Policy will not remove the configurations.

- Appending a policy to current configurations will not remove the configurations.

- You will need to overwrite the configurations with the correct configurations.

To overwrite the configurations with a new policy, you can use the `secedit` command. A more labor intensive method is to manually make the changes in the currently applied GPO, and at this workstation use the `secedit /refresh` command to force this new policy to be applied immediately. Either way, you'll need to somehow rewrite the settings that are amiss in your overall security configuration.

Troubleshooting Group Policy–Applied Templates

Not only do we need the skills necessary to apply security templates via GPOs or command-line tools, but we also need to know how to troubleshoot security templates when something doesn't work as expected.

In this section, we'll cover some basic troubleshooting tips for GPOs and discuss the "gotchas" for applying GPOs in a mixed client environment and after a server's operating system has been upgraded to Windows 2000 from Windows NT 4.

A GPO can be applied incorrectly for a number of reasons, but they can be distilled into two common occurrences:

- Network problems are preventing the GPO from being applied.

- The policy was assigned to the wrong AD container and, therefore, is not being applied to the desired objects in AD.

First, eliminate all your network connectivity issues. Check DNS to ensure proper name resolution, ping your servers, check your cables, and ensure that other traffic is passing over your network. Check the event logs to ensure that there are no warning or stop error messages. If there are, troubleshoot them as needed.

Second, if you've applied the GPO to the wrong container—maybe you wanted to apply it to one OU and instead it was applied to another OU—explicitly apply it to the correct OU and then use the `secedit /overwrite` command to apply a default template to the first OU to remove the unwanted configurations.

If you find that your policies are not being applied after waiting an appropriate amount of time, use the `secedit` command to refresh the policies in the folder. In other words, if the policy is applied to the correct container and you have eliminated connectivity issues, perhaps the problem is that you haven't waited long enough for the policy to be applied on its own. Remember that domain controllers update their policies every 5 minutes, but member servers and workstations update every 90 minutes with a randomized offset of 30 minutes. Hence, you may need to run the `secedit` command to force the policies to refresh before their scheduled interval. The `secedit` command is run from the command prompt.

Troubleshooting after Upgrading Operating Systems

Remember that Windows NT 4 policies will not migrate to Windows 2000, so any `*.pol` files that were created in your Windows NT 4 domain will not be migrated to Windows 2000.

In addition, after you upgrade a Windows NT 4 server to Windows 2000 Server, group policies are not automatically applied to that server. Hence, after upgrading a Windows NT 4 server to Windows 2000, apply the `basic*` templates to the server to apply at least a baseline of values to the server.

Troubleshooting Mixed Client Environments

If you have a mix of Windows 9*x*, Windows NT, and Windows 2000 clients on your network, pushing out security templates via group policies will not be easy. But you can enable a policy setting to allow the use of Windows NT 4–style policies for your legacy clients.

When configured this way, legacy clients will connect to the Netlogon share to find their `.pol` file and apply it during logon or logoff. However, if you change the policy, your legacy clients will need to log off and log back on to effect those changes right away. Unlike a Windows 2000 client that refreshes its policy settings every 90 minutes, legacy clients apply policies only during logon or logoff. This inefficient method can create some real headaches for administrators who might be more comfortable having their policy changes applied without client intervention.

If the new policies conflict with the old settings, some clients can be in conflict with others: for example, some clients can access a resource and others cannot.

The only real solution here is to adapt to the legacy clients and implement changes during times when you know your legacy clients will soon be logging off or on to the network.

Summary

This chapter started with an overview of Group Policies and then discussed what security templates are, how you can modify them, and how you can use them to update a GPO. You learned about the various security templates, including the basic and incremental templates. You also learned how to create a new template using the SCA tool, as well as how to troubleshoot templates.

You also learned that you can use the SCA tool to create new templates for GPOs. And you saw how to use the `secedit` command-line utility to push out new policies using customized templates to workstations and servers.

This chapter also covered troubleshooting policies, which can be a bit tricky, but the main thing to remember is that most problems occur from either applying the policy to the wrong container or configuring the wrong settings on the container. Best practice is to always apply a new template to an offline server first to observe the results of the policy before applying it to your production servers.

Exam Essentials

Know how to configure security templates.   Be sure that you understand which templates to use when configuring a new template. For example, if the server has recently been upgraded from Windows NT 4 to Windows 2000 Server, you can't just apply a customized template immediately. You'll first need to apply one of the basic templates to write a new set of basic configurations to your server. Be sure that you understand which templates write an entire set of configuration values and which ones merely write new information and assume that a base set of values in already in place.

Know the methods for deploying templates.   Be sure to understand that templates can be deployed in several different ways. You can deploy policies by importing them into an existing or a new Group Policy, or you can deploy them by using the `secedit /configure` command. You can use the `secedit` command to push out templates immediately. You can use a Group Policy to push out changes that don't need to be pushed out immediately.

Understand the potential hazards of working in mixed client environments.   Understand that you can enable the functionality of a Windows NT 4 policy in a Windows 2000 Server environment using a Group Policy. However, be aware of the timing differences between legacy systems and Windows 2000 Professional systems. Such differences can result in significant headaches when trying to reconfigure policies on your network.

Key Terms

Before you take the exam, be certain you are familiar with the following terms:

Access Control Entries (ACEs)	Group Policy Container (GPC)
Active Directory (AD)	Group Policy Template (GPT)
Active Directory Sites and Services (ADSS)	Security Configuration and Analysis tool (secedit.exe)
Active Directory Users and Computers (ADUC)	security templates
Discretionary Access Control List (DACL)	

Review Questions

1. You have 50 Windows 2000 Professional computers and 4 Windows 2000 domain controllers. Seven of your workstations are running an old application that has not been upgraded to be Windows 2000 compatible. You need to enable this application to run on those seven Windows 2000 Professional computers. What actions should you take? (Choose all that apply.)

    A. Apply the `basicws.inf` template. Modify the local policies to allow the application to run.

    B. Apply the `compatws.inf` template to the computers OU.

    C. Apply the `compatws.inf` template.

    D. Move the seven computers into their own OU and apply the `compatws.inf` template to this new OU.

2. You have recently upgraded your Windows NT 4 primary domain controller to be the root domain controller in your Windows 2000 forest. You apply the `hisecdc.inf` template to the domain controllers OU. After applying the template, you discover that its settings are not being applied. What should you do?

    A. Apply the `compatws.inf` template first.

    B. Apply the `notssid.inf` template first.

    C. Apply the `DC Security.inf` template first.

    D. Apply the `basicdc.inf` template first.

3. You have 200 users running a legacy application through Terminal Server on your Windows 2000 server. You've just been informed that a new version of this application will be arriving later this week that is Windows 2000 compliant. You have been charged with installing this application. After installing this application, you want your Windows 2000 server to be as secure as possible. What should you do?

    A. Create a new Group Policy to apply security at the Local Policies level.

    B. Create a new Group Policy to apply the `hisecdc.inf` template.

    C. Create a new Group Policy to apply the `notssid.inf` template.

    D. Convert the new application to work with Windows Terminal Server, and then apply the `notssid.inf` template.

4. The Maximum Lifetime For User Ticket Renewal is an example of what kind of policy setting?

    A. Password

    B. Local

    C. Kerberos

    D. User Rights Assignment

    E. System Services

5. You have a new Windows 2000 server that was upgraded from Windows NT 4. On this server, you have an industry-specific application that needs a unique set of system rights applied. You have applied those rights correctly. Now, you want to install a new security template. You decide to first apply the basicdc.inf template. What will be the result of this action on the permissions you've created for your application?

   A. Permissions will be modified.

   B. Permissions will not be modified.

   C. Permissions will be retained.

   D. Permission will be overwritten.

6. You have a special legacy application that needs to run on your Windows 2000 server. You do not want to apply the basic.inf template. What should you do?

   A. Add all the user accounts that need to use this application to the Power Users security group.

   B. Give the Everyone security group Write permissions to the Netlogon share.

   C. Give the Authenticated Users security group Read permissions to the Sysvol folder.

   D. Add all the user accounts that need to use this application to the Authenticated Users security group, and then add this group to the Power Users security group.

7. You want to implement a high degree of security on three of your Windows 2000 member servers. Which template should you use?

   A. hisecws.inf

   B. hisecdc.inf

   C. DC security.inf

   D. rootsec.inf

8. You want to enforce a minimum password length of eight characters. You create a new Group Policy object, open the Account Polices node, and select the Minimum Password Length setting. What should you do after double-clicking this setting? (Choose two.)

   A. Click the Reset All Passwords To This Length check box.

   B. Click the Define This Policy Setting In This Template check box.

   C. Clear the Define This Policy Setting In This Template check box.

   D. Clear the Reset All Passwords To This Length check box.

   E. Select 8 as the number of characters for the minimum password length.

9. You want to enable auditing on the company's payroll printer. You believe that a malicious user is attempting to use the printer to print bogus payroll checks. You want to find out who this user is before they are successful. What is the best way to do this? (Choose all that apply.)

   A. Enable failed logon events.

   B. Enable failed object access.

   C. Enable successful object access.

   D. Enable privilege use tracking.

   E. Audit the Authenticated Users security group in the printer's Properties dialog box.

   F. Audit the Power Users security group in the printer's Properties dialog box.

10. You need to audit all successful and failed logon attempts for 40 Windows 2000 member servers and 15 Windows 2000 domain controllers. Which option should you use to ensure that all servers are covered by your policy?

    A. Account Logon Events

    B. Account Management

    C. Directory Service Access

    D. Logon Events

    E. Privilege Use

11. You need to audit who is backing up and restoring files as part of a larger effort to track user activity on your network and ensure overall security. What action should you take?

    A. Audit Privilege Use.

    B. Audit Process Tracking.

    C. Enable Audit Use Of Backup And Restore Privilege under the Security node.

    D. Enable Audit Use Of Backup And Restore Privilege under the Local Policies node.

12. You have a folder named Confidential Memos that is accessed only by executives in your company. Inside this folder are two other folders: Current Memos and Past Memos. You need to ensure that auditing is set on all three folders and their files so that your manager can track who is accessing these folders and their contents. What actions should you take? (Choose all that apply.)

    A. Enable successful object access on the domain GPO.

    B. Enable Authenticated Users group in the Properties dialog box of the Confidential Memos folder.

    C. Select Reset Auditing Entries On All Child Objects in the Confidential Memos folder.

    D. Select Apply These Auditing Entries To Objects And/Or Containers Within This container Only.

13. Your manager has told you that a new Authorized Users message must appear when users log on to your Windows 2000 network. Which node will you need to look inside to find the Message Text For Users Attempting To Logon setting?

A. Local Policies

B. User Rights Assignment

C. System Services

D. Security Options

14. You have opened the `hisecdc.inf` template in the Security Template snap-in. You attempt to modify a permission setting on a Registry value. You discover that the Registry entries are missing. What is the problem?

A. You are working with a template that won't display the Registry entries.

B. You are working with a corrupt template. Copy an uncorrupted version of the template from another Windows 2000 server.

C. You need to refresh your view to display the Registry entries.

D. You need to be logged on as a member of the Enterprise Administrators security group to see these Registry entries.

15. When applying an audit policy on your network, what part of the object is modified?

A. The object's properties

B. The object's System Access Control List

C. The object's Discretionary Access Control List

D. The object's advanced properties

16. Which of the following are the two methods for deploying a security template to one or more computers?

A. Systems Management Server

B. Group Policy Object

C. `secedit /export`

D. `secedit /configure`

17. In your site Group Policy, you selected to remove the Run command from the Start menu. In your computers OU Group Policy, you deselected to have the Run command removed from the Start menu. In your domain Group Policy Object, you selected Not Defined for the Remove The Run Command From The Start Menu. What is the effective result of these three policies?

A. The Run command will appear on the Start menu.

B. The Run command will not appear on the Start menu.

C. The Run command will appear, but will be grayed out on the Start menu.

D. The Run command will not appear on the Start menu but will be published in Add/Remove Programs in Control Panel.

18. You've just implemented a change to your domain security policy. The Group Policy is being applied to the domain controllers OU and is also linked to the computers OU. After 45 minutes, you discover that only a few of the Windows 2000 Professional workstations on your network have the new settings applied. What should you do?

    A. Use the `secedit /export` command to force all the workstations to update with the new security settings.

    B. Use the `secedit /configure` command to force all the workstations to update with the new security settings.

    C. Reboot the PDC Emulator since this domain controller is the default domain controller on which all group policies are initially applied and modified. Rebooting the server will apply the Group Policy to all the machines on your network.

    D. Do nothing. This is expected behavior.

19. You configured new account policy settings in the domain Group Policy Object. You find that it is not being applied to your Windows 2000–based computers on your network. You run the `secedit /refresh` command on each domain controller and wait two hours. Network connectivity issues are not preventing nonpolicy traffic from working on your network. The policy settings are still not being applied. What should you do?

    A. Apply the account policy settings at the site level.

    B. Ensure that you have saved the Group Policy settings correctly by rebooting your PDC Emulator.

    C. Apply the account policy settings at the domain controllers OU.

    D. Ensure that you have refreshed all the workstations on your network by running the `secedit /refresh` command in their logon script. Have all users log off and log back on.

20. You have a user whom you have explicitly denied access to a folder on a Windows 2000 member server. How will Windows 2000 apply that configuration when the user attempts to open that folder? (Choose two.)

    A. By reading the SACL

    B. By reading the DACL

    C. By reading the ACL

    D. By reading the Access Token

Answers to Review Questions

1. C, D.   The `compatws.inf` template is written to "loosen" permissions on Windows 2000 computers and servers to allow older applications to work correctly. If you applied this template to the computers OU, all 50 computers would have their permissions loosened. Best practice is to move the seven computers to their own OU and have them apply the template to their own OU.

2. D.   The `basicdc.inf` file is used to create an initial base of security values on a domain controller and can be used in this situation when a domain controller was upgraded from Windows NT 4 to Windows 2000.

3. C.   The `notssid.inf` template will remove the Terminal Service SID from all permission sets. Since the new application is Windows 2000 compliant, the application can run under the tighter security of Windows 2000 Server. Removing the Terminal Services SID from the ACLs of all resources is the way to make your Windows 2000 Server the most secure.

4. C.   The Kerberos protocol uses tickets, session tickets, ticket-granting tickets, and user tickets.

5. C.   The default security templates do not include configuration values for user rights assignments, including rights assignments created by an application that is installed on Windows 2000 Server.

6. A.   The Power Users group enjoys additional permissions that will allow a legacy application not written for Windows 2000 to run on the Windows 2000 platform.

7. A.   Even though `hisecws.inf` may indicate that this is a template for workstations, it is also the template used for member servers (not domain controllers).

8. B, E.   By default, all settings are not selected in a new GPO. Therefore, you'll first need to define the setting in the Group Policy template and then indicate the number of characters you want to use in the setting.

9. B, E.   Because you know that the user has not been successful at printing any checks, it would be better to see who is attempting to print to the printer unsuccessfully. Auditing the Authenticated Users group will include all users who have logged on to your domain.

10. A.   This option tracks events related to user logon and logoff activity domain wide, and the events are recorded on the domain controllers.

11. C.   The Audit Privilege node does not track user activity related to backup and restore procedures. Therefore, under the Security node, you'll need to enable Audit Use Of Backup And Restore Privilege.

12. A, B, C.   The last option is set only when you want to limit the scope of the policies being applied to the local container and its objects. If more folders are created under the `Confidential Memos` folder and you have this folder selected, these folders will not inherit the policy settings.

13. C.   This node includes many options that you can select to strengthen security on your network.

14. A.   Some templates won't display the Registry entries. If you need to configure permissions on Registry entries for a new policy template, you'll need to work with a template that will display these entries.

15. B.   Auditing places entries in the System Access Control List.

16. B, D.   You can use the Group Policy Object or the `secedit / configure` command to deploy a security template. The `secedit /export` command is used to export a security template stored in a security database to a stand-alone template. You can use Microsoft's Systems Management Server to deploy a `secedit` script, but that would be unnecessary.

17. A.   The most local policy is applied last, and since the policy for the OU deselects this restriction, the Run command will appear.

18. D.   The workstations are configured to update every 90 minutes with a random offset of an additional 30 minutes. That the policy has not been applied after 45 minutes to most workstations is not a problem, and you should take no action.

19. C.   Domain controllers receive their account policy settings only from the Group Policy object that is applied to the domain controllers OU. Your domain controllers will not recognize account policies applied at any other level or object.

20. B, D.   The Windows 2000 operating system will find the explicitly denied access configuration in the discretionary portion of the ACL. The user's SID, which is found in the Access Token, will be compared to the list of SIDs in the DACL, and if there is a match, the match will be enforced. Since the user has been denied access, the user's SID will be found at the top of the DACL and marked as Denied Access. The Local Security Services on the Windows 2000 server will enforce this setting first, meaning that all other settings in the ACL will be ignored.

Chapter

2

Configuring Security Based on Computer Roles

THE MICROSOFT EXAM OBJECTIVES COVERED IN THIS CHAPTER:

✓ Configure additional security based on computer roles. Computer roles include Microsoft SQL Server computer, Microsoft Exchange Server computer, domain controller, Internet Authentication Service (IAS) server, Internet Information Services (IIS) server, and mobile client computer.

✓ Configure additional security for client-computer operating systems by using Group Policy.

You can apply security templates to your servers all day long, but if you don't understand the unique needs of your servers, you'll miss some important configurations that should be set for these servers.

As part of this exam, you'll be expected to understand these needs and know how to tweak the configurations on these servers to ensure that they are as secure as reasonably possible. These server platforms include:

- SQL Server 2000

- Exchange 2000 Server

- Internet Information Services

- Windows 2000 Server domain controller

- Wireless client computers

In this chapter, we'll also cover the security considerations for non-Windows clients.

Exam questions will probably incorporate this information into larger questions that will require you to integrate multiple server platforms into an overall security solution. So don't think that you can skip this chapter. You'll find this information peppered throughout the exam.

The information on securing a domain controller can legitimately be applied to the other server roles discussed in this chapter. Hence, although items such as SMB Signing are discussed in the "Windows 2000 Domain Controller Security" section, those items can be applied to other server roles as well.

SQL Server Security

Microsoft has released several versions of SQL Server in recent years. This section will focus on SQL Server 2000 (referred to as "SQL" in this chapter.)

SQL Server 2000 is based on the Windows 2000 Server security model. Therefore, a good understanding of the Windows 2000 Server security features is necessary to understanding how to secure SQL. However, SQL also has its own security features, which we'll discuss first. We'll then discuss how Windows 2000 Server security supports SQL Server 2000 security.

Security Features in SQL Server 2000

Right out of the box, SQL Server 2000 starts with an option to securely set up the server. During the installation of SQL Server 2000, an Authentication Mode dialog box is included as part of the setup routine, asking you to select your authentication mode: Windows NT Authentication Mode or Mixed Mode. Mixed Mode defaults the SA (System Administrator) account to a blank password. The Windows NT Authentication Mode uses the security context of the user for validation to a domain controller before allowing setup to continue. In Mixed Mode, this does not happen.

The Windows NT Authentication Mode also takes advantage of the Kerberos authentication system in Windows 2000 Server, and a token is requested on behalf of the user for authentication to the SQL server. The SIDs (security identifiers) returned from the domain controller are checked against the `sysxlogins` master database. If a match is found, that match is enforced. If a match is not found, the user cannot log in to the SQL server. For user accounts created on the SQL server itself, the Windows NT Authentication Mode allows for password expiration, auditing, account lockouts, and password attributes.

Second, SQL Server 2000 secures the folders that it installs to allow access to only the SQL service accounts and the built-in Administrators group. In addition, the SQL Registry key (`HKLM\Software\Microsof\MSSQLServer`) will have restricted access to only the service accounts for the SQL server that are selected during the setup process.

SQL Server 2000 also works with *Security Account Delegation* or *Delegation Authentication*, which is the ability to pass security credentials across multiple computers and applications on behalf of a user or a service account. This is a feature of Kerberos that is turned on by default in Windows 2000 Server. If a user has authenticated to ServerX and ServerX needs to access ServerY to fulfill a request by the client, ServerX requests a ticket on behalf of the client, and the client is authenticated on ServerY. This process is transparent to the user. This property is on all accounts in the folder, which can be turned on or off. NTLM (NT LAN Manager) does not support forwarding of credentials, but Kerberos does. This feature is thought to be a big improvement over Windows NT 4 Server and NTLM.

A word of caution is in order here when discussing Security Account Delegation. Essentially you are opening impersonation of a user account via a service account. The decision to enable this feature should not be entered into lightly, because this opens a security hole in your organization. For example, a hacker could take control of a service account and then impersonate user accounts to perform malicious activities. While not easy to do, it is certainly not outside the realm of possibility either.

Windows 2000 Security and SQL Server

From a security standpoint, you'll probably want to turn off delegation by default and then enable it for certain service and user accounts. When delegation is turned on, you are enabling delegation for all services that run under the Local System account on the computer. If an unwary administrator installs an untrusted service on the computer and configures it to run as Local System, it too is going to be able to gain access to network resources while impersonating other users. A better practice is to configure services that use delegation to run under their own domain user accounts managed by domain administrators.

To configure a user account for delegation, follow these steps:

1. In Active Directory Users And Computers, right-click User and choose Properties from the shortcut menu to open the Properties dialog box, which is shown in Figure 2.1.

FIGURE 2.1   The user's Properties dialog box, open at the Account tab

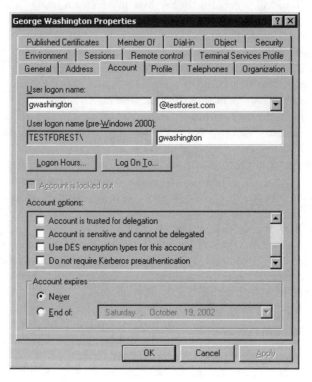

2. Click the Account tab.

3. Notice that in Figure 2.1 the Account Is Sensitive And Cannot Be Delegated check box is cleared by default; it should remain that way.

4. Click OK.

Now, if this is a service account, you'll have an additional choice to make. The options you select depend on whether the service runs under a computer's Local System account or under its own domain user account. If the service is configured to run under the Local System account, the computer on which the service runs must be trusted for delegation. To configure this setting, follow these steps:

1. In Active Directory Users And Computers, right-click the Computer object and choose Properties from the shortcut menu to open the Properties dialog box, which is shown in Figure 2.2.

FIGURE 2.2   A computer's Properties dialog box, open at the General tab

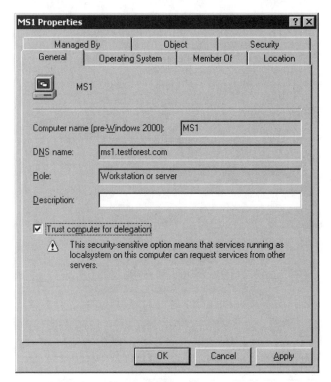

2. Click the General tab.

3. Click the Trust Computer For Delegation check box. This option is not selected by default.

4. Click OK.

If the service is configured to run under a separate user account that was specially created for the service, the user account of the service must be enabled to act as a delegate. To enable this account, follow these steps:

1. In Active Directory Users And Computers, right-click User and choose Properties from the shortcut menu to open the Properties dialog box.

2. Click the Account tab.

3. Click the Account Is Trusted For Delegation check box.

4. Click OK.

If you have multiple SQL servers or if there is interaction between the SQL Server and another application on another server, consider enabling Service Account Delegation. Doing so will increase response times to the user and create a better end-user experience.

FIGURE 2.3 The Properties dialog box for a service account, open at the Account tab

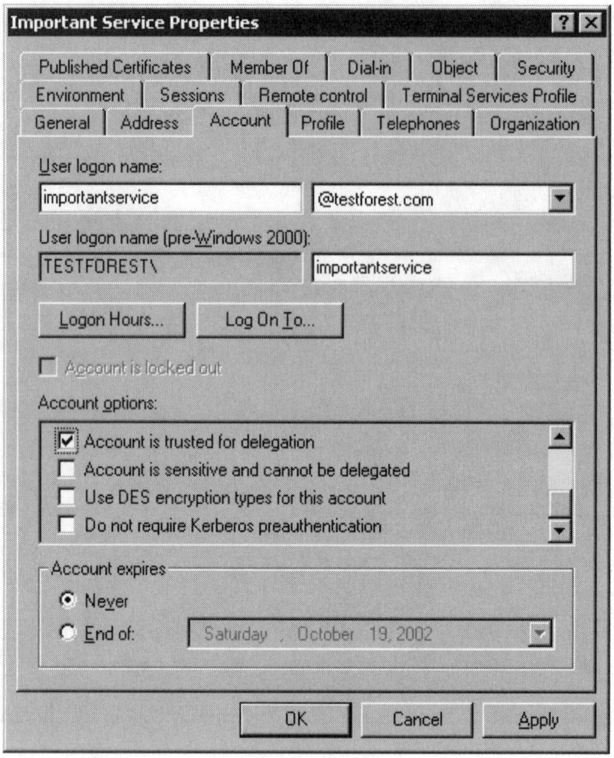

The BulkAdmin Role

This role is new in SQL Server 2000. Membership in this role allows users to load data from any file on the network or computer that can be accessed by the SQL service account. Do not add users to this role unless you are certain that they need it, because malicious users with this role can potentially corrupt large portions of a database by performing a bulk insert of bogus items.

The Encrypting File System and SQL Server 2000

SQL Server 2000 works with the Windows 2000 Server operating system to protect data files via the *Encrypting File System* (EFS). However, to use this correctly, you must assign an individual user account to the SQL Server 2000 service so that it doesn't run under the Local System account. Once you encrypt the account, if you need to change the service account for SQL Server 2000, you must first decrypt the files under the old service account, change the account, and then encrypt the files under the new service account.

Exchange 2000 Server Security

Most viruses enter a network through e-mail. This is why protection of your Exchange 2000 server is so important, both from an external and an internal viewpoint. Exploitation of the SMTP (Simple Mail Transfer Protocol) service on an Exchange 2000 server (or *any* SMTP server for that matter) can lead to significant loss of production as well as exposure to liability should unwanted or offensive content arrive in a person's inbox.

Because each Exchange 2000 Server database is exposed via the *Exchange Installable File System (ExIFS or just IFS)*, each item in the store can be accessed both through a URL and through *Server Message Blocks (SMBs)*. This means that folders in an Exchange server store can be shared to users on the local network and accept mapped drive assignments. Moreover, this means that if you open the Netbios ports on your firewall (something that is *not* recommended), then hackers could have a direct line into your Exchange databases. In addition, every item can be accessed through a browser over port 80 in a service known as *Outlook Web Access (OWA)*.

Like SQL Server 2000, Exchange 2000 Server also takes advantage of the Windows 2000 Server user and group accounts. Each item in the store, whether in a mailbox or a public folder, can be secured using regular NTFS (New Technology File System) permissions. What this means is that items found in a public folder can be filtered using NTFS permissions so that only those users who have explicit access to the item can access it. In fact, the ability to select who can *view* an item is also available to an Exchange Server administrator.

Securing the SMTP Service

The SMTP service is the most important service to secure. Port 25 is one of the most often attacked ports by hackers; hence, it is important to ensure that you have taken steps to guard inbound and outbound e-mail.

For instance, in most organizations, sexual harassment policies forbid certain types of conduct and conversation. These policies can be violated by pornographic spam arriving in a user's inbox. The exposure to liability for an employer in this instance is real. To ensure that this does not become a problem, install content scanning and anti-spam filters on your SMTP gateway server that will block e-mail messages based on their content both in the subject line and in the body of the message.

In addition, e-mail messages should be scanned for viruses before they arrive in a user's inbox. Hence, always ensure that antivirus scanning is turned on and is updating its definitions on a regular basis. The combination of content scanning, spam filtering and virus scanning will help ensure that your e-mail arrives clean of unwanted content and viruses.

NOTE   Many third-party content and virus-scanning products are available for Exchange 2000 Server. You can find more information at www.msexchange.org.

Securing Outlook Web Access

You can secure OWA in two ways: by using a front-end server and by using *Secure Sockets Layer (SSL)*.

In Exchange 2000 Server, you can place front-end Exchange 2000 servers in your *DMZ (De-Militarised Zone)* and transfer user calls for content from their inbox or a public folder to back-end database servers sitting inside your firewalls. This architecture provides a couple of benefits. First, users don't connect directly to the back-end database servers. Their calls for information are proxied to the back-end servers by the front-end servers. Because the front-end servers do not have any databases sitting on them, this architecture is more secure. For instance, you can require users to use SSL to connect to the front-end server and then require *IPSec (Internet Protocol Security)* to connect to the back-end server using an internal username and password from your local domain controller. If the front-end servers are brought down by a malicious user, you've really lost nothing (other than HTTP [Hypertext Transfer Protocol] access) because the databases sit on the back-end server.

Second, the front-end/back-end (FE/BE) architecture allows you to expose your entire Exchange 2000 Server deployment under a single name, IP address, and port number combination. Essentially, this hides your internal Exchange 2000 Server layout while providing services to your users through OWA.

Securing Outlook Web Access, URLScan, and IISLockdown

You can also "lock down" your OWA website using the URLScan and IISLockdown tools. The advantage of doing this is that since OWA runs inside IIS, these tools can treat OWA as another website. These tools are explained in detail in the "IIS Server Security" section.

Securing Public Folder Information

Items held in public folders are secured using NTFS file permissions. When it comes to securing information in a public folder, consider using these permissions to lock down folders and/or files that should only be viewed and read by certain individuals or groups. For instance, if you have ten items in a public folder and you want Sue to view only five of them, remove Sue from the permissions on the other five folders. This should result in only Sue being able to see the five remaining items.

Windows 2000 Domain Controller Security

Because Windows 2000 Server domain controllers (DCs) perform authentication and other network services, it is important to understand the actions you can take to secure a domain controller. Remember that implementing a security solution is always a trade-off between security and ease of use. The more secure a resource is, the more difficult it is to use that resource easily.

Good security usually means no ease of use. The challenge to every security architect is to find a balance between the two.

Domain controllers are the central servers that allow other member servers and clients to operate efficiently. One of the first tasks when securing a domain controller is to find out who the DC is talking to and who is talking to it.

Using Digital Signatures for Communication

If you want to ensure that the Windows 2000 Server DC is talking only to those servers that trust an internal Certificate Authority (CA) on your network, you can require that network traffic be digitally signed (called SMB Signing) for both servers and clients before a DC will accept an incoming transmission. Implementing digital signing helps to prevent impersonation of clients and servers or "man-in-the-middle" attacks. When enabled, SMB packet signing is required, meaning that a digital signature is placed in each packet and must be verified by both the client and the server before data transfer can occur.

If you require servers to have their communication digitally signed but you don't at least enable this setting on the clients, no data transfer can occur. To require digital signatures between servers and clients, apply a Group Policy to the Domain Controllers OU in Active Directory Users And Computers (see Figure 2.4 where these various options are illustrated). Be sure to enable Digitally Sign Client Communication (Always) and Digitally Sign Server Communication (Always). You will also need to do this on the OU or OUs that are hosting the client workstation accounts. Of course, for signing to work properly, you will need Certificate services running on your network, and all servers and workstations will need to obtain a certificate from the Certificate Authority.

FIGURE 2.4   Apply a Group Policy to the Domain Controller OU in Active Directory Users And Computers

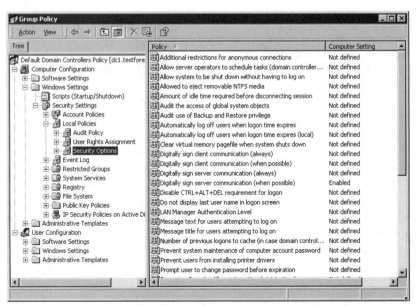

When SMB signing is implemented, you'll experience a performance overhead of up to 15 percent in order to sign and verify each packet between the client and server.

Securing DNS Updates

A second way to secure a Windows 2000 Server domain controller is to require secure updates to your DNS (Domain Name System) records if you are running Active Directory-Integrated DNS zones. When a client or a server then attempts to update the DNS records in Active Directory, a security session must first be established based on security tokens between the client and the server:

- The client generates the initial token and sends it to the server.

- The server processes the token and, if necessary, returns a subsequent token to the client.

- This negotiation continues until it is complete and a security context has been established.

The security context has a finite lifetime during which it can be used to create and verify the transaction signature on messages between the two parties. The lifetime depends on the protocol being used. In Windows 2000 Server, the lifetime is equal to the maximum service ticket lifetime (any time greater than 10 minutes and less than the maximum user ticket lifetime; the default is 10 hours).

Restricting Anonymous Access

Windows 2000 Server allows anonymous users to perform certain activities on the network, such as enumerating names of domain accounts and network shares. You might decide that such enumeration without authentication represents a security risk. To mitigate against this, you'll need to remove the Everyone and Network security groups from the anonymous user's token. To do so, you configure the No Access Without Explicit Anonymous Permissions option. When this option is configured, Anonymous user accounts will be able to access only resources to which they have been granted explicit permissions.

To configure this setting, you'll need to use a Group Policy that is applied at the domain level. As you can see in Figure 2.5, this setting is actually configured under the Additional Restrictions For Anonymous Connections policy under the Security Options node.

To configure this setting, follow these steps:

1. Double-click on the Additional Restrictions For Anonymous Connections setting to open the Security Policy Setting dialog box (see Figure 2.6) in which you can make choices about securing the Anonymous accounts.

FIGURE 2.5   Additional Restrictions For Anonymous Connections policy under the Security Options node.

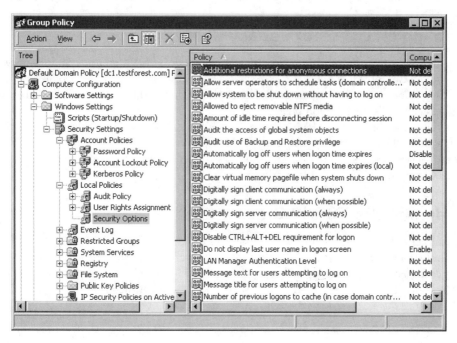

FIGURE 2.6   Configuring the No Access Without Explicit Anonymous Permissions policy setting

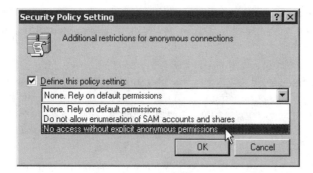

2.   Click the Define This Policy Setting check box.

3.   In the drop-down list box, select No Access Without Explicit Anonymous Permissions, and click OK.

4.   Click OK to close the Group Policy dialog box.

Once configured, this policy requires that Anonymous accounts be granted explicit permissions to a resource before the resource can be exposed to the account.

Enabling NTLMv2 for Legacy Clients

If you are running a mixed-client environment with Windows NT 4 and/or Windows 9x workstations, you can force these clients to use the NTLMv2 authentication protocol instead of the older NTLM protocol. Remember that these clients cannot authenticate using Kerberos, so forcing NTLMv2 is the best you'll get.

The difference between NTLMv2 and NTLM is that v2 introduces a secure channel that protects the authentication process, whereas NTLM does not. To enable NTLMv2, you'll need to install Service Pack 4 or later on the Windows NT workstations and install the Directory Service Client on the Windows 9x workstations.

Hardening the TCP/IP Stack

You can help prevent successful *Denial of Service (DoS)* attacks by hardening the TCP/IP (Transmission Control Protocol/Internet Protocol) stack on any server that is connected to the Internet. You modify the Registry to harden the stack. You will perform this work under the `HKL\System\CSS\Services\TCPIP\Parameters` key. Each key mentioned here will be added as a subkey to this key. All keys discussed here are DWORD type keys.

    Be sure to backup the registry before making any changes.

- The `SynAttackProtect` key allows you to configure TCP/IP to time out more quickly in the event of a SYN attack. Zero (0) is the default setting, and two (2) is the highest setting. Two is the recommended setting.

- The `EnableDeadGWDetect` Registry key allows TCP to perform dead gateway detection. With this setting enabled, TCP may ask IP to find another gateway to use if the current selected gateway is experiencing problems. This is a True/False setting, so 1 = True and 0 = False. The upshot here is that a server under attack may connect to an undesired gateway if this Registry key is set to True. Hence, the recommended setting is False. The default setting is True.

- The `EnablePMTUDiscovery` Registry key allows TCP to discover the largest packet size along the entire path that will be accepted without fragmentation. The value of doing this is that packets will be sent in a size acceptable to each router along the path and won't need fragmentation, increasing transmission speed of the packets to the destination. However, if this feature is enabled, an attacker could set the discovery size so low that your TCP/IP stack is unnecessarily overworked when transmitting data. Hence, best practice is to enter this Registry key and then set the value to zero (0) for False instead of one (1) for True. The default for this key is one.

- The `KeepAliveTime` Registry key controls how often TCP attempts to verify that an idle connection is still alive by sending a KeepAlive packet to the client. If the client is still there, the client will respond. If there is no response, the connection is killed. The default setting for this key is 7,200,000 milliseconds, or 2 hours. The recommended setting is 300,000 milliseconds, or 5 minutes. The reasoning is that if the packets are sent more often and there is no response, idle connections are killed more quickly.

While tedious and detailed, actions like this can help ensure that your domain controller is not brought down by a DoS attack. You can use a Group Policy Object (GPO) to push out these Registry settings to all your servers instead of modifying each server individually.

Disable Auto Generation of 8.3 Filenames

This feature is turned on by default in Windows 2000 Server and is there to allow for legacy compatibility with 16-bit applications. When this feature is enabled, an attacker needs only 8 characters to refer to any file in the folder structure. Unless you are running 16-bit applications, it is recommended that you turn off this feature. To do this, add `NtfsDisable8dot3Name-Creation (DWORD)` as a subkey to the `HKLM\System\CCS\Control\FileSystem` key with a value of one (1). Any existing 8.3 names will remain intact after this key is applied to your system.

Disable LmHash Creation

By default, Windows 2000 Server creates a hash of each password for the older LAN Manager (LM) and Windows NT (NTLM) and NTLMv2 authentication schemes. The LM hash is the weakest of all the hashes and can be vulnerable to a brute force attack. If you are running Windows 2000 only on your network, disable the LM hash creation. To do this, add the `NoLMHash (DWORD)` key as a subkey to the `HKLM\System\CCS\Control\LSA` key, and set the value to one (1).

Securing Built-in Accounts

A number of built-in accounts cannot be deleted in Windows 2000 Server, but you can rename them. Be sure to rename the Guest and Administrator accounts and do not enable the Guest account unless you have a specific reason for doing so. This advice is also true of the local Administrator account on member servers and workstations. Accounts can be renamed using a Group Policy. To do so, use the Rename Administrator Account policy under the Security Options node (see Figure 2.7). Just double-click on the policy setting, and inside the Security Policy Setting dialog box, select the Define This Policy Setting check box. Once selected, you'll be able to input the new name of the administrator account. Then click OK and exit the Group Policy.

FIGURE 2.7   Rename the Administrator account

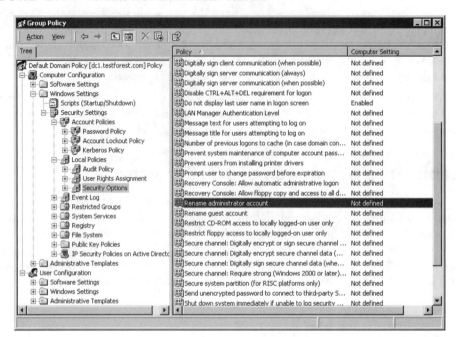

IIS Server Security

Port 80 is the most often attacked port on the Internet. Therefore, the likelihood of your IIS server being attacked is rather high. To make your IIS server as secure as possible, Microsoft has provided the IISLockdown tool. IISLockdown is a flexible tool that lets you specify the nature of your web server and then remove any functionality that is not required.

Before implementing the IISLockdown tool (or any recommendation in this chapter) in your production environment, be sure to test thoroughly any changes you want to make in a lab environment.

The IISLockdown tool is available as part of the Security Toolkit from Microsoft's security website (www.microsoft.com/security). After you download the tool, follow these steps:

1. Run the tool, agree to the license agreement, and click Next to open the Select Server Template screen, as shown in Figure 2.8.

2. In the Server Templates list, select the type of server you want to lock down, and click Next to open the Internet Services screen, which is shown in Figure 2.9.

FIGURE 2.8   The Select Server Template screen in the IISLockdown tool

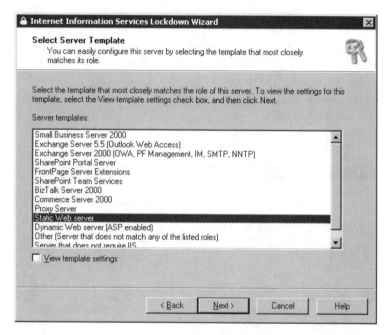

FIGURE 2.9   The Internet Services screen in IISLockdown

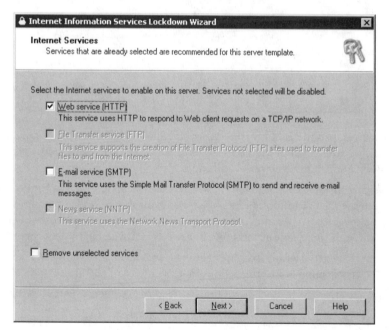

If you want to view the individual template settings, click the View Template Settings check box. This forces the tool to display the screens shown in Figures 2.9, 2.10, and 2.11. If this box in not checked, the tool will go directly to the URLScan screen, shown in Figure 2.12.

3. Select which services to enable on the server. If you select the Remove Unselected Services check box, those services not selected are removed instead of disabled. For a static web server, we'll select the Web Service (HTTP) only.

4. Click Next to open the Script Maps screen, which is shown in Figure 2.10. The default selection for a static web server is to disable support for all script maps.

FIGURE 2.10 The Script Maps screen in IISLockdown

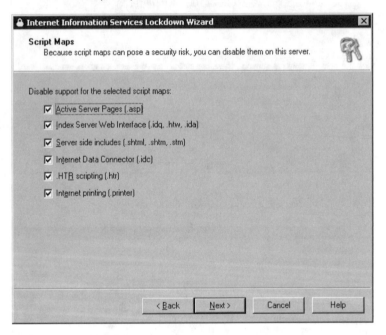

5. Click Next to open the Additional Security screen, which is shown in Figure 2.11. This screen allows you to remove unnecessary directories and change permissions for anonymous users. For a static web server, all choices are selected by default.

6. Click Next to open the URLScan screen, which is shown in Figure 2.12. The default selection is to install the URLScan tool. Before you do so, you should understand how that tool works and operates, so best practice is to install the tool in a lab environment and then put the tool through some serious tests. We'll discuss the URLScan tool later in this chapter.

7. Click Next to open the Ready To Apply Settings screen, which is shown in Figure 2.13. This screen displays a summary of the actions that the tool will perform.

8. Click Next to start the IISLockdown tool. Instead of getting a progress bar, you'll see a listing of the actions that the tool is performing as they are being performed, as shown in Figure 2.14.

FIGURE 2.11   The Additional Security screen in IISLockdown

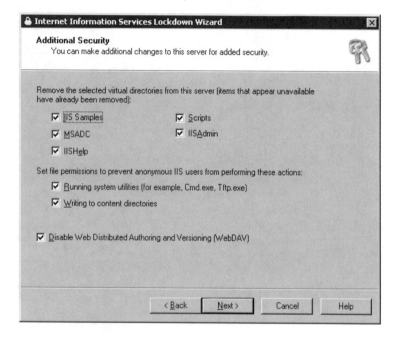

FIGURE 2.12   The URLScan screen in IISLockdown

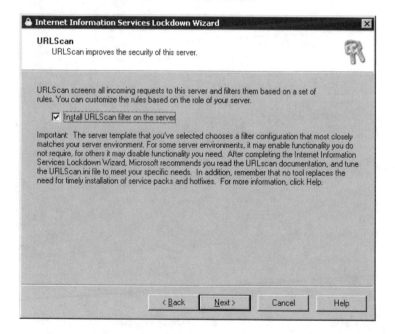

FIGURE 2.13   The Ready To Apply Settings screen in IISLockdown

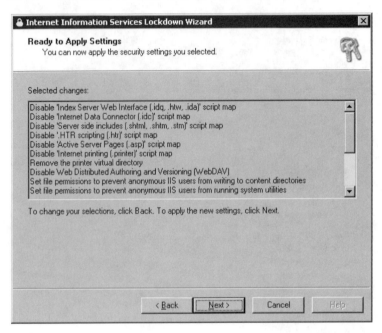

FIGURE 2.14   The Applying Security Settings screen in IISLockdown

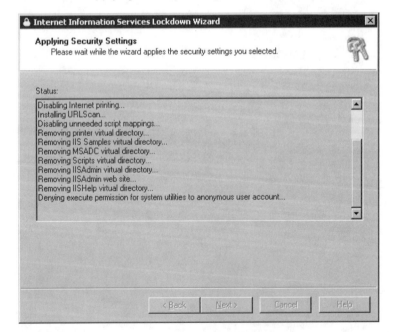

You can use the IISLockdown tool to lock down any number of server scenarios that rely on offering services through port 80, including OWA, SQL, SharePoint Portal Server, and Small Business Server. If you want to lock down an OWA server using IISLockdown, the tool will do the following:

- Leave HTTP and SMTP running on the OWA server

- Leave the .asp script map enabled; all others are disabled

- Leave WebDAV (Web Distributed Authoring and Versioning) enabled

To uninstall IISLockdown, simply run the tool a second time. The settings for the tool are on the server in the oblt-log.log file in the %windir%\system32\inetsrv folder and can be used to "reverse" the installation. Once IISLockdown is uninstalled, your server will be back to the state it was before running the tool.

> If you want to make changes to your web server, you'll need to uninstall and then reinstall the IISLockdown tool. In other words, you cannot change the configuration of the server without first uninstalling the current settings.

Figure 2.8, earlier in this chapter, lists most of the server types that this tool locks down. But the IISlockdown tool is not your only option in securing IIS. You can take further steps to secure your servers running IIS.

IP Address/DNS Restrictions

If possible, you can set the exact IP address or DNS names that are allowed access to your web server. Obviously, for publicly oriented websites, such as e-commerce websites, this is impractical. But for other sites that host sensitive or restricted information, you might be able to specify the clients for the website and set this accordingly.

Disabling the IIS Anonymous Account

It is pretty much common knowledge that the default IIS anonymous account is named IUSR_computername. A better way to handle anonymous access is to disable this account, create a new account, and use the new account as the anonymous account for your website(s). Adhere the account to strong password guidelines, which will make it more difficult for a hacker to guess the name and password combination.

The URLScan Tool

HTTP access to your websites can be analyzed and suspicious traffic rejected *before* that traffic hits IIS services. URLScan protects a server from attacks by filtering and rejecting certain packets that you define. When URLScan is first installed, it rejects the following request types:

- CGI (.exe) pages
- WebDAV

- FrontPage server extensions
- Index Server
- Internet printing
- Server side includes

This tool is configured via the urlscan.ini file, which is installed in the %windir%\system32\intesrv\urlscan folder. There are several sections to this file, and a typical section is shown in Figure 2.15.

FIGURE 2.15 The urlscan.ini file displaying the DenyVerbs section

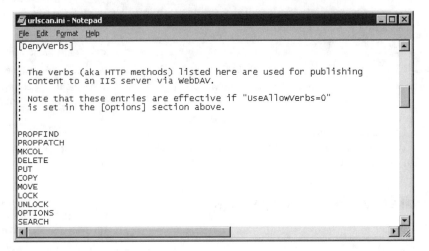

The Options section of the file defines how valid and invalid requests are handled. The options section includes the following:

UseAllowVerbs Allowed values for this option are either one (1) or zero (0). The default is one. When set to one, the tool rejects any request containing an HTTP verb that is not explicitly listed in the AllowVerbs section of the file. This section is case sensitive. If this option is set to zero, the tool rejects any request that contains verbs in the DenyVerbs section of the file. This section is not case sensitive.

UseAllowExtensions Allowed values for this option are either one (1) or zero (0). The default is zero. When set to the default, the tool rejects any request in which the file extension associated with the request is listed in the DenyExtensions section of the file. When set to one, the tool rejects any request in which the file extension associated with the request is not listed in the AllowExtensions section of the file.

NormalizeURLBeforeScan Allowed values for this option are either one (1) or zero (0). The default is one. When set to the default, the tool analyzes all packets after IIS has normalized the URL request. When set to zero, the tool analyzes all requests in their raw form. This option will open your server to canonicalization attacks.

Canonicalization

Canonical means the simplest or most standard form of something. *Canonicalization* is the process of converting something from one representation to its most simplest form.

Web applications must deal with lots of canonicalization issues from URL encoding to IP address translation. For example, a URL canonicalization vulnerability results when a security decision is based on a URL and not all possible URL forms are considered. If a URL is allowed access, it is possible to send a URL that appears as if it is pointing to one resource when, in fact, it is pointing to a different resource. When security decisions are based on canonical forms of data, it is therefore essential that the application is able to deal with canonicalization issues accurately. Only experienced administrators should configure the application.

VerifyNormalization   Allowed values for this option are either one (1) or zero (0). The default is one. When set to the default, this tool verifies the *URL normalization* and helps defend against canonicalization attacks. Best practice is to leave this at the default.

AllowHighBitCharacters   Allowed values for this option are either one (1) or zero (0). The default is zero. When set to the default, this tool rejects any request in which the URL contains a character not found in the ASCII character set.

AllowDotInPath   Allowed values for this option are either one (1) or zero (0). The default is zero. When set to the default, the tool rejects any URL that contains multiple dots (.). When set to one, the tool does not check for multiple instances of dots. In default mode, the tool rejects names with dots, such as `http://mail.domainname.com/exchange`.

RemoveServerHeader   Allowed values for this option are either one (1) or zero (0). The default is zero. When set to the default, the tool allows server headers in all server responses. When set to one, the tool removes the server header from all server responses.

EnableLogging   Allowed values for this option are either one (1) or zero (0). The default is one. When set to the default, the tool logs its actions in the `urlscan.log` file. When set to zero, no logging is performed.

PerProcessLogging   Allowed values for this option are either one (1) or zero (0). The default is zero. When set to the default, the tool does not associate the log file name with each process that is being logged. When set to one, the tool appends the process ID of the IIS process hosting `URLScan.dll` to the log file name.

AlternativeServerName   This option works in concert with the RemoveServerHeader option. When RemoveServerHeader is set to zero, the string of characters entered here replaces the default header in all server responses.

AllowLateScanning   Allowed values for this option are either one (1) or zero (0). The default is zero. When set to one, the tool registers itself as a low-priority filter, which means that other tools can scan and modify the incoming URL before URLScan. When set to the default, the tool scans in high-priority mode.

PerDayLogging   Allowed values for this option are either one (1) or zero (0). The default is one. When set to the default, a new log file is created for each day when the first log entry is written for that day. If there are no entries, no log is generated.

RejectResponseUrl   The input values are a string of characters in the form `/path/filename.ext`. This is the URL that is run when the tool rejects a request. The URL must be local.

UseFastPathReject   Allowed values for this option are either one (1) or zero (0). The default is zero. When set to the default, this option is ignored. But when set to one, the tool ignores the settings in the RejectResponseUrl and displays a 404 response to the client when it rejects a request.

The `urlscan.ini` file also contains sections for the following:

- Allowed verbs
- Denied verbs
- Denied headers
- Allowed extensions
- Denied extensions

If you install URLScan on each IIS web server, it acts as an end-point intrusion detection system (IDS). If you install URLScan on an ISA (Internet Security and Acceleration) server, it can act as a network-based IDS for all IIS servers on your network. At the network perimeter, you can block all types of requests instead of letting those requests traverse your network and then get blocked at the server level.

Although the IISLockdown tool works at the service level, URLScan works at the URL level to help secure your website. When you select one of the templates during the installation of IISLockdown, a preconfigured `urlscan.ini` file is also installed, easing the burden of administration for you. And, if necessary, you can go back and tweak the `urlscan.ini` file to work exactly the way you need it to work.

 Real World Scenario

Securing a Website Using the Anonymous Account

Let's say you want to present company files on the Internet for general public consumption, such as product and general information documents. Obviously, you want this site to be secure and yet accessible via the Anonymous account. Follow these steps:

1. Install the IISLockdown and URLScan tools.

2. Select the Static Web Site option in IISLockdown and accept the defaults in the `urlscan.ini` file.

3. Use a Group Policy to disable the Anonymous account membership in the Everyone and Network users security groups.

4. Explicitly give permissions to the Anonymous user account to the resources that will be presented in the website.

5. Rename the Anonymous user account with a name that "blends in" with the other names in your Active Directory so that a hacker cannot readily discern which accounts are intended for web access and which are not.

6. Require SSL for client connectivity if you want to ensure that data communications between your visitors and the web server are encrypted. With public documents, this might not be a desired outcome, but it is certainly available if you'd like to use it.

Securing Mobile Communications and Internet Authentication Service (IAS) Server

There is little doubt that wireless communication has exploded in the last few years. Along with this explosion, however, are real security concerns that have not been fully resolved. Like the other types of servers in this chapter, these technologies also raise specific security concerns, which include the following:

- No per-packet authentication.
- Vulnerability to disassociation attacks.
- No central authentication support.
- RC4 stream cipher is vulnerable to plaintext attacks.
- Some *WEP (Wired Equivalent Privacy)* keys are derived from passwords.
- No support for advanced security, such as smart cards, biometrics, and so on.
- Key management issues, such as rekeying global keys and no dynamic, per-station unicast key.

The WEP algorithm defines the use of a 40-bit secret key for authentication and encryption. The 802.11 standard allows for each station to hold two different shared keys: a unicast session key and a multicast/global key. The WEP is a symmetric algorithm in which the same key is used for both cipher and decipher.

Wireless technology can be used in conjunction with an IAS or any *Remote Authentication Dial-In User Service (RADIUS)*. Because most wireless communications need to access resources sitting on a cabled network, there is a need to marry these two technologies. When a wireless user connects to the network, the access point (AP) forwards the user's identity to the RADIUS server to initiate authentication services in Active Directory. Once authenticated, the RADIUS server sends back to the user via the AP an authentication key to be used to access information on the cabled network. The key is sent in encrypted form, of course. The AP also uses the authentication key to securely transmit per-station unicast session and multicast/global authentication keys to the user's device. The user's device, called a station (STA), then has keys available to transmit information back and forth between itself and the AP for access to information on the cabled network. Hence, the RADIUS server works in conjunction with your *Certificate Authority (CA)* and the AP to provide secure communications with your wireless clients.

The IAS service is Microsoft's implementation (and name) for the industry-standard RADIUS service. IAS can check Active Directory for a wireless client's request for authentication. The use of IAS allows the remote access user authentication services to the cabled network.

You can take some steps to further secure your IAS server. First, as the number of wireless client types increases, it is reasonable to assume that not every client will want to authenticate to the IAS server using the same methods. This situation already exists for Windows9x clients, which use NTLM, and Windows 2000 clients, which use Kerberos. Best practice here is to create a different user account for each client-authentication method. This way, if a password on one account is compromised, it is only compromised for that client, not for all the clients the user is using.

Second, ensure that you are allowing all wireless traffic to come through on a specific IP address. This allows you to hide your internal IP scheme and use a single namespace for resolution outside your network.

Finally, you can use the remote access account lockout feature in Windows 2000 Server to configure the number of times a user's authentication can fail before future connection attempts using that account are denied.

 The Remote Access Account Lockout feature is not related at all to the Account Locked Out setting in the Properties dialog box for a user account.

To configure the Remote Access Account Lockout feature, you edit the Registry on the server providing user authentication. To enable account lockout, you must set the MaxDenials entry in the Registry (HKLM\SYSTEM\CurrentControlSet\Services\RemoteAccess\Parameters\AccountLockout) to 1 or greater. This setting specifies the maximum number of failed attempts before the account is locked out. The default setting is that this feature is zero (0), or disabled. If you set it to three, the account will lock out after 3 failed authentication attempts. If you set it to 5, the account will lock out after 5 failed authentication attempts.

The window of time in which the specified number of failed authentication attempts is set is called the ResetTime (mins). You can find this entry in the Registry under the HKLM\SYSTEM\CurrentControlSet\Services\RemoteAccess\Parameters\AccountLockout key. The default is set to 0xb40, or 2880 minutes (48 hours). You can increase or decrease as necessary.

If you need to manually reset a user account that has been locked out before the failed attempts counter automatically resets the account, delete the following Registry subkey that corresponds to the user's account name:

HKLM\SYSTEM\CurrentControlSet\Services\RemoteAccess\Parameters\
AccountLockout\domain name:*user name*

Applying Security to Client Operating Systems

When it is time to apply additional security to client operating systems, we can either walk around and touch each desktop, or we can use some type of method that automatically applies the settings to each desktop. The best (and easiest) way to apply security to a group of desktops is to use the Group Policy feature in Windows 2000 Server.

You can use Group Policy Objects (GPOs) to apply additional security to clients by configuring a template and than applying that template to a GPO. You then assign the GPO to a site, a domain, or an OU container, and the clients inherit the settings. Now, each operating system is unique and has its own needs. Let's take a look at these needs.

Unix Clients

Unix clients can authenticate using the Kerberos version 5 protocol. They can also use the Windows 2000 Server domain controllers as their Kerberos *Key Distribution Center (KDC)*. If they already have a KDC they are using, an inter-realm Kerberos trust can be created between their KDC and a Windows 2000 Server domain controller (DC). Either way, their account will need to be created in Active Directory in order to gain access to Windows 2000 resources. Account mappings may need to be created between the Unix KDC and the DC. Such mappings associate the Windows 2000 account SID with a defined account in the Unix domain.

Older Unix clients that use the Common Internet File System (CIFS), such as Samba, can use the NTLM protocol to authenticate with AD. In addition, Unix clients can use certificates for SSL and Transport Layer Security (TLS) connections. All that is needed is a trusted CA by both the Unix and the Windows 2000 server.

Finally, remember that clear-text passwords can be secured using either SSL or IPSec (Internet Protocol Security). You'll need to secure clear-text passwords because Unix clients use them in several utilities. To set clear-text authentication, enable the Send Unencrypted Password To Connect To Third-Party SMB Servers setting under the Security Node in the Local Policies node of the GPO template (see Figure 2.16). Once this policy is set, you can use IPSec or SSL to secure the transmission.

You secure FTP and Telnet traffic using IPSec. You secure HTTP traffic using SSL.

If your Unix clients need to use their native NFS (Network File System) for file services, you can design a secure resource topology in Windows 2000 Server by installing Services for Unix. In this scenario, the Unix clients authenticate to their own NIS (Network Information System) server. In order for them to access files on the Windows 2000 server, you need to map the User Identifier (UID) and Group Identifier (GID) from the NIS server to an account in Windows 2000 AD. This mapping assigns the Unix account a SID from the Windows 2000 domain and allows the Unix client to access files and servers in the domain. You'll set permissions on NFS resources by using the Windows 2000 AD accounts.

FIGURE 2.16   The policy setting for clear-text authentication

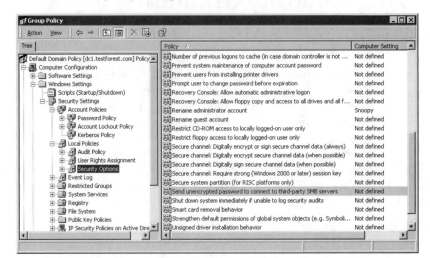

NetWare Clients

Microsoft provides three services to help NetWare clients interoperate with Windows 2000 Server:

Client Services for NetWare   This service allows Windows 2000 clients to access resources hosted on a Novell NetWare server. The clients have direct access to file services, print services, and Novell Directory Services (NDS). Do not install this if you are going to install Gateway Services for NetWare.

If you need to manage a large number of accounts for both AD and NDS, consider using the Microsoft Directory Synchronization Service to synchronize accounts between AD and NDS/3.x Binderies.

Gateway Services for NetWare (GSNW)   GSNW provides a single gateway through which Windows clients can access NetWare resources. Essentially, a Windows 2000 server acts as a proxy agent for requested resources to the Windows clients. Do not install this service if you are going to install Client Services for NetWare on all your workstations.

Authentication for this service uses a single account and must be a member of the NTGATEWAY group on the NetWare server. This account must be given permission to the NetWare resources if Windows 2000 clients are going to be able to access these resources. If this account is given Supervisor rights on the NetWare box, you could have a potential security hole if that account is compromised. Guard this account, and ensure that the password is changed regularly.

Services for NetWare   This add-on product from Microsoft provides several utilities to help Novell and Microsoft platforms coexist:

Microsoft Directory Synchronization Services (MSDSS)   This service provides two-way directory synchronization between AD and Novell Directory Services (NDS).

Microsoft File Migration Utility   This tool enables the migration of files from a NetWare server to a Windows 2000 server while preserving the directory structure and file permissions.

File and Print Services for NetWare   This service enables Windows 2000 Server to provide file and print services to NetWare clients. The Windows 2000 server will look and feel like a NetWare server to the NetWare clients.

There are security holes with the NWLink protocol, Microsoft's implementation of IPX/SPX (Internetwork Packet Exchange/Sequenced Packet Exchange). NetWare servers that use IPX/SPX advertise themselves to the network using the Service Advertising Protocol (SAP), which provides basic server information to everyone on the network, including attackers. For this reason, strive to use only TCP/IP on your network.

Macintosh Clients

By default, Macintosh clients use nonencrypted passwords. This should remain the case only for anonymous-accessed resources, such as public websites or public files. If you install File Services for Macintosh (FSM), you can have Macintosh clients who do not have accounts in AD authenticate as a guest user. This is best used for resources that do not require auditing or have liberal permission sets.

In addition, if you install FSM, you can instruct your Mac clients to authenticate using Apple Standard Encryption, which allows passwords up to only eight characters. You can also specify that they use the Microsoft User Authentication Module (MS-UAM). Using MS-UAM, passwords can be a maximum of 14 characters, but it does require the AppleShare client 3.8 or later to be installed on the Mac client.

For file security, set up volume passwords, which is somewhat analogous to share-level permissions. To access the volume, users must first supply the appropriate password.

As far as printing is concerned, there are no print permissions using the AppleTalk protocol. There is no user-level security for Macintosh printers.

Summary

In this chapter, we focused on securing different server platforms as well as how to secure non-Windows clients. Specifically, we focused on how to secure the following:

- SQL Server 2000
- Exchange 2000 Server
- Internet Information Services
- Internet Authentication Service Server
- Wireless clients

We also discussed how to secure a website using the IISLockdown and URLScan tools. Since these tools are unique to IIS, any server platform that uses IIS can (potentially) benefit from using them.

Non-Windows2000 clients need to be secured too, so we discussed how to secure a Unix client on your Windows 2000 network. Probably the best interoperability with Windows 2000 exists from the Unix world. We also discussed the interoperation with NetWare and how to secure these platforms when they must coexist. You learned that Microsoft has released a directory synchronization tool to ease administration when many accounts need access to both NetWare and Windows 2000. Finally, you learned to password-protect Macintosh volumes and to use the MS-UAM protocol for Macintosh clients.

Exam Essentials

Be able to list two or three actions you would take to secure each server platform discussed in this chapter.   Know what actions are recommended for each server and why you need to take them. Also, remember the interaction of the RADIUS server with wireless clients and the IAS server. You might also remember that you can use the IISLockdown tool for Exchange 2000 Server OWA.

Understand how IISLockdown and URLScan work together.   The IISLockdown tool works at the service level to add and remove services based on the configuration or template you choose when working with the tool. Once set, configuration choices must be uninstalled before they can be modified. The URLScan tool applies settings from the urlscan.ini file to incoming web services requests. Be sure you know that URL normalization and day-to-day security of your website is much more a function of the URLScan tool than the IISLockdown tool.

Understand how to secure each client type in a Windows 2000 environment.   Because so many of us run a mixed-client environment, it is important to understand how to secure each client type. You would also do yourself some favors by understanding the difference between the three NetWare services that Microsoft provides.

Key Terms

Before you take the exam, be certain you are familiar with the following terms:

Canonicalization	Kerberos Key Distribution Center (KDC)
Certificate Authority (CA)	Outlook Web Access (OWA)
Delegation Authentication	Remote Authentication Dial-In User Service (RADIUS)
De-Militarised Zone (DMZ)	Secure Sockets Layer (SSL)
Denial of Service (DoS)	Security Account Delegation (SAD)
Encrypting File System (EFS)	Server Message Blocks (SMBs)
Exchange Installable File System (ExIFS)	URL normalization
Internet Protocol Security (IPSec)	Wired Equivalent Privacy (WEP)

Review Questions

1. You have just installed SQL Server 2000 using Windows Authentication Mode. Which of the following statements is true?

   A. The SA account defaults to a predetermined password.

   B. NTLM becomes the default authentication protocol.

   C. Password expiration and account lockout are enabled.

   D. The SQL Server 2000 Registry keys will not be secured.

2. You are running 50 Windows 2000 Professional workstations and 30 Unix workstations. Mary, a user on a Windows 2000 Professional workstation, authenticates at Server1, a DC in the administration.testforest.com domain. She needs access to a SQL Server 2000 database that resides on a member server, SQL1. After authenticating to the network, Mary can access the SQL server. While working with data from the SQL server, she clicks a link that takes her to a secure intranet website on WS1. What will be the default behavior among these servers?

   A. SQL1 will request a ticket from Server1 on behalf of Mary for authentication to WS1.

   B. Mary's security credentials will be set to WS1 from Server1, and SQL1 will not be involved in her authentication to WS1

   C. Mary's security credentials will need to be created on WS1 after WS1 verifies her token with Server1.

   D. Mary's security credentials follow her everywhere in the forest. There is no need for SQL1 and WS1 to communicate directly.

3. When discussing Delegation Authentication, the best practice from a security standpoint is to do what?

   A. Leave the default settings alone.

   B. Modify the default settings.

   C. Change the default Delegation Authentication settings so that DA is enabled only for individual computers and user accounts.

   D. Remove Delegation Authentication, and then install it on individual servers and workstations that need it.

4. You are the administrator of a Windows 2000 network. You have 200 Windows 2000 Professional workstations, 20 Windows 2000 Server Member Servers and 5 Windows 2000 DCs. You want to make authentication to each server as fast and transparent as possible to your end users. You also want communication between your servers to be as secure as possible. What should you do? (Choose two.)

   A. Leave Delegation Authentication at the default configuration.

   B. Require digital signatures on all communication between servers.

   C. Enable Delegation Authentication on each server.

   D. Require digital signatures on all client communication.

5. You are the administrator of a SQL Server 2000 server. You have used the Encrypting File System to encrypt SQL-specific files. You then change the service account for your SQL server. You discover you cannot access the encrypted files. What should you do?

    A. Reinstall the SQL binary files. This will reset the SQL server to the default, and the files will be decrypted during the installation.

    B. Use the Local System account to decrypt the files. You can then encrypt them again using the new system account.

    C. Log on locally as the administrator. Use this account to decrypt the files.

    D. Change the service account to the old server account, and then decrypt the files. Change the server account again to the new account. Encrypt the files.

6. Items in an Exchange 2000 Server store can be accessed using which of the following methods? (Choose all that apply.)

    A. URL

    B. SMB

    C. MAPI

    D. HTTP

    E. HTTPS

    F. FTP

    G. Microsoft Office Application

7. Which of the following steps can you take as an Exchange 2000 Server administrator to further secure port 25 on your TCP filter?

    A. Install URLScan to scan incoming OWA requests.

    B. Install antivirus scanning of e-mail in the DMZ.

    C. Install IISLockdown to remove unnecessary services.

    D. Install content scanning of e-mail in the DMZ.

8. You are the system administrator for a large network of 2000 Windows 2000 Professional workstations, 50 Windows 2000 servers, and 300 Unix workstations. You have one intranet web server, WS1. You also have one Outlook Web Access (OWA) server. Your users use OWA to access their e-mail from the Internet. Because of heavy demand, you need to install a second OWA server. The OWA servers do not host any mailboxes or public folders. You also want your users to continue using the same URL they have been using to access OWA, but you want user calls balanced between the two servers. What should you do? (Choose all that apply.)

    A. Move your OWA servers to the DMZ.

    B. Transfer the databases to other Exchange 2000 servers.

    C. Use a DNS alias to load-balance client calls between the two servers.

    D. Install two Exchange 2000 Server front-end servers in your DMZ.

    E. Install Network Load Balancing to load-balance client calls between the two front-end servers.

    F. Use SSL for client connections to the front-end servers.

    G. Use IPSec to secure communication between the front-end and back-end servers.

9. You are the administrator for an OWA server. The server was installed using default settings. You want to further secure this server. Which two tools would you use to do this?

   A. Network Load Balancing

   B. URLScan

   C. IISLockdown

   D. SSL

10. Which of the following will help prevent impersonation on your network? (Choose two.)

    A. User authentication

    B. IISLockdown

    C. SMB signing

    D. Removing Delegation Authentication

11. You are the system administrator for 20 Windows 2000 servers and 2000 Windows 98 workstations. You also have 300 Unix workstations and two Novell NetWare file servers. You want to increase security for all client logon traffic. All clients connect to both Windows 2000 servers and the two Novell NetWare file servers. What actions should you take? (Choose three.)

    A. Enable NTLMv2 for the Unix workstations.

    B. Enable NTLMv2 for the Windows 98 workstations.

    C. Use only TCP/IP protocol on your network.

    D. Use Directory Synchronization Services.

12. You are the system administrator of a network consisting of 600 Windows 2000 Professional workstations and 30 Windows 2000 servers. One of your servers, Web1, hosts your company's e-commerce website. You discover that this server has been compromised using the Anonymous user account. You want to quickly secure this server and all resources to which the Anonymous user account has permissions. What should you do?

    A. Require SSL for all connections to your e-commerce website.

    B. Enable auditing for all packets on your router.

    C. Configure the No Access Without Explicit Anonymous Permissions Group Policy setting. Apply to all servers on your network.

    D. Run the IISLockdown and URLScan tools.

    E. Rename the Anonymous user account.

13. You find that your web server is receiving a large number of SYN packets. You suspect that you are being hit with a DoS attack. What should you do?

   A. Audit the packets and perform reverse DNS on the attacker's IP address. Block all packets from this IP address at the router.

   B. Configure the SynAttackProtect key on your web server to cause your web server to time out more quickly when it receives too many SYN packets.

   C. Configure the EnablePMTUDiscovery key on your web server to cause your web server to time out more quickly when it receives too many SYN packets.

   D. Block the sender's IP address in the Properties dialog box for your web server.

14. You are the system administrator for 10 Windows 2000 servers. You have no 16-bit applications running on your servers. What should you do to increase security?

   A. Modify the `NtfsDisable8dot3NameCreation` Registry key.

   B. Remove the `NtfsDisable8dot3NameCreation` Registry key.

   C. Uninstall the thunking process by removing the `win32onwin16.dll` file

   D. Do nothing. There is no security issue.

15. You are the system administrator for a network with 800 Windows 2000 Workstations and 40 Windows 2000 servers. You want to increase your password security. What actions should you take? (Choose all that apply.)

   A. Require complex passwords.

   B. Do not allow users to publicly expose their passwords.

   C. Disable LmHash creation.

   D. Do not allow users to use recently used passwords.

16. You have run the IISLockdown tool on your web server. You need to deliver dynamic, streaming content from your web server and use the FTP service for file transfers. You also need to reconfigure the settings for the IISLockdown tool to allow this new content to be delivered efficiently. What should you do?

   A. Edit the `urlscan.inf` file. Reinstall IISLockdown.

   B. Edit the `protocol.ini` file. Reinstall IISLockdown.

   C. Edit the `urlscan.ini` file.

   D. Uninstall and then reinstall the IISLockdown tool.

17. You need to launch a private website that will be accessed by 20 of your users and 10 partners from other companies. It is required that this site be highly secure. What actions should you take? (Choose all that apply.)

   A. Accept connections only from predetermined IP addresses and DNS names.

   B. Disable anonymous connections. Require user authentication.

   C. Use SSL for all client communications.

   D. Install the IISLockdown and URLScan tools.

18. You have been charged with designing a secure solution for wireless access to your network. Although you don't have any wireless users right now, your manager wants to update the remote sales force to use wireless PCs and connect to inventory data on your intranet without plugging into their customers' networks to gain Internet access. How should you design this network?

A. Require SSL connectivity between the wireless workstation and the intranet server.

B. Install an access point on your network.

C. Install Internet Authentication Service.

D. Require IPSec at the network layer between the users and the access point.

E. Have the web server trust an internal Certificate Authority, and have your wireless users trust an external Certificate Authority.

F. Have everyone trust the same Certificate Authority.

G. Disable LmHash.

19. You are the administrator for 3000 users who are running a mix of Windows 98, Windows NT 4, Windows 2000, and Unix workstations. You also have 400 wireless workstations in your warehouses and portable buildings. Many of the wireless users also log on to the network from their desktops. What should you do to increase security?

A. Disable Routing and Remote Access for the wireless workstations.

B. Require each user to use a different account for each device they use to log on to the network.

C. Enable Routing and Remote Access for the wireless workstations. Require IPSec.

D. Set the KeepAlive time to 120 seconds

20. You are the administrator of a network that has 30 Windows 2000 workstations and 30 Macintosh clients. You want to secure the Macintosh clients' passwords as much as possible. What actions should you take? (Choose two.)

A. Require Kerberos for all Macintosh clients.

B. Install File Services for Macintosh.

C. Specify that the Microsoft User Authentication Module be used.

D. Do nothing. Kerberos is the default authentication protocol for Macintosh clients.

Answers to Review Questions

1. C.   When you install SQL Server 2000 using Windows Authentication Mode, the security context of the user is used for validation to a DC before allowing setup to continue. Kerberos becomes the default authentication protocol, and the directories and Registry keys are secured in this mode as well.

2. A.   Security Account Delegation, or Delegation Authentication, is the ability of one server to request a ticket on behalf of a user or service account when that user is currently connected to the local server but needs to connect to another server. Answer A is the only answer that fits the description of this behavior. Delegation Authentication is enabled by default in Windows 2000 Server.

3. C.   Best practice is to turn off delegation by default and then enable it for certain services and user accounts. This will guard against an easily hacked service account name and password combination being used to access the server via impersonation.

4. A, B.   What is described in the question is Delegation Authentication, and it is enabled by default on all Windows 2000 servers. Requiring digital signatures, among the other answers, is the best way to secure communication between your servers. Answer D would not be appropriate since client-to-server communication was not a focus of this question.

5. D.   SQL 2000 Server works with the Windows 2000 Server EFS, but it encrypts files under its service account name and password assignment. If you change this account without decrypting any encrypted files, this data will be totally lost to you until they are decrypted. The only way to decrypt the files is to use the account under which they were encrypted for the decryption process.

6. A, B, C, D, E, G.   Because of the ExIFS, every item in an Exchange 2000 Server store can be accessed using a number of different protocols. This allows for flexibility in how information is managed and stored. However, the different access points also create security concerns in that the information must be secured on multiple fronts. Items are secured using Windows 2000 Server user and group accounts and NTFS permissions.

7. B, D.   Two actions you can take on inbound SMTP mail is to run that mail through both a content scanner and an antivirus scanner. Doing both will protect your mail from viruses, unwanted attachments, and unwanted content. The URLScan and IISLockdown tools are suited for HTTP and port 80, not SMTP and port 25.

8. D, E, F, G.   You might be surprised that you don't have to move any databases to achieve this solution. Because the OWA servers are not hosting any mailboxes or public folders, all you need to do is configure them to be front-end servers and then install security for communication between the clients and the front-end server and again between the front-end servers and back-end servers. The best security for information between the front-end servers and your clients is SSL. IPSec can be used for calls between the servers. Because you are using front-end servers, you'll need to install Network Load Balancing to load-balance calls between these two servers. By default, Network Load Balancing uses a single IP address and namespace.

9. B, C.   Although using SSL is a way to secure client-to-server communication over port 80, only URLScan and IISLockdown are tools that secure the server directly.

10. C, D.   SMB signing, when required, is a method to ensure that all communication on your network is digitally signed at the packet level. In addition, Delegation Authentication is a type of impersonation that servers perform on behalf of clients. This can be removed to eliminate the possibility of an attacker using this feature to impersonate another user.

11. B, C, D.   Since Unix workstations can use Kerberos, enabling NTLMv2 would be a step back for them. By using only TCP/IP, you eliminate IPX/SPX from the network and its need to use SAP to advertise the presence of each server to the clients on the network. And in installations in which a large number of clients need to authenticate to both NetWare and Windows 2000 Server, directory synchronization can increase security by using the same accounts in both directories.

12. C, E.   Because the compromise occurred using the Anonymous user account, first limit what this account can do and its group memberships. By default, the Anonymous account is a member of the Everyone and Network security groups. Enabling this policy setting will require that you explicitly set permission to all resources for the Anonymous user account. Although you might be able to think of other things that should be done in this scenario, only answers C and E directly mitigate against the threat of a compromise using the Anonymous account.

13. B.   Because this is a SYN attack, configure the SynAttackProtect Registry key on your web server. Obviously, you might take other actions, but this one will help mitigate against the DoS attack on that individual server.

14. A.   If you have no Windows 16-bit applications, turn off the 8.3 auto generation of filenames. With this feature turned on, an attacker only needs eight characters to refer to a filename. With this feature turned off, the attacker will need the entire filename in order to use a file.

15. A, B, C, D.   Since most resources are password-protected, this is one of the favorite techniques that an attacker uses to compromise your network. All these measures will help increase the password security on your network. And all of them are recommended, except for the LmHash answer, which you must leave enabled if you have legacy clients, such as Windows NT 4 or Windows 98 clients.

16. D.   If you were just allowing more verbs on your website, answer C might suffice. However, if you need to redo the service structure on you website after running the IISLockdown tool, you'll need to uninstall and then reinstall the tool choosing the option during installation to secure this new type of server.

17. A, B, C, D.   All these actions will help secure your website. By accepting connections only from certain IP addresses or DNS names, you significantly limit who can even connect to the web server. And then requiring user authentication will mean that hackers must not only spoof an IP address, but also compromise a username and password combination and then impersonate a user to gain access to the website.

18. A, B, C, F.   To connect, wireless workstations need an access point. You can use SSL for port 80 connections between the workstation and the access point. To authenticate on the network, a RADIUS server can be employed to proxy the authentication requests from your users to the DC. Since all this communication will occur using encryption and signatures, you'll need a Certificate Authority available that both sides trust.

19. B.   Because each wireless device may have a different way to authenticate on the network, require a different username and password combination for each client device. This is because client devices will vary in their security when passing the password from the client to the access point.

20. B, C.   The default password security for Macintosh clients is 8 characters and clear-text passwords. When you install File Services for Macintosh, you can then select the MS-UAM, which allows for password characters up to 14 characters in length.

Chapter 3

Installing, Managing, and Troubleshooting Hotfixes and Service Packs

MICROSOFT EXAM OBJECTIVES COVERED IN THIS CHAPTER:

✓ Determine the current status of service packs. Tools include MBSA and HFNetChk.

✓ Install service packs and security updates. Considerations include slipstreaming and using Remote Installation Services (RIS), custom scripts, and isolated networks.

 ▪ Install service packs and security updates on new client computers and servers. Considerations include slipstreaming and using RIS, custom scripts, and isolated networks.

✓ Manage service packs and security updates. Considerations include server computers and remote client computers. Tools include Microsoft Software Update Services, Automatic Updates, and SMS.

✓ Troubleshoot the deployment of service packs and security updates. Typical issues include third-party application compatibility, permissions, and version conflicts.

Probably the best way to keep your servers secure on an ongoing basis is to install the latest service packs and hotfixes. Because new vulnerabilities are discovered every day, new hotfixes (sometimes referred to as "patches") are released to shut down each vulnerability. A *hotfix* is nothing more than a small piece of code that has been rewritten to eliminate the vulnerability in the software product.

Microsoft will keep you informed of these updates if you subscribe to their security notification e-mail service at www.microsoft.com/security.

This chapter will focus on service packs and hotfixes. We'll look at installing, managing, and troubleshooting them. And we'll discuss the tools that are available to help in this process.

Determining the Current Status of Hotfixes and Service Packs

If you need to see the current status of a service pack that is installed on an individual workstation or server, right-click My Computer, choose Properties to open the System Properties dialog box, and click the General tab (see Figure 3.1).

However, if you need to find out the service pack level of many workstations or servers at the same time, you'll need to run the Microsoft Baseline Security Analyzer (MBSA) tool. When you're working at the enterprise level, it is possible that some service pack and/or hotfix installations won't be distributed to every machine at the same time. It is also possible that some workstations or servers will be missed when using manual installation techniques. Hence, you may need to poll a group of target machines to determine their service pack level and then get all the updates and hotfixes installed in a uniform manner across the enterprise.

We'll discuss the MBSA tool later in this chapter, but first, let's go over how to install a service pack and a hotfix.

FIGURE   3.1   The System Properties dialog box, open at the General tab

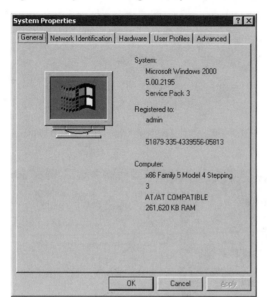

Installing Service Packs and Hotfixes

To install a new service pack on a Windows 2000 workstation or server, you'll first need access to the service pack file. Microsoft wraps service packs into a single installation file (see Figure 3.2) that, when invoked, expands into the local temp directory (see Figure 3.3) on the machine and then begins the installation process (see Figure 3.4). Microsoft also does this for hotfixes and updates.

FIGURE   3.2   Notice that the Windows 2000 service pack is encapsulated in a single file, which is highlighted in this illustration.

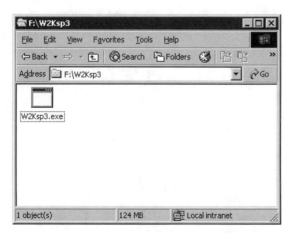

FIGURE 3.3   After the service pack file is invoked, the file is verified and then expanded in the temp directory.

FIGURE 3.4   After the file has been expanded, the Setup Wizard appears and starts the service pack installation.

To complete the installation, follow these steps:

1. At the Welcome screen, click Next to open the licensing screen.

2. If you agree to the terms of the license, select the I Agree radio button, then click Next to open the Select Options screen:

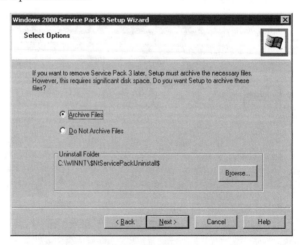

3. Choose whether to archive the files the service pack will overwrite, and then click Next to start the installation.

> Archiving the files means that the earlier versions will be retained and the current service pack can be uninstalled to revert to the earlier version in case the current service pack causes problems that cannot be resolved. If you choose not to archive the files, the service pack cannot be uninstalled.

The Setup Wizard first runs some diagnostic routines to determine how much disk space your machine has (see Figure 3.5) and to find out about some of the environment variables. It then begins the process of installing the updated files to your hard drive. If you selected to archive your files, setup first backs up all the files it intends to overwrite before installing the updated files from the temp directory.

FIGURE 3.5 Setup checks for adequate disk space.

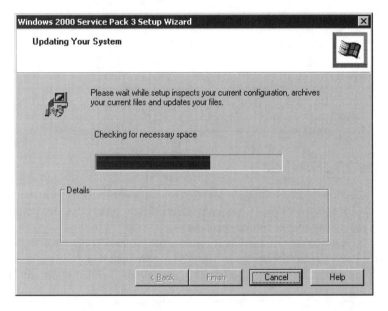

Once setup has completed, you'll be given a choice on the Finish screen to either reboot the machine now or reboot later. What this allows you to do is to install the service pack during the day and then reboot the machine later when client use is at low demand. Earlier versions of service packs did not include this feature. But remember, you must reboot the server in order for the new files that were installed to be registered and used. Until you reboot, you are operating under the old service pack, even though the new one has been installed.

In Exercise 3.1, you will install a new service pack for Windows 2000.

EXERCISE 3.1

Installing a Service Pack for Windows 2000

1. Double-click the service pack file.

2. Wait for the file to be verified and then expanded in the temp directory.

3. At the Welcome screen, click Next to open the licensing screen.

4. Read the licensing agreement, click the I Agree radio button, then click Next.

5. Make your archiving selection on the Select Options screen, and click Next to start the installation.

6. Wait for setup to run.

7. Click Finish.

8. Reboot your computer.

 You can download the latest Windows 2000 service pack from Microsoft's website at www.microsoft.com/windows2000.

Using the MBSA Tool

The Microsoft Baseline Security Analyzer (MBSA) tool is designed to perform much of what the Microsoft Network Security Hotfix Checker (HFNetChk) tool performs, but with a graphical front end (we like that!) and expanded capabilities.

You can scan one computer or a group of computers and check the installed operating system and the service pack level to determine which hotfixes are installed. You can find out about misconfigurations and missing hotfixes that have been recommended by Microsoft.

 You can download the MBSA tool, free of charge, from Microsoft's security website at www.microsoft.com/security.

MBSA can scan the following platforms:

- Windows 2000
- Windows NT 4

- Windows XP Professional
- Windows XP Home Edition

You can run MBSA from any Windows 2000 or XP platform, but you cannot run it from a Windows NT 4 machine. MBSA uses the HFNetChk tool to discover security updates that have been applied to a given machine or group of machines. How does MBSA know if all the required security updates have been installed? Well, it downloads an XML (Extensible Markup Language) file from Microsoft that contains all the hotfix updates that should be applied to each platform. It then checks for Registry keys, file version numbers, and checksums for each file or key that should have been installed with the hotfix. If there is a match to the XML file, the hotfix is presumed to be installed. If not, MBSA notifies you of this misconfiguration.

Each hotfix is stored under the Registry key HKLM\Software\Microsoft\WindowsNT\ CurrentVersion\Hotfix\Q######. Each hotfix has its own name with the syntax Q######_ XXX_YYY_ZZZ_LL.exe:

- Q###### is the number of the Knowledge Base article that discusses the hotfix.
- XXX indicates the platform or operating system to which this hotfix should be applied.
- YYY indicates the service pack level the system should be at before installing the hotfix.
- ZZZ indicates the hardware platform for which this hotfix was written.
- LL indicates the language of the hotfix.

MBSA not only scans for Windows 2000 hotfixes, but also for hotfixes associated with Windows XP, IIS (Internet Information Services), SQL Server 7 and 2000, and Internet Explorer 5.01 and later. This tool also checks for simple passwords and informs you if the passwords are either simple or blank.

Installing MBSA

To install this tool, follow these steps:

 MBSA will not install via Windows 2000 Server Terminal Services.

1. Download MBSA from Microsoft's website.
2. Double-click the mbsasetup.msi file to start Microsoft Baseline Security Analyzer Setup.
3. At the Welcome screen, click Next to open the licensing agreement screen.

4. Read the licensing agreement, agree to it, and then click Next to open the User Information screen:

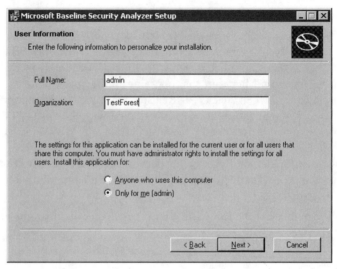

5. Enter your name and organization information, choose whether you want the tool available for all users of the computer or just you, and then click Next to open the Destination Folder screen.

6. Specify where you want the MBSA files installed, and then click Next to open the Choose Install Options screen. You can choose to do the following:

-   Launch the application after it is installed.
-   View the Readme file after installation.
-   Place a shortcut to MBSA on the Desktop after installation.

7. Make your selections, and then click Next to open the Select Features screen.

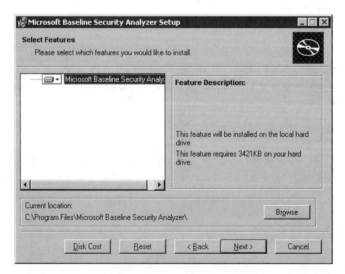

8. If you are unsure whether you have enough disk space to install MBSA, click the Disk Cost button to display a screen that shows you the amount of space that MBSA will consume and the amount of free disk space after installation (see Figure 3.6).

FIGURE 3.6   Click the Disk Cost button to display information about drive space.

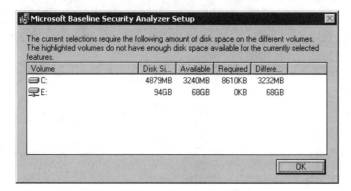

The Select Features screen really doesn't give you much in terms of additional features. About all you can select here is whether you want the MBSA installed on the local hard drive or whether you want all the features installed on the local hard drive. This is a bit of playing with semantics, since both choices lead to the same end.

9. Click Next, and Setup will tell you that it is ready to install the application.

10. Click Next to begin the installation.

In this Exercise 3.2, you will install the MBSA tool.

EXERCISE 3.2

Installing the MBSA Tool

1. Double-click the `mbsasetup.msi` file to start Microsoft Baseline Security Analyzer Setup.

2. At the Welcome screen, click Next to open the licensing agreement screen.

3. Agree to the licensing agreement, and then click Next to open the User Information screen.

4. Specify whether you want the tool available for everyone or only yourself, fill in the identifying information, and then click Next to open the Destination Folder screen.

5. Select your destination folder, then click Next to open the Choose Install Options screen.

6. Make your install option choices, then click Next to open the Select Features screen.

7. Click Next, and Setup will tell you that it is ready to start the installation.

8. Click Next again to start the installation.

9. Click Finish.

When you first run the tool, you'll see a rather nifty opening splash screen, as shown in Figure 3.7.

FIGURE 3.7   The opening menu screen for the MBSA tool

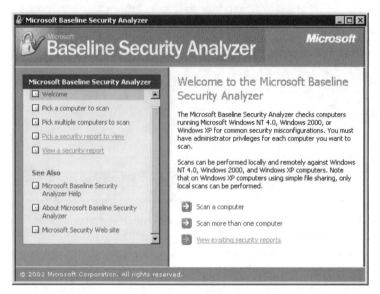

From this point, you can scan one or multiple computers, view security reports, or access online help.

We think it would be worthwhile, as a running example here, to scan both test computers in the testforest.com domain. It will be interesting to see how the default installation of Windows 2000 compares with the service packs and hotfixes that Microsoft recommends. By the way, we already have Service Pack 3 installed on our domain controller, DC1. So, what we'll do is click the Pick Multiple Computers To Scan link to display in the right pane input fields that let you enter a domain name and/or range of IP (Internet Protocol) addresses (see Figure 3.8).

Armed with this information, the tool finds all the computers that have a match and then scans them for the selected items, which include the following:

- Windows vulnerabilities
- Weak passwords
- IIS vulnerabilities
- SQL vulnerabilities
- Hotfixes

After the tools runs, it displays a report listing the computers that it scanned and its evaluation of their security status. Needless to say, the default installations of Windows 2000 will incur a Severe Risk assessment (see Figure 3.9).

FIGURE 3.8   Configuring MBSA to scan the testforest.com domain

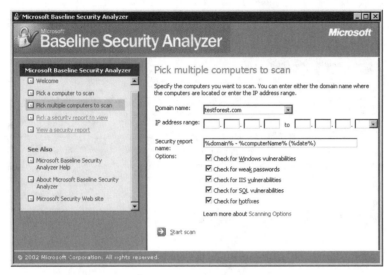

FIGURE 3.9   The results of running the MBSA tool on the two servers in the testforest.com domain

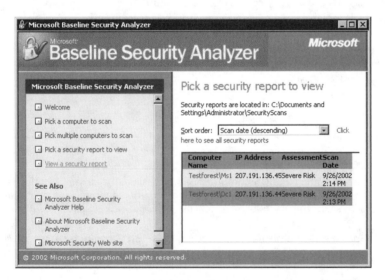

Clicking an individual machine in the report displays a detailed report for the machine (see Figure 3.10). If you run this tool on a default installation of Windows 2000 Server, you'll find that the default is really not very secure!

Although the MBSA tool has lots of whistles and bells, you can also use the HFNetChk tool to take care of many of the same tasks.

FIGURE 3.10   An individual server report from the MBSA tool

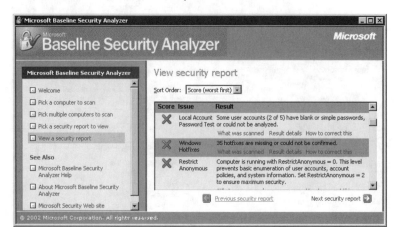

The HFNetChk Tool and MBSA

MBSA uses HFNetChk to scan the target computer(s). HFNetChk is really a command-line tool that MBSA uses or that you can run independently of MBSA. The reason you'll probably want to run MBSA as opposed to HFNetChk from the command line is that MBSA has a GUI front end that makes it easier to manage and navigate. In addition, HFNetChk checks only for hotfixes and services packs, whereas MBSA performs additional functions discussed previously in this chapter.

To view the syntax for HFNetChk, type **hfnetchk /?** at a command prompt. Table 3.1 describes each of the switches.

TABLE 3.1   The HFNetChk Switches

Switch	Description
-h	Specifies the NetBIOS computer name to scan. The default location is the local host. You can scan multiple host names if you separate each host name entry with a comma, as follows: hfnetchk -h computer1,computer2,server1,server2.
-fh	Specifies the name of a file that contains NetBIOS computer names to scan. There is one computer name on every line, with a 256 maximum in every file.
-i	Specifies the IP address of the computer to scan. Similar to NetBIOS names, you can scan multiple IP addresses if you separate each IP address entry with a comma.
-fip	Specifies the name of a file that contains IP addresses to scan. There is one IP address for every line, with a 256 maximum for each file.

TABLE 3.1   The HFNetChk Switches *(continued)*

Switch	Description
-r	Specifies the IP address range to be scanned, with *ipaddress1* and ending with *ipaddress2* inclusive, for example: hfnetchk -r 172.16.1.1-172.16.1.35.
-d	Specifies the domain name to scan. All computers in the domain are scanned.
-n	Specifies all computers on the local network to be scanned. This switch is similar to the -d switch for a domain, but all computers from all domains in My Network Places are scanned.
-history	Displays hotfixes that have been explicitly installed. Explicitly installed hotfixes are individually installed as opposed to being installed in a group via a rollup package.
-b	Scans your computer for hotfixes that are marked as baseline critical by the Microsoft Security Response Center (MSRC). To perform a baseline scan, your computer must be running the latest service pack that is available for your operating system.
-t	Displays the number of threads that are used to run the scan. Possible values are from 1 through 128. The default value is 64. You can use this switch to throttle down (or up) the speed of the scanner.
-o	Specifies the desired output format. The (tab) outputs in tab delimited format. The (wrap) outputs in a word-wrapped format. You'll use the tab output when scanning more than 255 hosts. The default is wrap.
-x	Specifies the XML data source for the hotfix information. The default file is the Mssecure.cab file from Microsoft's website.
-s	Eliminates the NOTE and WARNING messages in the output of the tool. The number 1=NOTE messages only. The number 2=both NOTE and WARNING messages. The default is no suppression.
-nosum	Prevents the tool from performing checksum validation for the hotfix files. The checksum information is found in the Mssecure.xml file for all hotfixes.
-z	Specifies that you do not want the tool to perform Registry checks.
-v	Displays the reason a scan did not work in wrap mode.
-f	Specifies the name of a file to output the results to.
-u	Specifies the user name to use when scanning a local or remote computer(s). You must use this switch with the -p (password) switch.

TABLE 3.1 The HFNetChk Switches *(continued)*

Switch	Description
-p	Specifies the password to use to help create the security context under which the tool will run. This switch must be used with the -u switch.
-about	Displays information about HFNetChk.
-?	Displays a help menu.

You can find a public newsgroup dedicated to the HFNetChk tool at microsoft.public .security.hfnetchk on the news.microsoft.com.

HFNetChk is a good tool to use for scanning individual computers or a range of computers. If you want a quick and clean report on which updates are installed on a single computer or a range of computers, HFNetChk is a great tool to use. The differentiating factor between using HFNetChk vs. MBSA is not the number of computers scanned, but the desired information: if you just want a report listing the updates that are not installed, HFNetChk is the tool to use. If you want to check for other items, such as IIS and SQL vulnerabilities, use MBSA.

Slipstreaming

Slipstreaming is a method for incorporating a service pack into the base install files on an installation point so that when a new installation occurs, the service pack is automatically installed. Slipstreaming removes the need to install the service pack separately.

To slipstream a service pack into a distribution share point, first create a distribution folder where you want the installation files to be held. Second, copy the I386 folder contents from the Windows 2000 CD-ROM. Be sure to copy all of the subfolders too. Third, run the service pack with the following syntax:

```
Update.exe -s:c:\<folder_name>
```

This command copies all the service pack files over the original installation files. Then, whenever a new installation is performed using these files, the service pack that was slipstreamed into the installation point is automatically installed.

In Exercise 3.3, you will slipstream Service Pack 3 into a Windows 2000 installation share point.

EXERCISE 3.3

Creating a Slipstreamed Installation Share Point

1. Create a distribution folder on your server.

2. Copy the contents of the I386 folder into the folder you just created.

3. Place the CD for Service Pack 3 in your CD ROM drive.

4. Run this command: update.exe -s:c:\<*name_of_distribution_folder*>.

5. Allow enough time for the installation to finish.

Using Remote Installation Services (RIS)

We've chosen not to go over how to create a RIS image and how to deploy it. This is a long, involved topic that would provide great background information, but probably not prepare you for the exam. You can't use RIS to keep your new workstations up-to-date with the latest service packs. This is not a solution for workstations that have already been deployed. Instead, this is a solution for creating a new workstation with the latest service packs and hotfixes when initially installing the workstation's operating system.

When new hotfixes become available, you can install these fixes on test servers and workstations. Once installed, you can then run Sysprep and store the new baseline image for future server and workstation installations. If the image is a Windows 2000 Professional image, you can push out this image using RIS.

The good part of this is that new workstations can be installed completely updated. The down side is that you'll need to keep re-creating the image, which means rebuilding a source workstation every time a new service pack or hotfix becomes available. This is probably a solution for larger environments only, in which the time spent rebuilding the source image is less than the time spent updating new machines after they have been deployed.

Working with Custom Scripts

If you are running a scripted installation of Windows 2000 or Windows XP, you can include in a script the hotfixes and updates. For both hotfixes and service packs, the -q switch allows the installation to run in quiet mode, which means that no user interaction is required for the installation to complete. Since every installation can be scripted, there are ways to ensure that a full, unattended installation occurs without any user intervention and with every update and fix installed.

Here are the command-line switches for update.exe:

-u	Unattended mode
-f	Force other applications to close at shutdown
-n	Do not back up files for uninstall
-o	Overwrite OEM files without prompting
-z	Do not restart the computer after installation has completed
-q	Quiet mode—no user interaction
-s:<foldername>	Use integrated installation mode

Here are the command-line switches for hotfix.exe:

-y	Uninstall hotfix
-f	Force other applications to close at shutdown
-n	Do not back up files for uninstall
-z	Do not restart the computer after installation has completed
-q	Quiet mode—no user interaction
-m	Unattended mode
-l	List installed hotfixes

If you have installed multiple hotfixes that replace the same file and you want to roll back your installation, you'll need to uninstall the hotfixes in reverse order of how they were installed.

You can also include the QChain tool in your scripts to ensure that you don't have version conflicts between hotfixes when they are installed with only one reboot. Be sure to read the section on QChain later in this chapter, as this is an outstanding tool that helps install multiple updates with only one reboot of the server.

Working on Isolated Networks

In a nutshell, Microsoft feels that the best way to keep your system up-to-date is to use their Software Update Services. This service (discussed in detail later in this chapter) allows you to set up a dedicated server to download and locally host new updates from Microsoft. This server will also manage offering these updates to the computers on your network.

However, if you are on an isolated network, meaning you have *no* Internet connectivity, you'll need to install the updates and fixes using an alternative method. This means that you might need to order the service pack CD ROMs or find an offsite location with good Internet connectivity, download the updates, burn them to a CD ROM, and then bring them into your network, or find another way to import the updates into your network.

The Software Update Services lets you manually download updates; so in a highly secure environment, it might be wise to completely disconnect the network from the Internet and connect only the Software Update Services server long enough to download the updates. Although more time-consuming for the administrator, this ensures that your network has all the updates installed, yet is only connected for discreet periods of time to the Internet.

Installing on New Clients and Servers

If you don't use RIS or any imaging system to install new clients and server, but yet you want to ensure that the initial installation contains all the latest service packs and hotfixes, this section is for you. Essentially, what you'll be doing is using a `.ini` file to specify the hotfixes you want run after you've installed a slipstreamed version of Windows 2000 Server or Professional.

Follow these steps:

1. Create a distribution share point on your network, and slipstream the latest service pack into the Windows 2000 installation files.

2. Prepare the hotfixes for installation. Because the Windows 2000 Setup program requires the 8.3 naming convention for all files and folders in the distribution folder, you must change the hotfix filenames from Q######_XXX_YYY_ZZZ_LL to Q######.

3. Open the `dosnet.inf` file located in the I386 folder on your distribution share point.

4. Add `svcpack` under the `[OptionalSrcDirs]` section. Save this file.

5. Create a `svcpack` folder under the I386 folder on your distribution share point, and copy the `sp3.cat` file to this folder.

6. Copy the hotfix(es) to this folder using the 8.3 naming convention.

7. Expand the hotfix, and then copy the hotfix binary files to the I386 folder. There is no need to copy `hotfix.exe`, `hotfix.inf`, `spmsg.dll`, or the symbol files.

8. Under the I386 folder, delete the `svcpack.inf` file.

9. Create a new `svcpack.inf` file and include the following information:

   ```
   [Version]
   Signature="$Windows NT$"
   [SetupData]
   CatalogSubDir="i386/svcpack"
   [ProductCatalogsToInstall]
   sp3.cat
   [SetupHotfixesToRun]
   Q######.exe </switches you want to use>
   ```

As the number of hotfixes increases or changes, all you'll need to do is expand the hotfix, copy the binary files to the I386 folder, ensure that the old binary files are deleted, and note the new hotfix in the `SetupHotfixesToRun` section of the `svcpack.ini` file.

Once complete, you can then use the regular setup commands to run this command in unattended mode.

If you don't want to slipstream the installation files, you can install Windows 2000 integrated with the latest service pack. To do this, follow these steps:

1. Copy the installation files for Windows 2000 to a distribution share point.

2. Expand the service pack files to another distribution share point.

3. Run the `update.exe` program in integrated mode, using the following syntax:

   ```
   Update.exe -s:x:\Windows2000
   ```

   - The -s switch specifies integrated mode.

- `x:\` is the drive letter of the partition holding your Windows 2000 installation files.

- `\Windows2000` is the name (and path) of the folder holding the installation files.

After `Update.exe` builds the integrated installation, you can deploy Windows 2000 to your users' computers from the distribution share point in either attended or unattended mode.

Managing Service Packs and Hotfixes

To say on top of the latest security issues from Microsoft, you can check several resources.

- Sign up to receive the latest Microsoft security bulletins from the Microsoft Security Bulletin Service. Whenever a new bulletin is released, you will receive an e-mail outlining the security problem and a link to the fix(es) for the problem.

- The Microsoft Software Update Services sends automatic notifications to your servers and workstations when security updates are posted to Microsoft's website. Microsoft has also released free software that lets an individual server on your network act as a Windows Update server. This is a nifty way to keep your network up-to-date with the latest security fixes and updates. We'll discuss this server and Windows Update a bit later in this chapter.

- Windows BugTraq is an independent website that maintains a mailing list that reports reproducible security bugs in Windows NT, Windows 2000, Windows XP, and related applications. You can find this website, shown in Figure 3.11, at `www.ntbugtraq.com`.

FIGURE 3.11   The home page for `ntbugtraq.com`

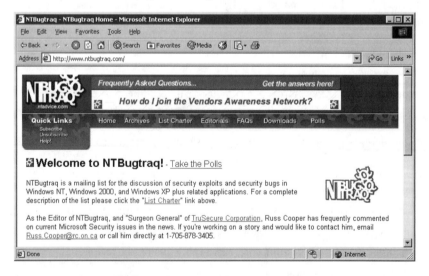

- You can use the MBSA, which we discussed earlier in this chapter.

These four resources, when combined, can provide a powerful solution for keeping your workstations and servers up-to-date. This section will focus largely on the Software Update Services, since this is a free software package that you can deploy on your servers and workstations.

Software Update Services: Keeping Servers and Clients Up-To-Date

You can find the Software Update Services at `www.microsoft.com/windows2000/windows-update/sus`. This software will help you manage and distribute critical Windows updates and fixes. What this software relieves you of is the responsibility of having to constantly check for new updates or download those updates when they become available. The Software Update Services (SUS) does this automatically. And only one server requires access to the Internet; the rest of your servers and workstations can be on an isolated network without Internet connectivity.

Here are the features of the SUS:

Content synchronization between your SUS server and the Windows Update service at Microsoft   The synchronization feature resides on the SUS server and retrieves the latest updates from Microsoft. As new updates are added to the Windows Update service at Microsoft, the SUS server automatically downloads and stores those updates locally. You can schedule this automatic downloading, or you can download manually.

Intranet-hosted Windows Update Server   Because the updates are downloaded to your SUS server, what you'll essentially have is a Windows Update server on your own network. This local server will handle the updates from Microsoft to all the servers and workstations on your network.

The opportunity to test new updates before deployment   Because the updates are downloaded to the SUS server, you can test the effects of installing each update before deploying it on your network. You can schedule the updates to run on your network, and you can deploy them according to options you select.

Integration with the Automatic Updates feature   Automatic Updates is a Windows feature that can be set up to automatically check for updates published on Windows Update. SUS can publish downloaded updates, and the clients can obtain their updates from your local SUS server instead of Microsoft's Windows Update server.

The SUS solution has both server- and client-side software that is intended to run on only Windows 2000 Professional, Windows 2000 Server, Windows 2000 Advanced Server, Windows XP Professional, and Windows XP Home Edition. It will also run with the new .NET server platforms once they are released.

If you are operating in a mixed environment of Windows 2000, Windows NT, Windows 9x, Unix, Novell, Macintosh, and/or DOS, you'll need to find other ways to install the updates. For example, you can use Microsoft's Systems Management Server.

The SUS solution has three main components:

- *Windows Update Synchronization Service*, which downloads content to your server running SUS

- The installation of an SUS website that services update requests from clients

- The installation of an SUS administration web page

From a client perspective, the SUS solution provides a number of features that are attractive, including:

- Background downloads

- Chained installations

- Built-in security

- Manageability

- Multilanguage support

Creating an SUS Server

After you download the software, you will need to install it. Your server must meet the following requirements:

- A P700 processor or higher

- 512MB RAM

- 6GB of available disk space

- Windows 2000 with Service Pack 2 or later

- Windows .NET RC1 or later

- Not a domain controller

- Not a Small Business Server (SBS)

- NTFS file system

To install the SUS software on a server, follow these steps:

1. Double-click `sussetup.msi` file to start an inventory of your server, which will give you context-sensitive error messages, such as not enough memory, not enough available disk space, or domain controller status.

2. When the inventory is complete (it's performed transparently in the background), you'll see the Welcome screen to the Microsoft Software Update Services Setup Wizard.

3. Click Next to open the licensing agreement screen.

4. Agree to the licensing terms, and then click Next to open the Installation Choices screen.

5. You can choose to perform a typical or a custom installation. We'll demonstrate a custom installation. However, the typical selection is just fine if you want to perform the installation quickly with default settings. Select Custom, and then click Next to open the Choose File Locations screen.

You can select the location for the updates to be stored by specifying the path when you click the Browse button. The default is c:\sus\. Most administrators will want to select a path other than the root drive.

You can also specify whether you want the updates pushed down to each machine on your network and then installed locally or whether you want all the machines to connect to your internal SUS and install the updates from that server.

6. Make your selection, and then click Next to open the Language Updates screen.

7. You can select all languages, which is the default, you can select English, or you can specify another language. Again, just make your choices, and then click Next to open the Update Approval Settings screen.

8. Here, you can tell SUS whether you want to manually approve new updates or have the tool automatically approve the updates. If you select the manual choice, you'll have the opportunity to test the updates in your environment before they are deployed on your network. In this running illustration, select the Manual option, and then click Next to open the Client URL Information screen.

9. This screen gives you the default URL your clients should connect to for updates. The default URL is http://<servername>. This screen is for information only, and when you click Next, the installation will commence.

Setup will run the IIS Lockdown tool. This means that URLScan will be automatically installed as well. Once this tool has been installed and installation is complete, you'll see a screen indicating the URL for administration of the tool, which is, by default, http://<servername>/susadmin.

Configuring the Software Update Services

Once installed, the SUS will need to be configured. To do this, you'll need to be running Internet Explorer 5.5 or later. Go to http://<*servername*>/susadmin (see Figure 3.12). You'll also find a shortcut to this site under the Administrative Tools.

FIGURE 3.12   The home page for administration of the Software Update Services

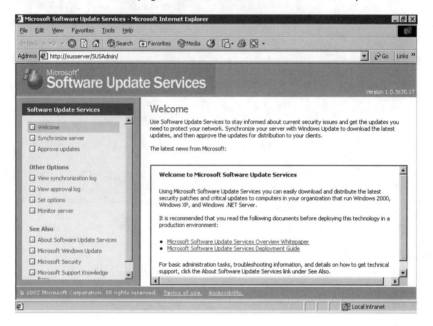

 You must be logged on as a local administrator to view the administration website for Software Update Services.

Click the Set Options link in the left pane to open the Set Options page (see Figure 3.13) on which you can configure a proxy server for SUS. Enter the information that is needed. In addition, on this page, you can specify the name of the server that your clients use to connect to the server.

Notice that you are entering the NetBIOS name of the computer. If you need to use DNS, enter the Fully Qualified Domain Name (FQDN) for the server or enter its IP address. Finally, you can select to have this server synchronize directly with Microsoft's Window Update server or synchronize with another update server that is hosted locally on your network. The second option allows you to deploy a farm of update servers on your network to provide load balancing for numerous client connections. This would only be applicable in large environments. Again, if you are using DNS for name resolution on your network, you'll want to enter the FQDN of the server from which this server should obtain its updates. Otherwise, NetBIOS name resolution is assumed.

FIGURE 3.13   The Set Options page for Software Update Services

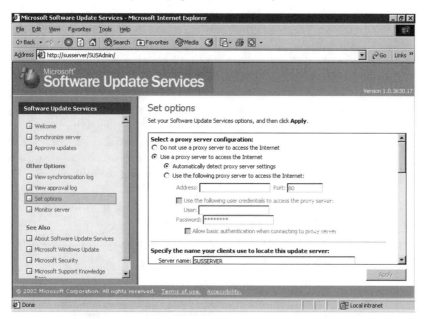

You can configure the synchronization schedule of the server with the Windows Update server at Microsoft by clicking the Synchronize Server link in the left pane of the home page (see Figure 3.12 earlier in this chapter). On the Synchronize Server page are two buttons: Synchronize Now and Synchronization Schedule. Click the Synchronize Now button if you want your server to synchronize itself with Microsoft's Windows Update server. This is best used when the server is first installed and you want to get all the updates downloaded right away to your SUS server. When you click this button, the Windows catalog is downloaded first and then the updates. A progress bar inform you of the progress of the downloads. The catalog is important to download because the SUS server will compare its version of the catalog with the version on the Windows Update server. Should they match, there are no updates to download. However, if there is not a match, the server will download the missing updates and make them available to the other computers on your network.

After all the updates are downloaded, you will be prompted to click OK and approve the updates. Remember that updates cannot be installed on computers on your network until they are approved. When this package is initially downloaded, you'll need to click a number of check boxes to approve the updates you want installed on your network if you selected the Manually Approve option. This can be time-consuming because there is no Select All button in the user interface. Also, if you did not select a specific language to install, all language versions will be downloaded. You'll need to scroll through that list and select the updates you want installed and the language you want to use as well.

Clicking the Synchronization Schedule button displays a simple schedule page that allows you to set a basic synchronization schedule so that you don't have to manually update the SUS server. Best practice here is to download updates when the server is not being backed up.

Installing the SUS Client

Except for your SUS servers, all your other machines will be SUS clients. If you are running Service Pack 2 or earlier for Windows 2000, you can install the SUS client, wuau22.msi. However, the SUS client is included in Service Pack 3 for Windows 2000, so by installing this service pack, you also install the SUS client.

Now, you might think that if you open the client, you can make your configuration choices there. Not true. Instead, you will configure the client via Group Policies Objects (GPOs) or push out Registry settings to non–Windows 2000 clients.

When Service Pack 3 is installed, a wuau.adm file is also installed, which can be imported as a template into a GPO. Once installed, the GPO can be applied to the client machines. After you add the .adm template to the GPO (see Chapter 2 for information about how to add templates to GPOs), you can find the Windows Update node under the Administrative Templates section.

To install the SUS client, you'll apply a GPO that has imported the wuau.adm. Here are the steps you'll follow to install the SUS client:

1. Under the Windows Update node inside the Administrative Templates of your GPO, double-click the Configure Automatic Updates setting to open the Configure Automatic Updates Properties dialog box:

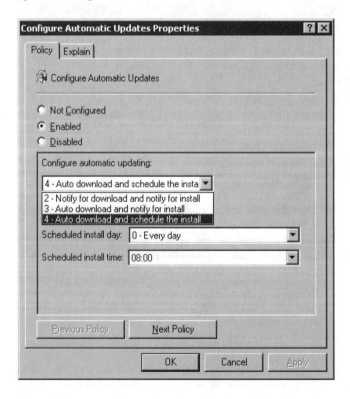

2. You'll see that you can configure the update method, how the updates are applied to the client, and a schedule of when you want the updates installed. Make your selections and click OK, or if you want to go to the next policy, click the Next Policy button.

If you select Notify For Download And Notify For Install or Auto Download And Notify For Install options in the Configure Automatic Updating section, you need to understand that these options only work with a logged-on administrative user account. User accounts that are not members of the local administrative group will not receive these notifications.

The other policy setting in the Windows Update node is Specify Intranet Microsoft Update Service Location Properties. Double-click this setting to open the Specify Intranet Microsoft Update Service Location Properties dialog box, as shown in Figure 3.14.

FIGURE 3.14   The Specify Intranet Microsoft Update Service Location Properties dialog box

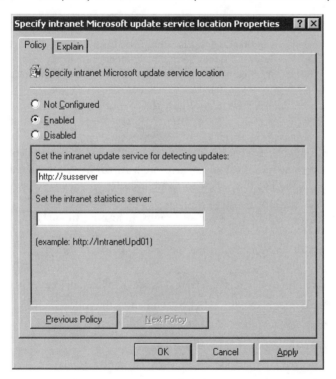

In this dialog box, you can specify the update server from which your clients will download and install the updates. You'll also need to specify the statistics server. This server is the server to whom clients will upload their statistics information so that from the SUS Admin page, you can determine aggregate numbers about updates on your network.

The statistics server must be running IIS. Statistics are stored in the IIS logs. The client returns to the statistics server the following information:

- During self-update: self-update pending

- After self-update: success or failure
- During detection: initialization success or failure
- After detection: detection success or failure
- After download: download success or failure
- After installation: installation success or failure

If you plan to use a server other than your SUS server as a statistics server, you'll need to copy the \<*website root*>\Vroot\wutrack.bin file to the root of your statistics server. This file is necessary to log SUS stats to the statistics server. Moreover, if you want only SUS statistics to appear in the logs (instead of all the HTTP traffic), you'll need to turn off logging in the website Properties dialog box. Then right-click wutrack.bin, and choose Log Visits from the shortcut menu.

 When Automatic Updates is configured through Group Policies, the policy will override the preferences set by the local administrator for the Windows client. If the policy is removed, the settings for the local client are used once again.

The nice thing about using GPOs to configure the clients is that by applying different settings to different OUs (organizational units), different SUS servers can be specified for a group of computers and thereby load-balance calls to your SUS servers.

If you are not running Service Pack 3 for Windows 2000, you'll need to deploy the SUS client. You can do so in several ways. First, you can use IntelliMirror (for Active Directory clients only) by configuring a GPO and creating a new software installation package. Assign the software package instead of publishing it, and then allow time for the policy to replicate throughout the forest. Ensure that you configure the package to install at boot time. Then reboot your client computers.

You can also deploy the SUS client using the Critical Update Notification (CUN) service. Set this Registry key as follows:

HKLM\Software\Microsoft\Windows\CurrentVersion\WindowsUpdate\CriticalUpdate

Create a SelfUpdServer key as a REG_SZ and enter the following value:

http://<*Servername*./SelfUpdate/CUN5_4

Do the exact same thing under the following key:

HKLM\Software\Microsoft\Windows\CurrentVersion\WindowsUpdate\
CriticalUpdate\Critical Update SelfUpdate

To confirm this has been successful, find the wuaueng.dll file and check its version number, which should be equal to or later than 5.4.3626.2.

SUS and Disaster Recovery

To successfully recover your SUS server in the event of a disaster, you will need to back up the website directory in which the SUS administration website was created, the SUS directory that contains the content, and the *IIS Metabase*.

You can back up the IIS Metabase from within the IIS MMC (Microsoft Management Console). In the IIS console, follow these steps:

1. Select the server to back up.

2. Choose Action ➢ Backup/Restore Configuration to open the Configuration Backup dialog box.

3. Enter a configuration backup name, and then create the backup.

You can now use your backup software to back up the metabase backup file.

Deploying SUS in the Enterprise

If you are using a proxy server to access the Internet, be sure to configure your proxy server on the Set Options page in the SUS Admin website. If you need to bypass the proxy server for local addresses, select the Bypass Proxy Server For Local Addresses check box. If your proxy server requires a user ID and password to access the Internet, select the Use The Following User Credentials To Access The Proxy Server check box, and then enter the needed credentials. You can also specify that basic authentication is used if your proxy server requires basic authentication.

You can deploy a farm of SUS servers to ensure there is load balancing of client requests for updates. You can synchronize content between servers running SUS or from a manually configured distribution point. Such a farm is useful when you have multiple SUS servers and you don't want all of them going to the Internet to update their content. In addition, if you have sites that do not have Internet access, or if you want to pull content only from a test lab (after the updates have been tested) into your production environment, synchronizing content between SUS servers is an excellent solution.

The server that obtains the updates from Microsoft's website is considered the *Parent server*. Other servers on your network that update their information from the Parent server are considered Child servers. On the *Child server*, click the Set Options link in the home page of Software Update Services to display the Set Options page. Enter the correct server name, and select the Synchronize From A Local Software Update Services Server radio button (see Figure 3.15). Moreover, if you select the Synchronize List Of Approved Items Updated From This Location (Replace Mode) check box, the Child server synchronizes the list of approved items along with the content. However, if you make this selection, you will not be able to alter the list of approved items on the Child server since that list is the same list as the one on the Parent server. If you need to make changes to this list, do so on the Parent server.

When you first install SUS, a default distribution point is created under the virtual root /Content folder. If you want to manually create a content distribution point, you must create a folder named Content and copy all the items from the Content folder on the source SUS server to the distribution server. You then create an IIS virtual root called http://<servername./ content and point that root to the Content folder. Remember that you can only deploy content that has been synchronized via SUS to other manually created content distribution points.

In larger environments, you can configure the SUS farm in conjunction with Network Load Balancing (NLB) to balance client connectivity to the Child servers. In this scenario, you'll only have one server downloading content from Microsoft's website; then the Child servers will synchronize their content and offer it to your users. NLB works best when there is good connectivity between all your Child servers and your clients. The nice thing about using NLB is that you can assign the same IP address and host name to all the Child servers in the "cluster" (*cluster* is the term used by NLB to designate which servers are load balanced by this service) and thus publish only one URL for all users to connect to. In large environments, this eliminates the necessity of having to create different GPOs and move computer accounts to different OUs to achieve load balancing across Child servers.

FIGURE 3.15   The Set Options page of the Software Update Services website

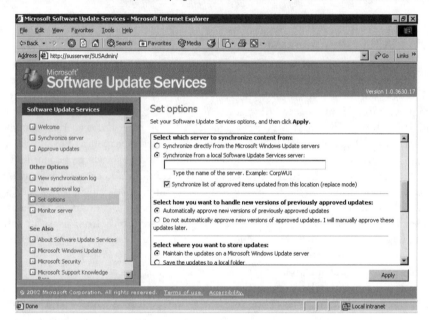

When working with Child servers, each server should store its content locally. In addition, you'll need to ensure that you have all the locales selected that will meet the needs of your users and choose the same locales for all the servers in the NLB cluster. Finally, each Child server in the cluster should obtain its downloads from the same source, whether that is a manual distribution point or another SUS server.

Troubleshooting SUS

Two logs are provided to the administrator to help determine SUS errors and activities: the synchronization log (see Figure 3.16) and the approval log. You can view both logs from the SUS Admin web page. You can use the logs to determine the point of failure and then use this information to further troubleshoot the problem.

In addition, the synchronization service generates event log messages for every synchronization action performed by the server and notes any major errors that were encountered. Moreover, a Monitor Server page (see Figure 3.17) in the SUS Admin website keeps information about available updates. This page displays the current contents of the metadata cache on the IIS server. From this page, you can find out how many updates are available for each platform on your network. You'll also see the last time the cache was updated next to each platform.

FIGURE 3.16   The synchronization log on a SUS server

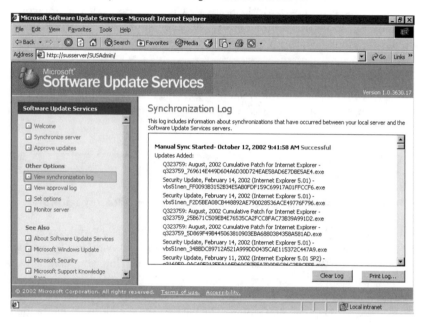

FIGURE 3.17   The Monitor Server page in the SUS Admin website

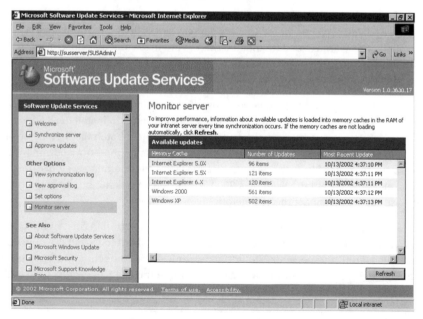

The white paper, "Deploying Microsoft Software Update Services," contains a list of all the event log messages and error codes for the Software Update Services. If you are working with SUS, it would be a good idea to print a copy of this paper and have it available for reference. You should also read through this paper to prepare for the exam.

You can fine the white paper, "Deploying Microsoft Software Update Services" at www.microsoft.com/windows2000/windowsupdate/sus/default.asp.

 Real World Scenario

Using SUS to Deploy Updates to 20,000 Windows Workstations

You work in a large installation of 20,000 workstations, with 10,000 Windows 2000 Professional workstations, 5000 Windows NT 4 workstations, and 5000 Windows 98 workstations. In addition, there are 400 Windows 2000 servers. Generally speaking, your company deploys roughly 550 new workstations each month. Because building new workstation images for all three workstation platforms every time a new update is released is too time-consuming, your CIO has directed you to develop a plan to install new workstations in unattended mode with all the updates and service packs. All new workstations are Windows 2000 Professional workstations.

Moreover, your CIO is tired of trying to keep all the security updates installed on the servers and workstations. And your CIO has stated that the servers can only be rebooted once when hotfixes are installed. He wants to ensure that the servers are up as much as possible. And he has made a requirement that no workstation can be connected to the network at any time without the latest updates and service packs installed.

The solution for this scenario is as follows. First, use slipstreaming to update the I386 installation folder for Windows 2000 Server. Then create an unattended script to install the Windows 2000 Professional workstation operating system. Fold the script into a batch file that includes the unattended script commands for the operating system, plus all the hotfix commands run with QChain. Run the batch file on the new workstation, allow the operating system to install with the hotfixes, and then reboot the Windows 2000 Professional workstation. It should now be up-to-date and ready to connect to the network.

To keep the Windows NT 4 and Windows 98 workstations up-to-date, install the SMS (Systems Management Server) client and require the SMS client to install the new updates as they are released to the network. Do not allow your users to decline the installation. Since some users rarely reboot their workstations, force the SMS packages to install at log on.

For your Windows 2000 server and current Windows 2000 Professional workstations, install a dedicated SUS server and have that server download the updates from Microsoft's website. Make this first SUS server a Parent server. Then, build a farm of five Child SUS servers that synchronize their content with the Parent server. Use NLB to balance calls between the Child SUS servers and publish a single URL for SUS connectivity. Then create a GPO that instructs all the Windows 2000 machines to download and install the updates from the SUS server farm. Ensure that the schedule for the updates does not occur when backups, indexing, or other regular database maintenance utilities are running.

Ensure that your servers install updates at a time when they can be rebooted with minimal user interruption, usually overnight.

Systems Management Server

The main use of Systems Management Server (SMS) is to push out updates to non–Windows 2000 clients. This includes Windows NT 4 and Windows 9x clients. You can set up software packages to install when the user logs on and even give the user a choice as to when the software is installed. Using SMS, you can also schedule software to be installed when users are not logged on to your network too.

Remember that if you need to upgrade computers that have an operating system already installed, you can use SMS. However, you cannot use SMS to perform the operating system installation. You must use other means to install the operating system on your client computers.

QChain

QChain.exe is a command-line utility that gives you the ability to install multiple hotfixes with only one reboot of the server, even if each individual hotfix would require a reboot on its own. The updates are "chained" together into a single installation, and then the server is rebooted only once. This allows more uptime for each server.

If you try to install multiple hotfixes before rebooting a server without QChain, you can run into a situation in which one hotfix replaces a file in the Pending File Rename queue that another hotfix already placed in the queue. The potential to overwrite a more recent version of a file with an older version is great, and you can end up with version conflicts.

The answer to this problem is to use QChain. To install multiple hotfixes with only one reboot, first run each hotfix with the -z switch to instruct the hotfix to not reboot after installation. After you install all the hotfixes, run QChain.exe, and then reboot the computer.

 Knowledge Base article Q296861 provides sample code for performing this operation using a simple batch file.

As you might have noticed by now, you can ensure that all the hotfixes are installed with one administrative act in two ways: you can use QChain, or you can use the method described earlier in this chapter that incorporates a .ini file, a distribution share point, and the manual expanding of hotfix files into the I386 distribution folder.

Which is better? Well, it all depends on your environment, but here are some guidelines:

When you need short installation times for your workstations, manually expand the hotfix binary files into the I386 distribution folder.   If you are going to use imaging to create a new workstation, it makes sense to take the time to manually expand each hotfix back into the I386 distribution folder and then create a new image for use on your new machines. Although it's time-consuming to expand each hotfix, this method ensures that the installation of the image doesn't take long and is up-to-date the moment the machine has complete installation.

When you need to ensure your servers are up as much as possible, use QChain.   Because multiple hotfixes can be installed with only one reboot, it makes sense to use QChain to install hotfixes on your Windows 2000 or Windows NT 4 servers.

When you install new workstations using unattended mode, but don't want to run a batch file after installation to install the updates, manually expand the hotfix binary files into the I386 distribution folder.   Then add command lines in the Cmdlines.txt file to run the hotfixes during Windows 2000 Setup. Using this method, only one command—the unattend command—will need to be run because the hotfixes are already present in the I386 distribution folder. Just run the setup as you normally would, and the installation of each workstation will be up-to-date.

In Exercise 3.4, you'll use QChain to install a series of hotfixes.

EXERCISE 3.4

Using QChain to Install a Series of Hotfixes

1. Place the hotfixes that need to be installed in the same folder location as the QChain utility.

2. Create a batch file that runs each hotfix as follows:

```
@echo off
setlocal
set PATHTOFIXES=<directory_path_to_fixes>
%PATHTOFIXES%\q######.EXE -Z -M
%PATHTOFIXES%\q######.EXE -Z -M
%PATHTOFIXES%\q######.EXE -Z -M
%PATHTOFIXES%\q######.EXE -Z -M
%PATHTOFIES%qchain.exe
```

3. Run the batch file.

4. Reboot the computer.

Troubleshooting the Deployment of Service Packs and Hotfixes

In our experience of working with SUS, it is best to install the server software on a new installation of IIS. For instance, if you have previously installed a heavily dependent software product, such as Microsoft's SharePoint Portal Server, uninstalled this product, and then tried to install SUS, chances are good that SUS will install but you won't be able to display the home page from which to perform administration.

Hence, it is a good idea that, before you install SUS, you uninstall IIS, then reinstall IIS, and then reinstall the latest service pack. We think you'll bypass a number of difficult-to-troubleshoot issues using this method.

Other troubleshooting scenarios will crop up, and it is impossible to discuss each possible scenario in this chapter. However, some common scenarios deserve attention, and we'll discuss them next. Some of these common scenarios have to do with third-party compatibility, some with SUS itself, and others with version conflicts.

Third-Party Application Compatibility Issues

You will need to ensure that after SUS is installed, your third-party applications continue to run. Best practice is to install those applications on a test server and then install SUS and observe any negative effects before doing this on a production server. Another best practice is to quarantine SUS services on an individual server that is performing no other role. Doing this will ensure that your third-party applications are not interrupted with the introduction of SUS into your environment.

However, if you are not so fortunate as to have a plethora of servers sitting around, be aware of the changes that will be made to IIS when SUS is installed:

- The `AspProcessorThreadMax` Registry key is set to one (1).
- The `AspThreadGateEnabled` Registry key is set to TRUE.
- ASP (Active Server Pages) files are enabled.
- IDQ (Internet Data Query), SHTML (Secure Hypertext Markup Language), SHTM (Secure HTM file), STM (Server-Side Include file), IDC (Internet Database Connector), printer, and HTR (hard-return) mappings are all disabled.
- Sample web files and the scripts virtual folder are removed.
- The MSDAC (Microsoft Data Access Components) virtual directory is removed.
- WebDAV (Web Distributed Authoring and Versioning) is disabled.
- IIS anonymous user is prevented from executing system utilities.
- IIS anonymous user is prevented from writing web content.

The IIS Lockdown tool is not applied when SUS is installed on a Windows .NET server since IIS 6 defaults to secure mode.

If any of your third-party applications need any settings different from those listed here, don't install SUS on that server.

Permissions

Some hotfixes and service packs will require administrative privileges on the local machine to successfully install. SUS is a great way to ensure that these updates and service packs are installed properly without having to log on to each workstation as an administrator and run the updates. For new machines, you can either manually expand the hotfix binaries into the I386 distribution folder or use QChain to install the hotfixes using a batch file.

Another way to ensure that you don't run into permissions issues is to use SMS to install on legacy platforms, such as Windows NT 4 and Windows 9x.

Version Conflicts

Version conflicts sometimes arise when you install incompatible service packs or hotfixes on the same computer. This is most often the case when multiple hotfixes are installed without the use of QChain. The best way to ensure that you don't have version conflicts between hotfix installations is to use QChain.

Less often, but still not uncommon, is the scenario in which you attempt to install an earlier version of a service pack over a later version. Microsoft does not allow this to happen because the service packs check the current service pack level of the workstation or server that is being run and return the error you see in Figure 3.18 if the current service pack level is greater than the one being installed.

FIGURE 3.18   The Service Pack Setup Error message

Summary

In this chapter, we discussed a number of different issues, including how to use the MBSA tool to determine which updates need to be installed on each computer on your network and how to use SUS to ensure that these updates are automatically downloaded and installed throughout your environment.

We also discussed the HFNetChk tool, which is used by MBSA to poll the target machines to determine what hotfixes, if any, need to be installed on them. HFNetChk can be run by itself, but is more useful when run inside MBSA.

We spent a fair amount of page space on the Software Update Services, which replaces the Critical Notification Service. If you are working with an older version of the test's domains and objectives, you'll see the Critical Notification Service mentioned. We did not neglect to cover this. On the contrary, SUS replaces this service and is the preferred method to ensure that you have all the updates and hofixes installed on each Windows 2000 machine on your network.

For legacy platforms, you'll want to use SMS to install updates on machines that already have an operating system. For new machines, you'll want to use slipstreaming and perhaps some scripting to run a batch of hotfixes using the QChain tool. However, when compared to SUS, slipstreaming and writing scripts seems rather time-consuming. If you are in an environment that doesn't allow any machine to not have the latest updates installed—even for a short period of time—slipstreaming and scripts using QChain will be the best way to ensure that new machines are up-to-date right from the start.

Exam Essentials

Know how to install Software Update Services.   You'll need to understand how to install the SUS server software. You'll also need to remember that the client software needs to be installed on all Windows 2000 machines that are running Service Pack 2 or earlier and that it is included in Service Pack 3 and later.

Know how to use NLB to balance client demand for updates from an SUS server farm. Essentially, NLB balances calls between IIS servers placed in a single NLB cluster. In large environments, calls for updates to SUS servers can be high, and this would indicate a need for NLB.

Know when to use QChain, when to use SMS, and when to manually expand hotfix binaries into the I386 distribution folder to install hotfixes.   QChain gives you the ability to install multiple hotfixes with only one reboot. This can be advantageous on both servers and workstations if a number of hotfixes need to be installed at the same time. You'll use SMS when installing updates on legacy platforms, and you'll manually expand the hotfix binaries when you need to keep your source installation files up-to-date for new workstation installations.

Know how to use the MBSA tool and its expanded features.   Remember that the MBSA tool uses HFNetChk to find out which target computers have which updates installed. But MBSA has expanded features that allow you to perform an expanded diagnosis of your workstations and servers.

Remember that version conflicts can occur without the use of QChain.   QChain gives you the ability to install multiple hotfixes and not experience version conflicts between individual binary files. If multiple hotfixes are installed with only a single reboot, the possibility exists for the wrong version of an individual file to be installed last, thereby creating a version conflict. QChain will solve this problem for you.

Key Terms

Before you take the exam, be certain you are familiar with the following terms:

Child server	Parent server
hotfix	Slipstreaming
IIS metabase	Windows Update Synchronization Service

Review Questions

1. You recently installed a service pack on your Windows 2000 server. You now need to uninstall this service pack. Which installation choice should you have made to allow for the removal of the service pack?

    A. The -q switch

    B. Archive files

    C. Unattended mode

    D. Native mode

2. You have just been hired as the new system administrator for a company with 20 Windows 2000 Server machines, 400 Windows 2000 Professional workstations, and 100 Windows 98 workstations. You need to quickly find out what service packs and hotfixes are installed on each machine. You want a complete report for your network. What action should you take?

    A. Run the HFNetChk tool.

    B. Run the MBSA tool.

    C. Run Update.exe.

    D. Run hotfix.exe.

3. You need to install the MBSA tool. The server you want to install this tool on is located in another building, so you connect to that server using the Terminal Services client. You proceed through the setup process and receive an unspecified error. After the error, setup will not continue. What should you do?

    A. Update your Terminal Services client and rerun setup.

    B. Turn off antivirus scanning during the installation.

    C. Ensure that the setup file is not infected with a virus.

    D. Walk to the server and install MBSA in person.

4. When using MBSA to scan for multiple computers, which two options are available to specify the target computers?

    A. One or more IP subnets

    B. One or more IP addresses

    C. Domain name

    D. Forest name

5. You have recently acquired a small competitor who has five Windows 2000 Professional workstations and one Windows 2000 Server machine. You want to quickly find out what service packs and hotfixes need installing on these six machines. What action should you take?

   A. Run MBSA.

   B. Run HFNetChk.

   C. Run `Update.exe`.

   D. Run `hotfix.exe`.

6. Which command should you run to slipstream a service pack into a distribution point for Windows 2000 Server?

   A. `Update.exe -q`

   B. `Update.exe - m`

   C. `Update.exe -1`

   D. `Update.exe -s`

7. You have 400 new Windows 2000 Professional workstations you need to deploy. You want to deploy them with the latest updates installed with the initial installation. You are not using imaging to create these new machines. What method should you use?

   A. Slipstream the service packs and hotfixes into the source files, and then perform the installations on the workstations.

   B. Create a batch file that will run `unattend.exe`, `update.exe`, and `hotfix.exe`.

   C. Update your test workstation. Then run `Sysprep` and install the new image to each workstation.

   D. Run a basic installation of Windows 2000 Professional. Then allow the Software Update Services server to update the workstation automatically.

8. You are the administrator of a highly secure network. One requirement of this network is that it be isolated from all external connectivity, including dial-up and dedicated technologies. However, you need to ensure that all the servers and workstations have the latest updates from Microsoft. Every update must be tested before being deployed on your network, and you must import the updates in the most secure method possible. What actions should you take to ensure that all workstations and servers are kept up-to-date with the latest updates, service packs, and hotfixes? (Select all that apply.)

   A. Install a dedicated Software Update Services server.

   B. Connect this server to the Internet only long enough to download the latest updates from Microsoft.

   C. Install a Parent Software Update Services server.

   D. Connect this Parent server to the Internet only long enough to download the latest updates from Microsoft.

   E. Test the updates on an isolated network in a lab environment.

   F. Synchronize an internal Child server with the Parent server.

9. You are the administrator for a network of 600 Windows 2000 Professional workstations and 50 Windows 2000 Server machines. Each Windows 2000-based machine is running Service Pack 2. You want to deploy the Software Update Services client and upgrade each machine to Service Pack 3. What action or actions should you take? (Select all that apply.)

   A. Use a Group Policy to install the Software Update Services client on each machine.

   B. Use a Group Policy to install Service Pack 3.

   C. Use SMS to install the Software Update Services client on each machine.

   D. Use SMS to install Service Pack 3 on each machine.

   E. Reboot the machines.

10. Which of the following are the three main components for the Software Update Services?

   A. Critical Notification Service

   B. Windows Update Synchronization Service

   C. Software Update Services website

   D. Software Update Services Administration website

   E. Windows Update service

11. You are the administrator of a network with 200 Windows 2000 Professional workstations and 7 Windows 2000 Server machines. All servers are domain controllers. You want to install the Software Update Services. What should you do?

   A. Install the Software Update Services on the root domain controller.

   B. Install the Software Update Services on any domain controller.

   C. Create a new domain controller and install the Software Update Services.

   D. Create a new member server and install the Software Update Services.

12. You are the administrator of your network. There are 1000 Windows 2000 Professional workstations on your network and 150 Windows 2000 Server machines on your network. All machines are running Service Pack 3. You need to ensure that all software updates from your Software Update Services server are installed on all workstations and servers on your network with as little administrative effort as possible. What actions should you take?

   A. Create a new GPO and assign it to the Domain object.

   B. Open the Configure Automatic Update dialog box, and select the Auto Download And Notify For Install option.

   C. Open the Configure Automatic Update dialog box, and select the Auto Download And Schedule The Install option.

   D. Create a new GPO and assign it to the Domain Controllers Organization Unit object.

   E. Specify an Intranet Update server and Intranet Statistics server in the Specify Intranet Microsoft Update Service Location Properties dialog box.

13. You are the administrator for 400 Windows 2000 Professional workstations and 35 Windows 2000 Server machines. Some of your workstations are not receiving software updates from your Software Update Services server. You want to log update activities only. Which two actions should you take?

A. Turn on logging in IIS on the Software Update Services website.

B. Turn off logging in IIS on the Software Update Services website.

C. Enable logging on the `wutrack.bin` file.

D. Disable logging on the `wutrack.bin` file.

14. You are the administrator for 50 Windows 2000 Professional workstations and 10 Windows 2000 Server machines. All machines are running Service Pack 3. You have successfully installed a Software Update Services server and have successfully used a GPO to configure the clients to download their updates from the SUS server. You now have decided to have all your Windows 2000-based machines obtain their updates directly from Microsoft's website. You disable the policy settings in the Windows Update node in the Group Policy Object. What will be the result of this action?

A. Current updates will be uninstalled.

B. Current updates will be unaffected, but new updates will not be downloaded.

C. Current updates will be unaffected; new updates will require an administrative intervention to install them.

D. New updates will be successfully downloaded with no more intervention.

15. You are running a mixed environment of Windows 2000 Professional and Windows NT 4 workstations. You need to deploy the Software Update Services client. One group of Windows 2000 Professional clients in the East OU are running Service Pack 1. All other Windows 2000 clients are running Service Pack 3. The Windows NT 4 clients are running Service Pack 6a. You are not running Systems Management Server. How should you deploy the Software Update Services client?

A. Create a software package and use Group Policies to push the client down to the Windows 2000 computers in the East OU.

B. Use the Critical Update Notification service to set the Registry entries on your Windows NT 4 workstations.

C. Use the Windows Update service to set the Registry entries on your Windows NT 4 workstations.

D. Create a software package and publish it to all workstations in your domain.

16. What must you restore in order to fully restore a Software Update Services server?

A. IIS Metabase

B. IIS Database

C. Extensible Storage Engine

D. The Content folder

E. Software Update Services websites

17. You need to push out software updates to a group of Windows 98 clients. What is the best way to accomplish this task?

    A. Create a Group Policy Object, and assign the software package to the workstations.

    B. Use Systems Management Server to push out each update's installation at logon.

    C. Use QChain to push out the installation packages.

    D. Use the Critical Update Notification service to push out the update installations.

18. You have six hotfixes you need to install on 26 Windows-based workstations. What should you do?

    A. Create a script that installs each hotfix individually and then runs QChain.

    B. Create a script that installs each hotfix serially and then runs QChain.

    C. Expand each hotfix into the I386 folder and run `Update.exe -q`.

    D. Expand each hotfix into the I386 folder, and then run `winnt32.exe -q`.

19. You have to install 400 new Windows 2000 Professional workstations each month and rebuild 100 deployed workstations. You need to perform these installations in the fastest time possible, but install all the latest updates as well. You cannot use imaging to perform this task. What should you do?

    A. Run an unattended installation, and then run a batch file that installs all the hotfixes using QChain.

    B. Slipstream the latest service pack into the source files, and then use QChain to install necessary hotfixes.

    C. Slipstream the latest service pack into the source files, and then manually expand each hotfix into the source files.

    D. Assign a software package to the desktop that will install the operating system with the necessary hotfixes.

20. You have recently installed eight hotfixes on your Windows 2000 server. Now, some third-party programs won't run correctly. You are also receiving version conflict errors in the event logs. What should you have done to prevent this?

    A. Run the `wutrack.bin` file

    B. Run RIS to install the hotfixes

    C. Run QChain to install the hotfixes

    D. Installed each hotfix individually and then performed one reboot of your server

Answers to Review Questions

1. **B.** During the installation of a service pack, you can select to archive the files that will be over-written. When you do this, the old files are placed in a special folder and kept there in the event that you want to uninstall the service pack. During the uninstallation process, the current files are replaced with the old, saved files and then deleted.

2. **B.** Although the HFNetChk tool will give you a list of all the updates and hotfixes that have not been installed on your servers and workstations, only the MBSA tool will give you a complete report that includes IIS and SQL server platforms as well as other items such as weak passwords and platform-specific vulnerabilities. Hence, to get the most complete report, you'll need to run MBSA. `Update.exe` is the command used to install a service pack, and `hotfix.exe` is the command used to install a hotfix.

3. **D.** You cannot install the MBSA tool using the Terminal Services client.

4. **B, C.** When running the MBSA tool, you can group your target computers based on either domain name or IP address range. Since all four octets of the IP address range are available for configuration, it would not be fair to say that you can specify only an IP subnet. You need to specify the exact starting and ending IP addresses, even if this means specifying the starting and ending address for a given subnet.

5. **B.** HFNetChk is a great tool for pinpointing which updates need to be applied to the scanned machines. If you don't need the additional scanning options that MBSA offers, use the HFNetChk tool.

6. **D.** The `-s` switch is the integrated mode switch. You can also think of this as the slipstream switch. When you specify a folder path and name after the `-s` switch, the service pack files are expanded and then copied over the current installation files. Then, when the installation is run from these files, the service pack will be installed along with the rest of the operating system.

7. **A.** Only answer A meets every need of the scenario described in the question. Answer D would be correct if the scenario described did not require the updated files to be installed at the time of initial installation. The batch file also doesn't meet the requirements of the scenario since this is a series of individual installations.

8. **C, D, E, F.** By installing a Parent server, you can accomplish two goals at the same time. First, you can further protect the isolated network by placing a firewall between the Parent and Child servers and ensure that the Child server is never connected to the Internet. Second, you can use the Parent server and another workstation as a test bed to test the updates before they are synchronized to the internal Child server. Also, this architecture keeps the SUS server on the isolated network from ever having any direct Internet connectivity.

9. **B, E.** When Service Pack 3 is installed on a Windows 2000-based machine, the Software Update Services client is installed as well. Although you can use SMS to perform the same function, pushing out a software update and assigning it to the workstation or server at the next reboot is the easiest way to get this software out to all your machines in a consistent and uniform manner.

10. B, C, D.   The Critical Notification Service is the old iteration of the current Software Update Services. The Windows Update service is the client-side service that works with the Windows Update service from Microsoft's website. The Windows Update service on the client is installed with the operating system and exists whether the Software Update Services client is installed or not.

11. D.   You cannot install the Software Update Services on a domain controller or a Small Business server. In addition, the server must have at least a PIII/700 processor, 512MB RAM, and 6GB of disk space. You must also be running Windows 2000 Server with Service Pack 2 or later and be using the NTFS file system. Only answer D meets some of the criteria for server requirements for Software Update Services.

12. A, C, E.   Answer B is incorrect because the Notify option means that someone must log on as an administrator and approve the installation. Answer D is incorrect because a policy applied only to the domain controllers OU would be applied only to the domain controllers and not to the computer accounts that exist in other OUs. A policy applied to the domain object will be inherited by all your computers in all OUs. The correct answers outline the basic steps you'll need to take in making sure that the software updates are pulled from your local SUS server and not from the Windows Update server on the Internet.

13. B, C.   In order to log only SUS traffic on the SUS server, you'll need to turn off IIS logging of that website and then enable logging on the `wutrack.bin` file.

14. D.   When Automatic Updates are configured through Group Policies, the policy will override the preferences set by the local administrator. However, if the policy is removed, the old settings will take effect and be used once again.

15. A, B.   For Windows NT 4 workstations, you can use the CUN to set Registry entries on each workstation that will tell the workstation to pull its updates from your internal SUS server. For the Windows 2000 workstations in the East OU, a Group Policy that assigns the package to the computer is the easiest way to install the client.

16. A, D, E.   The three main parts to back up on an SUS server are the websites, the metabase, and the update content. Obviously, you'll need to restore this information to fully restore an SUS server.

17. B.   When working with legacy clients, it is best to use SMS to push out update installations and assign the installation to run at a specific time. Since many people leave their computers turned on most of the time, you can select to have the software installed at logon.

18. B.   QChain is designed to run after a series of hotfixes has been installed. Only answer B fits the purpose for running QChain.

19. C.   What you are doing in answer C is updating the source installation files with the latest service pack and hotfixes. Because you can't use imaging here, the fastest way to get all these updates installed on new workstations is to use a combination of slipstreaming and hotfix expansion into the source files.

20. C.   Qchain is designed to eliminate version conflicts between system files that have been updated by different hotfixes. RIS installs an entirely new operating system, and the `wutrack.bin` file is designed to help track calls between SUS servers and SUS clients.

Chapter

4

Configuring IPSec and SMB Signing

THE MICROSOFT EXAM OBJECTIVES COVERED IN THIS CHAPTER:

✓ **Configure IPSec to secure communication between networks and hosts. Hosts include domain controllers, Internet web servers, databases, e-mail servers, and client computers.**

- Configure IPSec authentication.
- Configure appropriate encryption levels.
- Configure the appropriate IPSec protocol. Protocols include AH and ESP.
- Deploy and manage IPSec certificates. Considerations include renewing certificates.

✓ **Troubleshoot IPSec. Typical issues include IPSec rule configurations, firewall configurations, routers, and authentication.**

✓ **Configure Server Message Block (SMB) signing to support packet authentication and integrity.**

In this chapter, we will focus on Internet Protocol Security (IPSec) protocol: how we implement, manage, and troubleshoot it. IPSec is an important tool for ensuring that IP traffic is encrypted over untrusted networks, such as the Internet. We'll cover the considerations you must make for using IPSec in a variety of environments.

Server Message Block (SMB) signing is also an integral part of securing your network, so we'll go over SMB in this chapter as well.

Understanding IPSec

Internet Protocol Security (IPSec) is an open framework for ensuring private, secure communications over IP (Internet Protocol) networks using cryptographic security services. IPSec is a method widely employed that ensures that IP traffic is encrypted over untrusted networks, such as the Internet.

IPSec guards against several types of network attacks:

Eavesdropping When you use TCP/IP (Transmission Control Protocol/Internet Protocol) in its native format, information passed between computers is sent in clear text, which allows an attacker to "listen in" or read the traffic by simply copying the packets from the network line to their own computer. The ability to monitor and capture packets is generally thought to be the largest internal security concern for network administrators.

Data modification Because an attacker can read clear text data, it would stand to reason that the attacker could also alter the data without the sender or receiver of that data knowing that it had been altered. Altering data can result in incorrect and perhaps illegal activities, such as altering amounts ordered, messages sent, or sums of money. The ability to modify data can lead to a number of different types of attacks:

> **Identity spoofing or impersonation** If you can alter the contents of packets passed on the network, it is possible to spoof the sender's IP address or impersonate a different sender to the recipient of the message. This means that messages can be sent to a recipient that appear as if they came from a person who never sent them. In addition, real messages can be altered to have a different, malicious meaning. Such ability to disrupt real, authentic communication can wreak havoc on an organization.

> **Password attacks** Older applications may not protect passwords well. And if you are using Basic Authentication, all passwords are passed in clear-text format. The ability to intercept a password and then use it to gain access to secure data could place the attacker in a powerful position and put the organization in a vulnerable position.

Denial-of-Service Attacks   *Denial of service (DoS)* attacks result in servers going down or being unavailable because of all the SYN packets it is trying to service. Resources can be blocked by a DoS attack and your IS staff's time totally consumed in stopping the attack. Meanwhile, the attacker can concentrate on other secure targets and work unhindered while the IS staff defends against the DoS attack.

Compromised-key Attack   In this type of attack, an attacker copies a key off the network line and then breaks the key and uses it to gain access to secured resources. Such keys are referred to as compromised keys because they can no longer ensure the integrity of the data sent or secured.

IPSec is a real defense against these types of attacks. It provides a key line of defense against private network and Internet attacks.

IPSec has two basic foci. The first is to protect the packets sent across the line, and the second is to defend against network attacks. Both goals are achieved though the use of a public-key infrastructure for users on the network, users on the internet, and users accessing the network remotely through dial-up technologies. Because IPSec operates at the network layer, it provides a method of secure data transmission that is transparent to most applications. Deploying IPSec requires no changes to existing applications or operating systems, and IPSec policies can be centrally managed through Group Policies or locally on a computer.

The use of IPSec provides the following security benefits:

Nonrepudiation   This means that the sender of the message is the only one who could have sent the message. Nonrepudiation is accomplished through the use of digital signatures by which the sender's private key is used to sign the message.

Antireplay   IPSec ensures that each packet is unique. No packet can be captured, opened, modified, and then sent again, or replayed.

Integrity   IPSec ensures that the packet was not modified during transit and that the information contained in the packet is the information the sender intended to place in the packet before sending it. Because only the sender and receiver have the key to encrypt and decrypt the packet, it stands to reason that only the sender and receiver can read its contents, ensuring the integrity of the packet's contents.

Confidentiality   At first glance, you might be tempted to think that confidentiality and integrity are the same thing, but they are not. Whereas integrity ensures that the packet's contents have not been altered, confidentiality ensures that only the sender and receiver can read the packet's contents. This is accomplished through the use of data encryption, which is accomplished by a key that is known only to the sender and receiver of the data.

IPSec encrypts the data in packets for secured transmission. The Data Encryption Standard (DES) is one encryption method used by IPSec. IPSec's implementation of DES has the ability to frequently regenerate encryption keys during a communication. This prevents the entire data set from being encrypted by the same key and thus (potentially) having the entire data set compromised if the key is compromised.

IPSec supports the use of an advanced form of DES, called *3DES*, which processes each block of data three times in the following manner:

- Encryption on the block with key 1

- Decryption on the block with key 2
- Encryption on the block with key 3

The receiving computer reverses this process to decrypt the packet.

 Windows 2000 Server uses the United States *Data Encryption Standard (DES)* to encrypt data in its IPSec implementation.

Within the IPSec policies, you can also control how often a new key is generated during the communication between both computers. This regeneration of a new key is called *dynamic rekeying*. As computers send messages back and forth, their messages are divided into blocks, which are then encrypted to ensure confidentiality and integrity. Dynamic rekeying allows us to use a different key to encrypt each block of data; even if one key is compromised, only that portion of the overall communication is compromised. This is a secure method of transmitting data.

IPSec can share keys between communicating computers without sending the key across the network line. Windows 2000 uses the *Diffie-Hellman (DH) algorithm* to perform this function. First, the two computers publicly exchange some keying information, which Windows 2000 Server protects with a hash function signature. Second, with this shared information, each computer can generate the identical shared key. Now, each computer can use the key to communicate using IPSec. After the DH material exchange, identities are authenticated. Notice that the DH algorithm does not perform authentication; it merely provides a method of creating an environment using keys in which authentication and communication can take place.

Before data can be securely exchanged, the two computers must setup a *Security Association (SA)*, which is an agreement about how to protect information during transit. If your policies allow unsecured communications with non–IPSec-based computers, a *soft* SA is established. However, if the client is compatible with your IPSec policies and can securely communicate with your server, a *hard* SA is established with the client. Once IPSec SAs are established (one in each direction) between the client and server, they remain in effect for one hour after the last packet is sent between them. After that hour, the client drops the association and returns to the "respond only" state.

To build this contract, the two computers must engage in a key exchange resolution, called the *Internet Key Exchange (IKE)*.

IKE is a two-phase process. The first phase is a policy negotiation phase in which four parameters are agreed on:

- The encryption algorithm—either DES or 3DES
- The hash algorithm—either MD5 (Message Digest 5) or SHA (Secure Hash Algorithm)
- The authentication method—either certificate, pre-shared key, or Kerberos
- The exchange of DH material for key generation

In the second phase, the computers agree on the following parameters:

- The IPSec protocol—either AH or ESP
- The hash algorithm—either MD5 of SHA
- The algorithm for encryption, if requested—either DES or 3DES

As part of the second phase, session key material is refreshed again, and a new pair of keys is generated. The generation of new keys prevents bogus session material being inserted into the data stream by an attacker.

After these two phases are completed, the SA is said to be set up, and IPSec is ready to send secured data back and forth between the two computers. In the following sections, we'll show how to use IPSec and then discuss what happens when things go wrong.

Configuring and Administering IPSec Authentication

IPSec is implemented in Windows 2000 via the use of Group Policies. The policy rules are enforced by the IPSec driver, which is responsible for matching every incoming and outgoing packet against the security settings defined in the IPSec Group Policy.

These policies are managed from the IP Security Policy Management template underneath the Security Settings template in the object's Group Policy (see Figure 4.1).

FIGURE 4.1   The IPSecurity Policy Management template in the default Group Policy

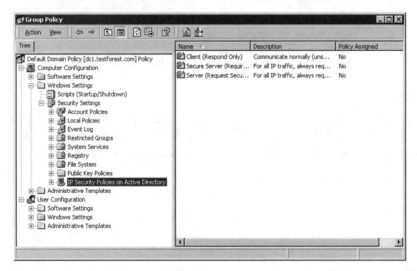

You can also create a custom MMC (Microsoft Management Console) that focuses only on the IP Security Policy Management node. After adding this node to the MMC, you'll need to select the computer for which you want to manage the IPSec policies as follows (see Figure 4.2):

- If you want to manage only the computer on which you are running the console, leave the default, which is the Local Computer option.

- If you want to manage the IPSec policies for any domain member server, select Manage Domain Policy For This Computer's Domain.

- If you want to manage the IPSec policies for a remote domain that the local computer is not a member of, select Manage Domain Policy For Another Domain.

- If you want to manage the IPSec policies for a single, remote computer, select Another Computer.

After making your selection, you can save the MMC for future use.

FIGURE 4.2   Management selections for IPSec policies when creating a customized IPSec MMC

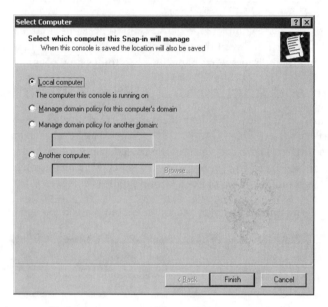

In Exercise 4.1, you will create a custom IPSec MMC.

EXERCISE 4.1

Creating a Custom MMC for IPSec Management

1. Choose Start ≻ Run to open the Run dialog box, and in the Open box, type in **MMC** and press Enter to open the Microsoft Management Console (MMC).

2. Choose Console ≻ Add/Remove Snap-In to open the Add/Remove Snap-in dialog box.

3. Click Add to open the Add Standalone Snap-in dialog box.

4. Select the IP Security Management snap-in, and then click Add to open the Select Computer selection box.

5. Make your selection on the Select Which Computer This Snap-In Will Manage.

6. Click Finish to close the Select Computer selection box.

7. Click Close to close the Add Standalone Snap-in dialog box.

8. Click OK to close the Add/Remove Snap-in dialog box.

9. Save the MMC Console.

Three predefined IPSec policies are installed with Windows 2000 Server (see Figure 4.1 earlier in this chapter). These policies can be left alone or modified as needed or used to help define a custom security template for future use. The policies are as follows:

Client (Respond Only)   This policy is for computers that do not require secure communications. If secure communications are requested, this policy instructs the computer to respond in a positive fashion.

Server (Request Security)   This policy is for computers that require secure communications. These computers will accept unsecured traffic, but they will always attempt to secure subsequent communications by requesting security from the sending computer. If the sending computer does not respond positively, all communications are sent without using IPSec.

Secure Server (Require Security)   This policy will require computers to use IPSec and secure their communications. Computers assigned to this policy will always reject unsecured communications, and outgoing traffic will always be secured.

To assign a policy to a given computer, you must enable the policy. Enabling the policy means that it is assigned to the object that it is modifying. You can either assign or unassign a policy, but you cannot assign more than one policy to any given object. Hence, you cannot assign both Client (Respond Only) and Server (Request Security) to the same Active Directory object. Instead, all you can do is assign one of the three policy settings to any given object.

Tunnel Mode versus Transport Mode

IPSec can be configured for either transport or tunnel mode. The *transport mode* authenticates and encrypts data moving between computers. This is the default mode for IPSec in Windows 2000.

To specify transport mode, open the Properties dialog box of the policy setting you want to modify. Click the rule you want to modify, and click Edit to open the Edit Rule Properties dialog box. On the Tunnel Setting tab, select This Rule Does Not Specify An IPSec Tunnel (see Figure 4.3).

FIGURE 4.3   Setting IPSec to run in transport mode

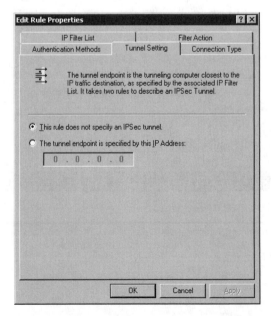

In Exercise 4.2, you will set your IPSec policy to run in transport mode.

EXERCISE 4.2

Setting IPSec to Run in Transport Mode

1. Open the Group Policy in the Properties dialog box of the object you want to modify.

2. Navigate to the IP Security Policies In Active Directory node.

3. Select the setting in the right pane for which you want to set transport mode.

4. Open the setting's Properties dialog box.

5. Select the Rule you want to modify and click Edit to open the Edit Rule Properties dialog box.

6. Click the Tunnel Setting tab.

7. Select This Rule Does Not Specify An IPSec Tunnel.

8. Click OK.

9. Close the Properties dialog box, and exit the Group Policy object.

Unlike transport mode, which secures the packet from the source to the destination, *tunnel mode* places a secure, existing packet inside a new IP packet that is sent to a tunnel endpoint. The tunnel endpoint is probably not the final destination of the inside packet, but it is the final destination of the outside packet. The outside packet is stripped off at the tunnel endpoint and the internal packet can be further routed to the final destination.

Tunnel mode does not provide security within each network that the packet will traverse. It simply provides security to the packet itself and guarantees that security to the endpoint (IP address) that you specify.

   IPSec tunnel mode is not designed to be used for virtual private network (VPN) remote access.

In Exercise 4.3, you will set IPSec to run in tunnel mode.

EXERCISE 4.3

Setting IPSec to Run in Tunnel Mode

1. Open the Group Policy in the Properties dialog box of the object you want to modify.

2. Navigate to the IP Security Policies in Active Directory node.

EXERCISE 4.3 *(continued)*

3. Select the setting in the right pane in which you want to set tunnel mode.

4. Open the setting's Properties dialog box.

5. Select the rule you want to modify and click Edit to open the Edit Rule Properties dialog box.

6. Click the Tunnel Setting tab.

7. Select the This Tunnel Endpoint Is Specified By This IP Address radio button.

8. Enter the IP address of the device that will act as the endpoint for the tunnel.

9. Click Apply.

10. Close the Properties dialog box and exit the Group Policy object.

Transport mode and tunnel mode are not available for the Client (Respond Only) setting. In addition, if you need to set up multiple tunnels, you will need to configure multiple rules because each tunnel requires its own rule in the policy setting. Finally, Windows 2000 supports multiple tunnel mode connections, but only one tunnel at a time.

Configuring an IPSec Rule

You can create customized IPSec policies, each with its own set of rules. Each policy can host more than one rule, and it is important to understand how these rules work because these rules govern how and when a policy is invoked. Any number of rules can be active simultaneously. You can create or modify existing rules to meet your requirements. Filters are applied in the order of most-specific filters first.

A rule consists of the following components:

Tunnel endpoint   A tunnel endpoint defines the IP address to which the tunnel will guarantee secured communications. There must be two rules to define an IPSec tunnel, one rule for each direction.

Network type   Use this setting to select the scope of the rule. You can select All Network Connections, Local Area Network (LAN), or Remote Access (see Figure 4.4)

Authentication method   You select the authentication method on the Authentication Methods tab. The default is Kerberos, as shown in Figure 4.5. If you click Add, you can select the other supported authentication methods in Windows 2000 Server, which are shown in Figure 4.6 and then described.

FIGURE 4.4   You configure the scope of the rule in the Connection Type tab

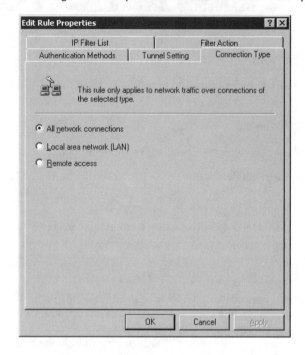

FIGURE 4.5   The Authentication Methods tab

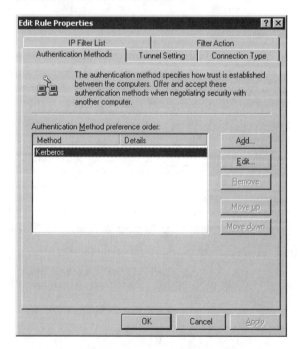

FIGURE 4.6   Supported authentication methods in Windows 2000 Server that can be selected for any given rule

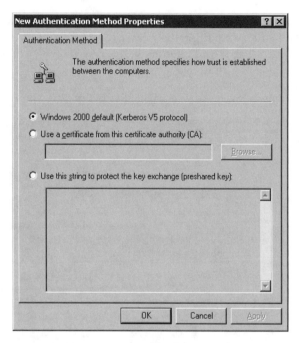

Windows 2000 Default (Kerberos V5 Protocol)   This is the default for Windows 2000 Server. This selection uses the Kerberos V5 authentication protocol. Any Kerberos-compliant clients can use Kerberos V5 even if they are not Windows-based clients. However, every client must be a member of a local or trusted domain.

Use A Certificate From This Certificate Authority (CA)   This selection requires that a trusted CA be available and that both the sender and the receiver use a certificate issued by the trusted CA.

Use This String To Protect The Key Exchange (Preshared Key)   This setting specifies a secret, shared key that both computers will use to encrypt and decrypt the packets. Obviously, this selection requires manual preconfiguration prior to its use.

IP filter list   This selection defines which traffic will be secured by this rule. You can use the defaults of All ICMP Traffic (Internet Control Message Protocol) or All IP Traffic, or you can select the type of traffic you want to include in the rule.

The filter is rather granular, allowing you to make selections in two areas: addressing and protocols. In addressing, you can select to filter traffic against any of the following defined addresses (see Figure 4.7):

- IP address
- Any IP address

- A specific IP address
- A specific IP subnet

To access the tab in Figure 4.7, first highlight the filter list you wish to edit in the IP Filter List tab (either All ICMP Traffic or All IP Traffic), then click the Edit button, This will invoke the IP Filter List dialog box. Click the Edit button on this box and you will be presented with the Filter Properties dialog box illustrated in Figure 4.7.

FIGURE 4.7   The Addressing tab in the Filter Properties dialog box

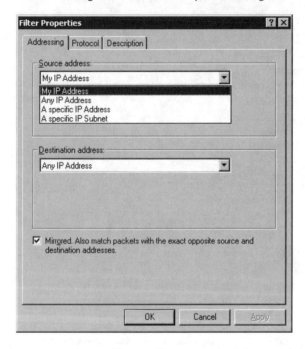

On the Protocols tab, you can select to filter traffic against the following defined protocols and either any port number or a predefined port number (see Figure 4.8):

- Any
- EGP (Exterior Gateway Protocol)
- HMP (Host Monitoring Protocol)
- ICMP (Internet Control Message Protocol)
- Other
- RAW (protocol 255)RVD (MIT Remote Virtual Disk Protocol)
- TCP (Transmission Control Protocol)
- UDP (User Datagram Protocol)
- XNS-IDP (Xerox NS IDP)

FIGURE 4.8   The Protocols tab in Filter Properties dialog box

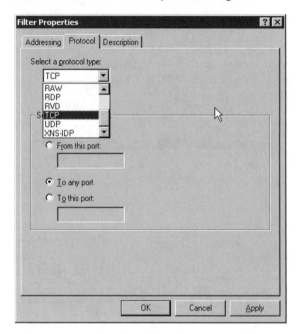

Filter action   The filter action lists the security actions that will occur when traffic matches the IP filter. These actions appear on the Filter Action tab in the Edit Rule Properties dialog box. There are three basic default settings (see Figure 4.9):

- Permit, which permits unsecured IP packets to pass.

- Request Security (Optional), which means that the server will request secure methods of communicating, but will transfer data in an unsecured manner too.

- Require Security, which means that the server will accept unsecured connections but then will require clients to communicate using only secured methods. This selection instructs the server to not communicate with untrusted clients.

What is interesting here is how granular the filter action can be. Figure 4.10 shows the default settings for the Request Security (Optional) security methods, which can be navigated to by clicking on the Protocols tab in the Filter properties dialog box. Notice that this method will allow unsecured communications, but that each connection will be responded to with IPSec. What this means is that the server will attempt IKE with each computer that connects to it in an attempt to communicate using IPSec.

The Session Key Perfect Forward Secrecy setting is cleared by default. *Perfect Forward Secrecy (PFS)*, when selected, means that every time rekeying occurs, a new master key is also generated. Although this is the most secure setting possible, it also generates additional overhead for your server and should only be selected in highly secure environments. Because a new master key is generated, both server and client will need to renegotiate new key material, and this can create interoperability problems with some non-Microsoft products.

FIGURE 4.9   The Filter Action tab in the Edit Rule Properties dialog box

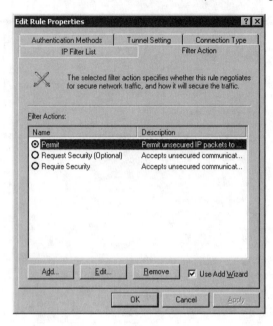

FIGURE 4.10   The default settings for the Request Security (Optional) security method

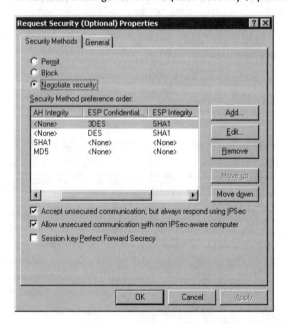

So when you put of these parts together, here is what you have: the ability to create a rule that defines the following:

- The scope (tunnel endpoint and network type)
- The authentication method
- Which traffic to secure (the IP filter list)
- The actions to take when the rule is met (the filter action)

When taking the exam, it will be easy to get lost in the details of the question. Keep yourself focused on the larger picture and remember how to further secure traffic using an IPSec filter rule. For instance, if you need to secure traffic over the Internet, ensure that you have selected a tunnel endpoint. If you need to authenticate using certificates, you'll need a CA trusted by all parties involved in the process. If you only want to secure certain types of traffic, understand that you are working with the IP filter list to select a protocol and port combination. And if you want to tweak the actions to be taken when traffic meets the defined rules, you are working in the Filter Action area.

If, after applying a rule, you don't like the results, you can restore default policies. Right-click the IP Security Policies Local Machine, choose Restore Default Policies from the shortcut menu, and then click Yes from the pop-up IP Security Policy Management message box.

Testing IPSec Policy Assignments

You can test your IPSec policy assignments in two ways: by using the `ping` command, and by using a resource kit utility called the IP Security Monitor.

The `ping` (Packet Internet Groper) command sends four echo packets to the server and expects to receive four echo replies back. A server running under the default IPSec policies will respond to the `ping` command. However, if there are problems with establishing a secure channel, you will receive a response "Negotiating IP Security." You can expect this response while the secure channel is established before the echo packets are responded to by the server.

The IP Security Monitor (see Figure 4.11) is a handy tool that will give you statistics about what Security Associations have been established and with whom. Moreover, you'll find good information on basic IPSec statistics. The tool automatically refreshes every 15 seconds, but this option is configurable using the Options button.

To run the IP Security Monitor, choose Start ➤ Run, enter the following syntax in the Open box, and press Enter:

```
Ipsecmon <computername>
```

in the lower-right corner of the IP Security Monitor dialog box is a message indicating whether IPSec is enabled on the computer.

FIGURE 4.11   The IP Security Monitor

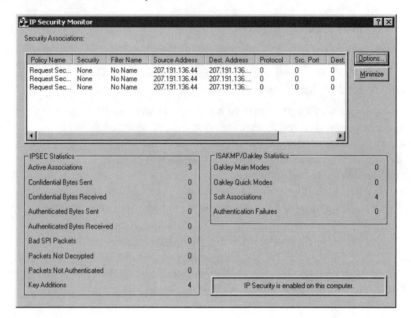

IPSec Policy Inheritance

IPSec policies follow the Group Policy inheritance model. Group Policies are applied in the following order:

- Site
- Domain
- OU

Policies applied last take precedence over policies applied first. However, you need to bear a couple of points in mind when it comes to policy inheritance and IPSec. First, IPSec policies assigned to a domain policy override any local IPSec policies when the computer is a member of the domain. Second, IPSec policies assigned to an OU will override domain-level policies.

Hence, if you need to assign a policy to a group of domain controllers but not to the other computers on your network, you'd want to do this at the OU level, not at the domain level.

Configuring the Appropriate IPSec Protocol and Encryption Levels

At a high level, Hash Message Authentication Codes (HMAC) are used to sign packets to verify that the information sent is the same information received (think "integrity" here). The hash function is really an algorithm that combines with the sender's private key to produce a cryptographic checksum or Message Integrity Code (MIC). Each party must compute this checksum to ensure that the data has integrity.

When configuring the IPSec protocol, you can select two functions:

MD5   *Message Digest 5 (MD5)* makes four passes over the data blocks which results in a 128-bit key used for the integrity check. MD5 is the fifth iteration of the Message Digest hash function.

SHA   The Secure Hash Algorithm (SHA) is closely modeled after MD5 but produces a 160-bit key that is used for the integrity check. Obviously, the longer key length provides greater security, so SHA is considered stronger than MD5.

The IPSec protocols further protect each packet by adding their own security protocol header to each IP packet. There are two protocol header types.

The Authentication Header (AH)

The *Authentication Header (AH)* does not encrypt the data, but it does provide authentication, integrity, and anti-replay for the entire packet. Although the data is in clear text, an attacker cannot modify it. AH uses the HMAC (Hash Message Authentication Codes) algorithms to sign each packet to ensure integrity. In the AH, a checksum is inserted between the network and transport layer headers. If the receiving computer's checksum does not match that which is in the AH, the packet is discarded. Anti-replay is achieved by inserting a sequence number in the AH. AH can be used with or without the Encapsulating Security Payload (ESP).

The Encapsulating Security Payload (ESP)

The *Encapsulating Security Payload (ESP)* ensures everything: confidentiality, authentication, integrity, and anti-replay. ESP can be used with or without AH.

When ESP is used with a tunneling protocol, it encrypts the entire packet. However, in the absence of a tunneling protocol, ESP encrypts only the data in the packet, not the headers. Like AH, ESP provides a sequence number and a checksum in its own header and provides authentication in a trailer via the Integrity Check Value (ICV) and a message authentication code that is used to verify the sender's identity and message integrity.

Since the ESP header is inserted between the IP and upper layer headers, the IP header itself is not protected, leaving this part of the packet open to attack.

Deploying and Managing IPSec Certificates

Before you can run IPSec on your network, you need to issue two different certificate types: IPSec and Computer. Without these two certificates issued by the CA, IPSec cannot work.

The default setting of the Policy Module in the Microsoft Certificate Authority is to always issue a certificate upon request. But you will also need to configure a Group Policy so that your computers automatically request the certificates from the CA. Because best practice is for all the computers in your domain to be issued certificates, best practice here is to perform this task on the domain object.

Open your Group Policy, expand Computers, expand Security Settings, and then expand Public Key Policies. Right-click the Automatic Certificate Request Setting, point to New, and select Automatic Certificate Request (see Figure 4.12) to start the Automatic Certificate Request Setup Wizard.

FIGURE 4.12 Selecting the Automatic Certificate Request menu option

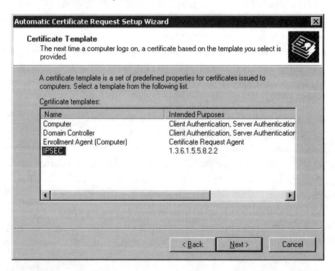

Now follow these steps:

1. At the Welcome screen, click Next to open the Certificate Template screen, as shown in Figure 4.13.

FIGURE 4.13 Certificate Template screen

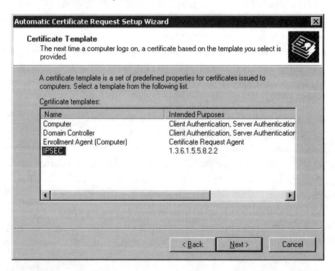

2. Select the certificate from the template list, and click Next to open the Certificate Template screen.

3. Select the CA from whom you want to have this certificate issued, and then complete the wizard.

You'll now see the certificate in the right pane of the Group Policy window, indicating that this certificate will be automatically issued to every computer the next time the computers boot up and connect to the network (see Figure 4.14).

FIGURE 4.14   The IPSec certificate is now being automatically issued

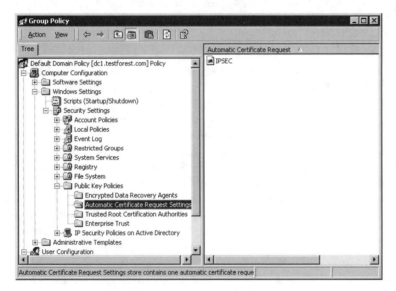

Notice the difference in the right pane of this screen in Figure 4.12 and the right pane in the screen in Figure 4.14. The IPSec certificate is now listed in the right pane.

You'll need to do this for both the IPSec and the Computer certificates. In addition, you'll need to specify the trusted root CA(s) for your network. You can specify more than one trusted root CA to accommodate remote users who may not be able to be issued a certificate from an internal Microsoft CA.

When your run through the wizard, you'll be prompted to specify the file that contains the certificate from the CA. Enter the path and filename, click Next, and finish the wizard. The certificate from the CA will now be trusted by all who have the Group Policy applied to them.

Renewing Certificates

When your users need to renew their certificates, they can do so by using the certificate website that installs automatically with Certificate Services. The default URL is *servername/certsrv*. If users navigate to that website, they can renew their certificate and continue to engage in secure communications using IPSec.

If your users are remote, you may need to open this website so that they can renew their certificates too. If they are trusting third-party CAs, they will need to purchase their renewal certificates from the third-party vendor.

When taking the exam, remember that certificates need to be current and trusting the same CA as the server.

Securing Communication between Server Types with IPSec

Securing different server types requires an in-depth knowledge of the type of packet traffic that each server will experience. In this section, we'll take a look at the specific attention and hurdles different types of servers might require.

Securing Web Servers

Securing a web server using IPSec is going to be difficult if the website is public. Although you can configure IPSec to request secured communications, chances are good that most clients will not be IPSec-ready and will only communicate using unsecured transmissions.

However, if the website is either secured through authentication or is an extranet with defined, known users, you can require IPSec for communications between your server and the site's users.

If the secured server is directly accessible from the Internet, or if the first client packets contain sensitive data, the client must receive an IPSec policy so that it requests IPSec security for traffic when it attempts to communicate with the server. This is the best practice for a secure website because a server set to request security instead of requiring security is easily open to a DoS attack. Remember that the server is set to request security, and then every client connection is responded to with an IKE request over port 500. Such additional traffic is unwarranted on the Internet and, through the smart use of a DoS attack, could render the server useless to legitimate client traffic.

One way to work with a secured website that has a defined group of users is to use a certificate known to everyone in advance and require that certificate for authentication. Doing this will prevent any unauthorized access to the website. Of course, if the certificate becomes compromised, another certificate will need to be generated and distributed to the users.

Best practice for unsecured Internet websites is to allow unsecured traffic. Best practice for secured websites is to require secure communications using IPSec.

Securing E-Mail Servers

If your e-mail servers connect directly to the Internet to pass SMTP (Simple Mail Transfer Protocol) traffic, it would be very unwise to require secured communications because most SMTP servers on the Internet are not configured for this type of communication. However, between your SMTP relay server in your DMZ (Demilitarized Zone) and your internal SMTP servers, you can require secure communication.

Doing this will mean that an attacker can only compromise your SMTP server in the DMZ, which is not a big loss since no critical data is sitting on that server. Because the internal SMTP servers will require secured communication before accepting mail, an attacker would need to impersonate the SMTP server in the DMZ with a valid certificate before being able to communicate directly with the internal SMTP server.

Securing Clients

Not all clients will be IPSec complaint. For these clients to successfully communicate with your IPSec servers, you'll need to ensure that you have assigned the Server policy, not the Secure

Server policy. The Server policy always requests security, but allows unsecured communication with clients by falling back to clear text communication if the client doesn't respond to the IKE request.

Note, however, that if a client does respond to the IKE request and then the negotiation fails, the client will be blocked from communicating with the server for one minute, and, thereafter, another negotiation will commence.

When working with remote clients, it is important to remember two facts. First, you cannot use IPSec in a VPN solution for remote clients. Second, the remote clients must trust the CA that your server is trusting for key generation. This means that if you work with a number of remote clients, you may need to trust an external third-party CA instead of a local CA on your network. Although it is easier (and cheaper) to create an internal Certificate Server and make that server the root enterprise CA, it may not be the best way to ensure a common, trusted CA.

In addition, the list of authentication methods for remote clients must include certificates, and at least one valid certificate must be installed on each client and peer server. And, finally, if you need to remotely administer a client computer, you must allow RPC TCP traffic in your IPSec rules for the internal network.

Troubleshooting IPSec

At a high level, IPSec problems can be grouped into several categories. IPSec won't work if the same CA isn't trusted. IPSec also won't work if different authentication methods are used in the rules for client and server. If you are working over the Internet, you must open port 500 and allow protocol IDs 50 and 51 for both inbound and outbound traffic. And, finally, IPSec won't work for remote access clients unless they first tunnel into a Windows 2000 RRAS (Routing and Remote Access Services) server using L2TP (Layer 2 Tunneling Protocol).

You may also find that you'll receive bad SPI (Security Parameter Index) messages in the event viewer. These messages may indicate that one party continued to send data after the SA expired. It may also indicate that the number of rekeys is too large compared with the amount of time the SA has been active. You can reduce the bad SPI messages by setting longer key lifetime values in the policy.

Rule Configuration Issues

You need to verify several things when working with the rules. First, even if you have multiple rules, you must make certain that those rules allow the client and server to use the same authentication method. If not, the client and server will not be able to talk to each other. To avoid authentication method problems, don't use protocol- or port-specific filters for the purpose of negotiating security for traffic. Instead, use protocol and port filters for permitting and blocking actions.

Also bear in mind that IPSec cannot be configured for one-way, secured traffic. If you create a rule that secures traffic from Server A to Client B, a rule needs to be created to secure traffic from Client B back to Server A. This is most easily done by creating two filters in the same filter list. However, what we've said here should not be confused with a one-way blocking rule. You can create a rule that blocks traffic in one direction, but this is different from creating a rule that secures traffic in one direction. To secure traffic more easily, you can select the Mirror check box (see Figure 4.7 earlier in this chapter), which will automatically generate the rule you are creating for both directions.

Certificate Configuration Issues

It is possible that certificates obtained incorrectly may result in a situation in which the certificate exists and is chosen for IKE authentication, but fails to work properly because the corresponding key in the key pair is not present on the local computer. You can see this by creating a new MMC that has the Certificates snap-in focused on the local computer. If the private key is not present, the certificate can't be used with IPSec.

In Exercise 4.4, you will create a new MMC that will allow you verify that a private key is installed.

EXERCISE 4.4

Creating a New MMC with the Certificate Snap-In

1. Open a new MMC.

2. Choose Console ➢ Add/Remove Snap-In.

3. Click Add to open Add Standalone Snap-in.

4. Find the Certificates snap-in, and click Add.

5. From the Certificates Snap-in dialog box that will automatically appear, click the computer account for which this snap-kin will manage certificates. Then click Finish. Doing so will close this box.

6. Then, click Close to close the Add Standalone Snap-in box.

7. Click OK to close the Add/Remove Snap-in dialog box.

8. Expand Certificates-User (local computer).

9. Expand Personal.

10. Click the Certificates folder.

11. In the right pane, double-click the certificate you want to use to open it.

12. Verify that you see the text "You have a private key that corresponds to this certificate."

Why might a private key fail? Well, for a couple of reasons. First, if the certificate in the personal folder doesn't have a corresponding private key, it is likely that the certificate enrollment process failed in some manner. Second, if the certificate was obtained from a Microsoft CA that was configured with the Strong Private Key Protection option, the user needs a PIN (Personal Identification Number) to access the private key. Since the PIN cannot be supplied for IKE negotiation, this certificate can't be used for this purpose.

If the IKE negotiations are failing, enable auditing for success and failed events for the audit attribute Audit Logon Events. The IKE service will report entries in the security log, which will give you an explanation as to why the negotiations are failing.

If you feel you need to clear all IKE negotiations and start "fresh"—perhaps when secured communications suddenly fail—you can do so from a command prompt by typing the following command:

```
Net stop policyagent
```

To resume IKE negotiations, use the Net Start command, as follows:

```
Net start policyagent
```

Remember that when you stop the policy agent, all IPSec filters will be deactivated for the time the service is stopped. In addition, your VPN tunnels will no longer be protected with IPSec. In addition, RRAS will be restarted as well.

If you have recently updated the policy settings and they don't seem to be taking effect, you can verify that the changes made to any policy have been updated in Active Directory by testing the policy's integrity. To do this, right-click the policy in the IP Security Settings for Active Directory, select Actions, point to All Tasks, and then click Check Policy Integrity.

Firewall and Router Configuration Issues

Firewalls generally reject IPSec packets by default. You'll need to configure your router or proxy server for some specialized filtering to ensure that packets secured with IPSec are not rejected. Here are some recommended filters for your router:

- Allow protocol ID 51 for inbound and outbound IPSec AH traffic.
- Allow protocol ID 50 for inbound and outbound ESP traffic.
- Allow UDP port 500 for inbound and outbound IKE traffic.

Without these ports and protocol IDs allowed, your firewall will not pass IPSec traffic.

Authentication Issues

You must use the same authentication methods for both rules between the client and server. Remember that there must be a rule for each direction, and if the authentication methods do not match, IPSec won't work. You must also verify that there is at least one compatible security method in both rules. Authentication can fail if the security methods do not match. If you are using IPSec tunneling, verify that the DNS name and IP address are correct and that the destination computer is up and running.

Domain Controllers and SMB Signing

If you want to secure communications at the packet level, then you'll want to use SMB Signing. SMB signing can be an integral part of securing your network. *Server Message Blocks (SMB)* date from 1984 when IBM first introduced NetBIOS (Network Basic Input Output Service).

In the years since, SMB has played a central role in passing information between computers and has been extended several times. The SMB protocol was developed jointly by Microsoft, Intel, and IBM. More recently, the *Common Internet File System (CIFS)*, an advanced version of the SMB protocol was introduced. We'll discuss CIFS later in this chapter.

SMB is an application-level protocol that is used to implement network session control, network file and print sharing, and messaging. Up to a point, SMB is analogous to the Apple-Talk Session, Filing and Printer Access protocols, and Novell's NetWare Core Protocol (NCP).

At a granular level, SMB defines a series of commands that the client and the server use to coordinate passage of information between each other. The redirector packages network control block (NCB) requests or responses into an SMB structure, which are then sent over the network to the target machine. Like other protocols, such as SMTP, the commands passed back and forth between the client and the server are based on a request-response architecture. One computer initiates the connection and sends requests (the client), and the other computer responds to those requests (the server).

To make the initial connection with the correct server, a method of addressing was needed. Until the advent of the CIFS, the SMB protocol used the NetBIOS name for addressing. One of the upgrades to SMB in the CIFS is its ability to use DNS-based host names for addressing.

SMB Commands

The core SMB protocol commands execute basic functions. Here are some examples (in no particular order):

- Create Directory (SMBmkdir)
- Open File (SMBopen)
- Commit All Files (SMBflush)
- Rename File (SMBmv)
- Start Connection (SMBcon)
- End Connection (SMBtdis)
- Create Spool File (SMBsplclose)
- Get Machine Name (SMBgetmac)

This list is not exhaustive. The core list in the original protocol consisted of 37 commands. You can group the core commands into four types:

Session Control Messages   These commands start and end a redirector connection to the shared resource on the server.

File Messages   These commands are used by the client to access files that reside on the server.

Printer Messages   These commands are used to send data to a printer on a print server and receive status information about the printer and the data that is being held in the queue.

Message Messages   These commands allow the sender and receiver to send messages back and forth.

As the protocol developed, commands were added that extended SMB's functionality. Commands such as Lock Then Read Data (`SMBlockreadr`), Write Then Unlock Data (`SMBwriteunlock`), Copy (`SMBcopy`), Open and X (`SMBopenX`), Tree Connect and X (`SMBtconX`), or Session Set Up and X (`SMBsesssetup`) can all be found in nearly every packet trace between two Windows-based computers.

> The "...and X" designation in an SMB command is a batching mechanism whereby multiple commands can be batched and sent over the line to the target computer and then processed asynchronously at the other end.

Configuring SMB

Since there are several versions of the SMB protocol, during the dialect negotiation of the TCP handshake, the client and the server agree on the version of the SMB protocol they will use to pass information back and forth. Agreement on the dialect indicates which set of commands will be considered valid by both machines.

Because the SMB protocol is an application-layer protocol, it can run over different transport and network layer protocols including Network Extended Basic User Interface (NetBEUI), Internetwork Packet Exchange/Sequenced Packet Exchange (IPS/SPX), and TCP/IP.

The SMB security model has two levels: Share and User. The Share level model applies protection at the share on the resource that resides on the server. Each share can have a password, and a client needs only to present that password to the server to access all files under that share. Once a client is authenticated, all SMB commands are available for use between the client and the server. This was the default SMB dialect that was selected between Windows for Workgroups machines.

The User security model requires the user to log in to the server and be authenticated by the server. In addition, protection is applied to individual files in each share, and access is based on user rights configured for each file or folder. When the user is authenticated, the user is given a User ID (UID), which it must present on all subsequent accesses to the server. This model was first introduced in the LAN Manager 1 dialect and was available starting with Windows 95.

The Common Internet File System (CIFS)

The CIFS is a public version of the SMB protocol that will be essentially the NT LM 0.12 dialect with some modifications for easier use over the Internet. The CIFS is the protocol used by Windows 2000. As you may have noticed, SMB did not contain any method for ensuring security in the packets as they are passed back and forth. CIFS has this capability—and more.

The CIFS protocol requires server authentication of users before file accesses are allowed. The server requires the client to provide a user name and (usually) a password. (Actually, any method whereby a client provides proof of identity is acceptable to CIFS. Passwords are the most common form of accomplishing this goal.) How the user is authenticated is not a concern to the CIFS protocol. Hence, the Kerberos authentication protocol can be used in conjunction with the CIFS protocol to authenticate the client to the server.

In addition, messages passed between the client and server can be authenticated by computing a message authentication code (MAC) for each message and attaching it to the message. The MAC key is computed from the session key. The MAC can either sign and/or encrypt the message text plus a sequence number, which prevents replay attacks. What the CIFS calls the MAC is what Microsoft calls SMB signing.

Enabling SMB Signing

SMB signing places a digital security signature into each SMB message, which is then verified by both the client and the server to deter impersonation and man-in-the-middle attacks.

> **NOTE**   SMB signing will impose a 10 to15 percent overhead hit on each server and client due to the additional processing required for each packet. Additional bandwidth is not required, however, to implement SMB signing.

SMB signing must be enabled on both the client and the server before it can be used. It is not turned on by default in Windows 2000 Server. SMB signing requires that both parties trust the same CA. If the client and the server do not trust the same CA, SMB signing won't work.

To use SMB signing, you must either enable it or require it on both the client and the server. If SMB signing is enabled on a server, clients that are enabled for SMB signing will use SMB signing when connecting to the server. If SMB signing is required on a server, a client will not be able to establish a session unless it is at least enabled for SMB signing. SMB signing is enabled in a Group Policy in the Security Options node under the Local Policies node (see Figure 4.15).

FIGURE 4.15   The SMB signing options under the Security Options node

Policy	Computer Setting
Additional restrictions for anonymous connec...	Not defined
Allow server operators to schedule tasks (do...	Not defined
Allow system to be shut down without havin...	Not defined
Allowed to eject removable NTFS media	Not defined
Amount of idle time required before disconne...	Not defined
Audit the access of global system objects	Not defined
Audit use of Backup and Restore privilege	Not defined
Automatically log off users when logon time ...	Disabled
Automatically log off users when logon time ...	Not defined
Clear virtual memory pagefile when system s...	Not defined
Digitally sign client communication (always)	Not defined
Digitally sign client communication (when pos...	Enabled
Digitally sign server communication (always)	Not defined
Digitally sign server communication (when po...	Enabled
Disable CTRL+ALT+DEL requirement for logon	Not defined
Do not display last user name in logon screen	Enabled
LAN Manager Authentication Level	Not defined
Message text for users attempting to log on	Not defined
Disabled	Not defined
Number of previous logons to cache (in case ...	Not defined

Here is an explanation of what each policy setting does:

Digitally Sign Client Communication (Always)   When this option is selected, the computer will require that SMB messages be digitally signed before accepting a network connection. Only do this in a pure Windows 2000 environment because other platforms will not work with this feature.

Digitally Sign Client Communication (When Possible)   When enabled, this policy causes the client to perform SMB packet signing when communicating with a Windows 2000 server that is enabled or required to perform SMB packet signing.

Digitally Sign Server Communication (Always)   When this policy is enabled, you are requiring the Windows 2000 server to perform SMB packet signing. If the clients are not set to at least Digitally Sign Client Communication (When Possible), the server will not be able to communicate with the client.

Digitally Sign Server Communication (When Possible)   When this policy is enabled, the Windows 2000 server will attempt to perform SMB signing when communicating to another Windows 2000 machine on the network. This policy is enabled by default on the Domain Controllers OU.

To enable SMB signing in Windows NT 4, you'll need to be running at least Service Pack 3 and then enter the following edits in the Registry:

`HKLM\System\CCS\Services\LanManServer\Parameters`

In Windows NT Server 4, open the Registry Editor, choose Edit ➢ Add Value to open the Add Value dialog box, and then add the following two values:

Value name: `EnableSecuritySignature`

Data type: REG_DWORD

Value: 0 (disable), 1 (enable)

Enter a value of 1 for this Registry key.

Value name: `RequireSecuritySignature`

Data type: REG_DWORD

Value: 0 (disable), 1 (enable)

Enter a value of 1 for this Registry key.

You will need to restart Windows after making these Registry entries before they will take effect. Obviously, you will not enable both keys. If you want to require SMB signing, you will need to use the `RequireSecuritySignature` Registry key. If you want SMB signing to be used when possible, use the other key.

To enable SMB signing on a Windows NT 4 workstation 4, open the Registry Editor and navigate to the following key:

`HKLM\System\CCS\Services\Rdr\Parameters`

Choose Edit ➢ Add Value, and then enter one or the other value, depending on whether you want to merely enable SMB signing or require it:

Value name: `EnableSecuritySignature`

Data type: REG_DWORD

Value: 0 (disable), 1 (enable)

Enter a value of 1 for this Registry key.

Value name: `RequireSecuritySignature`

Data type: REG_DWORD

Value: 0 (disable), 1 (enable)

Enter a value of 1 for this Registry key.

You'll need to restart the Windows NT 4 workstation for these changes to take effect. If you are running a Windows NT 4 network and need to require SMB signing, first require signing on the servers and then reboot them. You will then need to require signing on the workstations and reboot them as well.

To enable SMB signing on a Windows 98 client, open the Registry for the Windows 98 client, and then navigate to the following key:

`HKLM\System\CCS\Services\VxD\VNetsup`

Add the following two values to the key listed previously:

Value name: `EnableSecuritySignature`

Data type: REG_DWORD

Value: 0 (disable), 1 (enable)

Enter a value of 1 for this Registry key.

Value name: `RequireSecuritySignature`

Data type: REG_DWORD

Value: 0 (disable), 1 (enable)

Enter a value of 1 for this Registry key.

Just like Windows NT 4, you will need to add both keys, but not enable both keys. After adding these items in the Registry, you will need to reboot the Windows 98 client in order for the changes to take effect.

If you are running in a mixed environment, you may find that SMB signing doesn't work between Windows 2000 clients and Windows NT 4 servers. This is actually a problem with the Windows 2000 client and is fixed by installing the latest service pack. The error message is "Network name is no longer valid," which is a result of the initial attempt being made with an invalid password.

Also, in a mixed environment, you may find that SMB signing doesn't work if different CAs are trusted. This can be especially problematic if you have been running a Windows NT CA and now want to use a new, Windows 2000 CA. Best practice would be to upgrade your Windows NT CA to Windows 2000 so that you can retain the root certificate. Otherwise, you'll need to install new certificates system wide if you want to start fresh with a Windows 2000 CA.

Now, what happens if you lose your CA altogether? Well, here are some tips to both ensure this doesn't happen and to help you out if it does. First, you should not be running your Enterprise Root CA in your production environment. Best practice says that once you've installed your Enterprise Root CA, immediately install a Subordinate Enterprise CA, and then take your Enterprise Root CA offline and park it somewhere. Actually, taking out the hard drive and placing it in a fire-proof safe would be an excellent way to "store" your Enterprise Root CA.

Then, if the Subordinate Root CA becomes corrupted or compromised, you can still trot out the Enterprise Root CA and use it to install another Subordinate Root CA. All the certificates that have been deployed would still work because the trusted root CA still exists.

The problem comes when the trusted root CA no longer exists or the time period for the root CA certificate expires. At that point, you'll need to rebuild your certificate server infrastructure.

 SMB signing is really a LAN-based security measure and should only be employed between Windows-based computers.

Summary

In this chapter, we covered the important topics the IPSec Protocol and SMB signing.

We spent a great deal of page space on IPSec: how to configure this service and how to manage it. You learned that IPSec is rather complicated in that the rules that govern how IPSec operates can be configured at a granular level and applied via Group Policies. You also learned that IPSec depends on a successful deployment of a Public Key Infrastructure and that deployment of client certificates and their renewal is essential to a successful deployment of IPSec.

We also spent some time discussing the different authentication and encryption standards that are used by IPSec in Windows 2000. And we discussed some ideas about how to implement IPSec for web, database, and e-mail servers.

We finally ended the IPSec section by discussing troubleshooting tips and ideas to work with when taking the exam. One of the paramount ideas to keep in mind is that both client and server must trust the same CA, and successful certificate renewal is essential to an ongoing IPSec deployment.

In addition, you also learned that SMB signing is really placing a digital signature in each packet to allow the receiver to verify that the sender is who they claim to be. This can be of great help in overcoming security threats.

Exam Essentials

Understand the role of a certificate authority for IPSec.   Having a trusted CA is essential to a successful deployment of IPSec.

Understand the difference between an authentication protocol and an encryption protocol. It will be easy to mix up the different protocols on the exam. Be sure you understand which protocols are involved in encryption and which are involved in authentication.

Understand how to configure IPSec using Group Policies.   Because so much of an IPSec deployment is accomplished through Group Policies, it is important to understand how IPSec is deployed and then managed.

Understand how to fix problems when they occur.   You will be presented with scenarios on the exam that will be problematic: a certificate isn't working, the wrong protocol was selected, and so on. Be sure you spend some time thinking about what could go wrong with IPSec and the basic steps you would take to fix the problem.

Key Terms

Before you take the exam, be certain you are familiar with the following terms:

3DES	Internet Protocol Security (IPSec)
Authentication Header (AH)	Message Digest 5 (MD5)
Common Internet File System (CIFS)	Perfect Forward Secrecy (PFS)
Data Encryption Standard (DES)	Security Association (SA)
Denial of service (DoS)	Server Message Block (SMB)
Diffie-Hellman (DH) algorithm	SMB signing
dynamic rekeying	transport mode
Encapsulating Security Payload (ESP)	tunnel mode
Internet Key Exchange (IKE)	

Review Questions

1. The architecture of SMB signing is which of the following:

   A. Client-server

   B. Peer-to-peer

   C. Request-response

   D. Offer-acceptance

2. The Common Internet File System (CIFS) contains which new features over traditional SMBs? (Choose all that apply.)

   A. Clients must connect using IPSec.

   B. Clients must be authenticated before using CIFS.

   C. A message authentication code can be used.

   D. Clients must connect to the CIFS using a secure messaging channel.

3. One of the goals of secure communication is to ensure that the sender of the message is the only one who could have sent the message. Which security goal does this represent?

   A. Anti-replay

   B. Confidentiality

   C. Nonrepudiation

   D. Integrity

4. You are the system administrator for your Windows-based network. You have one Active Directory domain. Your domain controllers are in the default Domain Controllers OU. You have 50 Windows 98 workstations, 25 Windows 2000 member servers, and 200 Windows 2000 Professional workstations. The Windows 98 workstations are in the Research OU, and the Windows 2000 Professional workstations and Windows 2000 member servers are in the Admin OU. You need to require SMB signing for all computers on your network. What should you do? (Choose three answers; all three represent one part of one solution.)

   A. On the Windows 98 workstations, set the EnableSecuritySignature to one.

   B. On the Windows 2000 workstations, set the RequireSecuritySignature to one.

   C. In Active Directory, enable Digitally Sign Server Communication (Always) on the domain controller OU.

   D. In Active Directory, enable Digitally Sign Server Communication (Always) on the domain object.

   E. In Active Directory, enable Digitally Sign Client Communication (Always) on the domain controller OU.

   F. In Active Directory, enable Digitally Sign Client Communication (Always) on the Research OU.

   G. In Active Directory, enable Digitally Sign Server Communication (Always) on the Admin OU.

5. You are the system administrator of an Active Directory domain. You have 200 remote users who have Windows 2000 Professional installed on their laptops. You have another 200 users who have Windows XP Professional installed on their desktops in your network. Your remote users trust a third-party certificate authority, and your network users trust your internal Microsoft Certificate Authority. Your remote users need to trust the external CA in order to access secured databases shared by your company and three other partner companies. You need to enable SMB signing for all 400 users. What should you do first?

   A. Install a certificate on every remote client laptop. Have the client trust your internal CA.

   B. Use the Encapsulated Payload to transfer certificates between CAs.

   C. Use Active Directory to add a trusted root certificate from the external CA. Apply this to all machines on your internal network.

   D. Ensure that the Security Associations are trusting both CAs.

6. When a packet has been altered by an attacker to look like the sender is someone other than the real sender, the attacker has engaged in which of the following?

   A. Eavesdropping

   B. Impersonation

   C. Man-in-the-middle attack

   D. Identity spoofing

7. Which of the following is responsible for key exchange between two computers during the session authentication negotiation?

   A. 3DES

   B. Diffie-Hellman

   C. Dynamic rekeying

   D. Authentication headers

8. Which of the following are considered hash algorithms? (Choose two.)

   A. DES

   B. MD5

   C. Pre-Shared Keys

   D. Diffie-Hellman

   E. 3DES

   F. SHA

   G. ESP

9. Which of the following is the module responsible for enforcing IPSec rules against every packet?

   A. IPSec Driver

   B. Certificate Authority Policy Module

   C. Security Association

   D. Encapsulated Payload Protocol

10. You are the system administrator for an Active Directory domain. You have 4 Windows 2000 Server machines and 50 Windows 2000 Professional workstations. You want to ensure that the computers on your network use secure communications on your network. Which selections should you make? (Choose two.)

   A. Client (Respond Only)

   B. Server (Request Security)

   C. Secure Server (Require Security)

   D. Encapsulated Payload Protocol

11. You are the system administrator for an Active Directory domain, You have 50 Windows 2000 Professional workstations in the Research OU. You have 4 domain controllers in the Domain Controllers OU. You also have 50 Windows 98 computers in the Admin OU. The Admin OU is a child OU of the Research OU. You have 20 Windows 2000 member servers. The member servers are members of the Marketing OU. You want to assign IPSec to each computer on the network with the least amount of administrative effort. What should you do? (Choose all that apply.)

   A. Assign the Client (Respond Only) setting to the Research OU.

   B. Block policy inheritance on the Admin OU.

   C. Assign Secure Server (Require Security) on the Domain Contoller OU and the Marketing OU.

   D. Create a policy to assign the correct Registry key on the Admin OU.

   E. Assign Secure Server (Require Security) on the Marketing OU.

12. You are the system administrator for a Windows 2000 Active Directory domain. You need to securely transfer files every day to a Windows 2000 file server on the Internet. You want to use IPSec to perform this task. What should you do?

   A. Use the Encapsulated Payload service.

   B. Use Authentication Headers.

   C. Use IPSec transport mode.

   D. Use IPSec tunnel mode.

13. When two computers use IPSec to secure their transmissions, how many IPSec rules need to be in place in order for the transmissions to be successful?

   A. One

   B. Two

   C. Three

   D. Four

14. You are the system administrator for an Active Directory domain. You have just implemented IPSec to secure internal data transmissions. However, two hours after you implement this policy, no one can communicate with anyone else. You suspect that your configurations are wrong, and you need to get communications going again as fast as possible. What action should you take?

   A. Unassign the policy settings in Active Directory.

   B. Select Restore Defaults and reapply the policy.

   C. Disable all enabled policy settings and reapply the policy.

   D. Use the `secedit` command.

15. You have four servers on the Internet to which you need to set up secure communications. You decide to use tunnel mode for IPSec to securely transmit data to these four servers. Each server is directly available on the Internet, and each server has a unique IP address. How many IPSec rules will you need to configure?

   A. One

   B. Four

   C. Eight

16. Using the information in Question 15, how many tunnels can be active at any given time?

   A. One

   B. Four

   C. Eight

17. You want to implement IPSec in the most secure fashion possible. Of the answers provided, which of the following choices should you select? (Choose three; each correct answer represents one part of the overall solution.)

   A. Encapsulated payload

   B. Perfect Forward Secrecy

   C. Server (Request Security)

   D. Secure Server (Require Security)

18. You ping a Windows 2000 server that is configured for Server (Request Security). You receive the "Negotiating IP Security" message. What does this mean?

    A. The server responded to the `ping` command using secure data transmissions.

    B. The server did not respond to the `ping` command because the Security Association was being established.

    C. The Security Association was not able to be established.

    D. You should use Authentication Headers and DES instead of the Encapsulated Payload and 3DES.

19. You are the system administrator for a Windows 2000 Active Directory domain. You have a member server, Server1, in the Research OU. Your domain is named Corp. You have configured IPSec policies in the following manner: Corp: Secure Server (Require Security); Local Policies of Server 1: Server (Request Security). Unix-based users on your network are complaining that they cannot communicate with the Server1. What should you do?

    A. Change the policy setting on the Corp domain object to Server (Request Security).

    B. Change the policy setting on the Research OU to Secure Server (Require Security).

    C. Create a new policy and configure it with Server (Request Security). Link the new policy to the domain object.

    D. Create a new policy and configure it with Client (Respond Only). Link the new policy to the domain object.

20. You need to allow IPSec traffic past your IP filter on your network. Which of the following should you do? (Choose three.)

    A. Open port 53, inbound only.

    B. Open port 500, inbound only.

    C. Open port 500, inbound and outbound.

    D. Open port 53, inbound and outbound.

    E. Allow protocol ID 43.

    F. Allow protocol 50.

    G. Allow protocol 51.

Answers to Review Questions

1. **C.** The SMB architecture is a request-response architecture. The client sends requests to the server, and the server responds to those requests. For instance, when a client wants to perform a file move function, a request is sent to the server, and the server performs the function and then responds to the client.

2. **B, C.** One of the two main upgrades to SMB in CIFS is the ability to use a message authentication code on each packet. This is what Microsoft calls SMB signing. Each packet can be digitally signed to deter impersonation and ensure confidentiality.

3. **C.** Nonrepudiation is the assurance that the person who sent the message is the only one who could have sent the message. Confidentiality is the assurance that only the sender and receiver of the message can actually read the message. Similar in concept is the notion of integrity, which ensures that the packet was not altered during transit. Finally, anti-replay means that the packet cannot be captured, modified, and then replayed with bogus information.

4. **C, F, G.** To require SMB signing in a mixed environment, you will need to use the RequireSecuritySignature on Windows NT and 9x machines in their Registry. Then, in Active Directory, you will need to require SMB signing on all the domain controllers, member servers, and workstations. This is accomplished by creating a Group Policy on the correct objects and then applying it. The correct objects, in this instance, are the Domain Controller and Admin OUs. Applying the policy at the domain level will work, but is not the best answer because a more granular, more specific correct answer was available.

5. **C.** You can use a Group Policy to add a trusted certificate authority to your local network. All you'll need is a root certificate from the CA that will be used as a basis for trusting the CA. Then, when the remote users need to perform SMB signing, everyone can use the third-party CA as a common, trusted CA for the SMB digital signatures.

6. **D.** If the attacker had created new packets to look like they came from someone else when they really came from him, that would be impersonation. Impersonation is a form of identity spoofing. Here, the attacker is changing who the sender is and is not altering the data. Hence, this is a more generalized form of identity spoofing.

7. **B.** The Diffie Hellman algorithm provides a way for the two computers to send keying information to each other so that both can generate the keys of the other system and thereby engage in secure communications. The keys themselves are never passed over the line, just the keying information, and that information is hashed by Windows 2000 to ensure the information's integrity and confidentiality.

8. **B, F.** The purpose of this question is to ensure that you have a good understanding of which protocols and technologies are used for which purpose. In the answers to this question, we have inserted encryption and hash algorithms, authentication methods and the DH key generation exchange method. It is easy to confuse DES with MD5, thinking that they are both encryption methods. To a point, perhaps they are, but when used in conjunction with the Security Association setup, DES is thought of as an encryption algorithm and MD5 as an algorithm. Since the question was about hash algorithms, the correct answers are MD5 and SHA.

9. **A.** The IPSec Driver is responsible for rule enforcement in Windows 2000-based machines.

10. **A, C.** If you need to ensure that all computers on your network will use secure transmissions, A and C are the correct answers. If you need to provide secure transmission, but not require them, answers A and B would be correct.

11. **A, B, C, D, E.** Because the Windows 98 workstations are in a child OU, you'll need to block policy inheritance and then assign the correct Registry keys to the Windows 98 workstations via a Windows 98 Group Policy. All other answers are actions that you would need to take in order to implement IPSec in your environment.

12. **D.** The tunnel mode is designed to protect the packet as it flows over an untrusted network. The Internet is considered an untrusted network, so it is important to ensure that packet flow is encrypted to the destination you specify. The endpoint of the tunnel is really an IP address that is used to define the end of the tunnel. The packet may continue to travel on from there, but it will not be secure.

13. **B.** The number of rules depends on the type of traffic each rule is configured to secure. A rule is created for each direction of packet flow. Although you can have many active rules on the server, only one rule per server/client relationship can actually be used; hence, the answer is two—one rule for each direction.

14. **B.** If you want to return the IPSec rules and settings to default quickly, click the Restore Defaults button and then reapply the policy.

15. **B.** The answer depends on the type of data you want to secure. If you need to set up multiple tunnels, you will need to configure multiple rules—one rule per tunnel—because each tunnel requires its own rule in the policy settings.

16. **A.** The answer depends on the resources of the server and available bandwidth. Even though you can have multiple tunnels configured and created in Windows 2000, only one tunnel can be used at any given time.

17. **A, B, D.** The Encapsulated payload is a higher, more secure method of encrypting the data than Authentication Headers. Perfect Forward Secrecy regenerates the master key during rekeying from which other keys are derived during secure transmissions, and Secure Server (Require Security) requires your servers to interoperate using only secure transmissions.

18. **B.** When you receive the response "Negotiating IP Security" after using the `ping` command, the client from whom the `ping` command was initiated is setting up the secure channel with the server. Once the Security Association is set up, the `ping` command will work.

19. **A.** IPSec policies set at the domain level override local policies of member servers. If you want to allow the Unix-based workstations to communicate with Server1, changing the policy on the domain object will override the local policies of the server.

20. **C, F, G.** Protocols 50 and 51 should be allowed passage on your firewall. Port 500 should be opened for inbound and outbound traffic to allow the Internet Key Exchange protocol to work properly.

Chapter

5

Implementing Security for Wireless Networks

MICROSOFT OBJECTIVES COVERED IN THIS CHAPTER:

✓ **Implement security for wireless networks.**

- Configure public and private wireless LANs.

- Configure wireless encryption levels. Levels include WEP and 802.1x.

- Configure wireless network connection settings on client computers. Client-computer operating systems include Windows 2000 Professional, Windows XP Professional, and Windows CE 3.0.

Almost every business and aspect of life will change in the near future as result of the drastic changes in Internet implementation and wireless device support. Sure, many things won't change because of the Internet and wireless technologies, but those things probably have not changed much in the last 50 years. Anything impacted by technology will be impacted by mobile solutions.

So why wireless? Well, first, dragging that really long category 5 cable around can be a bit of a killjoy. Second, if businesses want to implement more technology connected to the Internet, Joe User cannot be running category 5 cables around his house to support all his home devices. Nor can we expect to add more network cable for all business applications. At last count, there were six network drops running to one of our desks. It just makes sense to provide a means for connecting all these devices, quickly, to the home network and the Internet. Wireless is convenient.

As wireless networks begin taking hold in business, we have a new problem—securing these networks. Just as our normal networks need to be secured, so do our wireless networks. Actually, our wireless networks need to be secured even more than our wired networks because the wireless aspect often means that the network is not only available within the office, often outside the office and even outside the building. Using a wireless network is much like having Ethernet ports on the outside of your office building. Anyone can bring a wireless device within the range of your network and start attacking it. Implementing security is extremely important if we want to properly protect our company network resources from intruders.

In this chapter, we'll cover the important aspects of securing your wireless networks.

Configuring Public and Private Wireless LANs

Remember the days when people would come to a big budget meeting with their laptops and fight over the wall jacks so they could get on the network? Well, now, we can easily deploy wireless to locations such as conference rooms and other common areas where workers gather to discuss their projects. We can also set up WLANs for our clients to use when they visit our place of business. *Wireless LANs (WLANs)* are wonderfully convenient and can really increase user productivity. In this section, we'll look at how to set up such a network.

To set up a WLAN, you need some hardware, software, and configuration settings such as:

- A *wireless access point* (AP), sometimes referred to as a WAP
- A network connection and power for the AP
- Wireless Ethernet adapters or wireless network interface cards (NICs) usually in the form of a PCMCIA (PC Memory Card International Association) or PCCardProximity, meaning you have to be within range of the radio signals emitted by the AP

Configuring a Public Wireless LAN

The idea behind a public WLAN is that getting on the network should be easy, so let's go through the rudimentary steps of building a public WLAN, now that we have looked at the necessary components. In Exercise 5.1, we'll configure a public wireless LAN for a Windows XP Professional client.

The SSID is an alphanumeric string identifier that distinguishes one wireless LAN from another. It is similar to an address for the wireless network. For example an SSID might be a simple string such as "CorpA", "CompanyB", or even "JoeSnuffy" that identifies an AP or a group of APs.

EXERCISE 5.1

Configure a Public Wireless LAN with a Windows XP Professional Client

1.   Connect the AP to the Ethernet network and plug in its power cable or use the inline power option for the AP if no power outlet is available. Turn on the AP if it has a power switch. Refer to the hardware vendor documentation if needed. We cannot address each and every AP and wireless NIC because so many are available.

2.   Connect to the AP using the serial port or use either telnet or the Web browser after IP address assignment through DHCP. Each AP will have its own process. Refer to the hardware vendor documentation as needed.

3.   Set the SSID to be used, and configure the IP address of the AP as a static IP address. Refer to the hardware vendor documentation as needed.

4.   Start up a client system and install the wireless NIC. Depending on the vendor and the version of the operating system, you may have to download the proper drivers for the wireless adapter.

5.   In Control Panel (in Category view), click Network And Internet Connections, then click Network Connections.

EXERCISE 5.1 *(continued)*

6. Right-click the Wireless Network Connection and choose Properties from the shortcut menu to open the Wireless Network Connection Properties dialog box. Click the Wireless Networks tab.

7. Select the SSID in the Available Networks box, and then click Configure. If the SSID is found, proceed to step 10.

8. If you don't find a network name (SSID) in the Available Networks box (because the AP is not broadcasting the SSID), click the Preferred Networks check box. If the SSID is there, select it, click Properties, and proceed to step 10.

9. If you don't find an SSID in the Preferred Networks box or in the Available Networks box, click Add to manually add the SSID information.

10. Update the SSID information in the Network name (SSID) box.

At this point, the client and the AP should be able to communicate, and the client should also be able to talk to the rest of the public network.

This will normally be all that is needed for a Windows XP Professional client. Setting up a Windows 2000 Professional client is similar. In Exercise 5.2, we'll configure a public WLAN with Windows 2000 Professional.

EXERCISE 5.2

Configure a Public Wireless LAN with a Windows 2000 Professional Client

1. Connect the AP to the Ethernet network and plug in its power cable or use the inline power option for the AP if no power outlet is available. Turn on the AP if it has a power switch. Refer to the hardware vendor documentation if needed. We cannot address each and every AP and wireless NIC because so many are available.

2. Connect to the AP using the serial port or use either telnet or the Web browser after IP address assignment through DHCP. Each AP will have its own process. Refer to the hardware vendor documentation as needed.

3. Set the SSID to be used, and configure the IP address of the AP as a static IP address. Refer to the hardware vendor documentation as needed.

4. Start up a client system and install the wireless NIC. Depending on the vendor and the version of the operating system, you may have to download the proper drivers for the wireless adapter.

5. In Control Panel, select Network, and then right-click the Wireless Network Connection and choose Properties from the shortcut menu to open the Wireless Network Connection Properties dialog box.

6. On the General tab, click Configure to open the wireless NIC Properties dialog box.

7. Click the Settings tab, enter the SSID in the Wireless LAN Service Area box (this is for a 3Com wireless NIC), and click OK. Steps 6 and 7 may be a bit different for other wireless NICs.

At this point, the client and the AP should be able to communicate, and the client should also be able to talk to the rest of the public network.

Generally, if you know the SSID, you can get on the wireless network. This is true for almost all public WLANs, and it is also true for the majority of private WLANs. Using DHCP to provide the IP address and all the IP configuration information streamlines the process of adding new wireless clients and decreases the administration involved.

Configuring a Private Wireless LAN

The idea behind a private WLAN is that it is secured so that only authorized people with the appropriate credentials can get on the network. In this section, we'll look at how to build a private WLAN.

As we mentioned in the previous section, DHCP can reduce the administration required to configure and maintain a WLAN whether it is public or private. Configuring a private WLAN is much the same as configuring a public WLAN except you will need to take some additional steps.

Many private WLANs are misconfigured when it comes to security. Many companies use DHCP for their wireless networks, and they do not use WEP, MAC filtering, or 802.1*x* to increase the security levels. SOHO (small office, home office) networks are almost always wide open and are not configured securely. To make it even easier to join a wireless network, Windows XP Professional can detect the SSID broadcasts of APs and automatically set up the wireless connection configuration for you. Connecting to a wireless access point is looking rather easy now, right? Well, in many cases, it is extremely easy.

Figure 5.1 shows how most companies install an AP, directly connecting it to their company network. In this configuration, the wireless devices connect to the AP and gain access to the company network through the AP so that they are on the same network as the wired clients. This configuration is not a best practice; however, it is a good starting point for this chapter. In this configuration, all the company client systems are behind the firewall and protected from the Internet.

FIGURE 5.1 A basic wireless network

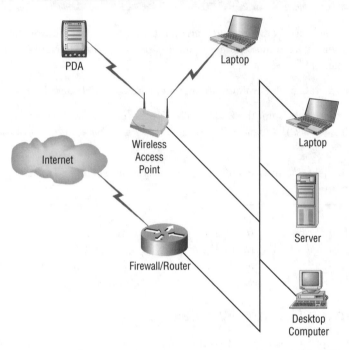

This configuration is easy for most administrators to support, especially with wireless devices that can receive the SSID information through broadcasts and also receive all their TCP/IP (Transmission Control Protocol/Internet Protocol) configuration information through DHCP servers on the local network. You will learn to love that Windows XP Professional is self-configuring in this sense; it is incredibly easy to get up and running. Windows 2000 Professional takes a little more work, but it is also easy to configure as a wireless client. In this configuration, all the company client systems are behind the firewall and protected from the Internet. In Exercise 5.3, we'll configure a private wireless LAN for a Windows XP Professional client, and in Exercise 5.4, we'll do the same using a Windows 2000 Professional client.

EXERCISE 5.3

Configure a Private Wireless LAN with a Windows XP Professional Client

1. Connect the AP to the Ethernet network and plug in its power cable or use the inline power option for the AP if no power outlet is available. Turn on the AP if it has a power switch. Refer to the hardware vendor documentation if needed. We cannot address each and every AP and wireless NIC because so many are available.

2. Connect to the AP using the serial port or use either telnet or the Web browser after IP address assignment through DHCP. Each AP will have its own process. Refer to the hardware vendor documentation as needed.

3. Set the SSID to be used, and configure the IP address of the AP as a static IP address. Refer to the hardware vendor documentation as needed.

4. Set the allowed MAC address range, set the WEP key, and configure 802.1*x* if available in the AP configuration tools. Refer to the hardware vendor documentation as needed.

5. Start up a client system and install the wireless NIC. Depending on the vendor and the version of the operating system, you may have to download the proper drivers for the wireless adapter.

6. In Control Panel (in Categories view), select Network And Internet Connections, and then select Network Connections.

7. Right-click the Wireless Network Connection, and choose Properties from the shortcut menu to open the Wireless Network Connection Properties dialog box. Click the Wireless Networks tab.

8. Use the Add button to manually add the SSID information in the Association tab. You will need to do this since the AP is not broadcasting the SSID. Enable WEP, and then click the Authentication tab.

9. In the Authentication tab, enter the 802.1*x* configuration information, and then click OK.

At this point, the client and the AP should be able to communicate, and the client should also be able to talk to the rest of the public network.

Again, since Windows 2000 Professional is a bit different than Windows XP Professional, its steps are a little different and are outlined in the following exercise.

Configure a Private Wireless LAN with a Windows 2000 Professional Client

1. Connect the AP to the Ethernet network and plug in its power cable or use the inline power option for the AP if no power outlet is available. Turn on the AP if it has a power switch. Refer to the hardware vendor documentation if needed. We cannot address each and every AP and wireless NIC because so many are available.

2. Connect to the AP using the serial port or use either telnet or the Web browser after IP address assignment through DHCP. Each AP will have its own process. Refer to the hardware vendor documentation as needed.

3. Set the SSID to be used, and configure the IP address of the AP as a static IP address. Refer to the hardware vendor documentation as needed.

EXERCISE 5.4 *(continued)*

4. Set the allowed MAC address range, set the WEP key, and configure 802.1x if available in the AP configuration tools. Refer to the hardware vendor documentation as needed.

5. Start up a client system and install the wireless NIC. Depending on the vendor and the version of the operating system, you may have to download the proper drivers for the wireless adapter.

6. In Control Panel, select Network, and then right-click the Wireless Network Connection and choose Properties from the shortcut menu to open the Wireless Network Connection Properties dialog box.

7. On the General tab, click the Configure button to open the Wireless NIC Properties dialog box.

8. Click the Settings tab and enter the SSID in the Wireless LAN Service Area.

9. Click the Advanced button and then click the Wireless Client tab. In the Operating Mode drop-down list box, select the proper level of WEP encryption and the proper key. These last few steps may be a bit different for other wireless NICs.

At this point, the client and the AP should be able to communicate, and the client should also be able to talk to the rest of the public network.

Exercises 5.1 through 5.4 may be a bit difficult to work through because of the unique tools and menus for all the APs and wireless NICs, but it is important to understand the process of setting up a wireless network. Now let's look at the differences between a public and a private WLAN when it comes to the security settings and configurations.

Configuring Windows CE as a Wireless Client

With the heavy emphasis on mobile devices, Windows CE has become important to the future of wireless and to the future of wireless security. Windows CE is widely used in a large number of handheld devices, including personal digital assistants (PDAs). Pocket PC standards usually specify a version of Windows CE for certain types of hardware. The current version of Windows CE is 3.0, and the .NET version of Windows CE is under development.

Windows CE 3.0 can participate on the company network using Ethernet adapters and can also participate on the company wireless network. Since Windows CE 3.0 can be a wireless client, we need to review which technologies can be used to secure CE devices. Windows CE currently supports the following security measure for wireless access:

- 64- and 128-bit WEP, with the high encryption pack installed
- MAC address filtering
- VPN *(virtual private network)* clients
- Personal firewalls
- 802.1x using Cisco components

Again, you must deal with the same limitations when it comes to wireless security and Windows CE devices. You can implement the same security components as you implement on Windows XP Professional clients with the exception of 802.1*x*, which is available only through vendor-specific solutions. Obviously, you should use 802.1*x* where possible.

> At this time, Windows CE does not support mutual authentication for wireless connectivity. According to the latest information, Windows CE .NET will not be supported for the newer releases in the near future.

Windows CE can use different authentication methods that can be plugged in to 802.1*x* through the EAP (Extensible Authentication Protocol) "extensible" capabilities that will allow some choices for the authentication methods. Vendor-specific solutions at this time include the ability to support usernames and passwords, certificates and certificates on smartcards, and even fingerprints. The EAP-MD5 supports usernames and passwords, and the EAP-TLS (EAP using Transport Layer Security supports certificate-based authentication. Again, 802.1*x* is vendor specific, with Cisco currently taking much of the initiative in this area.

Wireless Components

As far as hardware is concerned, a WLAN consists of two components: APs and wireless NICs. The AP is an important piece of equipment for a WLAN. After all, it is your main radio transmitter and receiver for the network and its devices. The decision about which technology to use and how to place the APs is also important. You need to give strong consideration to the type of AP that you purchase for your network. Some are really better than others. Look for the following key features:

- Support for *802.11a* as well as *802.11b* for easy upgrades to 802.11a.

- Support for multiple radio cards. This will allow you to have one 802.11b card and one 802.11a card so that the device can support two different network architectures with a single AP.

- Support for external antennas using *RP-TNC* connections. This will allow the AP to be well hidden for cosmetic reasons and expose just the antenna.

> Reverse polarity threaded naval connectors (RP-TNCs) are the standard connections used for external antennas for wireless access points.

- Support for inline power. This allows the AP to draw its power through the Ethernet cable and makes it much easier to deploy APs where they are needed, such as in drop-down ceilings, without separate power connections.

- Support for multiple SSIDs (Service Set Identifiers).

- Support for 802.1*x* authentication.

- Support for *RADIUS (Remote Authentication Dial-In User Service).*

Wireless NICs are supposed to be fully compatible with the various brands of APs. However, in practice, we have found this is not true. We highly encourage you to purchase APs and wireless NICs from the same vendor to avoid any potential compatibility problems. The key will be mostly how the NICs interact with the APs installed in the organization. A few brands let you install an external antenna to supplement the antenna built in to the PCMCIA card to help extend its range.

Choosing between 802.11a and 802.11b is difficult for many organizations. The 802.11a standard is still fairly new, and equipment can be a good bit more expensive than 802.11b equipment. Equipment based on 802.11a is even more expensive, though, because the range is significantly smaller. Notice in Figure 5.2 that 802.11a has significantly higher bandwidth, but that bandwidth decreases dramatically with distance from the AP. Equipment based on the 802.11b standard requires few APs; however, it does not provide the high bandwidth that many of today's applications need.

FIGURE 5.2   Comparing 802.11a and 802.11b

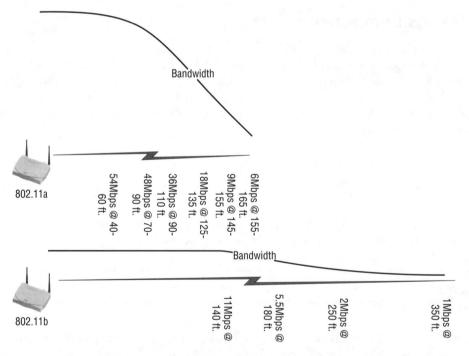

So, we plug in the AP, hook it up to the network, install our wireless cards, and away we go? Well, close. We need a little information about the network first. You need to answer some questions:

- Does the wireless network support Dynamic Host Configuration Protocol (DHCP), or do we need to get a static address for our card?

- What is the *Service Set Identifier (SSID)* for the AP?
- Are we using *Wired Equivalent Privacy (WEP)*, and what level of encryption?
- Are we using *MAC (media access control) filtering*?
- Do we use *802.1x* security?

The answers to these questions depend on whether this WLAN is public or private. A public wireless network is set up without any regard to security. It is built to allow anyone to use it, but usually it is built by a business so that their customers can use it. For example, Millennium Trenz Wireless, a business in Denver, Colorado, offers free 802.11b access, but it is intended for customers who come in to purchase wireless devices. You can find information about Millennium Trenz Wireless at www.80211hotspots.com, along with many other business and government entities that offer 802.11b access to the general public. A private wireless network is closed to the public and is intended for the private use of an individual or group of people defined by the owner of the AP.

 Real World Scenario

Extending the Capabilities of Wireless

Let's say you want to connect two buildings that are about 700 feet apart via a WAN link. You can't afford a dedicated T-1 between the buildings, you can't run fiber-optic cable between the buildings because of the costs of protecting it, and there is property between the two buildings that your company doesn't own.

Purchasing and deploying two wireless access points with RP-TNC for external antennas and connecting external directional antennas, it is easy to go beyond normal 802.11b distances and still get better bandwidth than a T-1 link. The best part of the solution is that no monthly fees are involved.

Configuring Secure Wireless Network Settings

As we previously discussed, you need to answer the following questions before you can add clients to an existing WLAN:

- Does the wireless network support DHCP, or do you need a static address for your card?
- What is the SSID for the AP?
- Are you using WEP, and what level of encryption?
- Are you using MAC filtering?
- Do you use *802.1x* security?

The answers to these five questions are the basis for controlling access to the wireless network and the ability to control whether others can listen in on your radio traffic. Another way to put it is that the answers to these five questions are the basis on which to implement security for your wireless network. Securing wireless networks involves a great deal of effort.

Dynamic Host Configuration Protocol (DHCP)

Implementing DHCP for the wireless network is a good plan if the goal is to reduce administration. However, it is not a good plan if security is more important. Giving intruders a working IP address is like giving them a hall pass to roam around the network. With this level of access, intruders can probe the many resources on the network to identify targets for further intrusion. An anonymous user attached directly to your network can cause incredible amounts of damage from the information they gather.

It's a trade-off between reduced administration and security issues. This is not a fun decision to make. Last year, reduced administration would have won, but in today's computing environment, security has to come out on top.

Using static IP configurations for wireless devices eliminates the DHCP issues. However, this also means that you either have to talk the users through this configuration or do it yourself, plus you have to manage the list of IP addresses that are being used and who has them. In either case, the more you handle such tasks manually, the greater the chance that the settings will be entered incorrectly, and the more time you will have to spend troubleshooting the configuration.

Another option provides a little administrative relief and also provides security to a degree: use a scope of addresses that are all set up with reservations. Using DHCP to provide addresses to certain MAC addresses as provided in the DHCP request can be both secure and helpful to administrators. First, with DHCP, you can change configuration information from the DHCP server without touching the client systems. This is, of course, a very good thing. Second, with DHCP options such as DNS (Domain Name System), WINS (Windows Internet Naming Service), domain names, and default gateways, you can eliminate the problems of users fat-fingering the information in their configurations. At the same time, you can stop potential intruders from getting an address and configuration options from your DHCP servers.

Without valid IP address information, an intruder really can't cause too many problems. However, if an intruder is in proximity, they can still attack your AP, consume bandwidth with their attacks, and listen in on your radio traffic to get the information they need to potentially connect to your AP. The best you can really do when it comes to IP configuration information is make it a bit harder on the potential intruders by using either statically assigned IP addresses or DHCP reservations.

Let's look at some other configuration options that can help secure wireless network.

Service Set Identifier (SSID)

The SSID is really just a network name. In many APs and wireless NIC configurations, it is even referred to as a network name. All that we are doing with SSIDs is providing a unique name for our wireless network to distinguish it from other wireless networks. The SSID is extremely important for connecting to a wireless network. The main problem with SSIDs, though, is that few administrators understand the security issues around wireless and do not know that the standard SSID for each vendor is part of the default configuration for each AP. The following SSIDs are implemented right out of the box:

- 3Com uses "101".

- Addtron uses "WLAN".

- Cisco uses "tsunami".

- Compaq uses "Compaq".

- Intel uses "intel".

- Linksys uses "linksys" and "default".

- Lucent uses "RoamAbout Default Network Name".

Administrators that do change the defaults often choose names that are easy to remember such as the name of their company and terms such as *wireless*, *default*, and *WAP*. It is highly recommended that you change all APs from their default SSIDs as well as default administrative passwords to settings that are not easy to guess or successfully use for brute force attacks.

> SSIDs can be case-sensitive. Be sure to consult your manufacturer's documentation for more information.

Figure 5.3 shows an example of how the wireless card configuration might look when a wireless network has multiple APs.

FIGURE 5.3   Configuring the SSID

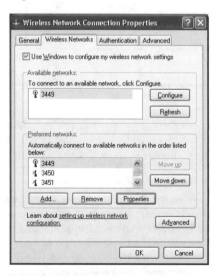

In Figure 5.3, multiple SSIDs are configured with a priority given to the 3449 SSID. In this example, SSID 3449 is the preferred AP, and 3350 is next on the list.

Generally, the SSID is used to segment the wireless network devices into networks of one or more APs. A large organization might have APs in the marketing area with one SSID, and all the marketing laptops are set up to use that SSID. The research engineers might also have some APs in their area of the building, and they are all set up with a different SSID. Research engineers users use only their APs, and the marketing team uses only their APs. This is one way for the client systems to handle overlapping coverage areas when multiple APs provide service. Figure 5.4 shows an example in which two APs overlap. If a user brings their computer from their office to the conference room in the middle, they can connect to either AP. Setting the preference as in Figure 5.3 allows the system to remain configured to its preferred AP and lets it switch over to its secondary AP if it is out of range of the preferred AP.

FIGURE 5.4   A sample office layout

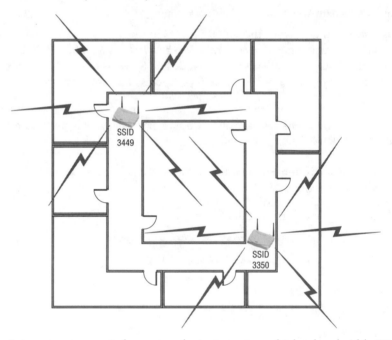

Overlap is important to a wireless network since you want higher bandwidth. Walls and other factors such as interference from devices like microwave ovens and 2.4GHz wireless phones can reduce the broadcast distances and make them much shorter than those specified.

Overlap of wireless zones can also be a problem with wireless networks because limited frequencies are available, and overlap can cause interference with devices. In 802.11b, of the 11 (numbered 1-11) channels available, only 3 channels are within the frequency that will not interfere with each other and cause interference when their zones overlap; channels 1, 6, and 11 do not overlap with each other. This means that, even in the best design, more than 3 wireless zones cannot overlap without causing communications problems.

Now, so far in this chapter, we have looked at the basics of connecting a client to a wireless access point, and we have seen how a connection can be made to a standard AP using a standard wireless NIC in Windows XP Professional or Windows 2000 Professional by setting the SSID. The primary security issues are controlling who can access the APs to connect to the network resources and preventing others from listening in on our radio traffic. As Figure 5.4 clearly shows, signals do not always remain within the building. Many times, radio signals cover areas outside the building. This excess coverage is much like putting network jacks on the outside of the building. Most everyone would agree that this is a bad idea. So how do we remove these wireless jacks? We use SSIDs, WEP, 802.1x, and VPNs, which will all be covered in the rest of the chapter.

SSID Security Concerns

You can implement network access control using an SSID associated with an AP or with a group of APs. The SSID provides a mechanism to segment a wireless network into multiple networks serviced by one or more APs. Every AP is configured with an SSID for a specific wireless network. To access the network, client computers must be configured with the correct SSID. An office or a building might be segmented into multiple networks by floor or department. Normally, you can configure a client computer with multiple SSIDs for users who require access to the network from a variety of different locations. Look back at Figure 5.3 for an example.

Because a client computer must present the correct SSID to access the AP, the SSID acts as a simple password, and it provides a measure of security. Although this security is fairly basic, you can configure the normal user's computer on the wireless network with the appropriate SSID for the department or group within the company, and you can segment their network traffic away from other APs that have different SSIDs. For example, if accounting has APs in their area and doesn't want everyone in the company using their APs, they can create an SSID for the accounting team APs. Anyone else in the company who doesn't have this SSID configured would be unable to connect to their APs.

However, this minimal security is easily bypassed and compromised, primarily as a result of. The improper configuration of the AP itself. If the AP is configured to broadcast its SSID, it can be picked up off the radio waves fairly easily. When this broadcast feature is enabled, any client computer that is not configured with a specific SSID is allowed to receive the SSID and access the AP. Windows XP Professional is really good at sniffing out these broadcast SSIDs in order to configure its wireless network settings automatically and make it easy for the user. Applications such as NetStumbler and AirMagnet can also sniff out these SSIDs even if the AP isn't broadcasting them.

SSID broadcasting is usually configured in the AP by changing the *Beacon* settings. This beacon broadcasts information to the wireless network, including the SSID.

The default configuration of most APs enables broadcasting of the SSID on the channel being used by the AP. Obviously, if you shout out your configuration information, your network is not very secure. So, here is the first area in which you can tighten up security. Most vendors' APs can turn off this broadcasting. We would be negligent if we didn't at least do that much.

OK, so we turn off the broadcasting of the SSID at the AP, but that doesn't eliminate the problem. After all, a hacker can use an 802.11 analyzer to sniff the radio packets. Any time a system associates or reassociates with the AP, the SSID is passed in the clear. Even if the broadcasting is turned off, the SSID can be found out easily enough. To top it off, we know that our network users do really odd things like share SSIDs with their friends so they can also use the wireless network.

Association in wireless networks is the process of the wireless NIC getting the data rates and other bits of info from the AP as it connects to it. Once the association is complete, the client and the AP can send data back and forth.

Protecting the SSID really isn't possible. All it will really do is keep authorized users from accessing the wrong APs. When it comes to keeping out knowledgeable intruders, the SSID is pretty much worthless.

Configuring Wireless Encryption Levels with WEP

You can use WEP to improve the security of your wireless networks. The idea behind WEP is to make wireless traffic as secure as traffic traveling a wired network. WEP encrypts the body of each wireless frame. As you have learned, encryption is a good thing because it keeps data and communications private. E-mail, Instant Messaging, Usernames, Passwords, and other extremely important information should be encrypted if it contains proprietary data. This is even more important with wireless networks that are accessible from outside the office because of their broadcast range.

The Basics of WEP

The concept is simple. If WEP is activated at both the AP and the client, the wireless NIC encrypts the data payload and the CRC (cyclic redundancy check) of each and every frame sent to the AP using RC4 ciphers. All data between the AP and the wireless NIC is protected. The seed used to create the RC4 ciphers is a combination of the WEP base key and the *initialization vector (IV)* to create a 64-bit or 128-bit encryption key. The data sent between the AP and the client includes the IV along with the encrypted payloads. The IV just happens to be transmitted in the clear. "Transmitted in the clear" is a phrase that makes most security guys shudder, and for good reason. Anyone listening in on the traffic can read the IV in their packet sniffer. The IV is used on the receiving end along with the base key to decrypt the payload.

The transmission is encrypted with the IV combined with the WEP base key, which is stored in the configuration information for the NIC and the AP. The receiving side then decrypts the data using the IV that it receives as part of the transmission and combines it with the WEP base key that is part of its configuration information. Assuming that the WEP base keys are the same on both ends, the data will be successfully decrypted. It is a little more complex than this quick explanation, but there isn't any real value in going deep into the hows and whys of WEP encryption. The basics will do here.

In many access points, WEP is optional. Even if WEP is enabled and the encryption is turned on, it is not enforced by the AP. A client without encryption can still access that base station if they have the proper SSID.

You can typically configure WEP in three modes:

- No encryption

- 40-bit encryption

- 104-bit encryption

There is some confusion with the number of bits, so let's take a second to straighten that out. The IV is 24 bits. The IV is combined with the 40-bit key to create a total of 64 bits for use in encrypting and decrypting. In the 104-bit mode, the 24 bits for the IV are added to get 128 bits. Thus, the total encryption is 64 or 128 bits.

Almost every AP has WEP disabled by default. Going from 64-bit encryption to 128-bit encryption does not help with the known problems of WEP. A 128-bit encryption can be broken almost as easily as a 64-bit encryption. The steps for configuring WEP are rather basic, as you'll see in Exercise 5.5.

EXERCISE 5.5

Configuring WEP

1. Configure and enable WEP and the AP using the tools and processes described in the vendor's hardware guide.

2. In Control Panel (in Categories view), select Network And Internet Connections, and then select Network Connections.

3. Right-click Wireless Network Connection, and choose Properties from the shortcut menu to open the Wireless Network Connection Properties dialog box. Click Wireless Networks tab.

4. Select the SSID (Network Name) in the Available Networks box, and then click the Configure button to open the Wireless Network Properties dialog box. Click the Data Encryption (WEP Enabled) check box to enable WEP.

5. In the Network Key box, type the key from the AP, and confirm it if necessary. Click OK twice to close the open dialog boxes.

6. Restart the AP.

At this point, the client and the AP should be able to communicate, and the client should also be able to talk to the rest of the public network.

Enabling WEP

What is really unsettling is that few companies turn on WEP for their access points. This can be the case for several reasons:

- It is not easy to change the default configurations on most APs.

- Many administrators deploy APs for evaluation and forget to secure them once they decide that wireless is making life easy for the company employees.

- Some administrators are just plain overworked and can't take the time to change the default configuration of the APs that they deploy and all the client configurations.

Figure 5.5 shows the WEP base key that will be used along with the IV to encrypt the payload.

FIGURE 5.5   Enabling WEP

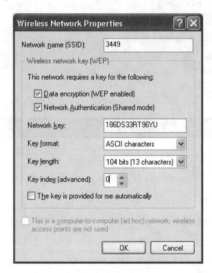

In the Network Key box, you can see the 13 characters of the WEP key used for this client to connect to the AP using SSID 3449. Notice that the Data Encryption check box is checked, which means that WEP is enabled. The Network Authentication (Shared Mode) check box is also checked. Again, keeping it basic, we provide another means of authenticating the client to the AP by checking this check box. Using the WEP key, much like using the SSID as a password of sorts, you can prevent clients from attaching to your wireless network unless they have the correct key. Not only is the key used to encrypt the payload of each frame, but it is used to authenticate client and AP to each other.

The basis of all the issues with WEP is the IV. In most WEP implementations, the base key is static, meaning it does not change from frame to frame. The base key is the shared secret that you enter in the APs and in the wireless NIC configuration settings as the WEP key. Even with the IV being rotated, the IV will be repeated fairly often over a day or two since the IV is only 24 bits. A hacker that captures enough packets with the same IV (remember it is in the clear) can decrypt the base key. Once the base key is decrypted, the encryption itself is worthless. With the base key in the possession of an intruder or somebody trying to listen in, each and every frame traveling on the radio signal can be easily decrypted, since the IV is traveling in the clear and those are the only two pieces used to build the encryption keys.

This is not saying that the RC4 algorithms are defective. In fact, the RC4 ciphers are strong and reliable. It is a weakness in the implementation of WEP with the IV being in the clear. If the encryption is based on the combination of the IV and the base key, and the IV is a problem, the only way to really address the problem is to rotate the base key using some automated method or to change it manually on a regular basis. Compounding the difficulty is that wireless data is easy to capture compared with data transmitted over wired networks. You don't even have to be in the building to get to it in most cases.

Let us add to your woes. If a client system is stolen or lost, standard security practices require that you rekey each and every system in your wireless network. You can't afford the risk of somebody getting the WEP key from the lost or stolen system. Since 802.11 standards do not specify tools or processes for mass updates, it all has to be done manually.

OK, so WEP is broken too. Great! So why in the world would you want to even go through the trouble of using WEP? The answer is simply that WEP is better than not doing anything at all. At least you can make your intruders work for it. You can only hope that they find other targets that are easier to penetrate and leave you alone.

If you have been keeping up with security bulletins, some of the driest reading in the known world, you have either heard of the problems with WEP, or you have fallen asleep at your desk more than you care to admit. WEP has flaws. WEP has serious flaws. WEP has easily exploitable, serious flaws. WEP, meant to be equivalent to a wired network for security, isn't.

MAC Filtering

Yes, a *Media Access Control (MAC)* address is not exactly friendly and easy to use. Anyone that has done MAC filtering with other devices knows how difficult it is to configure. Just entering the MAC, 12 hexadecimal numbers, can be a pain all its own. It is easy to read the wrong number or mistype it.

A MAC address is unique to the network device. At least it is supposed to be unique. Assuming it is unique and that you can identify a single network device from its MAC address, this may have some potential for security. If we can somehow identify each system by its MAC address and then grant it access or deny it access based on a list of those MAC addresses, we are in business.

But can we actually do this? The answer is, of course. Why else would it be here in the book?

 You can find the MAC address of your wireless network cards by entering IPConfig/all at a command prompt in Windows 2000 or Windows XP. Also, many NICs print the MAC address on the outside of the network card.

To administer the AP, we can use telnet over IP, a direct serial connection, or a web browser, and we can dig around in the AP configuration until we find MAC filtering. It is as simple as adding the MAC addresses that we are willing to allow on our wireless network. In Figure 5.6, you can see how a 3Com AP can be managed using a web browser to make changes to the security. It is as simple as clicking the View/Add/Delete button next to Ranges Of Allowed Wireless Clients and adding the MAC addresses of the wireless NICs that you want to allow on your network. Anyone trying to gain access to the network will be denied unless they have a NIC with an appropriate MAC address.

Clicking the View/Add/Delete button next to Disallowed Wireless Clients lets you manage a list of MAC addresses not allowed on the network. OK, since there is likely some confusion, let's look at why there is a list to allow and a list to disallow. Assuming you really want to know, think of it this way. In the list to allow access, you can enter in a range of MAC addresses. Entering a range of addresses makes much more sense than adding many MAC addresses to the list one at a time, right? Well, if you do that, and an employee quits or is about to be terminated because of some fishy things they are doing, you can take action right away and place them on the disallow list, which removes their access.

FIGURE 5.6   Configuring MAC filtering

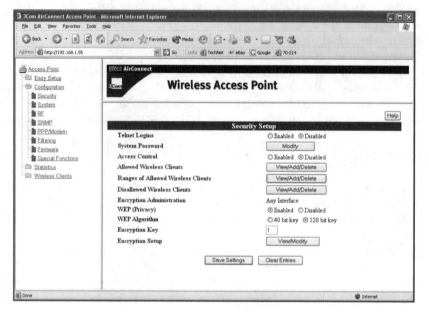

You can use SSIDs to identify APs, and you can use MAC addresses to identify client network cards. Combining the two can definitely help secure the wireless network from unauthorized users. Two pieces working together can definitely be better than one.

But, are you ready for the bad news? MAC addresses are fairly easy to spoof. Some Unix and Windows applications allow the user to spoof a MAC address. With a little monitoring of the network, valid MAC addresses can be found, and these addresses can be used to get past the MAC filtering that is in place. Sometimes it just seems that we can't win when it comes to wireless security. Despite the ability to spoof MAC addresses, you should still filter on them if it is possible. Again, you don't want to make it easy for intruders. If you make it hard enough, they might go onto other more inviting targets.

MAC address filtering (along with SSIDs) provides improved security. Combine the two with WEP and some security around IP addressing, and you are actually getting a fairly secure environment. The biggest problem with using MAC filtering, though, is the administration involved. With large networks, keeping track of each adapter's MAC address and the owner of each card can be difficult. Using MAC filters is best suited to small networks for which the MAC address list can be efficiently managed. Each AP must be manually programmed with a list of MAC addresses, and the list must be kept current. Even with tools from the manufacturer that let you update multiple APs simultaneously, this can be cumbersome. Administrative overhead limits the scalability of MAC filtering just as it limits changing WEP keys regularly, and it limits the ability to control IP configurations. Administration is a major impediment.

Configuring Wireless Encryption Levels Using 802.1x

The IEEE (Institute of Electrical and Electronics Engineers) 802.1x standard is the next big step in wireless security. This standard manages and controls access to the wireless network using *Extensible Authentication Protocol Over LANs (EAPOL)* in combination with *Protected Extensible Authentication Protocol (PEAP)*, *Extensible Authentication Protocol with Transport Layer Security (EAP-TLS)*, Kerberos, or Message Digest 5. The 802.1x standard is not just for wireless implementations; it can also be used for LAN-based devices.

 Windows XP Professional is the only client that fully supports 802.1x. Windows 2000 Professional cannot use the features at this time, and Windows CE (discussed later) supports only certain vendor implementations through the vendor's drivers and other tools.

The 802.1x standard is a great step forward for security; however, setting it up requires some extensive resources and a Private Key Infrastructure (PKI) to provide the certificates. The necessary resources include the following:

- Wireless clients such as Windows XP Professional that support 802.1x
- Active Directory running on Windows 2000 Server, SP3
- A *Certificate Authority*
- A remote access policy for wireless clients
- RADIUS servers

 The IEEE is an international electrical standards organization.

In Figure 5.7, you can see the additional infrastructure needed to make this all work. DC1 and DC2 are the Active Directory domain controllers (you want at least two for redundancy), IAS1 and IAS2 are the *Internet Authentication Servers* (again, two for redundancy) that will be used for RADIUS, and CA is the Certificate Authority.

The main goal of 802.1x is to securely authenticate clients associating with APs and to exchange encryption keys. The process is somewhat confusing, but it can be clarified a bit. See Figure 5.7 for the visual of the process; the steps are outlined here.

1. The AP sees that a client exists on the network and initiates contact. Access is blocked by the AP until authentication is completed by the client. If authentication fails, no data is ever forwarded onto the wired network.

2. The AP sends an EAPOL-encapsulated EAP Request-ID to the client.

3. The client sends an EAPOL-encapsulated EAP Response-ID message that contains the user's identification information to the AP.

4. The AP then forwards this EAP Response-ID by encapsulating it in a RADIUS access request packet and sending it to a RADIUS server. This could be either IAS1 or IAS2.

FIGURE 5.7   Authentication for 802.1*x*

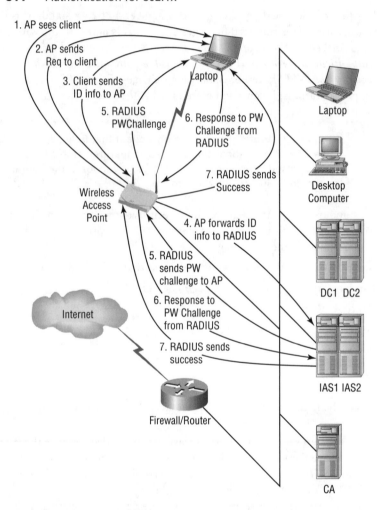

5. The RADIUS server responds with an EAP-Request, encapsulated in a RADIUS packet, that contains a password challenge for the client, and it is forwarded by the AP to the client after the AP encapsulates it using EAPOL.

6. The client responds to the challenge with EAPOL-encapsulated response information that is sent to the AP and then forwarded to the RADIUS server in an encapsulated RADIUS packet.

7. The RADIUS server responds with a RADIUS-encapsulated EAP success message to the AP. The AP then forwards this EAP success message to the client encapsulated with EAPOL.

Once all these steps have taken place, the client is considered properly authenticated and can start transmitting data on the wireless network to the wired network. In this exchange, all traffic between the client and the AP is encapsulated using EAPOL. All traffic between the AP and the IAS (RADIUS) servers is encapsulated using RADIUS.

OK, so you now understand the architecture of it at a high-level. Now let's look at the client configuration. Figure 5.8 shows how to enable 802.1x access control for a wireless client. You need to enable it, and then you need to set the EAP type. Normally, this is set to use a certificate in the Registry or a certificate on a smart card.

FIGURE 5.8   Configuring an EAP type

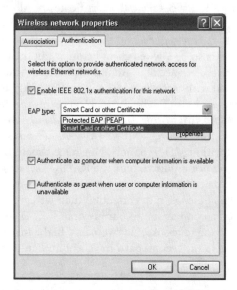

When a Windows XP Professional client starts, it broadcasts three EAP messages in an attempt to prompt the AP to start the process discussed previously and illustrated in Figure 5.7. Remember, the AP needs to see the client on the network to start the process. If the AP does not send the request, the client will not attempt to connect via 802.1x authentication and will send normal wireless data to the AP. If the AP, however, does send the request, the client will respond and start the 802.1x authentication process.

If the Enable IEEE 802.1x Authentication For This Network check box check box is checked and the AP is not set to use 802.1x or does not support it, it the client will not be prevented from properly accessing the AP and participating in the wireless network. If the Enable IEEE 802.1x Authentication For This Network Enable =802.1x check box is cleared and the AP is enforcing 802.1x authentication, the client will not connect.

In the EAP Type drop-down box list box, shown in Figure 5.8, the Protected EAP (PEAP) option will be available along with Smart Card Or Other Certificate after you apply SP1.

Prior to SP1, the default types available include MD-5 Challenge and Smart Card Or Other Certificate.

EAP Authentication Methods

Windows XP Professional, prior to SP1, supports EAP-TLS and EAP-MD5 authentication methods. MD5 is not recommended because it is not a mutual authentication method, and it is susceptible to offline dictionary attacks. TLS utilizes certificates stored in either the Registry or on Smart Cards and can provide mutual authentication as well as an encrypted means of transferring keys.

EAP-TLS is the default EAP type. TLS is intended for wired networks, but can also be used in wireless environments. Using TLS requires that that RADIUS server and the client both have certificates and that both devices have the certificates residing within a trusted CA. In order for the client to get a certificate for use with wireless access, though, it must first have wired access to the CA to make the request and then apply the certificate. This is a problem in that each wireless client must also be a wired client before it can then become a wireless client. It just doesn't make sense on the surface of it. Administrative overhead for TLS can be a bit high.

Windows XP Professional with SP1 provides support for PEAP. Using PEAP, the initial communications are encrypted with TLS. Because TLS encrypts the data flow, password-based authentication protocols such as *Microsoft Challenge-Handshake Authentication Protocol version 2 (MS-CHAP v2)* can be used securely. MS-CHAP v2 is not susceptible to offline dictionary attacks if it is being passed within a TLS channel. One huge benefit of this solution is that user and computer certificates are not required; only the RADIUS servers require certificates for a fully secured association and authentication process for wireless users.

PEAP with MS-CHAP v2 deserves more attention than we can give it here, but it is important to know how it works in comparison to our previous 802.1x authentication process in Figure 5.7. PEAP authentication takes place in two parts. In the first part, the client and the AP create the TLS channel, and in the second part, the client authenticates using MS-CHAP v2.

MS-CHAP version 2 is a password-based challenge-and-response authentication protocol that uses Message Digest 4 (MD4) and Data Encryption Standard (DES) ciphers to encrypt messages and responses. Although MS-CHAP v2 is susceptible to offline dictionary attacks to break the encryption and find the passwords, adding TLS in PEAP provides strong security.

Creating the TLS Channel involves the following steps:

1. The AP sends an EAP Request-ID message to the wireless client.

2. The wireless client responds with an EAP Response-ID message that contains the ID of the client.

3. The EAP Response-ID message is forwarded by the AP to the RADIUS server.

4. The RADIUS server sends an EAP-Request/Start PEAP message to the client through the AP.

5. The client and the RADIUS server send TLS messages back and forth to establish the cipher for the TLS channel, and then the RADIUS server sends a certificate to the client for authentication.

Once the TLS channel is in place, the second part of the process begins, and it includes the following steps to establish authentication using MS-CHAP v2:

1. The RADIUS server sends an EAP Request-ID

2. The client responds with an EAP Response-ID that contains the client ID

3. The RADIUS server sends an EAP-Request/EAP-MS-CHAP-v2 challenge that contains a challenge string to the client for authentication

4. The client responds with an EAP-Response/EAP-MS-CHAP-v2 response that contains the response to the RADIUS server challenge, and it also issues a challenge string for the RADIUS server to establish mutual authentication

5. The RADIUS server sends an EAP-Request/EAP-MS-CHAP-v2 Success message, which tells the client that its response was accepted, and it also sends a response to the client challenge sent in step 4 to authenticate itself to the client.

6. The client sends an EAP-Response/EAP-MS-CHAP-v2 Ack message to the RADIUS server to verify that its response was accepted.

7. The RADIUS server sends an EAP-Success message, and this ends the mutual authentication process using MS-CHAP v2

At the end of this mutual authentication exchange, the wireless client has provided proof of knowledge of the correct password (the response to the RADIUS server challenge string), and the RADIUS server has provided proof of knowledge of the correct password (the response to the wireless client challenge string). The entire exchange is encrypted through the TLS channel created in PEAP in the first part of the process.

The real benefit to PEAP with MS-CHAP v2 is that passwords are used, not certificates. In the release of Windows .NET Server, the IAS (RADIUS) implementation will require using a certificate for it, but not for the clients. This is important because it will considerably reduce the overhead of the solution. Instead of having to implement a full PKI solution to support wireless client security, you can purchase a single certificate from a commercial Certificate Authority.

Problems and Attacks Specific to Wireless Networks

OK, now that your head is spinning from trying to figure out how wireless communications can be secured, it is time to apply some of this newly gained knowledge. First, let's identify some of the common problems and the common attacks. Although you have probably heard of most of them, this is still the perfect time to review them.

Rogue APs

The word *rogue* fits well here because it really does describe this problem of unsanctioned or unauthorized activity. Our users are supposed to come to us in the IT department to install things like APs for their use. However, sometimes our security department will not approve the installation. So what do our users do? Do they just gladly accept that security denied their request? Of course not. They read the manual and do it themselves. They participate in rogue activities and go to great lengths to hide their work. In some instances, APs have been found locked up in wooden file cabinets where employees have drilled holes to run the power and network cables inside the cabinet.

Being busy people, and bucking the system at the same time, they do the minimum to get it to work and do not seek advice from the IT staff about the proper way to do it because they are trying to keep it a secret. They aren't being malicious; they just want the benefit of using all those cool wireless toys, such as their pocket PCs and laptops, without hassling with wires and cradles and all that stuff. Gee, go figure—they want to be productive!

OK, we all know it happens, so how do we stop it? Well, we take advantage of the tools in our bag of tricks. We install NetStumbler, AiroPeek, AirSnort, or some of our other wireless tools that will find those rogue signals. We walk around the building with our laptop hooked up with a wireless card and run the applications looking for unauthorized radio signals. Our goal is simple: find the unauthorized APs, and then take action to either get rid of them or secure them properly.

War Driving

No, it is not a conspiracy to rid the world of WiFi. War driving is not against the law. *War driving* is the act of looking for and logging active wireless access points. In most cases, it has become a really sophisticated process using a laptop, a wireless NIC, some good software, and even a Global Positioning System (GPS) to provide exact coordinates for logging the find. A war driver can simply hook up their laptop, start up their software, and drive around the neighborhood or the business park while the software automatically logs the location and type of device using its wireless card and the attached GPS.

So why is it bad? Well, if you screwed up your implementation of wireless access, you might be found by a war driver. Worse yet, this war driver might be one of the many out there that participate in war-driving sites and then might upload your information to the Internet. There, on the Internet, all the information needed to come and attack your network will be made available. It is clear how bad this can be.

OK, how do we stop it? Basically we stop it the same way we stop rogue access points. We war drive our own buildings using the same software and tools that the culprits use, and if we find anything, we fix it right away.

War Chalking

War chalking is much like war driving. What is done with war chalking, though, is that somebody actually gets out of the car and puts a special symbol on your sidewalk, driveway, garage, or the middle of the street indicating that an unsecured wireless network is nearby. War chalking gets its name from two sources. First is the practice of war dialing, in which a user uses a modem and dials all the numbers it can find in the area to look for a modem that answers. Once a modem is found, the user can then start attacking it and attempt to break into the system. Second is the process during the depression when hungry and homeless people put chalk marks on homes to indicate to each other which ones were friendly and might give them a meal or a place to stay for a night.

What is most interesting about war chalking is that many of the chalk marks that people see on their buildings at work or on their driveway are readily dismissed as kids playing. Since the chalk is not permanent, they really don't pay too much attention to it.

OK, so how do we avoid being war chalked? Again, we check out our networks and secure them, so even if we are chalked, hopefully it will be with a symbol showing that we are secured.

Radio Interference

Remember, 802.11 traffic utilizes unlicensed radio frequencies. Did you know that the 2.4GHz phone that you just bought might interfere? How about that microwave oven right down the hall? It is really odd just how many electronic devices use the same unlicensed frequency that our wireless networks also use. So, if you can interfere with your network without even trying, can it be done on purpose? Absolutely!

Only 11 channels are available to us in 802.11b. Of those 11 channels, only 3 provide non-overlapping traffic between the other 8 channels. Most wireless administrators are aware of this, so they generally choose one of those 3. It makes perfect sense. Knowing that almost all wireless networks will be using one of 3 different channels, just how hard could it be to set up a transmitter that sends traffic on all 3 channels at the same time and then provide enough power to totally drown out and overpower all devices trying to use those bands? In practice, it is easy, and this is scary.

The real problem is that there are no known defenses against this type of attack. Since the frequency is unlicensed, you can't go to the FCC unless the user is exceeding the FCC power restrictions of 1 watt. To be honest, there are very few reports of this happening, but we do need to be aware that it is a possibility. Maybe, when we design a new building for construction, we might put thicker exterior walls in to defend ourselves from this kind of activity.

WEP Attacks

As you saw earlier, WEP is not fully secure. However, as we discussed, you should use it in combination with other measures to help secure your network.

Using an application such as NetStumbler or AirSnort, an intruder can capture the packets over time and then use tools to break the encryption key to find the base key for WEP. It really doesn't take too much effort for a high-end PC to break the encryption, and on a busy network, less than a day's worth of packets are all that are needed.

So how do you stop it? Well, you need to set some monitoring of your own. One way to beat those trying to break is in to do your best to secure your wireless network and then use AirSnort or some other tool to watch the network. Monitoring your traffic can help you identify when the traffic is higher than established baselines and let you know that something fishy might be going on. Of course, even then, it might not be enough, so what are the next steps? On to the next section for the answer.

The Next Steps

Now that you have learned more about wireless networking, you can see some challenges in deploying it and challenges in securing it. Going all the way back to Figure 5.1, you can see that this typical wireless network implementation is probably much more typical than we hoped. We can take our simple network and make one quick and easy change.

We simply move our AP to the DMZ (De-Militarized Zone), or if we only have a single firewall, we put the AP on the outside of it, as in Figure 5.9. Now, even if intruders defeat the security of the AP device, they still have to defeat the firewall to get access to the inside of our network and have access to our resources. That seems like a simple solution; however, it does present some challenges.

FIGURE 5.9   Moving the AP

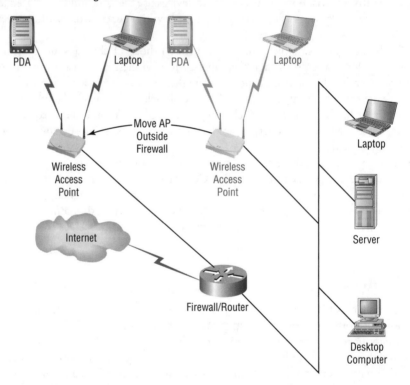

One of the biggest challenges that we will face with the AP outside the firewall is figuring out what ports we need to open and then doing it without compromising the security of our firewall. This is why we may end up with a DMZ implementation as the preferred solution. At least our external firewall will provide greater security for those attackers not in our general area of the AP.

Let's not forget about one key piece of security here; if our wireless clients are not protected by the firewall as in Figure 5.1, we need to provide personal firewalls for them. We can't have our client systems susceptible to attacks from the Internet, and we need to take measures to protect their local data as well as the applications they use. A personal firewall might be one of the best ways to do that.

Implementing VPNs to Protect Wireless Networks

The more that companies started looking at the option, of moving the AP outside the firewall, the more they started to think that it really looks like any other implementation in which we clients are outside the firewall. We can use the example of the user at home coming in via DSL (digital subscriber line) or cable modem. How are we, as an organization, currently providing the applications they need and access to the data that they need to do their jobs from home? Well, if we can properly provide secure access for them, why not our wireless users outside the firewall too?

If you use VPNs to secure all traffic from your clients on the Internet through the firewall and into your organization's network, you should be able to use them for the wireless side too. Figure 5.10 shows the use of the remote user coming in via the Internet. We have been using VPNs for these types of users for a couple of years now and have not had any problems with security with a proper VPN implementation. If you take that same VPN technology and use it for wireless access, you will have high levels of security for your wireless traffic. The wireless traffic will be secure, and you will not have to worry about having to punch additional holes through your firewall.

FIGURE 5.10   Using VPNs

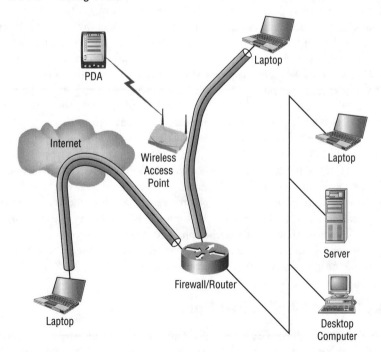

VPN technology has many advantages, including the following:

- It is preexisting on most enterprise networks.
- It is scalable.

- The administration is already in place, and the additional number of users in most cases will not adversely impact the environment.

- Wireless traffic cannot enter the private network until VPN authentication takes place.

- WEP implementations and MAC filtering are not as important because of the strong security found in the VPN implementation.

- Users will have a consistent process for connecting to the network whether at home using VPNs, while traveling and using remote Internet connections, or while using wireless access in the office.

The VPN solution for wireless network access may actually meet all the needs of the organization for security and still provide the conveniences of wireless access.

Combining VPN and 802.1x

You have seen that a VPN for wireless clients is a great way to really secure the traffic. You have also seen that 802.1x with the newer PEAP implementation can also secure your wireless network. Although many see these as competing technologies, we need to step back and look at them for what they really are: highly complementary technologies that can be used together in many cases.

First, using 802.1x allows us to use a RADIUS server inside our network to provide authentication for our clients, and we can combine this capability with certificates to fully encapsulate and encrypt the authorization traffic. However, even if we use authentication methods such as EAP-TLS and PEAP, we are not properly covering the traffic from end to end. We need to secure the traffic all the way from the wireless client and into the network so that it is not susceptible to attacks from outsiders. Our 802.1x solution only encrypts traffic from the wireless client to the AP. If the AP is outside the network, we are not protecting the traffic from the AP to inside the network. We have a gap that needs to be covered.

Second, you have seen that using VPNs to provide access to most enterprise networks is a fairly common solution. Accessing data and applications inside the network from the Internet requires the client to establish a VPN to the network. A VPN connection ensures data security all the way from the client end to the VPN server itself, inside the network.

If you combine the security of 802.1x, which protects the wireless side and provides extremely secure authentication using RADIUS with the high levels of security provided by a VPN solution, you can see how they work together and provide secure access to clients accessing the company network from the Internet from public places and homes and from the wireless network. A couple of layers of security can really make the difference.

Wireless Security Moving Forward

OK, we use 802.1x and VPNs. We also use WEP and MAC filtering and change our SSID to a difficult-to-guess string, and we turn off broadcasting of our SSID. We provide limited access to TCP/IP addresses for our wireless networks, and after all that, we have a rather nice, secure wireless implementation.

However, combining all these will only work if you have Windows XP Professional wireless clients. Windows 2000 Professional clients can still take advantage of many of the security provisions as discussed in this chapter; however, Windows 2000 Professional clients do not currently support 802.1*x*.

Wireless security is important, but it really isn't being implemented properly. Reports from war drivers still show about 50 to 60 percent of wireless networks implemented without changing SSIDs and without using WEP. Wireless security can be broken down into four basic levels of security:

No Security   A wide open network without WEP, using the default SSID, and probably even broadcasting its SSID

Basic Security   A network utilizing at least 40-bit WEP and renaming its default SSID and turning off broadcasting

Enhanced Security   A network utilizing mutual authentication and 802.1*x* along with implementing WEP, turning off the SSID broadcasts, and changing the SSID to a difficult-to-guess string

VPN Security   Utilizing VPN connectivity to secure wireless clients and combining it with enhanced security

It would be nice to see more of the enhanced level and to see more implementations utilizing VPNs. We really need to take wireless security seriously because it is absolutely one of the weakest entry points to our network resources.

Summary

This chapter covered wireless networking and how to secure a wireless network. We discussed some common configuration problems and described several ways to improve the security of an organization's network by making configuration changes.

In particular, we described how to configure wireless networks, including private and public networks, and how to configure encryption levels for wireless networks, including WEP and 802.1*x*.We also discussed how to configure different client operating systems, including Windows 2000 Professional, Windows XP Professional, and Windows CE.

Finally, we finished with a discussion on how to protect networks from attacks specific to wireless networks, including the utilization of VPNs to improve security for wireless networking.

Exam Essentials

Configuring public wireless networks   Make sure you understand the significance of the SSID and how and when to change the SSID to segment networks. Also understand how to configure Windows XP Professional and Windows 2000 Professional, and understand the major features of Windows CE.

Configuring private wireless networks   Make sure that you understand how private wireless networks operate and know how to implement security measures for a private wireless network, including:

- Implementing MAC Filtering
- SSID broadcast issues and how to fix them
- DHCP issues

Configuring wireless encryption levels   Make sure you can do the following:

- Enable and configure WEP
- Enable and configure 802.1x
- Implement VPNs for wireless

Key Terms

Before you take the exam, be certain you are familiar with the following terms:

802.11a	Microsoft Challenge-Handshake Authentication Protocol version 2 (MS-CHAP v2)
802.11b	PEAP with MS-CHAP v2
802.1x	Protected Extensible Authentication Protocol (PEAP)
AP (access point)	RADIUS (Remote Authentication Dial-In User Service)
beacon	RP-TNC (reverse polarity threaded naval connectors)
Certificate Authority	Service Set Identifier (SSID)
Extensible Authentication Protocol Over LANs (EAPOL)	virtual private networks (VPNs)
Extensible Authentication Protocol with Transport Layer Security (EAP-TLS)	war driving
initialization vector (IV)	Wired Equivalent Privacy (WEP)
Internet Authentication Servers (IAS)	wireless access point (WAP; AP)
MAC filtering	Wireless LANs
MAC (Media Access Control) filtering	

Review Questions

1. Your company has two groups that want to use wireless networks. Accounting is willing to fund their own hardware purchases to pay for the wireless network that will cover their part of the building, but they do not want any other groups using their hardware and reducing the performance for their users. Based on some testing, you will need to install two new APs to provide proper coverage for the accounting area. How should you configure their wireless hardware?

   A. Create a unique SSID for each of the APs and then configure the clients so that they have the SSID of the AP closest to their office.

   B. Create a new SSID, configure it for both APs, and then configure the accounting clients so that they have the SSID that goes to both APs.

   C. Create a unique SSID for each of the APs, then create a third SSID for the clients, and configure the clients to use both the SSID for the clients and the SSID of the AP closest to their office.

   D. Use the default SSID for the equipment so that accounting can get on the network easily. Make the other group change their SSID so that they don't interfere with the accounting network.

2. Your company has only five wireless clients that access the wireless network set up in the conference room. Recently, you were reviewing the configuration of the AP and noticed that it had eight wireless clients attached to it that were active. You verified that the five normal wireless clients were being used in the conference room, but could not find any others. You are sure that they are not authorized, and you want to kick them off and prevent them from ever connecting to your network again. How should you configure the AP without reconfiguring the client systems so that only the five approved users will be able to access the AP and the intruders will not be able to connect?

   A. Implement WEP on the AP.

   B. Implement 802.1x for the wireless network.

   C. Implement MAC filtering, and allow only the MAC addresses of the five client systems that are approved.

   D. Implement MAC filtering, and deny the MAC addresses of the intruders.

3. Your company has entered into a strategic partnership with another company. The other company often sends representatives to your office, and they need access to the Internet to get their e-mail and to browse the Internet as part of their research. They do not need access to the internal network. These visitors all use Windows XP Professional clients, and they use a wireless network in their office. Your boss has told you to provide this access to them using an AP that their company has sent to him. He wants the AP installed so that their users cannot access any of the internal company network resources, and he says that they do not want the AP security changed in any way from its current configuration. You set up a meeting with everyone involved, including your network architecture guys and the firewall team. They propose the following options. Which is the best option?

   A. Install the AP on a separate network in the company, and then configure a router to allow only HTTP (Hypertext Transfer Protocol) and SMTP (Simple Mail Transfer Protocol) traffic out of the wireless network.

   B. Install the AP on a separate network in the company, and then configure a router with VPN from the wireless network to a VPN device at the other company's network.

   C. Install the AP in a DMZ off the company firewall, and configure the firewall to allow AP traffic to go to and from the Internet and not into the company network.

   D. Install the AP outside the firewall, and purchase IP addresses from the ISP to support all wireless users.

4. Which of the following are valid 802.11 specifications for wireless networks commonly in use? (Choose all that are correct.)

   A. 802.11a

   B. 802.11b

   C. 802.11c

   D. 802.11t

5. Many APs provide support for inline power. What does in-line power actually provide?

   A. Power for the AP by drawing on the power through Ethernet cables

   B. A battery backup for the AP

   C. Support for changing out the radio card in an AP

   D. Additional power for external antennas

6. Internet Authentication Service (IAS) is required in Windows 2000 Server architecture to support 802.1x implementations. What other acronym is considered the same thing as IAS?

   A. ISA (Internet Security and Accelerator)

   B. AD (Active Directory)

   C. MS-CHAP v2 (Microsoft Challenge Handshake Authentication Protocol)

   D. RADIUS (Remote Authentication Dial-In User Service)

7. A good friend of yours comes to visit you at your office, and he pulls out his laptop to show you pictures of his new office. Once he powers up his laptop, he gets a notification balloon in the lower right corner saying that it found a wireless network. He shows you the notification balloon, and you recognize the SSID as the one for the AP you installed yesterday. After he leaves, you want to fix this so it doesn't happen again. What should you do?

   A. Change the default password on your AP.

   B. Change the AP from DHCP to a static IP.

   C. Change the SSID from the default to a new value.

   D. Turn off broadcasting for the SSID.

8. Your company will be buying three different APs in the near future, and their coverage areas will overlap once they are set up in the building. What channels should the APs be set on so that they will not interfere with one another?

   A. All three APs should be set up on channel 1.

   B. The APs should be set up so that one uses channel 1, one uses channel 2, and one uses channel 3.

   C. The APs should be set up so that one uses channel 9, one uses channel 10, and one uses channel 11.

   D. The APs should be set up so that one uses channel 1, one uses channel 6, and one uses channel 11.

9. You come into work after being on vacation and find that one of your co-workers has installed all the APs for the new 802.11b wireless network. He is just getting around to testing them and has found that one AP seems to have problems maintaining connectivity with clients, intermittently. This AP is installed in the conference room. Which device is most likely causing interference?

   A. The copier machine 30 feet and 2 walls away

   B. The conference room projector about 10 feet away

   C. The TV and VCR in the conference room about 5 feet away

   D. The microwave oven about 10 feet away on the other side of the wall

10. Which of the following are needed to install a wireless network? (Choose all that apply.)

   A. A wireless access point

   B. Wireless network cards for client systems

   C. Appropriate TCP/IP addresses for the network

   D. The DNS name of the wireless access point

11. You have decided to implement MAC filtering on your AP. How do you find the MAC addresses of the wireless NICs for your network? (Choose all that apply.)

    A. Run `IPConfig /all` from the command prompt.

    B. Copy the MAC address from the outside of the network adapter.

    C. Run `MACID` from the command prompt.

    D. Use the IP address if it is a static IP instead.

12. You must get a certificate from a certificate authority. Which of the following security measures requires getting a certificate?

    A. MAC filtering

    B. WEP encryption

    C. 802.1x

    D. All the above

13. Which 802.11 standard provides for the widest coverage, meaning, the signal travels farther than the others?

    A. 802.11a.

    B. 802.11b.

    C. 802.1x.

    D. They are all the same.

14. Your supervisor asks you to set up his laptop with wireless connectivity. The company standard is to use 802.1x. His laptop runs Windows 2000 Professional. What do you need to do to make it work?

    A. Install the high encryption pack from Microsoft's download site.

    B. Upgrade his laptop to Windows XP Professional first since Windows 2000 Professional does not support 802.1x.

    C. Buy a wireless NIC that supports 128-bit encryption.

    D. Select 128-bit Shared Key Algorithm for the Encryption Algorithm option.

15. You need to set up a conference room for wireless access. It is your first wireless project for the company, so there is no existing equipment. Your supervisor says that high bandwidth is important for wireless users in the conference room. Which 802.11 standard should you implement for the equipment?

    A. 802.11a.

    B. 802.11b.

    C. 802.1x.

    D. They all have the same bandwidth.

16. You replace all company 802.11b equipment with 802.11a equipment. When replacing the APs, you put in 802.11a APs in exactly the same places where the 802.11b APs were installed. Users report that they are finding a large number of areas in the office where wireless access is not working. What is the most likely cause of this problem?

    A. 802.11a APs do not cover the same amount of area as 802.11b APs, so more will need to be added to cover the dead zones.

    B. 802.11a APs must be overlapping and interfering with each other. The overlaps are causing dead zones.

    C. 802.1x authentication must have been configured, but not all APs are configured properly.

    D. 802.11a is more susceptible to fluorescent lights than 802.11b. Light filters are needed so that 802.11a can provide the same coverage area.

17. Your company uses 802.11b for wireless access. You accidentally break your wireless NIC. You buy another wireless NIC of the exact same brand, but it will not connect to the network. You know that your company uses WEP, and a quick call to the help desk. When talking to the help desk, you told them that your computer somehow lost its configuration information. The helpdesk walks you through inputting the custom SSID and enabling WEP. You still are not able to connect. What is the most likely cause of the problem?

    A. Your new NIC must be an 802.11a NIC

    B. You are out of range of an AP

    C. DHCP is not working

    D. MAC filtering needs to be reconfigured on the APs

18. Your company uses 802.11b for wireless access. Your company uses a mix of Windows 2000 Professional and Windows XP Professional wireless client computers. You have set up and configured DHCP for wireless clients. You review the DHCP logs and see that an unauthorized user it gaining access to the network. You do not want to set up WEP. What other methods can you use to secure your wireless network?

    A. Setup MAC filtering on the APs

    B. Set reservations in DHCP for all authorized MAC addresses and remove all other addresses from the DHCP scope

    C. Configure a custom SSID

    D. Implement 802.1x

19. Your company uses 802.11b for wireless access. You accidentally break your wireless NIC. You buy another wireless NIC of the exact same brand, but it will not connect to the network. You know that your company uses WEP, and then make a quick call to the help desk. When talking to the help desk, you told them that your computer somehow lost its configuration information. The helpdesk walks you through inputting the custom SSID and enabling WEP. You still are not able to connect. What is the most likely cause of the problem?

A. Your new NIC must be an 802.11a NIC

B. You are out of range of an AP

C. DHCP is not working

D. MAC filtering needs to be reconfigured on the APs

20. Your company uses 802.11b for wireless access. You configure several new laptop computers to join the wireless network in the accounting area. All users in the accounting area are reporting very poor wireless performance since the new laptops were deployed. What can you do to improve the wireless performance?

A. Upgrade all of the new accounting wireless clients with 802.11a adapters.

B. Setup MAC filtering on the AP in accounting so only accounting wireless clients can use the AP.

C. Add a new AP in the area with a new SSID. Configure the new laptops to use the new AP.

D. Add a new AP in the area with a new SSID. Configure all of the wireless clients in the accounting area to use the new AP.

Answers to Review Questions

1. B.   This solution allows accounting clients to roam and connect to the closest AP for best performance.

2. C.   Implementing MAC filtering will not affect the five approved users because the filter is implemented on the AP and does not require configuration changes for the clients. Also, setting up the filter to allow only the five MACs will prevent any and all other MACs from connecting.

3. C.   This option is the easiest, least expensive, and most secure solution to provide Internet access to the visitors.

4. A, B.   The 802.11a standard is the new 54Mb implementation that is now starting to make headway in the market, and 802.11b is the 11Mb solution that has been around for a few years.

5. A.   A is the proper description for in-line power.

6. D.   IAS is Microsoft's implementation of RADIUS in Windows 2000 Server.

7. D.   Broadcasting the SSID causes the behavior described in the question.

8. D.   Only three channels do not overlap and interfere with one another: channels 1, 6, and 11.

9. D.   Microwave ovens use the same 2.4GHz frequency used by 802.11b devices and can cause interference when they are running.

10. A, B, C.   The DNS name associated with an AP is not required to install and configure a wireless network.

11. A, B.   `IPConfig /all` displays the MAC address of all installed network adapters in a computer, and it is standard practice to print the MAC address on the outside of the NIC. There is no such command as `MACID`, and IP addresses will not work for MAC filtering.

12. C.   Of these options, only 802.1x requires using certificates.

13. B.   The 802.11b standard covers a much larger area than 802.11a, and 802.1x is not a transmission standard; it is an authentication standard for wireless.

14. B.   Windows 2000 Professional does not support 802.1x.

15. A.   The 802.11a standard has much higher transmission rates than 802.11b, and 802.1x is not a transmission standard.

16. A.   The 802.11a standard has much lower range than 802.11b. Using 802.11a will require installation of more APs to cover the same amount of area.

17. D. The helpdesk would not have asked for MAC information since you never told them it was a new wireless NIC.

18. A, B, C. 802.1x can not be used for Windows 2000 client computers.

19. D. The helpdesk would not have asked for MAC information since you never told them it was a new wireless NIC.

20. C. The new wireless clients and the old wireless clients all in the same area must be broken into groups so they do not all use the same AP.

Chapter 6

Deploying, Managing, and Configuring SSL Certificates

THE MICROSOFT EXAM OBJECTIVES COVERED IN THIS CHAPTER:

- ✓ **Deploy and manage SSL certificates. Considerations include renewing certificates and obtaining self-issued certificates versus public-issued certificates.**

  - Obtain public and private certificates.
  - Install certificates for SSL.
  - Renew certificates.

- ✓ **Configure SSL to secure communications channels. Communications channels include client computer to web server, web server to SQL Server computer, client computer to Active Directory domain controller, and e-mail server to client computer.**

Data needs to be secured in several places on the network: in databases, in file shares, in websites, on client computer hard drives, and in other areas such as public folders on Exchange servers. However, all these places are basically physical locations where data is stored. If you focus on these areas alone, you miss a large vulnerability, the transmission media. When you use the Internet or even an intranet in many organizations, the traffic from your client system to the web server can go through several servers or routers before it is received. All sorts of confidential information passes through these systems, including passwords, company private documents, Personal ID Numbers (PINs), credit card numbers, online purchase orders, electronic invoices, and other personal and company information. In between the client and server are many other systems that also might be monitoring the traffic and actively capturing the data so it can be used later to break into systems or to steal your personal identity and your company network credentials. This traffic needs to be secured so that information cannot be stolen from the packets traveling across the network.

In Chapter 5, you saw how to secure wireless networks. In Chapter 4, you saw how to use IPSec and SMB signing to secure communications. In this chapter, we will use *Secure Sockets Layer (SSL)* protocol to secure transmissions to and from the Internet as well as internally on an intranet. Initially, SSL was developed to secure web traffic; however, SSL has been adapted to other protocols.

In this chapter, we will look at using SSL to secure Internet traffic from the client system to the web server, to secure traffic from the web server to the SQL server, to secure traffic from a client system to Active Directory domain controllers, and to secure e-mail traffic from the e-mail server to the client system. We will cover how to get a certificate, install a certificate, and renew a certificate. We will also cover how to implement SSL for these different processes. Because knowing how to configure SSL is critical, this chapter will be fairly exercise oriented.

An SSL Primer

Before we look at how to implement SSL, we need to go over some basics. Once you understand how SSL works, it is much easier to understand how to deploy and support SSL implementations.

SSL provides two main services: *authentication* and *encryption*. When a client system and a server communicate using SSL, the client system can verify the identity of the server from the certificate installed on the server; this is authentication. Once the client system has verified that the server is who it says, to the client system can establish a secure tunnel in which all data traveling through this tunnel is encrypted. Once the server has properly installed its certificate, the process follows the steps shown in Figure 6.1 and detailed below.

FIGURE 6.1   The SSL process

1. The client system initiates SSL and sends its capability information to the server, including the SSL versions, cipher suites, and compression methods that it supports.

2. The server responds by sending its digital certificate to the client; the digital certificate contains information about the server such as its DNS (Domain Name Server) name, the public encryption key, the cipher suite, and the compression method it has selected for the session.

> *Public key cryptography* is the technique that uses a pair of *asymmetric keys* for encryption and decryption. Each pair of keys consists of a *public key*, which is widely distributed, and a *private key*, which is always kept secret. Data that is encrypted with the public key of the pair can only be decrypted using the private key, and, conversely, data that is encrypted with the private key can only be decrypted by using the public key.

3. The client verifies that the certificate is valid and that the certificate authority (CA) is in the list of trusted CAs. The client also checks the expiration date to make sure that the server certificate is still valid. All this proves the identity of the server to the client.

4. The client generates and sends a master secret (master key) to the server that is encrypted using the server's public key.

5. The server decrypts the master secret using its private key and then uses the master secret to generate encryption keys for bulk data encryption and for message authentication, and the client generates the same keys since it has the same master secret and is using the same algorithm as specified in Step 2.

6. The server sends a verification message to the client, and the handshake process is completed.

7. The tunnel is now established, and data can flow through it.

SSL provides the ability to encrypt all types of traffic as previously discussed and also provides message integrity since the data traveling through the encrypted tunnel cannot be altered in route. Message integrity is guaranteed through the use of the message authentication code inserted in the data between two systems. The message authentication code provides protection against message alterations by using a digest. If a message is altered during transport between the systems, the digest will not be the right one for the message, and the altered information will not be accepted. If enough altered messages are received, the two systems can stop communicating.

SSL also provides the ability to prevent replays. In a *replay*, a potential intruder captures all the data in a session and then later resends the messages to the server or the client to try to trick one of them into responding. SSL provides protection against replay attacks by using sequence numbers in both directions of the session. Any attempts to send packets at a later time with incorrect sequence numbers will result in the packets being disregarded.

When SSL is installed, many resources are accessed using a different port. Most system administrators know that by default HTTP uses port 80 and that HTTPS (SSL secured) uses port 443. Table 6.1 lists some of the common port assignments for the protocols we will discuss in this chapter.

TABLE 6.1   SSL Port Assignments

Protocol	Standard Port	SSL Secure Port
HTML	80	443
IMAP	143	993
LDAP	389	636
POP3	110	995
SMTP	25	465

Now that you've seen the basics of how SSL works, let's look at how to obtain certificates from both public certificate authorities and private certificate authorities, how to install certificates to support SSL, and how to renew certificates.

Obtaining Public and Private Certificates

Certificates are the basis of the security mechanisms discussed in this chapter. These certificates can be obtained from *public certificate authorities* and *private certificate authorities*. The general rule as to whether you use a public CA or a private CA is whether you will use the certificate externally or internally. If it is used internally, you can still choose to use a public CA rather than create your own *Public Key Infrastructure (PKI)* to support certificate use. External use is the main reason for using public CAs. Since the better public CAs have their information preinstalled on most current operating systems, the users of the secure links do not have to do anything special to start using them. With private CAs, you need to install the certificates for the CA in the trusts lists of the client systems that will be using the certificates. This can be difficult and time-consuming; so to avoid the additional work, we often use public CAs.

Obtaining Public Certificates

You obtain a certificate from a certificate authority. A certificate authority is a service that generates and maintains information about certificates. Some well-known certificate authorities include Baltimore, Comodo, Entrust, GeoTrust, Thawte, Valicert, and VeriSign. There are many others, but these are some of the best known. These CAs are public CAs because they interact with the general public. Basically, any company can get a certificate from one of these public CAs. The CA acts much like a driver's license office or a passport office. Before they can issue identification, they need proof of identity. Once you prove that you are a legal representative of a company, you can get a certificate. This certificate will include the following:

- Your organization name
- Additional information such as your physical address
- A unique serial number
- Your public key
- The expiration date of the public key
- The CA's digital signature showing that they issued it

Normally, the process of obtaining a certificate from a public CA takes a few days. First, you must submit some of the following documentation as proof of company identity. (Not all this information is needed; this is just an example of items that might be requested.)

- Business license
- Dun & Bradstreet number
- Articles of incorporation
- Trade name registration
- Proof of ownership of the domain name
- Names of corporate officers
- Full company name, address, and phone number
- Technical contact information
- Billing contact information

Second, you must provide proof of domain name ownership or of the authorization from the owner to purchase the certificate on their behalf. Generally, this step requires choosing the common name that will be used for the certificate. The common name is the fully qualified domain name of the server on which the certificate will be installed, for example, www.*companyname*.com. It is important that this common name be acceptable before the certificate is purchased since changing the common name requires purchasing a new certificate. Ownership of the domain name is usually proven by faxing or mailing documentation on company letterhead, stating ownership, and also faxing or mailing documentation showing legal ownership of the name.

The third step is to generate a *Certificate Signing Request (CSR)*. The process of generating the CSR depends on the operating system of the server. We'll describe this process in detail shortly. The CSR process will ask you for the following information:

Common name This is the same as the URL or fully qualified domain name for the server, such as www.*companyname*.com.

Organization or company This is the registered trade name or the corporate name of the company purchasing the certificate. You should use the full name and not any abbreviations.

Organizational unit This is an optional field that might be used to show which department or division in the company is purchasing the certificate, or it might be used if there is a Doing Business As (DBA) name. This field does not need to be filled out.

City/Locality This is used to show where the company is physically located. If this is a division or a department of the company, it is generally expected that you enter the local office location in this field.

State/Province U.S. and Canadian organizations must enter this information. Organizations outside the United States and Canada can skip this field as long as they enter a city/locality.

Country This is the two-character country code. For example, the United States is US, and Japan is JP.

The fourth step is to generate the certificate request. The information is dumped into a text file, so you will need to cut the information out of the text file and insert it in the enrollment form for the CA. The CSR information will look something like that in Figure 6.2.

FIGURE 6.2 CSR information

After the certificate request is generated and input into the online template, the fifth step is to complete the rest of the CSR form and submit it. Part of the application may require entering a challenge phrase. This is the same thing as a password. Make sure you remember this phrase or document it in a secure place since it will be needed to renew or revoke the certificate, and the account and pass phrase will make it easier to obtain certificates in the future.

The CSR password created during the process should be eight characters or fewer and should not use these special characters: ~ ! @ # $ % ^ & * ( ) _ { } | : " < > ? / \

Generally, you will need to provide payment during the application using a credit card, a purchase order, a bank draft, or a wire transfer. Once the payment has been properly received by the CA along with all the requested information, you will have to wait for the application to be completed by the CA. If there any problems, they will contact one of the individuals set up as contacts for the company to request clarification or more information. If everything goes as planned, you will receive your approval, and the certificate will be e-mailed to the technical contact. Once a certificate is received, you can install it on the server.

Backing up the certificate is a good idea. You can copy it to a floppy disk and then properly secure that disk in a safe location or in some other properly locked area.

Now that we have gone over the process at a high level, let's look at the individual steps. In Exercise 6.1, you'll obtain a certificate from a public CA.

EXERCISE 6.1

Obtain a Public Certificate

For this exercise, we will obtain a certificate from a public certificate authority for a web server running IIS 5. These are the steps for Comodo's InstantSSL. If you really want to purchase a certificate for SSL, go to the website of the CA that you want to use. For this exercise, we went to www.instantssl.com and then selected the InstantSSL Certificate without any upgrades for express credentials. This CA covers 99 percent of the existing browser market.

1. Provide your CSR. To get the CSR, you need to generate it on the web server. So, on your web server, run the IIS MMC snap-in.

   a. Choose Start ➤ Programs ➤ Administrative Tools ➤ Internet Services Manager to start the console.

   b. Right-click the website where you want to install the certificate and then choose Properties from the shortcut menu to open the Properties dialog box for the website.

c.   Click the Directory Security tab, and the click the Server Certificate button in the Secure Communications section of the Properties page to initiate the Wizard.

d.   At the Welcome screen, click Next.

e.   Select Create a New Certificate, and then click Next.

f.   Verify that the Prepare The Request Now, But Send It Later button is selected. If it isn't, select it and click Next.

g.   On the next screen, enter the Name of the site. This name is just to make it easier for you to refer to later. Also select the bit length for the CSR. The higher the bit length, the more secure the protection. A bit length of 512 will result in only a 40-bit SSL certificate. Most commercial CAs recommend 1024 bits for the CSR so that you can get the full 128-bit certificate. Higher bit lengths can cause performance problems, so don't get too carried away. Click Next.

h.   On the next screen, enter the organization and the organizational unit. Normally, the organization will be the company name, and the organizational unit will be the department or division. Click Next.

i.   On the next screen, enter the common name of the organization. This will be the fully qualified domain name for the server as it will be accessed from the Internet. Click Next.

j.   On the next screen, we will enter the country/region, state/province, and city/locality information as discussed earlier in this chapter. Click Next.

k.   Now you need to specify a filename and location for the CSR. This will be a text file, and we will use a text editor to open it later. Remember the name and location of the file. Click Next to open the Summary screen.

l.   Verify that all the information is correct. If anything is wrong, click the Back button and fix the problem. Otherwise, click Next, and then click Finish.

m.   Click OK to close the Properties dialog box for your website.

n.   Find the file that you saved in Step k, and open it using Notepad or some other text editor. Copy the entire file, including the dashes, in the Begin New Certificate Request and the End New Certificate Request lines in the template for the CA. (See Figure 6.2 earlier in this chapter.)

o.   Select the software used to generate the CSR and item 2 on the screen shown here. We will use the drop-down box in Step 2 and select Microsoft IIS 5.x And Later.

EXERCISE 6.1 *(continued)*

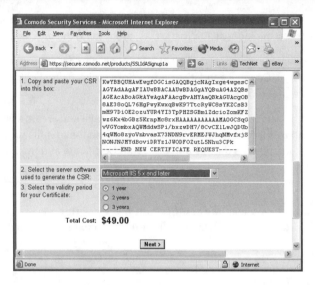

p. Select the length of the certificate and item 3 on the screen. Click Next in the browser to open the Company Details screen.

q. Fill in all the company information as seen in the following screen. On this same screen complete the blanks for the Administrative, Billing, and the Organizational Contact information. Enter the account name and password so you will not have to enter this information again in the future. Click the Submit Details & Proceed to Payment button.

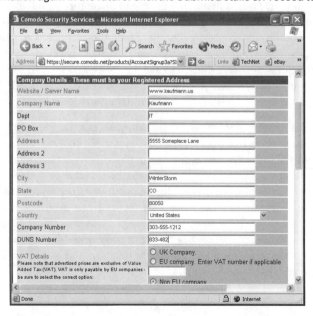

r.   Normally, payment will be via credit card or purchase order. Once payment information is submitted, finish the request. For many CAs, processing the request takes a few days.

s.   Once your request has been processed, the technical contact should receive an e-mail from the CA. Some CAs will send it to you on floppy disk using FedEx or some other delivery service that requires a signature receipt.

t.   Cut and paste the certificate information out of the e-mail and create a file with the `.cer` extension using this information as the content, or use the text file on the floppy disk sent by the CA. Include the dashes and the Begin Certificate and the End Certificate in creating the file.

At this point, you have obtained the certificate. It resides within that `.cer` file. However, just having the certificate doesn't really do much for us. The next step is to install the certificate.

 Real World Scenario

Using Multiple DNS Names

Let's say that you are the network administrator for a company that uses Outlook Web Access so that many people can access their e-mail from outside the office without having to install Outlook or configure Outlook Express.

The problem is that you have heard that many people in the company have been told to use `https://owa.`*companyname*`.com/exchange` to access their e-mail, and others have been told to use `https://email.`*companyname*`.com/exchange`. Since the certificate was purchased for the `email.`*companyname*`.com` common name, the `owa.companyname.com` DNS name causes a security alert to appear for the users that try to use the `owa.companyname.com` address saying "The name on the security certificate does not match the name of the site." This situation is causing excessive calls to the help desk employees, and they are not able to keep up with them.

The key here is that the name has to be `email.`*companyname*`.com` for the certificate. Since many users think they need to use `https://owa.companyname.com/exchange`, rather than redirecting the request through DNS, the requests can be properly redirected through a web page. Create another website for the `owa.`*companyname*`.com/exchange` address and secure it properly with SSL by purchasing another certificate using `owa.company.com` as the common name. Then create a web page on `https://owa.`*companyname*`.com/exchange` that redirects all requests to `https://email.companyname.com/exchange`. This way, all requests whether to `https://owa.`*companyname*`.com/exchange` or to the proper address of `https://email`*.companyname*`.com/exchange` will end up at the right location and will be able to use the certificate without getting any error messages.

Installing an SSL Certificate

In Exercise 6.2, you will install an SSL certificate on an IIS 5 Web server. At this point, the IIS administrator can start utilizing SSL to encrypt connections for the server. We will cover how to do this later in the chapter.

EXERCISE 6.2

Installing an SSL Certificate

For this exercise, we will use the certificate obtained in Exercise 6.1 and install it on an IIS 5 server.

1. On your web server, run the IIS MMC snap-in. Choose Start ➢ Programs ➢ Administrative Tools ➢ Internet Services Manager to start the console.

2. Right click the website where you want to install the certificate, and then choose Properties from the shortcut menu to open the Properties dialog box for your website.

3. Click the Directory Security tab, and then click the Server Certificate button in the Secure Communications section to start the wizard.

4. At the Welcome screen, click Next at the first page of the wizard.

5. Select Process The Pending Request And Install the Certificate. Click Next.

6. Navigate to the .cer file either on floppy or some other storage medium, and click Next once it has been found using the browse button.

7. The summary screen provides some details such as the name of the file, the common name of the server, the CA that issued it, the expiration date, and the certificate's intended use. It also includes other identifying information. Verify that the information is correct, click Next, and then click Finish to install the SSL certificate.

Renewing a Public CA Certificate

When you purchase a certificate, it has an expiration date. Normally, two years is considered the normal time frame for a certificate; however, it can be more or less. The certificate we obtained in Exercise 6.1 is a one-year certificate. It will expire. Our options, when it expires, are to either remove it or renew it. Removing it is a valid option; however, it is probably a bit quicker to renew an existing certificate. In Exercise 6.3, we'll renew a certificate.

EXERCISE 6.3

Renewing a Certificate

For this exercise, we will use the certificate obtained in Exercise 6.1 and installed for use by IIS 5 in Exercise 6.2.

1. On your web server, run the IIS MMC Snap-in. Choose Start ➢ Programs ➢ Administrative Tools ➢ Internet Services Manager to start the console.

2. Right-click the website on which you want to renew the certificate and then choose Properties from the shortcut menu to open the Properties dialog box for the website.

3. Click the Directory Security tab, and then click the Server Certificate button in the Secure Communications section to start the IIS Certificate Wizard. (Clicking View Certificate at this point will allow you to see when the certificate is to expire and will also tell you which CA provided it.)

4. At the Welcome screen, click Next to open the Modify The Current Certificate Assignment screen:

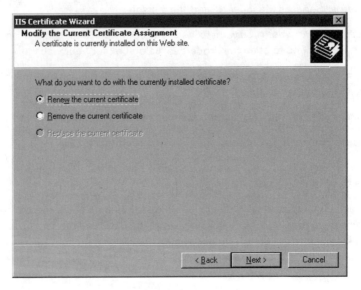

5. Select Renew The Current Certificate, and then click Next.

6. Verify that the Prepare The Request Now, But Send it Later button is selected. If it isn't, select it, and then click.

7. Select a filename and a location for the CSR. This will be a text file, and we will use a text editor to open it later. Remember the name and location of the file. Click Next to open the Summary screen.

8. Verify that all the information is correct. If anything is wrong, click the Back button and fix the problem. Otherwise, click Next, and then click Finish.

9. At this point, you will need to go to the website of the CA and follow their procedures for renewing the certificate. The process is similar to that of creation except that this time you will use the account and pass phrase from Exercise 6.1 to renew the existing certificate. You will not have to reenter all the information for all CAs; however, some will require that you enter the information for many of the fields again as a means of proving identity.

10. Select the renewal length and then proceed to the payment screen.

11. Make the appropriate payment arrangements and submit the request to renew the certificate.

12. The CA will distribute the renewal key in the same way it did the original key.

13. Upon receipt of the key, cut and paste the certificate information out of the e-mail and create a file with the .cer extension using this information as the content, or use the text file on the floppy disk sent by the CA. Include the dashes and the Begin Certificate and the End Certificate in creating the file.

14. On your web server, run the Internet Services Manager MMC Snap-in.

15. Choose Start ➢ Programs ➢ Administrative Tools ➢ Internet Services Manager to start the console.

16. Right-click the website on which you want to renew the certificate, and then choose Properties from the shortcut menu to open the Properties dialog box for the website.

17. Click the Directory Security tab, and then click the Server Certificate button in the Secure Communications section to start the IIS Certificate Wizard.

18. At the Welcome screen, click Next.

19. Select Process The Pending Request And Install the Certificate. Click Next.

20. Navigate to the .cer file either on floppy or some other storage medium using the browse button. Click Next once the file has been found using the browse button.

21. The summary screen provides some details such as the name of the file, the common name of the server, the CA that issued it, the expiration date, and the certificate's intended use. It also includes other identifying information. Click Next, and then click Finish to renew the certificate.

Renewing an SSL certificate is much like the process of obtaining an SSL certificate. It is a bit quicker, though.

Obtaining and Renewing a Private Certificate

To get a private certificate, you need an existing PKI implemented. Of course, you can always install one when it is needed, but doing so usually requires some significant planning. If the PKI is not rolled out properly, you might need to tear it down and rebuild it completely, which would make all the certificates that it had previously issued completely worthless. Installing a CA is covered in Chapter 9.

The process is similar to obtaining a public certificate; however, you can obtain a private certificate much more quickly and without all the painful paperwork.

The exercises in this chapter assume you have Certificate Services installed on a Windows 2000 Server computer. If you don't, see Chapter 9 for details about how to install Certificate Services.

In Exercise 6.4, we'll obtain a private certificate using the Web interface.

EXERCISE 6.4

Obtaining a Private Certificate Using the Web Interface

For this exercise, we will obtain a certificate from the Microsoft Certificate Authority residing on our internal network. You can obtain private certificates in two ways: by using the web interface for the private CA as shown in this exercise, and by sending the request directly to the CA online, as shown in Exercise 6.5.

1. On your web server, run the Internet Services Manager MMC Snap-in. Choose Start ➢ Programs ➢ Administrative Tools ➢ Internet Services Manager to start the console.

2. Right-click the website on which you want to install the certificate, and then choose Properties from the shortcut menu to open the Properties dialog box for the website.

3. Click the Directory Security tab, and then click the Server Certificate button in the Secure Communications section to start the IIS Certificate Wizard.

4. At the Welcome screen, click Next.

5. Select Create A New Certificate. Click Next.

6. Verify that the Prepare the Request Now, But Send It Later button is selected. If it isn't, select it, and then click Next.

7. On the next screen, enter the name of the site. This name is just to make it easier for you to refer to later. Also select the bit length for the CSR. The higher the bit length, the more secure the protection. Microsoft's CA supports from 384 to 1024 bits for the CSR. A bit length of 1024 is the recommended value. Click Next.

8. On the next screen, enter the Organization and the Organizational Unit. Normally the organization will be the company name and the organizational unit will be the department or division. Click Next.

9. On the next screen, enter the Common Name. This will be the fully qualified domain name for the server as it will be accessed from the network. Click Next.

10. On the next screen, we will enter the county/region, state/province, and city/locality information as discussed earlier in this chapter. Click Next.

11. Specify a filename and location for the CSR. This will be a text file, and we will use a text editor to open it later. Remember the name and location of the file. Click Next to open the Summary screen.

12. Verify that all the information is correct. If anything is wrong, click the Back button and fix the problem. Otherwise, click Next, and then click Finish.

13. Click OK to close the Properties dialog box.

14. Find the file that you saved, and open it using Notepad or some other text editor. Copy the entire file, including the dashes, in the Begin New Certificate Request and the End New Certificate Request lines into the template for the CA.

15. Open Internet Explorer and enter the URL for the certificate server, `http://servername/certsrv`, as shown here.

16. On the opening screen of the certificate server, click the Request a Certificate radio button, and Click Next.

17. Click the Advanced Request radio button and click Next.

18. Click the Submit A Certificate Request Using a Base64 Encoded Pkcs #10 File Or A Renewal Request Using A Base64 Encoded Pkcs #7 File button, and then click Next.

EXERCISE 6.4 *(continued)*

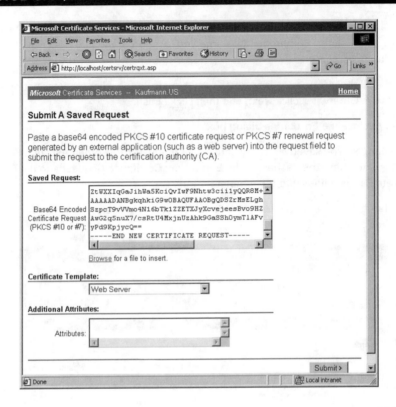

19. Insert the CSR, and in the Certificate Template drop-down list box, and select Web Server. Click Submit to open the Certificate Issued screen.

20. To download the certificate click the Download CA Certificate link.

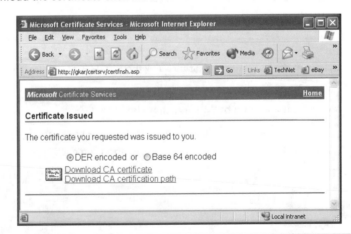

Clicking the Download CA Certificate link downloads the `.cer` file and saves it to disk. Make sure this file is saved to a secure area. Refer to Exercise 6.2 for details about how to install the SSL certificate. The process is exactly the same once the certificate has been received and is available to install on the web server. In Exercise 6.5, we'll obtain a private certificate using an online CA.

EXERCISE 6.5

Obtaining a Private Certificate Using an Online CA

For this exercise, we will obtain a certificate from the Microsoft Certificate Authority residing on our internal network.

1. On your web server, run the IIS MMC snap-in. Choose Start ➢ Programs ➢ Administrative Tools ➢ Internet Services Manager to start the console.

2. Right-click the website on which you want to install the certificate, and then choose Properties from the shortcut menu to open the Properties dialog box for the website.

3. Click the Directory Security tab, and then click the Server Certificate button in the Secure Communications section to start the IIS Certificate Wizard.

4. At the Welcome screen, click Next.

5. Select Create A New Certificate. Click Next.

6. Select the Send The Request Immediately To An Online Certificate Authority radio button and click Next.

7. In the Name field, enter the name of the site. This name is just to make it easier for you to refer to later. Also select the bit length for the CSR. The higher the bit length, the more secure the protection. Microsoft recommends 1024 bits for the CSR. Click Next.

8. Enter the organization and the organizational unit. Normally, the organization will be the company name, and the organizational unit will be the department or division. Click Next.

9. In the Common Name field, enter the common Name. This will be the fully qualified domain name for the server as it will be accessed from the Internet. Click Next.

10. Enter the county/region, state/province, and city/locality information as discussed earlier in this chapter. Click Next.

11. From the drop-down list box, select the name of the certificate server on the network, and click Next to open the Summary screen.

12. Verify that everything is entered properly, click Next, and then click Finish.

At this point, the server generated the request, received the certificate, and installed it all at the same time. Using the online CA really saves many steps and completely eliminates the process of cutting and pasting the CSR.

Renewing Private Issued Certificates

Renewing certificates with a private CA is easier than renewing public certificates. To renew private certificates, though, you must first install the Certificates MMC snap-in. In Exercise 6.6, we'll install the Certificates snap-in.

EXERCISE 6.6

Installing the Certificates Snap-In

This exercise will create an MMC console to manage certificates.

1. Choose Start ➢ Run to open the Run dialog box.

2. In the Open box, enter **MMC** and press Enter to open the MMC console.

3. Choose Console ➢ Add/Remove Snap-In to open the Add/Remove Snap-In window.

4. In the Add/Remove Snap-in window, click on Add down at the bottom.

5. In the list of snap-ins, select Certificates, and then click Add.

6. Since, in this chapter, the certificates are to be used for SSL, click the Computer Account button, and then click Finish.

7. Click Close to close the list of snap-ins.

8. Click OK to close the Add/Remove Snap-In window.

9. Choose Console ➢ Save As to open the Save As dialog box.

10. Enter the location and the filename for this MMC. We would recommend saving it either to the Desktop or to the Administrative Tools group.

Now that you have an MMC console with the Certificates snap-in, you're ready for the next step. In Exercise 6.7, we'll renew a private certificate.

EXERCISE 6.7

Renewing a Private Certificate

This exercise walks you through the steps of renewing a private certificate.

1. Start the Certificates MMC.

2. Right-click Certificates in the MMC, and choose Connect To Another Computer from the shortcut menu. Connect to the computer on which you installed the SSL certificate.

3. In the console tree, expand Personal, and then click Certificates to display the installed certificates.

4. In the pane on the right, select the certificate that you want to renew.

5. Choose Action ➤ All Tasks ➤ Renew Certificate With Same Key to start the Certificate Renewal Wizard. (Renew Certificate With New Key is actually recommended in most cases. After using the same key for a long time, it is a good idea to get a new key to reduce the risk of compromise. Both the Same Key and New Key renewal options are processed the exact same way.

6. Select Certificate Template if it is not already selected, and click Next to open the Certificate Friendly Name And Description screen.

7. Enter a Friendly Name and some Description information so that you can refer to the certificate better within the MMC console. Click Next, and then click Finish.

Configuring SSL to Secure Communications Channels

So far in this chapter, we have discussed how to get certificates from both public and private certificate authorities, and we have looked at the basics of how to install a certificate on a web server and how to renew a certificate. It is time to fill in the blanks a little in this section of the chapter. Although we may have shown how to install the SSL certificate on the web server, we never really showed how to use it. In this section, we will show how to use the certificate for a web server, and we will also show how to use certificates for traffic between the web server and the SQL server, between client systems and Active Directory domain controllers, and between client systems and e-mail servers.

Using SSL to Secure a Client Machine to Web Server Traffic

As you saw in the previous exercises, installing SSL on IIS 5.0 is really not difficult. Refer to Exercise 6.2 for the details. After a little practice, obtaining and installing the SSL certificate are both fairly straightforward processes.

SSL on IIS 5 can provide an extremely secure platform for secure commerce or for applications that use highly confidential information. The client system and the secure web server can transfer information back and forth in an encrypted form that is extremely difficult to decrypt unless you have the proper keys. Usually, we use SSL to protect our customers and their data while it travels the Internet and to protect our business interests.

Now that you have installed the SSL certificate on your web server, how do you use it? Well, that is the easy part. After completing Exercises 6.1 and 6.2, you have a secured web server.

Before installing SSL, you should have done some testing to make sure your IIS 5 server worked properly. If you did that, you might have created a test page and then verified that it worked by using a web browser on your network. Entering the address of your server as `http://testserver` and then pressing Enter sets the page up as the default page, as shown in Figure 6.3.

FIGURE 6.3   A standard web page

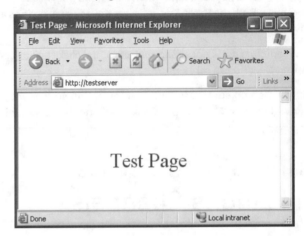

OK, this page is pretty bare, but it is only being used here to illustrate the difference between a standard web page and an SSL secured web page. After you install your certificate, SSL is available. So, simply changing the address in the browser to `https://testserver` will give you a page that looks like that in Figure 6.4.

FIGURE 6.4   An SSL web page

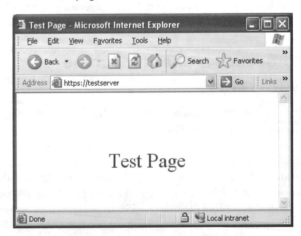

Notice that using `https://` instead of `http://` provided the cue from the browser to the web server that we wanted our page encrypted. You can see that it is properly encrypted by checking for the lock icon in the Status Bar in Internet Explorer. You can double-click the lock to display the certificate itself, and you can see which CA issued the certificate, the valid dates for the certificate, and many other details. There is a problem with this default IIS configuration, though. The browser can access the page regardless of whether it is using SSL. For secure websites, you really should force the browser to connect only using SSL. You can force this behavior by making a configuration change in IIS, which is what we'll do in Exercise 6.8.

EXERCISE 6.8

Enforcing SSL on IIS 5

In this exercise, we will configure IIS 5 so that any browser connections to the website on which the SSL certificate has been installed must use SSL.

1. On your web server, run the IIS MMC snap-in. Choose Start ➢ Programs ➢ Administrative Tools ➢ Internet Services Manager to start the console.

2. Right-click the website on which you want to install the certificate, and then choose Properties from the shortcut menu to open the Properties dialog box for the website.

3. Click the Directory Security tab, and then click the Edit button in the Secure Communications section to open the Secure Communications dialog box.

4. Click the Require Secure Channel (SSL) check box, as shown here, and click the Require 128-Bit Encryption check box if you want to enforce 128-bit encryption. Then click OK on all the boxes until the Properties page is closed.

Making this change in Exercise 6.8 will not impact the use of the `https://` address. However, now if you type **http://testserver** in your web browser, you will not get the test page. Instead, you will receive an HTTP 403.4 error page which says that this page is only accessible using SSL and that you need to use `https://` to access it, as shown in Figure 6.5.

FIGURE 6.5   The HTTP 403.4 error page

With SSL enforced on your sites, you can rest assured that your customers and their data as well as your business are secure from prying eyes. SSL encryption of 128 bits is strong and will do a great job of encrypting the traffic between a web client and an IIS 5.0 server with SSL configured properly. All traffic from the browser to the web server will now use port 443, the default port for HTTPS traffic, instead of port 80, the default port for HTTP traffic.

Using SSL to Secure Web Server to SQL Server Traffic

The ability to use SSL to secure SQL is new to SQL Server 2000. Installing and properly configuring it can be a problem because there are no wizards for this process, and there is no way to identify which connections are encrypted (Windows connections are not encrypted). So, this erodes some of the comfort level associated with using SSL and SQL. To verify that SSL is properly working, after the installation and configuration, you will likely need to use a packet sniffer of some kind to capture some transactions and then look at them.

The process involves some high-level steps with lots of little steps in between. Let's start with the high-level steps.

1.   Install a certificate on your SQL server.

2. Configure encryption for either every SQL client attaching to the server or for the client so that uses encryption when it connects to any SQL server.

3. Test.

Now, Steps 1 and 2 are much more in depth than just a couple of lines. You will need a SQL database administrator to assist you with getting this working in a lab or production environment.

Installing a Certificate on a SQL Server

To install the certificate on the SQL server, you will need to use the Certificate MMC Snap-in that we used earlier in this chapter to renew certificates. On the SQL server itself, install the MMC Snap-in as we did in Exercise 6.6. You will use the Snap-in to manage certificates for the computer account. Once the Certificate MMC is ready, open it, and verify that you are connected to your computer (the SQL server). You are now ready for Exercise 6.9.

 This process cannot be used for a SQL cluster, and it is only supported for SQL Server 2000.

EXERCISE 6.9

Install a Certificate on a SQL Server

We will install a certificate on a SQL Server 2000 server in this exercise to support encryption of SQL data between a web server and the SQL server.

1. Open the Certificate MMC.

2. Right-click the Personal folder, and choose All Tasks ➢ Request New Certificate to start the Certificate Wizard.

3. Once the Certificate Wizard opens, click Next, and verify that the Certificate Type Of Computer is selected. Click Next.

4. In the Friendly Name box and the Description, you will want to fill in information to make it easy to remember what the certificate is being used for once it is properly installed. Click Next to open the Summary screen.

5. Verify the information and click Finish.

6. Restart the MSSQLServer (SQL Server) service, click the Force Protocol Encryption check box, and then click OK if you want all SQL connections to the SQL Server server encrypted. If you want only the IIS server to connect using encryption, skip this step.

Notice that there is nothing really special about this certificate that distinguishes it from any other computer certificate. This same process can be used on any computer to install a computer certificate for a variety of uses. The real key to this exercise is Step 7 in which the Force Protocol

Encryption option is enabled. This option forces the traffic to the SQL server to be encrypted; if it is not encrypted, the request will fail. You can choose to encrypt only the web server connections and unencrpyt all other SQL connections. To encrypt only the IIS server connections, you need to configure the encryption for a specific client. If you want all connections to the SQL server encrypted, skip configuring encryption for a specific client and go right into testing.

Configuring Encryption for a Specific Client

OK, the SQL server is ready. Now you can configure the IIS server to use encryption when connecting to the SQL server. In order for the client system (the IIS server) to initiate the SSL encryption, it must trust the SQL server's certificate. To trust the SQL server's certificate, the CA must be on the Trusted Root Certification Authorities list on the IIS server. In Exercise 6.10, we'll add a CA to the Trusted Root Certification Authorities list.

EXERCISE 6.10

Adding a CA to the Trusted Root Certification Authorities List

In this exercise, we'll use the Certificates MMC Snap-in to export the SQL server's certificate Trusted Root Certificate Authority and then import this information into the IIS server.

1. Using the MMC console created on the SQL server in Exercise 6.9, open the Certificate Snap-in.

2. Select the Personal folder to expose the certificates.

3. Right-click the certificate name, and then choose Open from the shortcut menu to open the dialog box.

4. Click on the Certification Path tab. Note the name at the highest level of the path. This is the root CA. Click OK.

5. In the Certificate MMC, double-click the Trusted Root Certification Authorities folder to expand it, and then click Certificates.

6. In the right pane, scroll down the list of CAs until you find the one that was at the top of the Certification Path in Step 4.

7. Right-click the CA, and choose All Tasks ➢ Export to start the Certification Export Wizard.

8. At the Welcome screen, click Next.

9. The DER Encoded Binary X.509 (.CER) is selected by default. Click Next.

10. Enter the filename and location. It is a good idea to put this on a common file server since this location will later be used by the IIS server. Click Next to open the Summary screen.

11. Click Finish to complete the export process. Click OK when the confirmation message appears.

12. On the IIS server, create an MMC console with the Certificates Snap-in as we did in Exercise 6.6. Open the Certificates Snap-in when completed.

---

13. Right-click the Trusted Root Certification Authorities folder, and choose All Tasks ≻ Import to open.

14. Click the Browse button to find the file, or manually enter the location of the exported `.cer` file created in Step 10. Click Next.

15. Verify that the Place All Certificates In The Following Store radio button is selected and click Next.

16. Click Finish to complete the import process.

Now that the IIS server trusts the SQL server's certificate, it can establish an SSL connection to it. To complete the process for setting up the IIS server encrypted connection, you must use the SQL Server Client Network Utility. In this tool, enable the Force Protocol Encryption option, which will require all SQL traffic from the IIS server to the SQL server to be encrypted.

 Encryption can be enforced either at the client or at the SQL server. Trying to enforce encryption at both ends will cause it to fail.

Testing the Connection Encryption

Since we are not using a Web browser to pass the SQL data and requests, we can't look for that little lock icon to confirm that security is working. To test the IIS server connection, you can either use the Query Analyzer tool or an ODBC (Open Database Connectivity) application. To use an ODBC application, you must be able to change the connection string.

To use the Query Analyzer, you connect to the SQL server and run a simple query against it. If the Force Protocol Encryption option is properly set up, the SQL requests and responses will be encrypted. You can verify this using the Microsoft Network Monitor on either the IIS server or the SQL server. You can also verify by using any other packet sniffer to monitor the traffic between the two systems.

To use an ODBC application, you will need to modify the connection strings. Once the connection strings are modified, you can then test the connection by using Microsoft Network Monitor on either system or by using a packet sniffer to verify that the data is encrypted.

For ODBC, modify the connection string so that it looks like this:

```
Driver=SQLServer;Server=ServerNameHere;UID=UserIdHere;PWD=PasswordHere;
↳Network=DBNETLIB.DLL;Encrypt=YES
```

This will enable encryption from the client system for ODBC. For OLEDB, you will need to modify the configuration so that it looks like this:

```
Provider=SQLOLEDB.1;Integrated Security=SSPI;Persist Security Info=
↳False;Initial Catalog=dbNameHere;Data Source=ServerNameHere;Use Encryption
↳for Data=True
```

One of the main problems with encrypting the SQL communications between systems is not being absolutely sure that they are encrypted and that you did it right. The only way to tell for sure is to use some kind of packet analyzer or sniffer and look at the packets. This can be a pain for many people, but it is a good idea to become familiar with these tools for security purposes.

Using SSL to Secure Client Machine to Active Directory Domain Controller Traffic

One of the big concerns with Windows NT and Windows 2000 is the way that hackers can capture packets during the logon process and then use brute force to get the user names and passwords for user accounts. In security, it is important that we not give information to potential intruders. This information can easily be used against our systems. For example, to log in to the network, you need a user name and its associated password. With Active Directory and the *Lightweight Directory Access Protocol (LDAP)* used in Windows 2000, it can be fairly easy to get user information. So, this section will address what we need to do to secure LDAP traffic between the client systems and the Active Directory domain controllers in the network using SSL. Once SSL is configured, this traffic can be encrypted and properly protected.

Configuring SSL for Active Directory Domain Controllers

To install SSL for protecting LDAP requires installing certificates on all the Active Directory domain controllers. You must take a few steps make it all happen:

1. Install an Enterprise Certificate Authority on one of the Windows 2000 domain controllers.

2. Configure Group Policy Objects for the Domain Controllers Organizational Unit to automatically receive certificates.

3. Configure the client systems.

Installing an Enterprise Certificate Authority is discussed in Chapter 9, so we won't cover that information here. Once the CA is installed, though, you need to set up the rest of the domain controllers. Exercise 6.11 walks you through this configuration.

EXERCISE 6.11

Configuring GPO for Automated Certificate Distribution for Domain Controllers

In this exercise, we will set up the Group Policy Object (GPO) for the Domain Controllers Organizational Unit to distribute certificates to the domain controllers.

1. On an Active Directory domain controller, open the Active Directory Users And Computers MMC Snap-in by choosing Start ➤ Programs ➤ Administrative Tools ➤ Active Directory Users And Computers.

2. Right-click Domain Controllers and choose Properties from the shortcut menu to open the Default Domain Controller policy. Click the Group Policy tab, and then click Edit to open the default GPO.

3. Choose Computer Configuration ➤ Windows Settings ➤ Security Settings ➤ Public Key Policies to expand the policy.

4. Right-click Automatic Certificate Request Settings (as shown here) and choose New ➤ Automatic Certificate Request Wizard to start the Automatic Certificate Request Wizard.

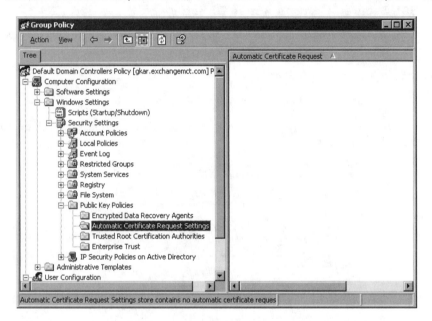

5. At the Welcome screen, click Next to open the Certificate Template screen.

6. Select Domain Controller, and then click Next.

7. Verify that the certificate authority is selected. Click Next and then click Finish to complete the wizard.

Testing SSL for Active Directory Domain Controllers

You can test for SSL security over LDAP by using the Address Book. Since the certificates were installed using the Domain Controller Organizational Unit GPO, all domain controllers will automatically install a certificate. Once the certificates are installed, the domain controllers will communicate over port 389 for standard LDAP or port 636 for SSL encrypted LDAP.

The Address Book is the default search client for Windows 2000 and Internet Explorer 5 and later. It uses LDAP to connect to a domain controller, and it can be configured to use secure LDAP. This process will work with Windows 2000 running IE 5 or later. In Exercise 6.12, we'll test SSL secured LDAP to Active Directory.

Windows 95 and Windows 98 clients with IE 5 are considered down-level clients and will not function like Windows 2000. See q238007 for instructions for down-level clients.

EXERCISE 6.12

Testing SSL Secured LDAP to Active Directory

In this exercise, we'll test the connection between a Windows 2000 client and an Active Directory domain controller.

1. Choose Start ≻ Search ≻ For People.

2. In the Look In drop-down list box, select Active Directory.

3. Right-click Active Directory (while this may look odd, it will work), and choose Properties from the shortcut menu to open the Active Directory Properties dialog box:

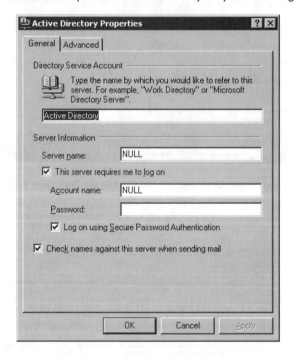

4. In the Server Name box, enter the domain controller's server name This must be the fully qualified domain name such as *servername.domainname*.com.

5. Leave the account name and password fields alone, unless you have set up special security on searching Active Directory. If Active Directory is set up so that only certain users or accounts have access, enter a user name and password. Make sure to enter the user name with the NetBIOS name of the domain such as domainname\username.

6. Click the Advanced tab.

7. In the Directory Service (LDAP) box, enter **636** (the secure LDAP port number).

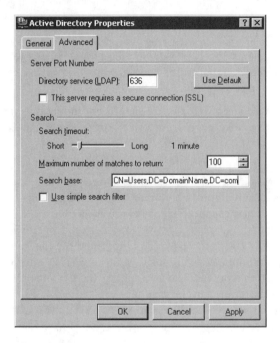

8. In the Search Base box, enter the Active Directory container to be used, such as, CN=Users,DC=domainname,DC=com, and then click OK.

9. In the Name box of the Find People dialog box, enter a user name such as Administrator.

Assuming that everything worked correctly, Step 9 will provide the results of the search you requested, using port 636.

Using SSL to Secure Client Machine to E-Mail Server Traffic

Exchange 2000 uses *Transport Layer Security (TLS)* protocol, which is a protocol based on SSL that is completely compatible with SSL. Enabling TLS in Exchange 2000 is the same thing as implementing SSL. When discussing SSL and Exchange 2000, the terms can be used interchangeably. For the sake of consistency, we will use SSL in this section, although we may use TLS along with it to remind you that they are one and the same thing in our discussions regarding SMTP (Simple Mail Transport Protocol) and encryption of SMTP traffic.

Securing e-mail through Exchange Server 2000 can be complicated. You need to secure the download of e-mail from the server to the client system, and you also need to secure the uploaded e-mail from the client system to the server. Think of e-mail as two completely different and distinct processes; one is receiving e-mail from the server and getting it to the client system, and the other is sending e-mail from the client system through the server to its final destination.

To send e-mail from the client system through the server and out to its final destination, you can use three methods:

MAPI   Microsoft's Messaging Application Programming Interface will get e-mail to and from client systems within the Exchange environment, but to send e-mail outside the company, you will need to use SMTP.

SMTP   Simple Mail Transport Protocol is the standard for e-mail between mail servers on the Internet. All standard Internet e-mail traffic between e-mail servers uses SMTP whether it is on the sending side or the receiving side.

OWA   Outlook Web Access is a web based e-mail client that allows the user to send and receive e-mail using the Exchange server from a web browser without needing any other e-mail client software installed on it.

MAPI is primarily used with the Outlook client or one of the older mail clients such as the Exchange clients that shipped with previous versions of Exchange Server. MAPI is not an Internet protocol in that you will probably never send MAPI messages from one system on the Internet to another except through VPN (virtual private network) tunnels. The main problem with securing SMTP is that the systems on the other side (the ones getting our mail and sending mail to us) all expect SMTP traffic to be sent and received using the standard process, which does not include SSL encryption. We will look at securing SMTP using SSL and show how to do it while still being able to send and receive e-mail to and from the rest of the world on the Internet. OWA will also be covered in this chapter.

To receive e-mail from the server to the client, we use MAPI, OWA, and the following two methods:

IMAP4   Internet Messaging Access Protocol version 4 is one of two common Internet standards for pulling e-mail from an e-mail server down to a client machine where it can be read and archived.

POP3   Post Office Protocol version 3 is the other of the two common Internet standards for pulling e-mail from an e-mail server down to a client machine where it can be read and archived.

Again, MAPI is primarily used with the Outlook client or one of the older mail clients such as the Exchange clients that shipped with previous versions of Exchange Server. MAPI is not an Internet protocol in that you will probably never send MAPI messages from one system on the Internet to another. IMAP4 and POP3 are both protocols used to pull e-mail off of the e-mail server and bring it down to the client system where it can be read using a client application that supports these particular protocols. What is important to remember with IMAP4 and POP3 is that the client application that uses either of these protocols must also use SMTP in order to send new e-mail out to or to respond to previously received e-mail. OWA is the web client that allows us to connect to the Exchange server and access our e-mail through a web browser. It is a nice, lightweight client that uses HTTP for reading and sending e-mail. You do not use SSL with MAPI, so we will not discuss it here. However, you can use SSL with IMAP4, POP3, and OWA, so we will go over the process to secure each of these methods. Figure 6.6 shows and explains the various methods.

FIGURE 6.6   Internet e-mail Methods

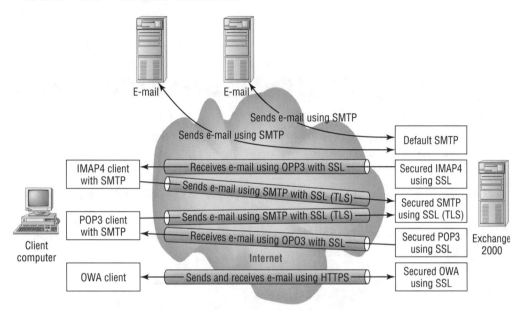

On Exchange Server are several *virtual servers* that are used to process messages. Exchange can have multiple virtual servers supporting multiple instances of each protocol as needed. In Figure 6.6, you can see that the Exchange 2000 server on the right has a Default SMTP virtual server and a Secured SMTP virtual server. Each of these secured virtual servers will be discussed in more detail in this chapter. However, you might want to mark the page for Figure 6.6 so that you can look back on occasion as we discuss each of the protocols and how to secure them. The ultimate goal is that your environment will look like Figure 6.6 in which our Exchange server is able to communicate with external e-mail servers of all types using standard SMTP on port 25, yet is also able to communicate with external e-mail clients that are accessing their e-mail on the Exchange server using IMAP4 and POP3 clients with SMTP through encrypted connections using port 465.

Securing SMTP

As we discussed earlier, securing SMTP can be problematic. Mostly because we need to protect our SMTP server from being used as a relay for spammers on the Internet. Therefore, we set up SMTP authentication for who can send e-mail, and we allow others to send us e-mail as anonymous users. When configuring SMTP security, the default SMTP virtual server is used as our Internet mail connector from the Exchange server to and from the rest of the Internet. This SMTP virtual server connects to remote Internet domains to deliver and receive messages to and from external organizations. This becomes a problem because we don't want others on the Internet to be able to see the e-mail being downloaded from the Exchange server by client systems on the Internet. To protect against that, we configure authentication or set up encryption for our POP3 and IMAP4 clients. This problem becomes even bigger though. If we make these changes, the inbound sessions from SMTP servers outside our location will be affected. We need to properly secure SMTP in order to support IMAP4 and POP3 clients too. To secure SMTP client access and avoid open relays that can be abused, you must first create a new SMTP virtual server to use with inbound client connections.

In Exercise 6.13 we'll go through the steps to properly secure SMTP using SSL.

EXERCISE 6.13

Creating a Dedicated SMTP Virtual Server

In this exercise, we will create a new virtual server on our Exchange 2000 server to be used for dedicated external IMAP4 and POP3 clients. We will use this virtual server in the next exercise and implement SSL encryption.

1. On the Exchange server, or on a system with the proper Exchange 2000 client tools, choose Start ➤ Programs ➤ Microsoft Exchange ➤ System Manager to open the System Manager.

2. Expand the Servers object, select the server to be used if you have more than one, expand Protocols, and then expand SMTP as shown here.

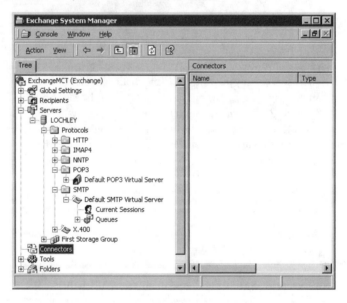

3. Right-click the SMTP folder and choose New ➤ SMTP Virtual Server.

4. Enter a name for this virtual server, something like Secure Server, and then click Next.

5. Select the IP address to use and click Finish. A dedicated IP address is required for this virtual server that is different from the one used for the default SMTP virtual server.

Now that you have an SMTP virtual server on the Exchange server, you can start configuring it. The nice thing about having these two SMTP virtual servers, the default and the new one, is that all normal e-mail can still continue processing. We have not changed that in any way. However, it is a good idea to test SMTP before continuing by sending and receiving a few e-mails. The next step, after you test the current configuration, is to install SSL. In Exercise 6.14, we will secure SMTP on Exchange 2000 Server.

 For the purpose of the following exercise, and several others in this chapter, we will use a private certificate from an internal CA. Generally, you will want to use a certificate from a public CA for external resources such as the Exchange server so that all external clients will automatically have the appropriate entries in their Trusted Root Certification Authorities list. We will use private certificates in these exercises so that you can also use private certificates.

EXERCISE 6.14

Securing SMTP on Exchange 2000 Server

In this exercise, we will install and configure SSL on the SMTP virtual server created in Exercise 6.13.

1. Choose Start ➢ Programs ➢ Microsoft Exchange ➢ System Manager to open the System Manager.

2. Expand the Servers object, select the server to be used if you have more than one, expand Protocols, and expand SMTP.

3. Right-click Secure Server (our new virtual SMTP server) and choose Properties.

4. Click the Access Tab, and then click Certificate in the Secure Communication section to start the Certificate Wizard.

5. At the Welcome screen, click Next to start the wizard and verify that the Create A New Certificate radio button is selected. Click Next.

6. Click the Send The Request Immediately To An Online Certificate Authority radio button, and then click Next.

7. Enter the name of the certificate, and set the bit length. The preference is 1024 bits. Click Next.

8. Enter the organization and the organizational unit. Normally, the organization will be the company name, and the organizational unit will be the department or division. Click Next.

9. Enter the common name. This will be the fully qualified domain name for the server as it will be accessed from the Internet. Click Next.

10. Enter the county/region, state/province, and city/locality information as discussed earlier in this chapter. Click Next.

11. In the drop-down list box, select the certificate server to be used. Click Next to open the Summary screen.

EXERCISE 6.14 *(continued)*

12. Verify that the information is correct, click Next, and then click Finish to complete acquisition of the certificate for the SMTP virtual server.

13. Click the Communications button on the Access tab in the Secure Communications section to open the dialog box.

14. Check the Require Secure Channel check box and the Require 128-Bit Encryption check box, and then click OK.

15. Stop and restart the Secure Server SMTP Virtual Server.

Configuring SMTP with SSL is only part of the solution. As previously stated, SMTP is the sending side of the e-mail client. Now, we need to address the receiving side of the e-mail client.

Securing IMAP4

Many companies set up IMAP4 for their external e-mail users who want to use Outlook or Outlook Express from home to read and respond to their e-mail. Using IMAP4, you don't have to worry about users dumping their entire e-mail from the e-mail server to their local client, which can happen with POP3 if it isn't set up correctly. IMAP4 is a good protocol to use externally because it will not remove e-mail from the server except when it is normally deleted from the server.

The main problem with using IMAP4 to download e-mail to an external e-mail client is that the messages travel in the clear. This means that the e-mail and all its contents, including attachments, can be captured off the Internet and viewed by a potential hacker. To prevent this, you need to use SSL to secure IMAP4. Exercise 6.15 walks you through the process of securing IMAP4 on the Exchange 2000 e-mail server.

In many of these exercises, we have been creating new certificates. In reality, we can use the Assign An Existing Certificate radio button and then select one of the certificates that we have already acquired and use it to secure the virtual server. We recommend using a new certificate for each virtual server because each service is not dependent on the same certificate in the event the certificate is compromised.

EXERCISE 6.15

Securing IMAP4 on Exchange 2000 Server

In this exercise, we will install the certificate for IMAP4 and configure Exchange Server to support secure IMAP4 connections from external clients.

1. On the Exchange server, or a system with the proper Exchange 2000 client tools, choose Start ➤ Programs ➤ Microsoft Exchange ➤ System Manager to open the System Manager.

2. Expand the Servers object, select the server to be used if you have more than one, expand Protocols, and expand IMAP4.

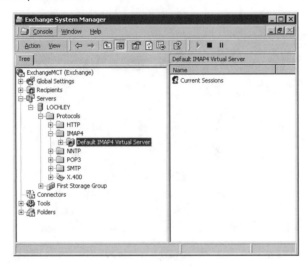

3. Right-click Default IMAP4 Virtual Server, and choose Properties from the shortcut menu to open the Properties dialog box.

4. Click the Access tab, and then click the Certificate button in the Secure Communication section to start the Certificate Wizard that we have used several times in this chapter already. Click Next.

5. Verify that the Create A New Certificate radio button is selected, and then click Next.

6. Click the Send The Request Immediately To An Online Certificate Authority radio button, and then click Next.

7. Enter the name of the certificate, and set the bit length. The preference is 1024 bits. Click Next.

8. Enter the organization and the organizational unit. Normally, the organization will be the company name, and the organizational unit will be the department or division. Click Next.

9. Enter the common name. This will be the fully qualified domain name for the server as it will be accessed from the Internet. Click Next.

10. Enter the county/region, state/province, and city/locality information as discussed earlier in this chapter. Click Next.

11. In the drop-down list box, select the certificate server to be used and then click Next to open the Summary screen.

12. Verify the information, click Next, and then click Finish to complete acquisition of the certificate for the IMAP4 virtual server.

13. On the Access tab, click the Communication button in the Secure Communication section to open the Security dialog box.

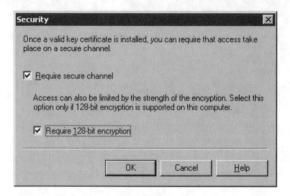

14. Check the Require Secure Channel check box and the Require 128-Bit Encryption check box to use the most secure setting, and then click OK.

15. Click the General tab and verify that the IP address is the same one that you used in Exercise 6.13 for the new virtual SMTP server. If it isn't, select the proper IP address from the drop-down list box, and then click OK.

16. Stop and Restart the IMAP4 virtual server to make the setting take effect.

Configuring IMAP4 for the Exchange server is now complete. We will test this, along with the SMTP and POP3 configurations shortly. With IMAP4 and SMTP properly secured, you can now safely connect client e-mail applications from the Internet and not have to worry about anyone capturing your e-mail and reading it. Next, let's look at how to secure POP3 using SSL.

Securing POP3

Many companies set up POP3 for their external e-mail users that want to use Outlook or Outlook Express from home to read and respond to their e-mail. Using POP3, though, you need to be careful in configuring the e-mail client so that it does not download all of your e-mail from the e-mail server. If you are not careful, the next time the user is in the office, they will find an empty e-mail box and may then ask for it to be restored from tape.

Just like IMAP4, the main problem with using POP3 to download e-mail to an external e-mail client is that the messages travel in the clear. This means that the e-mail and all its contents, including attachments, can be captured off the Internet and viewed by a potential hacker. To prevent this, you need to use SSL to secure POP3 from these unintended viewers. Exercise 6.16 walks through the process of securing POP3 on the Exchange 2000 e-mail server.

EXERCISE 6.16

Securing POP3 on Exchange 2000 Server

In this exercise, we will install the certificate for POP3 and configure the Exchange server to support secure POP3 connections from external clients.

1. On the Exchange server, or on a system with the proper Exchange 2000 client tools, choose Start ➢ Programs ➢ Microsoft Exchange ➢ System Manager to open the System Manager.

2. Expand the Servers object, select the server to be used if you have more than one, expand Protocols, and then expand POP3.

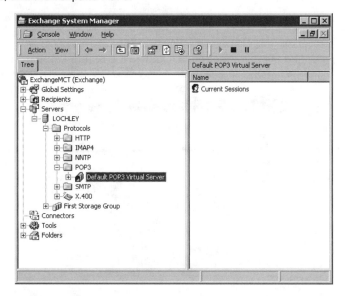

3. Right-click Default POP3 Virtual Server, and choose Properties from the shortcut menu to open the Properties dialog box.

4. Click on the Access tab, and then click the Certificate button in the Secure Communication section to start the Certificate Wizard that we have used several times in this chapter already. Click Next.

5. Verify that the Create A New Certificate radio button is selected, and then click Next.

6. Click the Send The Request Immediately To An Online Certificate Authority radio button, and then click Next.

7. Enter the name of the certificate, and set the bit length. The preference is 1024 bits. Click Next.

8. Enter the organization and the organizational unit. Normally, the organization will be the company name, and the organizational unit will be the department or division. Click Next.

9. Enter the common name. This will be the fully qualified domain name for the server as it will be accessed from the Internet. Click Next.

10. Enter the county/region, state/province, and city/locality information as discussed earlier in this chapter. Click Next.

11. In the drop-down list box, select the certificate server to be used, and then click Next to open the Summary screen.

12. Verify the information as correct, click Next, and then click Finish to complete acquisition of the certificate for the POP3 virtual server.

13. On the Access tab, click the Communication button in the Secure Communication section to open the Security dialog box.

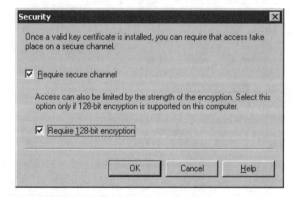

14. Check the Require Secure Channel check box and the Require 128-Bit Encryption check box, to use the most secure setting, and then click OK.

15. Click on the General tab, and verify that the IP address is the same one that you used in Exercise 6.13 for the new virtual SMTP server. If it isn't, select the proper IP address from the drop-down list box, and then click OK.

16. Stop and restart the POP3 virtual server to make the setting take effect.

At this point, configuring POP3 for the Exchange server is now complete. We will test this, along with the SMTP and IMAP4 configurations right now. With IMAP4, POP3, and SMTP properly secured, we can now safely connect client e-mail applications from the Internet using either of the two protocols for reading e-mail and SMTP to send e-mail and not have to worry about anyone capturing our e-mail and reading it.

Setting Up and Testing Secured IMAP4, POP3, and SMTP with Outlook Express

Going through all of these options and configurations can be tiresome, but now we can actually see them all work. So, let's dive right in with Exercise 6.17 and set up Outlook Express to test our configurations.

 To test IMAP and POP3, you will have to create the account for one, delete it, and create the account again using the other.

EXERCISE 6.17

Testing Secure E-Mail with Outlook Express

In this exercise, we will set up Outlook Express to connect to the Exchange server using the new secured virtual SMTP server and the secured IMAP4 and POP3 virtual servers.

1. Choose Start ➢ Programs ➢ Outlook Express to start Outlook Express.

2. Choose Tools ➢ Accounts to open the Internet Accounts dialog box.

3. Choose Add ➢ Mail to start the Internet Connection Wizard.

4. In the Display Name box, enter your display name, which is generally your full name, and then click Next to open the Internet E-Mail Address screen.

5. In the E-Mail Address box, enter the e-mail address that you want others to use to send you e-mail. This is the address that will be in your e-mails sent out to the Internet that others will use for their reply e-mails. Click Next to open the E-Mail Server Names screen.

6. From the My Incoming Mail Server Is drop-down list box, select IMAP or POP3, depending on which one you want to test. In the Incoming Mail (POP3, IMAP, or HTTP) Server box enter the IP address of the virtual IMAP4/POP3 server, which should be the same as the secured SMTP virtual server IP address used in Exercise 6.13. In the Outgoing Mail (SMTP) Server box, enter the same IP address as for the Incoming Mail Server. Click Next to open the Internet Mail Logon screen.

7. Enter the account name and password for the e-mail box that you want to access using Outlook Express. Check the Remember Password box, unless you want to enter your password every time you access Outlook Express. Click Next, and then click Finish.

8. In the Internet Accounts dialog box, click the Mail tab, click the account with the IP address of your secure SMTP virtual server, and then click Properties to open the Properties dialog box for that IP address.

9. Click the Servers tab.

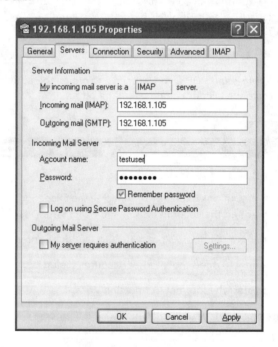

10. Check the My Server Requires Authentication check box, and then click Settings to open the dialog box.

11. Verify that the Use Same Settings As The Incoming Mail Server radio button is selected, and then click OK.

12. Back in the Properties dialog box, click the Advanced tab. You use the options on this tab to set up Outlook Express to use the secure virtual servers. Make sure the This Server Requires A Secure Connection (SSL) box is checked for both the Outgoing Mail (SMTP) and the Incoming Mail (IMAP) as shown here. (IMAP4 is on the left, and POP3 is on the right.)

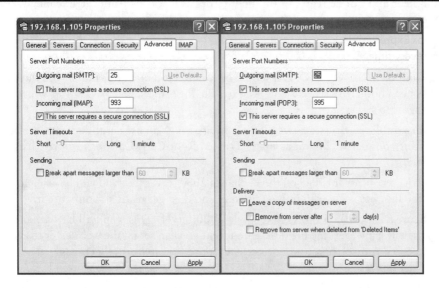

13. Click OK to close the Properties dialog box, and then click Close to close the dialog box.

14. In the Would You Like To Download Folders From The Mail Server You Added? dialog box, click Yes.

15. After the folders download, which should only take a minute or less, click OK. If you chose POP3, you can skip this step.

16. In Outlook Express, find the new mail account on the left, and expand it, if necessary. Click the Inbox, and you should see it start to fill with any messages that might be on the Exchange server for the mailbox used. Using a packet sniffer such as Microsoft Network Monitor, you can verify that these messages are being downloaded securely.

17. To test the ability to send using the secure SMTP virtual server, click Create Mail and create a test message. Again, you can test whether it is sent encrypted by using a packet sniffer.

For POP3 accounts, you will probably want to check the Leave A Copy Of Messages On Server box. If you do not check this box, Outlook Express downloads all the e-mail from your Exchange mailbox and removes the e-mail from the server. The e-mail box on the server will be empty if you do not check this box.

At this point, you can be confident that external e-mail users can connect to the secure virtual servers on the Exchange server for safe e-mail. With SSL encryption between the e-mail client and the e-mail server, nobody will be able to read the messages going back and forth between these two systems. However, you need to remember that if the e-mail is going out to another e-mail server on the Internet for its final destination, it will eventually end up going out in the clear and can be read out on the Internet as it travels from the Exchange server to other e-mail servers.

Securing Outlook Web Access

Securing Outlook Web Access (OWA) should be easy for you now. After all, if you think about it, OWA is just another IIS server. You need to take the same steps for OWA as you would for any other web server:

1. Obtain a public certificate as we did in Exercise 6.1. You use a public certificate because you want your certificate on as many Trusted Root Certification Authority lists as possible.

2. Install the certificate for IIS 5 on the Exchange 2000 server that you will be using for OWA from the Internet, as we did in Exercise 6.2, and then get ready to configure it.

3. Configure SSL for IIS 5 on the Exchange 2000 server. This step will be similar to Exercise 6.8. However, the big difference is that you can set up the web server to encrypt only the OWA directory, and not use encryption for any other web pages that may be on the server.

4. Test the configuration.

What makes configuring OWA different from configuring any other web server is that you may not have any other sites or directories on the IIS 5 server on the Exchange 2000 server that need encryption. In Exercise 6.18, we'll secure OWA.

 **Real World Scenario**

Secure E-Mail Required

Let's say you are the network administrator for a large banking organization with branches around the United States and that you use Exchange 2000 Server for your e-mail system.

You just acquired another bank. As part of this acquisition, you need to provide e-mail accounts for the new users at the new bank without installing an e-mail server at their location. The e-mail must be accessible from their location, and it must be secured using SSL. You do not have people to send to the bank to set up the client computers.

You could use the processes discussed in this section of the chapter to configure secure SMTP and secure IMAP4 to your Exchange 2000 server. You could then set up all the users on your current e-mail system and give them all directions on how to set up Outlook Express. However, a quicker solution is to have them use OWA and their web browsers as an e-mail client and secure OWA using SSL.

EXERCISE 6.18

Securing OWA

In this exercise, we will set up OWA so that any connections to it will be encrypted using SSL. This exercise assumes that you have already obtained and installed a certificate for IIS 5 on the Exchange server. If you want, you can do this exercise using a private CA and a private certificate.

1. On your web server, run the Internet Services Manager MMC Snap-in. Choose Start ➤ Programs ➤ Administrative Tools ➤ Internet Services Manager to start the console.

2. Double-click Default Web Site to expand it.

3. Right-click the directory, Exchange, as shown here, and choose Properties from the shortcut menu to open the Properties dialog box.

4. Click the Directory Security tab, and then click the Edit button in the Secure Communications section to open the Secure Communications dialog box.

5. Click the Require Secure Channel (SSL) check box, and click the Require 128-Bit Encryption check box if you want to enforce 128-bit encryption.

6. Click OK to close the Secure Communications dialog box, and then click OK again to close the Properties dialog box.

To test the configuration, open Internet Explorer and go to https://*servername*/exchange. The web browser will request a log on if you are not already logged on to the network. If you are already logged on to the network, the web browser will take you directly to your e-mail box. Verify that you can see the SSL lock on the bottom of Internet Explorer, and consider the implementation another success.

Configuring OWA using SSL is extremely popular. The employees of companies around the world all love the ability to access their e-mail without having to worry about configuring an e-mail client. With SSL, not only is OWA easy to access and use, but it is also secure.

Summary

In this chapter, you learned about Secure Sockets Layer (SSL) protocol. We covered the basics of how SSL works to encrypt traffic as well as how to do the following:

- Obtain certificates from public and private certificate authorities

- Renew certificates from public and private certificate authorities

- Install and configure certificates on the following:

  - IIS 5

  - Exchange 2000 Server

  - SQL 2000 Server

- Use SSL to encrypt and secure network traffic for the following:
  - Client to an IIS 5 server
  - Client to Active Directory domain controllers
  - IIS 5 to SQL 2000 Server
  - Client to Exchange 2000 Server

The exercises in this chapter provide step-by-step instructions for performing all these tasks. Although you may have understood that SSL is often used for web traffic, you can also use it in a number of ways to secure many types of traffic. Using SSL to properly secure your network is effective, and it meets almost all business needs for security when working with the Internet.

Exam Essentials

Deploy and manage public and private certificates   Make sure you understand the difference between public and private certificates and when it is appropriate to use each type. Understand how to generate a CSR for all the different servers discussed in this chapter, and understand how to renew certificates.

Configure SSL to secure communications channels   You should fully understand how to use SSL to secure network traffic by enforcing its use and not allowing unsecured traffic. Understand how to use SSL to secure the traffic between client systems and IIS 5, Active Directory domain controllers, and Exchange 2000 servers. Also understand how to secure traffic between an IIS 5 server and a SQL 2000 server.

Key Terms

Before you take the exam, be certain you are familiar with the following terms:

asymmetric keys	public certificate authorities
authentication	public key
Certificate Signing Request (CSR)	public key cryptography
certificates	Public Key Infrastructure (PKI)
encryption	Replay
Lightweight Directory Access Protocol (LDAP)	Secure Sockets Layer (SSL)
private certificate authorities	Transport Layer Security (TLS)
private key	virtual servers

Review Questions

1. Your company is about to bring two web servers both running IIS 5 back in house from a hosting facility. One server contains all your public company information. Customers can connect to it and learn about the company and its products. Clients can use the other server to purchase your products online and have them directly shipped using an e-business application developed in house. This server uses SSL to encrypt all the customer-entered data that is sent to the server to process the order. Which ports need to be opened on your firewall to support these two servers?

    A. 110

    B. 143

    C. 80

    D. 443

2. You are the administrator of your IIS 5 web servers in your company. You have set up SSL to protect Outlook Web Access. Your boss is concerned that somebody could be capturing all his session, even though it is encrypted, and then using it to try to break into the OWA server and read his e-mail. What will you explain to him to make him feel more comfortable with the technology and its ability to defend against this kind of attack?

    A. SSL provides message integrity checks and will break off communications with a system if the integrity checks fail.

    B. SSL provides the ability to prevent replay attacks by using sequence numbers in each direction of the session.

    C. SSL uses different port numbers for SSL-protected services than for standard services.

    D. The attacker would have to know the port number used for the Outlook Web Access server and would have a difficult time guessing it.

3. Your company needs certificates for deployments of SSL within the company. At no time will users outside the company be accessing these protected resources. Your supervisor is concerned about the high cost of purchasing certificates. What can you tell your supervisor?

    A. Using a private certificate authority, a service that can be installed on Windows 2000 servers without any additional charge, would not require spending money for each certificate used within the company.

    B. Public certificates may be expensive, but they are the only certificates that can be used to secure network traffic using SSL.

    C. SSL does not require that certificates be installed.

    D. Private certificates may be cheap, but they are not secure.

4. You purchased and installed a public certificate on your IIS 5 web server used for Outlook Web Access from the Internet. It has been working fine for several months. Now your supervisor wants to change the name of the server in DNS. Which of the following do you tell him?

   A. You will need to shut down the server and restart it to change the server name in DNS; however, this will not affect the users in any way other than the outage time.

   B. You can't do it. Once a certificate is added, it cannot be removed, and the name cannot be changed.

   C. You can do it, but it will mean purchasing another certificate since the old one will generate error messages if it used with a different name.

   D. You can't do it. To change the name of the server, you would have to rebuild the server completely.

5. You recently purchased a certificate. During the CSR generation, you entered the common name as email.*companyname*.com for the Outlook Web Access server that is accessed by company users from the Internet. You found out, after the server was deployed, that the DNS administrator also created a record so that owa.*companyname*.com also directs users to the same server. Many users use the email.*companyname*.com address, and many others use the owa.*companyname*.com web address. You heard that users trying to use owa.*companyname*.com always get the "The name on the security certificate does not match the name of the site" error message. What can you do to prevent this error message from appearing?

   A. Obtain another certificate with owa.*companyname*.com and replace the email.*companyname*.com certificate with the new one.

   B. Create another site for https://owa.*companyname*.com that has a valid certificate with its common name and a web page to redirect all requests to the proper address.

   C. Renew the email.*companyname*.com certificate and change its name at the same time. This renewed certificate will then support both common names.

   D. Send everyone instructions about how to update their Trusted Root Certification Authority list so that it will not generate the error message.

6. You recently installed a certificate for SSL on your IIS 5 web server named Server1, but you are not sure if it is working correctly. What is the easiest way to verify that SSL is working?

   A. Using Internet Explorer, connect to https://server1 and check the Status Bar to see if the lock appears.

   B. Using Internet Explorer, connect to http://server1 and then check the Status Bar to see if the lock appears.

   C. Install the Certificates Snap-in in the MMC and open the certificate to make sure it has not expired.

   D. Install the Certificates Snap-in in the MMC and open the certificate to verify that it is for a web server.

7. You are trying to get a certificate from a public certificate authority. You generate the CSR and paste it into the proper part of the template. When you submit the CSR, though, you receive an error message that the CSR is not compatible with a 128-bit certificate. What might be wrong?

    A. The common name is not the same as the DNS site name for the server on which you will install the certificate.

    B. The company name is not spelled correctly in the CSR.

    C. You did not copy the header and footer of the CSR into the template.

    D. If the CSR is generated using 512 bits, it isn't sufficient for 128-bit certificates. It must be at least 1024 bits.

8. When you test your installation of SSL on an IIS 5 server named Server1, you notice that the web server responds to both `http://server1` and `https://server1`. What steps do you need to take to ensure that the web server responds only to `https://server1`?

    A. Using the Internet Services Manager Snap-in, open the Properties dialog box for the virtual server. In the Directory Security tab, click the Edit button to open the Secure Communications dialog box, and verify that Enable Client Certificate Mapping is checked.

    B. Using the Internet Services Manager Snap-in, open the Properties dialog box for the virtual server. In the Directory Security tab, click the Edit button to open the Secure Communications dialog box, and verify that Require Secure Channel (SSL) is checked.

    C. Using the Internet Services Manager Snap-in, open the Properties dialog box for the virtual server. In the Directory Security tab, click the Edit button to open the Secure Communications dialog box, and verify that Enable Certificate Trust List is checked.

    D. Using the Internet Services Manager Snap-in, open the Properties dialog box for the virtual server. In the Directory Security tab, click the View Certificate button to open the Secure Communications dialog box, and verify that the certificate is not expired.

9. You implemented SSL for securing IMAP4 access to the Exchange 2000 server in your company. You also set up SMTP for secure access. When configuring Outlook Express, you check the This Server Requires a Secure Connection (SSL) check box. You notice that the IMAP4 configuration is set to use port 993, so you change it to 995. When you test the Outlook Express configuration, it fails. What is the most likely reason for the failure?

    A. IMAP4 uses port 143, and it will not work properly using anything else.

    B. Secure IMAP4 uses port 143. Port 995 is for secure POP3, so it should be changed to 143.

    C. The correct port for secure IMAP4 is 993, so it needs to be changed from 995 to 993.

    D. The Exchange 2000 server is configured incorrectly.

10. You recently set up a client system to use Outlook Express for secure access to Exchange 2000 with POP3 and SMTP both secured with SSL. You tested it, and everything seemed to be working fine as it downloads e-mail from the server and sends e-mail. The next day, a user calls to complain that all his e-mail in Outlook is missing and that he needs it restored. What is the most likely cause of the user's missing e-mail?

A. Outlook Express was configured with IMAP4, which will remove e-mail from the Exchange 2000 server.

B. Outlook Express was not configured to use secure POP3. Standard POP3 will remove all the e-mail from the Exchange 2000 server.

C. Outlook Express was not configured to leave a copy of the e-mail on the Exchange server, and all the e-mail was downloaded to Outlook Express.

D. The user deleted his e-mail accidentally and just didn't realize it.

11. You are trying to configure IIS 5 to use a certificate for SSL. When you open the Properties dialog box for the website and click the Directory Security tab, you see that the Edit key is grayed out in the Secure Communications section. What is the most likely reason it is grayed out?

A. A certificate has not yet been installed on the IIS 5 server.

B. The certificate is expired.

C. The certificate is from an untrusted certificate authority.

D. The certificate is 40 bits, and only 128-bit certificates can be edited.

12. Your company has been using an IIS 5 web server so that some customers can place orders from the Internet. Recently, a few customers have complained that the web traffic to this server is not secured because SSL is not being used for this server. You have never used SSL for web servers in your company before. You configure SSL and test it internally. It works fine. Now, customers are complaining that they are unable to access the server at all, even using SSL. What is the most likely reason for the web server to fail for external users?

A. The certificate authority is not trusted by most web browsers.

B. The certificate authority has not yet configured the certificate to make it available; they must be waiting for payment to clear before allowing it to be used.

C. The common name was not correctly entered when the CSR was generated.

D. The firewall between the IIS 5 server and the Internet is not allowing port 443 traffic to the IIS 5 server.

13. You recently configured Active Directory domain controllers to use SSL. When testing the configuration, you received the "The specified directory service could not be reached" error message. You start troubleshooting. You open Address Book, right-click Active Directory in the Look In box, and choose Properties from the shortcut menu to open the Properties dialog box. You notice in the Advanced tab that the Directory Server (LDAP) is set for port 366. You are certain that this is wrong and is the cause of the problem. How can you verify that you are correct?

A. Change the port to 636, and make sure that the This Server Requires A Secure Connection (SSL) check box is checked. Then retry the search.

B. Change the port to 3268, and make sure that the This Server Requires A Secure Connection (SSL) check box is checked. Then retry the search.

C. Change the port to 389, and make sure that the This Server Requires A Secure Connection (SSL) check box is checked. Then retry the search.

D. Change it to 993, and make sure the This Server Requires a Secure Connection (SSL) is checked. Then retry the search.

14. One of the guys on your team was recently trying to configure SSL on a SQL 2000 server so that it could use a secured communication channel to pass information back and forth from an IIS 5 server. He was unable to get it working. He described his steps to you and said that he used the IIS 5 server on the SQL server to get the certificate installed. You are sure this is not the proper method. What do you tell him to do?

A. Install the Certificates Snap-in in an MMC and use it to request a new certificate. Use a computer certificate, not a SQL certificate.

B. Install the Certificates Snap-in in an MMC and use it to request a new certificate. Use a service account certificate, not a web certificate. Configure it for the SQL service account.

C. Install the Certificates Snap-in in an MMC and use it to request a new certificate. Use an EFS certificate, not a web certificate.

D. Install the Certificates Snap-in in an MMC and use it to request a new certificate. Use a computer certificate, not a web certificate.

15. One of the members of your team installed a computer certificate on a SQL 2000 server as part of the process for configuring secure communications between the SQL 2000 server and an IIS 5 server. He tells you that he set up the SQL 2000 server with the Force Protocol Encryption option and that he then set up the IIS 5 server with the SQL 2000 client software to also use the Force Protocol Encryption option. He can't get the IIS 5 server to talk to the SQL 2000 server using encrypted channels. What should you tell him?

  A. Force Protocol Encryption can only be used from the SQL 2000 server side, not the client side.

  B. Force Protocol Encryption can only be used from the client side (IIS 5 server in this case) and cannot be used from the SQL 2000 server side.

  C. Force Protocol Encryption cannot be set up on both the SQL 2000 server and the client (IIS 5 server) at the same time. Choose one or the other, but not both.

  D. Using a computer certificate and then setting up the Force Protocol Encryption option are not required. The systems will automatically encrypt communications based on how the web application is coded.

16. SSL can be used on commercial sites to do which of the following? (Choose all that apply.)

  A. Encrypt the web traffic.

  B. Authenticate the web server to the client.

  C. Prevent replay attacks on the web server.

  D. Prevent port scanning.

17. You have employees in your company that want to access e-mail from home. Your supervisor has asked for the best solution to provide them secure access without having to spend much money. What would you recommend to your supervisor?

  A. Configure SMTP and POP3 using SSL for external access.

  B. Configure SMTP and IMAP4 using SSL for external access.

  C. Configure the e-mail server to send copies of all e-mail to employees' homes as well as to work e-mail addresses.

  D. Configure OWA with SSL for external access.

18. You configured an internal website for payroll reporting. Accounting wants the site secured so that private company data about pay rates does not get out to the employees. Accounting intends to use the site internally only. They want to minimize costs. What should you do?

  A. Use a private certificate authority to get a certificate and configure the website using SSL.

  B. Use a public certificate authority to get a certificate and configure the website using SSL.

  C. Move the web server onto the accounting network segment. Set up a firewall to filter HTTP between accounting and the rest of the network.

  D. Move the web server into a secured room behind a firewall. Configure a firewall to allow only accounting IP addresses to access the Web server.

19. A co-worker configured a web server with SSL about two years ago using a private certificate authority. You have been told that the certificate will expire in a couple of days. What should you do?

    A. Use the Web Enrollment pages on the private certificate authority to request a new certificate before the old one expires.

    B. Renew the certificate on the web server using the Certificates MMC Snap-in.

    C. Wait for the certificate to expire, and then get another one from the private certificate authority.

    D. Use the Web Enrollment pages on the private certificate authority to revoke the old certificate and get a new certificate.

20. Your co-worker implemented SSL for the SMTP service on the company e-mail server. Users report that they are no longer receiving e-mail. What is the most likely cause?

    A. Your co-worker did not create a new SMTP virtual server for the SSL implementation.

    B. Your co-worker forgot to use SSL on POP3 or IMAP 4 along with SMTP.

    C. Your co-worker didn't update the DNS server settings on the e-mail server.

    D. Your co-worker failed to reboot the e-mail server after making the changes.

Answers to Review Questions

1. C, D. HTTP uses port 80 for standard web traffic, and HTTPS uses port 443 for SSL protocol secured traffic.

2. B. The attack discussed is called a replay attack, and SSL provides protection against replay attacks by inserting sequence numbers in the packets.

3. A. Private certificates for internal use are feasible and can be deployed effectively in the organization.

4. C. A certificate requires that the proper name be entered when generating the CSR, and to change the name would mean generating a new CSR with the new name and obtaining a new certificate based on the new CSR.

5. B. If the page on `https://owa.companyname.com.` redirects users to `https://email.companyname.com`, this error message will not be generated.

6. A. When using the `https://` address type, the lock icon will appear in the Internet Explorer Status Bar if the connection is made using SSL.

7. D. A bit length of 512 for the CSR is only enough to generate a 40-bit certificate.

8. B. If Require Secure Channel (SSL) is not checked, IIS 5 will accept both secure and unsecure access to web pages.

9. C. SSL-enabled IMAP4 uses port 993. SSL-enabled POP3 uses port 995.

10. C. If you do not check the Leave A Copy Of Messages On Server check box, Outlook Express downloads all the mail from the Exchange 2000 server, and the e-mail box on Exchange 2000 will be empty the next time it is accessed using another e-mail client.

11. A. Once the certificate is installed, the Edit button will be accessible.

12. D. To access the server using HTTPS, the firewall must allow traffic using port 443 to the IIS 5 server.

13. A. LDAP secured with SSL uses port 636.

14. D. The SQL 2000 server needs a standard computer certificate in order to configure communications channels to use SSL.

15. C. Trying to use the Force Protocol Encryption for both the client and the server will cause the communications to fail between the systems.

16. A, B, C. SSL can be used for more than just encrypting the web traffic. It also prevents replays through the MIC and authenticates the server to the client system.

17. D.   OWA is easy to configure with SSL to secure it. As an administrator, you would never have to support external e-mail clients because all users will use their web browser to access e-mail.

18. A.   Private certificates are easy to configure and do not cost as much as the other solutions.

19. B.   You can use the Certificates MMC Snap-in to renew certificates as well as to request them.

20. A.   If the only SMTP virtual server for the company is configured to use SSL, nobody on the Internet will be able to send e-mail to the server because they are not sending encrypted e-mail to the company.

Chapter 7

Configure, Manage, and Troubleshoot Authentication

THE MICROSOFT EXAM OBJECTIVES COVERED IN THIS CHAPTER:

✓ **Configure and troubleshoot authentication.**

- Configure authentication protocols to support mixed Windows client-computer environments.
- Configure the interoperability of Kerberos authentication with Unix computers.
- Configure authentication for extranet scenarios.
- Configure trust relationships.
- Configure authentication for members of nontrusted domain authentication.

✓ **Configure and troubleshoot authentication for web users. Authenication types include Basic, Integrated Windows, anonymous, digest, and client certificate mapping.**

✓ **Configure authentication for secure remote access. Authenication types include PAP, CHAP, MS-CHAP, MS-CHAP v2, EAP-MD5, EAP-TLS, and multifactor authentication with smart cards and EAP.**

Authentication, to provide a loose definition, is the process of verifying the identity of a person. Of course, this is incredibly important; otherwise, anyone could log on to our networks and cause all sorts of problems. In Windows 2000, a network user must be authenticated to an account before gaining access to any of the network resources. One of our goals is to make the authentication process secure while still meeting the business goals of the organization.

We use authentication in our daily lives, so, of course, we will also use it in our electronic lives. For example, we use our driver's license (a commonly accepted form of authentication) to prove our identity when checking in at the airport, picking up a rental car, and writing checks as well as when processing other financial transactions. We use looser forms of authentication too. A great example of that is facial recognition. If somebody appears on your doorstep, and you recognize them as a relative, you will probably let them in. When you walk into your office, you may have electronic keycards, but people recognize you walking down the hall and going to your cube or office. If you don't belong, you will be identified as an intruder, will be questioned, and potentially even apprehended by internal security personnel.

But facial recognition is not be a reliable authentication method for larger organizations, and it can really cause problems for new employees; so many organizations have implemented stronger authentication methods for access to the organization such as private identification badges. When it comes to crossing international borders, even stronger authentication methods are required; so most countries use passports issued by the country where the traveler is a citizen. Well, in our electronic world, we also need to use defined protocols to authenticate our network users and gain some confidence that they are who they say they are, and some of these protocols are stronger than others.

In this chapter, we will look at the authentication protocols used for wired network authentication, web server authentication, and Remote Access Service (RAS) authentication. For each of these types, we will discuss how to implement the protocols, and we will point out security problems as well as provide some troubleshooting tips as appropriate.

Configuring and Troubleshooting Authentication

This first section is focused on local area network (LAN) *authentication* protocols, as opposed to Internet and RAS, which will be covered later in this chapter. Although much of the information here also applies to web and RAS users in Windows 2000, this is probably the best place to start.

The LAN Authentication Protocols

Two authentication protocols are used in a LAN environment:

NT LAN Manager (NTLM)   This is the default protocol used in Windows NT 4 and earlier.

Kerberos v5   First introduced in Windows 2000, Kerberos v5 is used with Windows XP and will also be used with Windows Server 2003.

NT LAN Manager (NTLM)

NTLM is used by down-level operating systems such as Windows 95, Windows 98, and Windows NT 4. NTLM is also used by Windows 2000 and Windows XP when logging in to a Windows NT 4 domain and when logging in to their own local computer databases (not Active Directory domains). There are three versions of NTLM:

LAN Manager (LM)   This form of NTLM is Windows 2000 and Windows XP so that computers running Windows 2000 and Windows XP can connect to file share points on computers running Windows 95 or Windows 98. This form of NTLM is the least secure of the three.

NTLM version 1   This is a more secure form of NTLM than LM. This version is available for connections to servers in a Windows NT domain that has at least one domain controller running Windows NT 4 SP3 or earlier.

NTLM version 2   This is the most secure form of NTLM authentication that is supported. It is used when computers need to connect to servers in a Windows NT 4 domain in which the domain controllers are all running SP4 or later or when a Windows NT 4 server running SP4 is a member server in a Windows 2000 Active Directory domain. Windows 95 and Windows 98 can also use this version of NTLM if they have installed the Directory Service client.

By default, all three version of NTLM are available in a Windows 2000 Active Directory domain so that down-level clients can continue to function. It is very important that you consider the capabilities of older client operating systems before disabling any of the levels of NTLM on the network. If they can all support NTLM version 2, you can disable the others using the LAN Manager Authentication Level security option in the Local Policy or using Group Policy Objects. The standard steps to authenticate when logging on are listed here.

1. In Windows 2000 or Windows XP, press Ctrl+Alt+Del, and the Winlogon will use the *GINA (Graphical Identification and Authentication dynamic-link library)* to display the logon dialog box.

2. After the user enters their user name and password, Winlogon sends the logon information to the *LSA (Local Security Authority)* for processing.

3. The LSA uses the local computer *SAM (System Account Manager)* database if the account and target name identify it as a local computer account. The LSA uses the Net Logon service to query the domain SAM on a domain controller if the target account is a domain account not local to the computer.

4.   Once the logon information is identified as correct, the SAM sends an acceptance message to the LSA. This acceptance message contains the user account SID (security identifier) and the SIDs of all groups associated with the account. The LSA creates an access token using this information.

5.   Winlogon then starts up the user interface and attaches the token to all processes.

This same process is valid whether using LM, NTLM version 1, or NTLM version 2. In the event there is no domain, NTLM can also be used for any peer-to-peer networking authentication needs. In Exercise 7.1, you will disable LM and NTLM version 1.

EXERCISE 7.1

Disabling LM and NTLM version 1

In this exercise, we will disable LM and NTLM version 1 so that any clients attempting to use these authentication protocols will be ignored.

1.   Choose Start ➤ Programs ➤ Administrative Tools ➤ Active Directory Users And Computers.

2.   If necessary, expand the MMC (Microsoft Management Console), right-click the domain name, choose Properties from the shortcut menu to open the Properties dialog box for the domain, and then click the Group Policy tab.

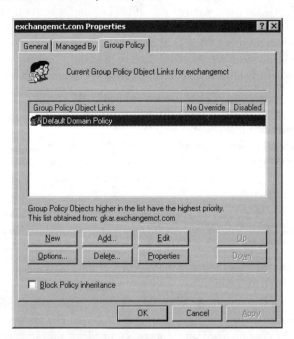

3.   Select Default Domain Policy, and then click Edit to open the Group Policy window. (You can also do this by creating a new policy, but since we would intend that this be done for all systems and as a permanent setting, it makes sense to edit the Default Domain Policy and use it.)

EXERCISE 7.1 *(continued)*

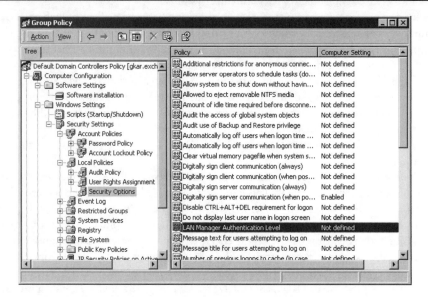

4. Expand Computer Configuration, expand Windows Settings, expand Security Settings, expand Local Policies, and then expand Security Options.

5. Double-click LAN Manager Authentication Level to open the Security Policy Settings dialog box.

6. Click the Define This Policy Setting check box, and in the drop-down list box, select Send NTLM Version 2 Response Only\Refuse LM and NTLM.

7. Click OK to close the Security Policy Settings dialog box, close the Group Policy window, and then click OK to close the Properties dialog box for the domain.

If you are working on a live network, now go back and undo this exercise. It is highly possible that you could interfere with your down-level clients, and they might not be able to log on. The options available for NTLM are discussed in the "Configuring Authentication Protocols to Support Mixed Windows Client-Computer Environments" section later in this chapter. There are many options when it comes to securing the use of NTLM on the network, and there are many issues with LM and NTLM version 1 being disabled. It may not be appropriate for your public network.

The Kerberos Protocol

Kerberos is used by Windows 2000 and Windows XP when logging in to an Active Directory domain. Kerberos is not a new technology; it has been around for many years in the Unix world. What Microsoft has done is use a well-proven authentication protocol for improved security and increased interoperability with Unix systems.

The Kerberos protocol provides mutual authentication between a client (which can be a user or a computer) and a server, meaning that not only does the client authenticate against the server, but the server authenticates itself against the client. With mutual authentication, each system can verify the identity of the other. Kerberos is extremely efficient for authenticating clients and has been proven in large network environments. Kerberos was designed and is implemented with the idea that all initial transactions between the clients and the servers occur in a semihostile environment, that is, on a network where potential intruders and hackers live and can try to appear to be either a client computer or a server on the network and capture and possibly even alter communications. Kerberos is designed to provide protection with secured authentication processes.

To provide security for the authentication process, Kerberos uses secret key encryption for authentication traffic from the client. The same secret key is also used on the server to decrypt the authentication traffic. The Kerberos *Key Distribution Center (KDC)* handles the decryption and is run on every domain controller as part of the Active Directory domain. As part of the security of Kerberos, an *authenticator* is used with the encrypted logon information. The authenticator contains information such as a time stamp that is used to prevent replays. As the logon information is received and accepted by the server, a new authenticator is inserted into the KDC response as part of the confirmation process. The KDC issues a *Ticket-Granting Ticket (TGT)*, which is then used by the client computer's LSA to get service tickets for other systems that it needs to access.

One of the benefits of Kerberos is that it does not require constant reauthentication by the client in order to access other resources on the network. The client system can use its TGT to request access to other resources. The process of authentication using Kerberos involves the following steps:

1. In Windows 2000 or Windows XP, press Ctrl+Alt+Del, and the Winlogon will use the GINA to display the logon dialog box.

2. After the user enters their user name and password, Winlogon sends the logon information to the LSA for processing.

3. The LSA passes the logon request to Kerberos. The client sends its logon information and an encrypted time stamp to the KDC as part of the authentication request. The TGT is requested in this step.

4. Using the secret key, the KDC decrypts the logon information and the time stamp and issues a TGT. This TGT contains a session key, the account name of the user authenticated, and the maximum lifetime of the ticket. Other information is also sent. The KDC then encrypts the response using the client key and is sent to the client. Included in the response is the TGT, which includes the SID for the user account and SIDs for any global and universal groups associated with the account.

The SIDs are provided to the LSA so they can be included in the *access token*. The maximum lifetime of the ticket is defined by the domain policy. The client will request new tickets if any tickets expire during an active network session.

5. Once the TGT is obtained, the client uses it to request a service ticket from Kerberos services on the domain controller. The Ticket Granting Service issues a service ticket. Service tickets are encrypted using the server's secret key. Also the SIDs for the account and its associated groups are copied from the TGT to all service tickets issued by the Kerberos service.

6. The client uses the service ticket to access the network services, and the ticket provides identification for the user and all the SID information for permissions.

Tickets received from the KDC are cached on the local client so that it can continue to use any tickets received until they expire. In the event that a ticket expires, the LSA negotiates the renewal by communicating with the KDC.

The main drawback with using Kerberos is that it is supported only on Windows 2000 and Windows XP operating systems. If the network has any down-level clients, NTLM is required.

The Logon Process

You can log on to a Windows network using either NTLM or Kerberos in three ways:

1. Using local computer accounts authentication

2. Using Windows NT 4 domain authentication

3. Using Windows 2000 Active Directory domain authentication

Using the Log On To drop-down list box in the Log On To Windows dialog box (see Figure 7.1), you can log on using the local computer database by selecting your computer name in the box, or you can select any of the domains that are available either through the computer being a member of the domain or through trust relationships established between your domain and other domains.

FIGURE 7.1   The Log On To Windows dialog box

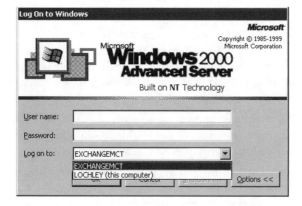

    If the Log On To drop-down list box does not appear, click the Options button to display it.

Whether the computer is running Windows NT 4, Windows 2000, or Windows XP, the local computer accounts database is on the computer itself, and Windows uses the local SAM database when logging on to the local computer. In Windows 2000 and Windows XP, Windows first attempts to use the KDC for Kerberos authentication. When the operating system fails to find the KDC, it falls back to using NTLM and attempts to log on locally using the following steps:

 Windows 2000 will fail to find the KDC on the local computer unless the local computer is a domain controller.

1. In the Log On To Windows dialog box, enter your user name and password.

2. The GINA collects the user name and password and then sends that information to the LSA for authentication.

3. The LSA takes the information sent by the GINA and passes it to the *Security Support Provider Interface (SSPI)*. The SSPI is works with the Kerberos and NTLM services and enables third-party developers to create security-aware applications without any in-depth knowledge of how Kerberos and NTLM work.

4. The SSPI then passes the user information to Kerberos where it checks to see if the logon target is the local computer or the domain. If it is the local computer, Kerberos passes an error message back to the SSPI. The computer then generates an error message behind the scenes, stating that the KDC could not be found.

5. This hidden error causes SSPI to start the logon process again, and the GINA sends the user logon information to the LSA again, and then LSA sends it to the SSPI again.

6. When the SSPI receives the logon information the second time, it sends the user logon information to the NTLM driver. The NTLM driver uses the Net Logon service to authenticate the logon information against the SAM database on the local computer.

The local logon process is quick, and it is secure since it happens within the confines of the computer. There is no network traffic to monitor and capture out on the wire.

The logon process for logging on to a domain can be of two domain types: the Windows NT 4 domain and Windows 2000 Active Directory domain. The steps are similar to the local computer logon discussed previously:

1. After you enter the user name and password in the Log On To Windows dialog box and click OK, the LSA of the computer passes the logon information to the SSPI, which can communicate with both Kerberos and NTLM services.

2. The SSPI then passes the user information to Kerberos where it checks to see if the logon target is the local computer or the domain. The Kerberos SSPI determines whether the target computer name is the local computer or the domain name. In this case, it identifies the name as the domain name.

3. The KDC checks for the user name and password, and the Kerberos authentication process proceeds if both are valid. The logon process ends at this point if the domain is an Active Directory domain.

4. If Step 3 fails because the user name is not found by the KDC, the KDC passes an error message to the SSPI. If the KDC cannot be found, a hidden error message is passed back to the LSA, letting it know that the SSPI could not find the KDC.

5. The hidden error message to the LSA causes the process to start again, and MSGINA passes the information to the LSA again, and then LSA passes the logon information to the SSPI.

6. The SSPI then passes the logon information to the NTLM driver, and it then uses the Net Logon service to finish the authentication process using NTLM authentication.

When Windows 2000 or Windows XP computers log in, they first check to see if the logon name is a computer name or a domain name. They then first try to use Kerberos and fail over to NTLM if Kerberos is not available.

Troubleshooting Authentication

Troubleshooting authentication is like troubleshooting anything else. The process requires some structure and a little art. So, imagine the standard help desk call in which the user complains about not being able to log in from their computer. What kind of questions should you ask?

Can you log in on a different computer?   If the answer is yes, something is probably wrong with that particular computer. Perhaps the network wire is loose, or perhaps the network port that it is attached to has been recently configured differently.

Can others log in on your computer?   If the answer is yes to this one, perhaps something is wrong with the user's password or they are mistyping either their user name or password. Maybe the password needs to be reset and the change synched to all the domain controllers before the user tries again.

What is the name of your computer?   A quick check or two can confirm whether the computer is properly attached to the network. Pinging by the name will verify whether it is registered in DNS (Domain Name Service) and will help identify any other problems that the computer might have.

What is the exact error message that you are receiving?   TechNet, www.microsoft.com/technet, is fantastic source for error messages. Look through for any articles that can help with troubleshooting the problem.

Have you changed your password recently?   Often, users change their password, log off the network, and try to log right back in again. They may not get back on right away if they didn't allow time for the password change to synchronize with all the domain controllers.

You can also ask the network administrator a couple of questions. After all, they may have made some changes to the configuration of the network that could be causing problems, such as changing the DNS server or even making some changes to Group Policy Objects that might impact the users. For example, did the network administrator make some changes to the NTLM configurations that disable LM and NTLM version 1. If so, you need to find out what operating system the user is trying to run and try to identify the change as a potential cause of the problem.

There are some other well-known problems regarding incompatibility with NTLM version 2. This list will probably grow over time as more administrators try to tighten security and disable the less secure LM and NTLM version 1.

- Keep passwords to 14 characters or fewer. Otherwise, problems can arise when logging on from Windows 95, Windows 98, and Windows NT 4 systems.

- Remote Installation Services (RIS) servers can exhibit problems with NTLM2 and may require NTLM1.

- Windows 2000 clusters do not respond properly using NTLM2; they need NTLM1 or LM.

Configuring Authentication Protocols to Support Mixed Windows Client-Computer Environments

As we just mentioned, only two protocols are available when logging on to the domain. You can use Kerberos if you have a Windows 2000 domain environment, or you can use NTLM. As we discussed, only Windows 2000 and Windows XP can use Kerberos. Even then, in a completely Windows 2000 and Windows XP network, at times you need to use NTLM to avoid significant problems, such as with clustering and RIS. As with any change, test it to the best of your abilities, and recognize that even with testing, you might not find a problem that surfaces when the change is made in production.

NTLM version 1 really was not that much of a security concern initially, but when computer hardware and software improvements made it easy to break NTLM version 1, it became a concern for many in the industry. Microsoft released NTLM version 2 with Windows NT 4 Service Pack 4, and it is a considerable improvement in security over version 1.

In Exercise 7.1, we set the Group Policy Object on the domain to enforce the LAN Manager authentication level. Setting this option determines which NTLM authentication protocol is used for network logons for connections to Windows 2000 and Windows XP systems, but since Group Policies do not apply to down-level clients, they take some additional work. Remember Windows 2000 and Windows XP use Kerberos if it is available and use NTLM only if Kerberos is not available or if you log in to the local computer. Setting the option will affect the version of NTLM authentication used by clients, the level of security negotiated, and the authentication levels accepted by servers. The following options are available, from the lowest to the most secure:

Send LM & NTLM Responses   Clients will use LM and NTLM version 1 authentication and will never use NTLM version 2 session security. Domain controllers will accept LM, NTLM version 1, and NTLM version 2.

Send LM & NTLM   Clients will use NTLM version 2 if negotiated. Clients will use LM and NTLM authentication and will use NTLM version 2 if the server supports it. Domain controllers will accept LM, NTLM version 1, and NTLM version 2 authentication.

Send NTLM Response Only   Clients will use NTLM version 1 authentication only and will use NTLM version 2 if the server supports it. Domain controllers will accept LM, NTLM version 1, and NTLM version 2 authentication.

Send NTLM Version 2 Response Only Clients will use NTLM version 2 authentication only and will use NTLM version 2 if the server supports it. Domain controllers will accept LM, NTLM, and NTLM version 2 authentication.

Send NTLM Version 2 Response Only\Refuse LM Clients will use NTLM version 2 only and will use NTLM version 2 if the server supports it. Domain controllers will refuse LM and accept only NTLM version 1 and NTLM version 2 authentication.

Based on these options, you can chose the most restrictive and implement it using Group Policy Objects. However, using Send NTLM Version 2 Response Only\Refuse LM may not be the best solution, especially if you have down-level clients such as Windows 95 and Windows 98, which do not support NTLM version 2 out of the box. If you want to use NTLM version 2, you need to use software that will fully support it, and that includes all operating systems. Of course, if you need to use NTLM version 2 whenever possible, but have the ability to fall back to NTLM version 1 for computers that cannot support NTLM version 2, you can get that by using the Send NTLM Response Only option. You need to weigh your security needs against the capabilities of your operating systems when making these decisions.

Configuring Authentication for Windows 95 and Windows 98 Clients

If you have down-level clients, your options are to either relax security in order to support them or to use additional software components to improve their capabilities. In the case of Windows 95 and Windows 98, you can use NTLM version 2 if you install the *Directory Services client* on each system running these older versions of Windows. In Exercise 7.2, you'll install the Directory Services client.

EXERCISE 7.2

Installing the Directory Services Client

In this exercise, you will install the Directory Services client on a Windows 98 computer and configure it to use NTLM version 2. For this exercise, you will need a Windows 98 system and the Windows 2000 Server CD. This exercise assumes that Windows 98 is already installed and on the network and that the latest version of Internet Explorer is also installed. (For Windows 95, you will need to follow all these steps, plus install the Distributed File System (DFS) client, WinSock 2.0 Update, and the Microsoft DUN Client 1.3.)

1. Insert the Windows 2000 CD in the drive of the Windows 98 system.

2. In Windows Explorer, navigate to the CD drive, expand the Clients folder, and then click the Win9x folder.

3. In the right pane, double-click the Dsclient file to start the Directory Services Client Setup Wizard. At the Welcome screen, click Next, and then click Next again to start copying files to the hard drive.

4. When the files are copied, click Finish.

5. Click Yes to restart your computer, and the Directory Services client will finish its installation.

EXERCISE 7.2 *(continued)*

6. After you reboot the system, the Directory Services client is fully installed.

7. Log in to the Windows 98 computer, choose Start ≻ Run to open the Run dialog box, and in the Open box, enter **Regedit** to open the Registry Editor.

8. Expand the HKEY_LOCAL_MACHINE key, expand System, expand CurrentControlSet, and then expand Control.

9. Verify that Control and the LSA exist. If the key is missing, add the LSA key. Select Control, choose Edit ≻ New ≻ Key. Enter in **LSA**.

10. Click LSA to open the LSA folder, and then click Edit ≻ New ≻ DWORD Value. For the value name, enter **LMCompatibility** and for the value, enter **3**. The result should look like this:

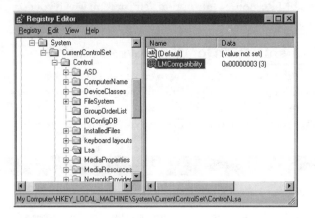

In Step 10, the value is either 0 or 3.

- Level 0 - Send LM and NTLM Response; Never Use NTLM 2 Session security. Clients will use LM and NTLM authentication and will never use NTLM 2 session security; domain controllers accept LM, NTLM, and NTLM 2 authentication.

- Level 3 - Send NTLM 2 Response Only. Clients will use NTLM 2 authentication and will use NTLM 2 session security if the server supports it; domain controllers accept LM, NTLM, and NTLM 2 authentication.

11. Close the Registry Editor.

Configuring Authentication in a Windows NT 4 Environment

Now, following the steps in Exercise 7.2 takes care of the NTLM version 2 concerns for Windows 95 and Windows 98 clients. However, that still leaves Windows NT 4 as a potential problem. If you have Service Pack 4 or later installed, you can use NTLM version 2. To disable LM authentication in Windows NT 4, you need to use the Registry Editor and configure the changes. We'll do so in Exercise 7.3.

EXERCISE 7.3

Disabling LM and NTLM version 1 Authentication in Windows NT 4

In this exercise, you will disable the LM authentication in Windows NT 4. This exercise assumes installation of Service Pack 4 or later. Service Pack 6a is highly recommended.

1. Choose Start ➤ Run to open the Run dialog box, and in the Open box, enter **RegEdt32** to open the Registry Editor.

2. Select `HKEY_LOCAL_MACHINE`, expand `System`, expand `CurrentControlSet`, expand `Control`, expand `LSA`, and then expand `MSV1_0`.

3. Choose Edit ➤ Add Value and then add the following Registry value:

   ```
   Value Name: NtlmMinClientSec
   Data Type: REG_WORD
   Value: 0x00080000
   ```

4. Close the Registry Editor.

You have the following options for supporting down-level clients in your networks:

- Allow LM and NTLM version 1 support to handle these older client operating systems by doing one of the following:

  - Enforcing NTLM version 2 and not allowing LM and NTLM version 1 to be used at all.

  - Choosing a configuration that will attempt to use NTLM version 2 and then fail back to support older versions.

- Make the necessary changes to your down-level clients so that they can support NTLM version 2.

The decision about how to support older operating systems without sacrificing higher levels of security can be troublesome and will always be a concern. As network administrators, we will have to explain our options, the risk associated with each option, and the potential problems with each option. Of course, our recommendations will be to have the network as secure as possible, but this will come at a cost in direct dollars for new purchases and the costs of teaching everyone how to support the new environment.

The Interoperability of Kerberos Authentication with Unix

As we mentioned earlier in this chapter, Kerberos is not a new authentication protocol. It has its roots in the Unix world where it has been proven to be secure, dependable, and scalable. In the Windows world, Kerberos was first included with Windows 2000.

Windows 2000 supports *RFC 1510* to ensure that the Kerberos in Windows 2000 will interoperate with the Kerberos used in other operating systems that also conform to the RFC. If all the operating systems in use in an organization comply with the RFC, it is possible to have a *single sign-on* implementation for the network. In a single sign-on environment, the network user will have to log in only once and will be able to gain access to all the resources on all operating systems on the network according to the permissions that have been granted.

To achieve this single sign-on, you must make a choice. Do you configure your client operating systems to authenticate against a third-party Kerberos implementation, or do you configure all third party-operating systems to authenticate against Windows 2000 domain controllers? It is possible to configure Windows XP Professional to log in to a third-party Kerberos implementation. However, to do this, you must take the computer out of the Windows 2000 Active Directory domain and make it a member of a workgroup. This is because a Kerberos realm is not the same thing as a Windows 2000 Active Directory domain. Although they have many things in common, Windows 2000 Professional and Windows XP clients must be configured differently to support a third-party Kerberos implementation.

On the flip side, other operating systems and their applications can authenticate against a Windows 2000 Kerberos implementation if they are based on the *Generic Security Service Application Program Interface (GSSAPI)*. If third-party operating systems support GSSAPI, they can obtain service tickets from a Windows 2000 Active Directory domain.

To configure Windows XP Professional to authenticate against a third-party Kerberos implementation, you will need to make some changes to the normal configuration. First, the computer has to be a member of a workgroup and cannot be a member of a Windows 2000 Active Directory domain. Second, you have to install the proper tools on the Windows client. Third, you have to run the Kerberos command-line tool Ksetup.exe to establish the link between the client system and the Kerberos KDC. In Exercise 7.4, you'll make these configuration changes.

EXERCISE 7.4

Configure Windows XP Professional to Use a Third-Party Kerberos version 5 Implementation

In this exercise, you will install the support tools on Windows XP Professional and then run Ksetup.exe to configure Windows XP Professional to use the third-party Kerberos implementation to log in, to change passwords, and to map the user account.

1. Insert the Windows XP Professional CD-ROM. In Windows Explorer, navigate to <*CD Drive Letter*>:\Support\Tools, and double-click Setup.exe to start the installation.

2. Verify that Ksetup.exe was installed with the rest of the support tools. It should be in the <*Root Drive*>:\Program Files\Support Tools folder.

3. Verify that the Windows XP Professional computer is not part of a domain. Choose Start ➢ Control Panel ➢ Performance And Maintenance ➢ System to open the System Properties dialog box. Click the Computer Name tab, and then click the Change button. This will indicate whether Windows XP Professional is part of a domain or is in a workgroup. Close all the dialog boxes. If the computer is part of a domain, remove it, and then restart the computer.

4. Choose Start ➢ Run to open the Run dialog box, and in the Open box, enter **CMD** to open the Command Prompt window.

5. At the command prompt, type **ksetup /addkdc** *realmname.domainname*.com *kdcservername*
    .realmname.mydomain.com and then press Enter to add a KDC to the Windows client. You
    can repeat this command if you have multiple KDCs on the network for redundancy.

6. If the realm supports the change password protocol, then using the proper servers can be
    configured to support changes to the password with the security dialog box when pressing
    Ctrl+Alt+Del on the Windows client. Type **Ksetup /addkpasswd** *realmname.domainname*
    .com kpasswdservername.realmname.domainname.com and then press Enter.

7. To log on to the computer, you will need a local computer account mapped to a Kerberos
    account using Ksetup.exe. So, first create a local computer account on the Windows client
    and then at a command prompt enter **ksetup /mapuser** *username@realmname.domainname*
    .com username and press Enter (username is the name of the local account). Without an
    entry, the user cannot log in on this particular computer. This is one way to prevent more
    than one user from using a particular computer. You can use a wildcard to map all users
    to the same local computer account.

8. Restart the computer so that the changes can take affect.

Since Windows 2000 complies with the Kerberos RFCs, it is also possible for a Unix system
to use the Windows 2000 Active Directory domain controllers as realm KDCs, using the
domain name as the realm name. Kerberos is flexible in that with proper support for the RFC,
it is operating system agnostic.

Configuring Authentication in Extranet Scenarios and with Members of Nontrusted Domains

The designers of Windows 2000 thought about the issues involved in extending networks to
business partners; this includes both suppliers and customers. In the classic *extranet* environment,
we configure our networks to allow our close partners to access our data, and they set up their
networks to allow us access to their data. For example, a retailer has a close relationship with
some of its suppliers. As sales increase and stock starts to dwindle, the supplier can automatically ship replacement stock based on prior agreements and save the retailer from having to
place the order themself. At the same time, the retailer can check the shipment from the supplier
to see when the order was shipped, check the quantity shipped, and find the expected arrival
date. The value of extranets is clear.

The key to making an extranet environment work is finding a way to allow outside users to
access internal resources in a secure fashion. In Windows 2000, you need an account in your domain
or in a trusted domain to apply security permissions so that the account has access to the resources
it needs. You need to give an extranet user an account that lets them access your resources.

Extranet users access your network in a couple of ways. You need to keep in mind that extranet
users are usually members of another domain that is a nontrusted domain, and often they

are also members of another company. To provide them access, normally, we use one of the following methods:

- Internet web access
    - Using accounts and passwords in your network. This is done using a prompt when trying to connect to the web resources that requires logon information.
    - Using certificates that map to accounts in your network. This is done using certificate mapping, which will be discussed later in this chapter.
- VPN (virtual private network) access (covered in depth in Chapter 8).
- Dial-up access (covered later in this chapter).

Thankfully, Windows 2000 can use these methods and support authentication protocols to prove the identity of external users as they enter your network. For example, you can authenticate external users over the Internet by using standard X.509 certificates. You can then map these certificates to user accounts and assign permissions to resources to these user accounts. You can also use a web front-end for the external user so they can perform the tasks needed through a web browser. Of course, you want to protect this web application using SSL as in Figure 7.2.

FIGURE 7.2   How an extranet works

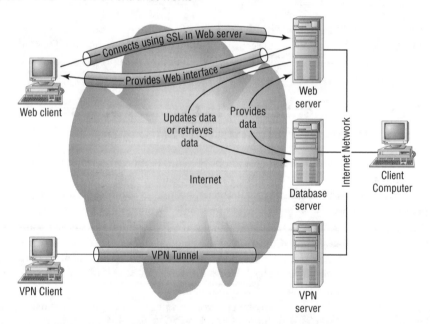

In an extranet environment, you probably don't want to distribute an application to external clients and then have to worry about supporting it. This is where the web interface is extremely valuable. (The various web authentication methods are covered later in this chapter, including certificate mapping.)

In our simple example, we can provide support for extranet users using a number of authentication protocols, including Kerberos. The process involves the following steps:

1. The extranet user connects to the web server using an SSL connection and is prompted for a user name and password. You can replace the user name and password prompt with a certificate mechanism.

2. IIS looks up the user account in Active Directory. If the user name is found and the password is the proper one, a credentials package is put together and a Kerberos ticket (TGT) is issued to the IIS server on behalf of the user. If a certificate was used, the information in the certificate is used to map it to an account in Active Directory, and a TGT is provided. At this point, Kerberos is being used to authenticate.

3. The IIS server uses the credentials of the extranet user to request access to the database server for the data requested using the web application and also for the ability to update or add new data. The IIS server passes the credentials to the database server with its requests using Kerberos.

4. The database server authenticates the user credentials provided in the Kerberos ticket and then uses the ACLs (access control lists) to decide whether to allow or deny access to the data.

In our example, it does not really matter whether a certificate is presented by the extranet client or whether a user name and password is used since everything then maps to an account in Active Directory, and this account is used in the ACLs on internal resources to determine whether access is allowed or denied. In either case, the logon process to the IIS server is protected using SSL, and the authentication using Kerberos is the same. As for the VPN client and the internal network client, they can access the application in the same way; however, the VPN client will be using much a smaller pipe and will have slower performance. The VPN client and the internal client can use either fat client software or the web application.

Extranets are extremely valuable to businesses, especially when they are used to access applications and other resources remotely. Whether our personnel or our partners are accessing the network, the process is similar.

Trust Relationships

Trust relationships allow Windows 2000 Active Directory domains to add users from one domain to the ACL for a resource that exists in another domain and for these users to access resources across the trust. Within a Windows 2000 Active Directory forest, all trusts relationships are two way transitional relationships so that each and every domain within a forest trusts the other domains and is also trusted by the other domains through these trust relationships.

Each trust relationship uses an authentication protocol for the trust as well as for the users across the trust. Windows 2000 supports only two protocols for trust relationship authentication:

Kerberos   The default Windows 2000 authentication service

NTLM   The default Windows NT 4 authentication service

The oddity here is that trust relationships between Windows 2000 forests do not use Kerberos; they use NTLM. For any trusts within a forest, Kerberos is used, but the only time Kerberos is used for external trusts is with third-party Kerberos realms. Figure 7.3 shows the trust types and the authentication protocol for each type of relationship.

FIGURE 7.3 Trust relationship authentication

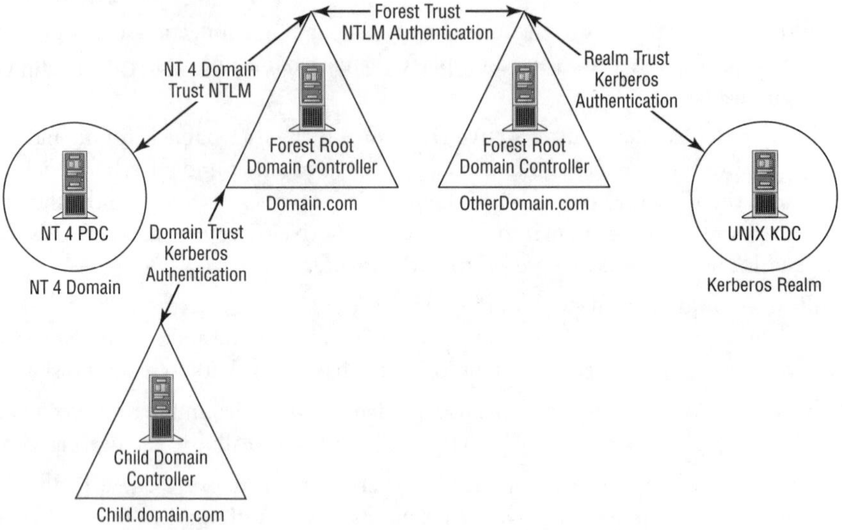

Basically, each trust relationship and the authentication used for the trust depends on the two entities joined in the trust:

Intraforest   These trusts are authenticated using Kerberos.

Forest-to-forest   These trusts are authenticated using NTLM.

Forest to NT 4 domain   These trusts are authenticated using NTLM.

Forest to realm   These trusts are authenticated using Kerberos.

At times, it is necessary to create a trust relationship between a Windows 2000 Active Directory domain and a Windows NT 4 domain. Windows 2000 lets you configure a one-way trust in either direction. These one-way nontransitive trusts can be helpful when used to connect small domains such as domains in screened subnets and domains used to house specialized systems such as Manufacturing Execution Systems (MESs) that manage production lines. You can configure one-way trusts between domains. A one-way trust from the screened subnet domain or the MES domain will allow accounts on the internal domain to be trusted by these other domains' external domain, but does not allow these external domain accounts to be trusted by the Windows 2000 Active Directory domain. Setting up these one-way trusts is explained in Exercise 7.5.

EXERCISE 7.5

Creating a One-Way Trust: A Windows NT 4 Domain Trusts a Windows 2000 Active Directory Domain

In this exercise, you will create a one-way trust between a Windows 2000 Active Directory domain and a Windows NT 4 domain.

1. Before configuring these trusts, make sure that the Windows 2000 Active Directory domain controllers and the Windows NT 4 domain controllers are registered in DNS and in WINS (Windows Internet Naming Service).

2. On the Windows NT 4 primary domain controller (PDC), log in as an administrator equivalent and choose Start ➤ Programs ➤ Administrative Tools ➤ User Manager For Domains to open User Manager For Domains.

3. Choose Policies ➤ Trust Relationships.

4. In the Trusted Domains section, click Add, enter the domain name of the Windows 2000 domain, and enter a password that will be used later on the Windows 2000 domain controller to establish the trust relationship. Click OK.

5. You can safely ignore any errors that may have been received since the Windows 2000 server side has not been done yet. The trust relationship is not complete. Close any error messages that you receive.

6. On a Windows 2000 domain controller, log in using an account with administrative privileges, and then choose Start ➤ Programs ➤ Administrative Tools ➤ Active Directory Domains And Trusts.

7. Right-click the domain name, choose Properties from the shortcut menu to open the Properties dialog box for the domain, and then click the Trusts tab.

8. In the Domains That Trust This Domain section, click Add. This is the bottom part of the Properties window.

9. Type the name of the trusting Windows NT 4 domain, and then provide a password to be used on the other side of the trust to establish the trust. Click OK to close the Properties dialog box.

10. In the dialog box, click Yes to display a user name and password prompt. Enter the user name and password for an administrative account on the Windows NT 4 domain, and then click OK.

11. When you receive a message verifying that the trust has been verified, click OK and close the remaining dialog boxes.

One of the keys to establishing and maintaining trusts between Windows NT 4 domains and Windows 2000 Active Directory domains is that the domain controllers all need to be registered in WINS or the Windows NT 4 domain controllers will fail to find the Windows 2000 domain controllers.

Configuring and Troubleshooting Authentication for Web Users

So far, we've only talked about authentication for LANs and intranets/extranets, but eventually you'll need to configure your network for authenticating web users using the Internet. IIS 5 supports several authentication protocols. Each provides a method for a user to authenticate their identity or account to the web server using a web browser. Once they establish their identity, the account associated with that identity is used to identify the permissions to access resources such as files and web content in the case of a web server.

The following protocols are available using IIS 5 on Windows 2000 servers:

- Anonymous
- Basic
- Digest
- Integrated Windows
- Certificate

Web authentication involves communications between the web browser and the web server. Normal web authentication occurs upon failure of Anonymous authentication. If the site does not support anonymous access, or if the content is protected with NTFS (New Technology File System) permissions, the web server will send an error message to the web browser specifying the type of protocol to use to authenticate. For example, when Basic authentication is used, a logon dialog box pops up asking for the user name and password in most web browsers, and the browser reissues the request with the new identity information.

Each authentication protocol has different configuration requirements and has varying degrees of compatibility and security. Some of the protocols have different system requirements as well. We'll look at each one in some detail.

Anonymous Authentication

Web authentication takes place when the browser tries to access web server content. If *Anonymous authentication* is enabled and the proper file permissions are in place, all connections are allowed. This is the most common setting for web servers; after all, can you imagine having to log in on every website that you visit? That would drive everyone over the edge. So, if you want others to have access to web servers that host public information, always configure those servers to use Anonymous.

If you configure IIS to allow anonymous access, IIS maps all anonymous users to the account defined as the guest account for IIS. By default, this account is named IUSR_*computername* (*computername* is the name of your IIS server). The IUSR_*computername* account is created during the installation of IIS and will have log on locally user rights on the server. Without log on locally user rights, the users of the web server will not be able to connect. You can use this IUSR account to secure the web server files and restrict anonymous users to just the content you want to make available. This IUSR account can be excluded from other files on the web server to secure them. In the event that you have content for anonymous users and content that should be restricted, you can run all this content off the same server by securing the restricted content using file and folder NTFS permissions. IIS will try anonymous authentication first; however, it will use other authentication protocols if access is restricted beyond anonymous users. If other protocols have not been configured or if the user does not have proper access to the content, IIS will send the user an "HTTP 403 Access Denied" error message.

The IUSR_*computername* account is created with a randomly generated password. Microsoft recommends that an administrator change this password using password standards for the organization so that the account can be used for troubleshooting permissions of content if needed. You reset the password in the Active Directory Users And Computers console and then change it on the Master Properties of the Internet Service Manager for each instance of IIS. The IUSR_*computername* account must be a valid user account accessible by the IIS server, but it does not have to be a local computer account. Many organizations change the accounts used for anonymous IIS access for all servers to one centralized account that can be used for all IIS servers to ease ACL administration and make auditing easier as well.

In Exercise 7.6, you'll configure a website for anonymous access.

EXERCISE 7.6

Configuring Anonymous Authentication in IIS 5

In this exercise, you will configure an IIS 5 web server to use Anonymous authentication.

1. On the IIS server, choose Start ➤ Programs ➤ Administrative Tools ➤ Internet Services Manager to open Internet Services Manager.

2. Expand Server to expose the sites, if necessary, and then right-click any site on which you want to set using Anonymous authentication. For example, the Default Web Site will work just fine. Right-click the site, and then choose Properties from the shortcut menu to open the Properties dialog box for the site.

3. Click the Directory Security tab.

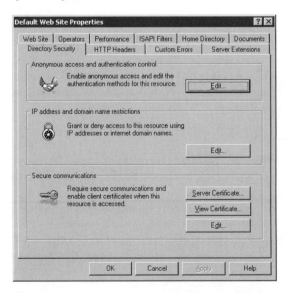

EXERCISE 7.6 *(continued)*

4. In the Anonymous Access And Authentication Control section, click Edit to open the Authentication Methods dialog box.

5. Be sure that the Anonymous Access check box is checked, and then click OK to close the Authentication Methods dialog box.

6. Click OK to close the Web Site Properties dialog box, and then close the Internet Services Manager.

You can combine Anonymous authentication with other authentication protocols. In the event that Anonymous authentication is enabled along with other methods, the browser will always try Anonymous first. If the content does not allow anonymous access or if the content is protected using NTFS file and folder permission that require user identification, Anonymous will fail back to another method of authentication and allow the user to still access the content if they have the proper permissions.

Basic Authentication

Basic authentication is supported by most browsers and most web servers in order to comply with HTTP specifications. When Basic authentication is implemented, IIS prompts users for a valid account and password that is then used to authenticate the user and to set file security so that the user is allowed to access data only according to permissions.

A major security risk is associated with using Basic authentication: the logon information passes unencrypted. This information is sent using Base64 encoding, which is easy to decode and reveals the logon information from the captured packets. Since the logon information is not secured and can be easily captured, few organizations use Basic authentication by itself. To provide the necessary security, most organizations combine Basic authentication with SSL so that the logon information cannot be captured. This is both a secure solution and a highly compatible solution since both technologies are Internet standards and are supported by most browsers.

In Exercise 7.7, you will enable Basic authentication.

EXERCISE 7.7

Enabling Basic Authentication in IIS 5

In this exercise, you will configure an IIS 5 web server to use Basic authentication.

1. On the IIS server, choose Start ➤ Programs ➤ Administrative Tools ➤ Internet Services Manager to open the Internet Services Manager.

2. Expand Server to expose the sites, if necessary, and then right-click any site on which you want to set Anonymous authentication. For example, the Default Web Site will work just fine. Right-click the site, and then choose Properties from the shortcut menu to open the Properties dialog box for the site.

3. Click the Directory Security tab.

4. In the Anonymous Access And Authentication Control section, click Edit to open the Authentication Methods dialog box.

5. Check the Basic Authentication (Password Is Sent In Clear Text) check box. A warning box should appear stating that using Basic authentication will cause passwords to be transmitted without encryption. Click Yes to confirm that you are aware of this.

EXERCISE 7.7 *(continued)*

6. In the Authenticated Access section, click Edit.

7. Enter the NetBIOS domain name. This will save users from having to enter their user name in a `domainname\username` format when logging in. If this information is not entered, it will likely cause problems for many users attempting to use this site.

8. Click OK to close the Authentication Methods dialog box, and click OK to close the Web Site Properties dialog box. If you see an Inheritance Overrides dialog box, click Select All, and then click OK.

9. Close the Internet Services Manager.

It is vital that you remember that Basic authentication is susceptible to intruders that can capture packets and then use Base64 decoding to gather logon information. Basic authentication is not secure, when using it, be sure to protect the site using SSL. You need to use SSL on more than just the initial logon page since every object request that is protected with NTFS permissions will cause the logon information to be resent to the server. To properly protect the password, the entire session needs to be protected using SSL.

In Exercise 7.7, we set up the domain name for Basic authentication. You can set this information for all sites on the server using the Master Properties for the server. Just edit the WWW Service and follow the steps in Exercise 7.7. Once the authentication option is set there, it will apply to all the sites on the server.

Configuring Basic authentication does not automatically configure the IIS server so that it authenticates users. The user accounts must be available, and the file and folder permissions must be set on the content. If the content does not restrict access for anonymous users and you have both Anonymous and Basic authentication configured, users can access the content without having to authenticate using Basic authentication. It is a good idea to set up a network sniffer or to use Network Monitor to monitor the network traffic and verify that the logon information is not going in and out without being encrypted.

Digest Authentication

Digest authentication is new to IIS starting with version 5. Digest authentication is similar to Basic authentication except that instead of using Base64 encoding, the credentials are hashed. This hash is known as a message digest, and it is then encrypted. It is secure in that it is encrypted, and it has protection against replay attacks.

Digest authentication works through both proxy servers and firewalls, but it has requires the following:

- HTTP 1.1 support. Any browsers that do not support HTTP 1.1 will be denied access.

- Internet Explorer 5 or later.

- The web server must be an Active Directory domain member with access to Active Directory.

- Active Directory must be configured for Digest authentication.

Digest authentication does not work the same way as Basic authentication. In Digest authentication, the browser tries to access the content using Anonymous authentication. When anonymous access fails because either the content is protected with NTFS permissions that will not let the IUSR_computername account access the content or the site does not allow anonymous authentication, then the following steps occur:

1. The IIS 5 server sends a response to the web browser indicating the authentication method to be used.

2. The browser takes the user name, password, and some additional information and creates a hash. The additional information is sequencing information to prevent replay attacks.

3. The browser sends the hash to the web server.

4. The web server performs the same hashing operation by using the plain text password information found in Active Directory.

5. If the hashes are equal, access is allowed to the content.

The hash is extremely secure because it is not based on information that can be guessed and brute force attacked. With the combination of the account, password, and the sequencing information, the hash is extremely difficult to break.

In Exercise 7.8, you will enable Digest authentication.

EXERCISE 7.8

Enabling Digest Authentication in IIS 5

In this exercise, you will configure an IIS 5 web server to use Digest authentication. First, though, you must configure Active Directory to support Digest authentication, and then you need to configure the IIS 5 website.

1. Choose Start ➤ Programs ➤ Administrative Tools ➤ Active Directory Users And Computers to open Active Directory Users And Computers.

2. Double-click the account you want to use with Digest authentication, and then click the Account tab.

3. In the Account Options section, click the Store Password Using Reversible Encryption check box, and then click OK.

4. You must reset the password after enabling Reversible Encryption for it to take effect. Right-click the account, and choose Reset Password from the shortcut menu.

5. Enter a new password and click OK.

After you configure all the accounts to support Reversible Encryption, you must configure IIS 5 to support Digest authentication.

6. On the IIS server, choose Start ➤ Programs ➤ Administrative Tools ➤ Internet Services Manager to open the Internet Services Manager.

7. Expand Server to expose the sites, if necessary, and then right-click any site on which you want to set Anonymous authentication. For example, the Default Web Site will work just fine. Right-click the site, and then choose Properties from the shortcut menu to open the Properties dialog box for the site.

8. Click on the Directory Security tab, and then in the Anonymous Access And Authentication Control section, click Edit to open the Authentication Methods dialog box.

9. Click the Digest Authentication For Windows Domain Server check box. A warning box should appear stating that Digest authentication requires storing passwords in clear text within Active Directory. Click Yes to continue.

10. Click OK to close the Authentication Methods dialog box, and then click OK to close the Web Site Properties dialog box. If you see an Inheritance Overrides dialog box, click Select All, and then click OK.

11. Close the Internet Services Manager.

Once Reversible Encryption is enabled and the password is reset, the new password is stored in Active Directory using clear text.

When troubleshooting Digest authentication, check for the following:

- Is IIS 5 a member of a Windows 2000 domain?
- Is Reversible Encryption enabled for the account?

- Has the account password been reset since Reversible Encryption was enabled?

- Is IIS 5 also using other authentication methods instead of Digest?

- Is the web browser Internet Explorer 5 or later?

Remember, Digest authentication works only if the domain server for which a request is made has a plain text copy of the requesting user's password. This is a security risk in itself because now that all domain controllers have plain text copies of passwords, they need to be secured from a variety of both physical and network attacks. Refer to the Windows 2000 Server Resource Kit for information on how to properly secure an Active Directory domain controller.

Integrated Windows Authentication

Integrated Windows authentication is also known as Windows NT Challenge/Response and NTLM. Integrated Windows authentication is fairly secure because it does not ever transmit actual passwords. Integrated Windows authentication uses either Kerberos or NTLM authentication protocols. Although Kerberos is considered secure, NTLM is no longer considered as secure as it used to be because in the last few years it has become more feasible to break the encryption using better software and faster processors.

Integrated Windows authentication enables the browser to use the current logon information to access secured data. If the user is already logged in to the network with a valid user name and password and tries to access web content that is secured using NTFS permissions, the browser can pass the logon information behind the scenes and authenticate the user without using any prompts for logon information. If the user has not logged on already, they are prompted for the logon information. When Integrated Windows authentication is used, a request for secured web content is handled as follows:

1. Anonymous access is attempted and fails because the content is either secured with NTFS permissions that do not allow anonymous access or the website is not configured to allow anonymous access.

2. The web server sends a response to the browser notifying it of the authentication protocols it supports.

3. The browser automatically supplies the logon information if the user has logged on to the network. If the user has not logged on to the network, the browser prompts the user for the logon information.

4. With the proper credentials supplied, access is granted.

The only issue with Integrated Windows authentication is whether it is using Kerberos or NTLM. Kerberos is used if all the following conditions are met:

- The client is running Windows 2000 or later.

- The client is running Internet Explorer 5 or later.

- The server is running IIS 5 or later.

- The client and the server are in the same Active Directory domain or are in trusted domains.

- The server name matches the website name, or the server has the Server Principal Name set to be equal to the site name.

You can set the Server Principal Name using the SetSPN tool in the Windows 2000 Server Resource Kit.

If any of these conditions cannot be met, Windows Integrated authentication will use NTLM. In Exercise 7.9, you will enable Integrated Windows authentication.

EXERCISE 7.9

Enabling Integrated Windows Authentication in IIS 5

In this exercise, you will configure an IIS 5 web server to use Integrated Windows authentication.

1. On the IIS server, choose Start ➢ Programs ➢ Administrative Tools ➢ Internet Services Manager to open the Internet Services Manager.

2. Expand Server to expose the sites, if necessary, and then right-click any site on which you want to set Anonymous authentication. For example, the Default Web Site will work just fine. Right-click the site, and then choose Properties from the shortcut menu to open the Properties dialog box for the site.

3. Click the Directory Security tab.

4. In the Anonymous Access And Authentication Control section, click Edit to open the Authentication Methods dialog box.

5. Click the Integrated Windows Authentication check box.

6. Click OK to close the Authentication Methods dialog box, and then click OK to close the Web Site Properties dialog box. If you see an Inheritance Overrides dialog box, click Select All, and then click OK.

7. Close the Internet Services Manager.

You need to remember the following when working with Integrated Windows authentication:

- It does not work across CERN-compliant proxy servers.

- It does not work with some firewall applications, but will work with others, such as ISA (Internet Security and Acceleration).

- It requires Internet Explorer 2 or later.

Authenticating with Client Certificate Mapping

Client certificate mapping is the process of mapping certificates on client computers to Active Directory accounts. Certificates are used in many applications, including data encryption, signing of data, and providing authentication. A certificate includes an encrypted set of authentication credentials, which includes the digital signature from the issuing certificate authority (CA). As you saw in Chapter 6, the process of obtaining a certificate from a certificate authority is a process of identification authentication, so it makes sense that we can use certificates to prove our identity and authenticate for network resources.

Using certificates for authentication requires that the client computer present its certificate to the server, and the server presents its certificate to the client computer for mutual authentication. The client stores its certificate on the local computer, and the browser can access the certificate when requested by the server.

On the server, client certificates are mapped to user accounts in Active Directory. These accounts can then be used and applied in ACLs on web server content. With a mapped account and a local certificate, the web browser can attach to the web server and request secured content without having to log in. All the authentication can take place behind the scenes, and the data can be downloaded without having to supply logon information like other authentication protocols. These certificate mappings can be one certificate to one Active Directory user account or multiple certificates to one Active Directory user account.

To use certificates for extranet users, you need to configure a certificate authority, which is covered in depth in Chapter 9, and then you need to obtain certificates for each client from the certificate authority. Each extranet user must request and install a certificate from the CA into their browsers. After each extranet user has a certificate installed, that certificate can be used to authenticate against an IIS server once the certificates have been mapped to an account or multiple accounts. In Exercise 7.10, you will configure certificate mapping.

EXERCISE 7.10

Configuring Certificate Mapping

In this exercise, you will obtain a certificate from a local certificate authority and then map that certificate in IIS to a user account in Active Directory.

1. Log in to the client computer that will be used to connect to the IIS 5 server. In the browser, enter the URL for the local CA, for example, http://*servername*/certsrv.

2. Click the Request A Certificate radio button, and then click Next.

3. Click Advanced Request, and then click Next.

4. Click Submit A Certificate Request To This CA Using A Form, and then click Next to open the Certificate Template screen.

5. From the drop-down list box, select User, set the key size to 1024, and then click Submit.

6. Depending on how security is set on your browser, you may see a Potential Scripting Violation warning message. If so, click Yes to proceed. If not, proceed to Step 7.

7. You will see a message asking you to wait for the server to process the request, and then the certificate will be issued.

8. Click Install This Certificate to install the certificate on the local computer.

9. You should then see a message that your new certificate has been successfully installed. Close the web browser window.

Now that you have installed the certificate on the local computer, you need to configure mapping for the certificate.

10. On the certificate authority server, choose Start ≻ Programs ≻ Administrative Tools ≻ Certificate Authority to open the Certificate Authority console.

11. Expand the left pane so that you can select Issued Certificates.

12. In the right pane, right-click the certificate that you just requested and installed on the client computer, and choose Open from the shortcut menu to open the dialog box.

13. Click the Details tab, and then click the Copy To File button to start the Certificate Export Wizard.

14. At the Welcome screen, click Next, and then select the Base-64 Encoded X.509 (.CER) radio button.

15. Enter the filename under which you want to save the exported certificate. This should be a shared file location accessible from the web server. Click Next, and then click Finish.

16. In the Success Notification window, click OK, click OK in the Certificate window, and close the Certificate Authority console.

Now that the certificate has been exported, you can map it to a user in the Internet Services Manager console.

17. On the IIS server, choose Start ➢ Programs ➢ Administrative Tools ➢ Internet Services Manager to open the Internet Services Manager.

18. Expand Server to expose the sites, if necessary, right-click the site that you want to configure to accept certificates, and choose Properties from the shortcut menu to open the Properties dialog box for the site.

19. Click the Directory Security tab, and then click the Edit button in the Secure Communications section to open the Secure Communications dialog box.

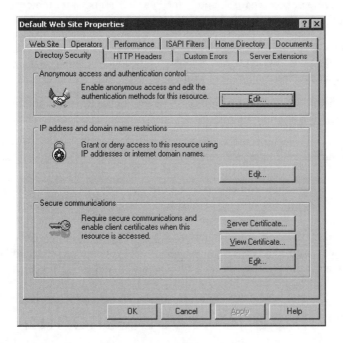

20. Click the Accept Client Certificates radio button, click Enable Client Certificate Mapping, and then click the Edit button to open the dialog box.

21. Click the 1-to-1 tab, and then click Add to create the account mapping.

22. Navigate to the shared file location where you exported the certificate in Step 15, and click Open to open the Map To Account dialog box.

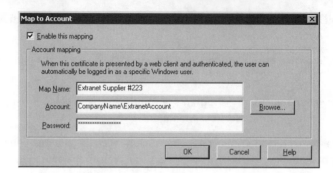

23. Verify that the Enable This Mapping check box is checked, and then in the Map Name box, enter a name for the mapping that will be easy to remember. In the Account box, enter the account name or browse for it, and in the Password box, enter the password for the account to be mapped. Click OK to close the Map To Account dialog box.

24. Click OK again to close the Account Mapping dialog box. Click OK to close the Secure Communications window. Click OK to close the Properties dialog box for the website. (If necessary, accept Inheritance Overrides, and click OK.)

25. In the left pane of Internet Information Services, right-click the server name and chose Restart IIS from the shortcut menu.

26. When the restart is finished, close the Internet Information Services console.

Using certificate mapping, you can extend your networks to enhance the relationships between customers, suppliers, and other business partners. Not only can you extend the network, but you can do so securely using extranet technologies. Stronger ties with those in your business world will result in better service to your customers and more efficient business practices. It just makes good sense all around. Of course, you need to be careful to weigh these added benefits against the added costs of deploying and maintaining this technology.

Configuring and Troubleshooting Authentication for Secure Remote Access

Remote access is one way to allow external users to access the internal network of the organization. We need to stress how important it is that you use proper authentication protocols for these connections. By proper, we mean that they should be secure. Remote access will be covered in more depth in Chapter 8 as we discuss virtual private networks. In this section, we'll look at how Remote Access authentication works and the protocols that you can use.

The scenario is simple: your client computer dials a Routing and Remote Access Server (RRAS) to connect to the organization's network. You use one of the following authentication protocols:

- *Password Authentication Protocol (PAP)*
- *Challenge Handshake Authentication Protocol (CHAP)*
- *Microsoft Challenge Handshake Authentication Protocol (MS-CHAP)*
- *Microsoft Challenge Handshake Authentication Protocol version 2 (MS-CHAPv2)*
- *Extensible Authentication Protocol Message Digest 5 (EAP-MD5)*
- *Extensible Authentication Protocol Transport Layer Security (EAP-TLS)*

You can select which protocols you want to use by configuring RRAS appropriately, as in Exercise 7.11.

EXERCISE 7.11

Configuring RRAS Authentication Protocols

In this exercise, you will configure RRAS authentication protocols on a server.

1. On the RRAS server, choose Start ➢ Programs ➢ Administrative Tools ➢ Routing And Remote Access to start the RRAS console.

2. Right-click the server name, and choose Properties to open the Properties dialog box for the server.

3. Click the Security tab, and then the Authentication Methods button to open the Authentication Methods dialog box.

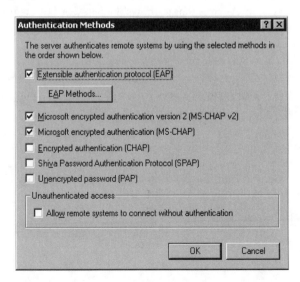

EXERCISE 7.11 *(continued)*

4. Select the authentication protocols to be used by checking the box next to each one that you want to configure.

5. Click OK to close the Authentication Methods dialog box, and then click OK again to close the Properties dialog box for the server.

6. Close the Routing And Remote Access console.

As you can see from the exercise, you can choose from several authentication protocols. By default, Windows 2000 enables MS-CHAP and MS-CHAP v2; however, there are other options to consider. Some of them will be required depending on your environment.

PAP If you select Password Authentication Protocol (PAP), the client computer sends the logon information in clear text. The server then authenticates the client access against the information in Active Directory. This is the least secure of all the authentication protocols and is typically used only when compatibility with a large number of clients is required. Don't use PAP unless it is not possible to use a more secure authentication method because the client cannot support it.

CHAP If you select Challenge Handshake Authentication Protocol (CHAP), the RRAS server sends a challenge to the client computer. This challenge contains session identifier information as well as an arbitrary string. The client computer sends an encrypted reply using a Message Digest 5 hash of the arbitrary string plus the session identifier and the logon information. The server then compares the hash received by the client with the hash that it builds using the same information to see if it is valid. If the hashes are equal, the logon is considered authenticated.

CHAP is considerably more secure than PAP because it does not send the actual password information to the server; it just proves that it knows the password by creating the hash for the server to compare to its hash. CHAP is an industry standard and is compatible with almost all third-party RAS devices.

 PAP and CHAP cannot be used if data encryption is required for dial-up or PPTP (Point-to-Point Tunneling Protocol) connections.

MS-CHAP Microsoft Challenge Handshake Authentication Protocol (MS-CHAP) is similar to CHAP, but it has been extended or enhanced by Microsoft. Just like CHAP, MS-CHAP uses a challenge-response process. The difference between the two is that MS-CHAP uses Microsoft Point-to-Point Encryption (MPPE) instead of Message Digest 5.

MS-CHAP works with all versions of Windows starting with Windows 95, but it not compatible with many non-Microsoft RAS devices. It is installed by default as an authentication method for RRAS in Windows 2000.

To use MS-CHAP for Windows 95, Dial-up Networking (DUN) version 1.3 is required.

MS-CHAP v2   Version 2 of MS-CHAP offers improvements in security. MS-CHAP v2 provides for mutual authentication, not just one way like MS-CHAP, and it provides strong encryption. Windows 2000 and Windows XP Professional use MS-CHAP v2 for both dial-up networking and VPN connections. Windows NT 4 and Windows 98 can only use MS-CHAP v2 for VPN connections. The backward compatibility is a problem if working with older client operating systems, and there is little compatibility with third-party RAS devices.

Windows 2000 uses MS-CHAP v2 as one of its default RRAS authentication protocols along with MS-CHAP. To try to improve on the security, though, Windows 2000 will try to negotiate with MS-CHAP v2 before it tries MS-CHAP so that version 2 is used whenever possible.

EAP-MD5   EAP-MD5 is an extension to the Point-to-Point Protocol (PPP). The Message Digest 5 challenge is the same type as used in CHAP, but the messages are sent using EAP, so they are even more secure.

EAP provides support for many authentication methods that might be added by third parties in the future—smart cards, token cards, one-time passwords, certificates, and biometric devices among others. EAP offers stronger authentication methods that provide greater protection than other password-based authentication protocols against password attacks such as brute-force attacks and dictionary attacks.

In Exercise 7.12, you will enable EAP on RRAS.

EXERCISE 7.12

Enabling EAP on RRAS

In this exercise you will enable EAP for a Routing and Remote Access Server and view the EAP types supported.

1.   On the RRAS server, choose Start ➢ Programs ➢ Administrative Tools ➢ Routing and Remote Access to open the RRAS console.

2.   Right-click the server name, and then choose Properties from the shortcut menu to open the Properties dialog box for the server.

3.   Click the Security tab, and then click the Authentication Methods button to open the Authentication Methods dialog box.

4.   Click the Extensible Authentication Protocol (EAP) check box, and then click the EAP Methods button to open the EAP Methods dialog box.

Notice that the EAP methods installed are the default methods as shown here, but you can add more using third-party plug-ins to support other EAP types in the future.

EAP-TLS EAP-TLS is used for certificate-based security. When using smart cards, for example, you must use EAP-TLS authentication to support the certificate stored on the smart card. EAP-TLS authentication provides for mutual authentication of the client to the server and the server to the client. During authentication, the client computer sends its user certificate and the server sends its computer certificate. If either computer certificate is not valid, not trusted by the other computer, or expired, the authentication fails, and the connection is dropped.

EAP-TLS is extremely secure because it also provides for the negotiation of the encryption method. EAP-TLS provides the strongest authentication available at this time.

EAP-TLS is supported only on Windows 2000 servers running RRAS that are configured to use Windows Authentication and are Active Directory domain members. EAP-TLS is not supported on standalone servers running RRAS. A remote access server running as a standalone server or a member of a workgroup does not support EAP-TLS.

Multifactor Authentication with Smart Cards and EAP

The key to accessing the network is having the proper user name and password combination. This is known as single-factor authentication. Anyone that happens to have your user name and password, or can guess it, can easily pretend that they are you on the network. The password alone is not enough to properly secure the network and to authenticate a user with extremely high levels of confidence.

A two-factor system is a great improvement over a one-factor system. The Automatic Teller Machine (ATM) is a good example of the two-factor system. You need the ATM card with the account information on it, and you also need a personal identification number (PIN). One item is not enough. You need both to access the ATM and withdraw money from it. Of course, the weakness of a two-factor system such as the ATM card is that if you lose the card, you cannot withdraw money, and to get a replacement card is not an easy process since the old one has to be canceled and a new one created. The lost time is a major cost for many organizations.

In Windows 2000 networks, you can use a number of multifactor systems:

Smart cards   A card that can store data, usually a certificate, for identification purposes. Smart cards can provide two-factor authentication by using a PIN in combination with the card.

Tokens   RSA security has the best-known token system. A small device carried by the user generates special codes that must be entered during logon along with the user name. This is also an example of two-factor authentication.

Biometric devices   Some common biometric devices are fingerprint scanners and retinal scanners. These devices are fairly expensive in comparison with other multifactor devices, and other issues can render them worthless, such as a badly burned finger or an eye patch after getting poked with a sharp stick while doing yard work.

Generally, smart cards are the best solution for multifactor authentication. With a smart card and the PIN for the card, multiple factors must be met to prove identity to the network. Smart cards happen to have other advantages such as the ability to provide mutual authentication with the domain controller and to provide encryption keys to protect the logon information.

Windows 2000 and EAP allow for multifactor authentication systems to be used to increase security. Soon, multifactor authentication will become the industry standard as the prices of smart cards and smart card readers come down. Not only is EAP more secure than other authentication methods because of the certificate use, but when combined with the requirement for the smart card and the PIN, the reliability of the system is much greater as well.

Summary

In this chapter we looked at various ways to authenticate users. We also discussed the security concerns with some authentication methods and made some recommendations about which authentication protocols should be used and when. We discussed authentication in relationship to the following:

- Supporting older versions of Windows such as Windows NT 4 and Windows 9x clients
- Supporting Kerberos with Unix systems
- Supporting remotely located clients
- Supporting extranet environments
- Supporting web servers
- Supporting smart cards

Authentication is one of the most important concerns with security in any network. After all, without knowing for sure who is on the other side of a network connection, you cannot be sure that a user should have access to the data they are using. You need to be sure that the clients on our network belong there and did not break in, and you can help increase the security of your network by using the best authentication protocols available for the environment.

Exam Essentials

Make sure you understand the issues with older Microsoft clients such as Windows 9x and Windows NT 4.   Know which authentication protocols each can support and understand the benefits of the Directory Services client.

Be aware of the interoperability between Kerberos and Unix.   Make sure you understand that Kerberos in Windows 2000 follows the RFCs and will interoperate with Unix clients and Unix servers.

Make sure you understand the needs of most businesses to provide access to external partners.   Be aware of the tools you'll need in order to provide secure authentication for those client computers.

Understand trust relationships.   Make sure you understand the authentication protocols that are used in establishing and maintaining trust relationships between Windows 2000 Active Directory domains and Windows NT 4 domains as well as Unix Kerberos realms.

Make sure you can configure authentication protocols for IIS 5 web servers.   Understand the benefits and problems with each of the following authentication protocols:

- Basic authentication
- Integrated Windows authentication
- Anonymous authentication
- Digest authentication
- Client certificate mapping

Know the authentication protocols used for secure remote access.   Make sure you understand each of the authentication protocols used for Windows 2000 Routing and Remote Access Services servers. In particular, know when each should be used and the value of each authentication protocol, including:

- PAP
- CHAP
- MS-CHAP
- MS-CHAP v2
- EAP-MDS
- EAP-TLS

Understand multifactor authentication with smart cards and EAP   Understand the value of multifactor authentication and the options available in Windows 2000 through EAP. Understand the benefits of smart cards.

Key Terms

Before you take the exam, be certain you are familiar with the following terms:

access token	Key Distribution Center (KDC)
Anonymous authentication	LAN Manager (LM)
authentication	LSA (Local Security Authority)
authenticator	Microsoft Challenge Handshake Authentication Protocol (MS-CHAP)
Challenge Handshake Authentication Protocol (CHAP)	Microsoft Challenge Handshake Authentication Protocol version 2 (MS-CHAPv2)
Client certificate mapping	NT LAN Manager (NTLM)
Digest authentication	NTLM version 1
Directory Services client	NTLM version 2
Extensible Authentication Protocol Message Digest 5 (EAP-MD5)	Password Authentication Protocol (PAP)
Extensible Authentication Protocol Transport Layer Security (EAP-TLS)	RFC 1510
extranet	SAM (System Account Manager)
Generic Security Service Application Program Interface (GSSAPI)	Security Support Provider Interface (SSPI)
GINA (Graphical Identification and Authentication dynamic-link library)	single sign-on
Integrated Windows authentication	Ticket-Granting Ticket (TGT)
Kerberos v5	Trust relationships

Review Questions

1. Your supervisor told you to set the Default Group Policy for the domain to tighten security for LAN Manager Authentication Level to Send NTLMv2 Response Only\Refuse LM. Since making this change, Windows 98 users are unable to log in. How can you fix this problem without changing the Group Policy Object?

    A. Install the Dial-up Network (DUN) v 1.3 client on Windows 98.

    B. Install the Directory Services client and configure the Windows 98 computer's Registry to Send NTLMv2 responses only.

    C. Upgrade to Windows 98 Second Edition.

    D. Upgrade all Windows 2000 domain controllers to Service Pack 3 or higher.

2. You implemented a peer-to-peer network in a small branch office using Windows 2000 Professional and Windows XP Professional for the operating systems. Performing a security audit, you find that these computers are not using Kerberos. Why is Kerberos not being used?

    A. Kerberos requires an Active Directory implementation for the user to log in to.

    B. Service Pack 1 for Windows XP Professional and Service Pack 3 or later for Windows 2000 Professional are needed to support Kerberos in a peer-to-peer configuration.

    C. The local computer policies need to be configured to refuse LM, NTLMv1, and NTLMv2 in order to force Kerberos to be used.

    D. At least one Windows 2000 Professional computer needs its KDC service set to automatic.

3. You want to implement a single sign-on solution so that all the Windows 2000 Professional and Windows XP Professional computers can access all Windows 2000 server resources and all Unix server resources. The Unix administrator says it is not possible. You say it is if the Unix servers and their applications support which of the following?

    A. Generic Security Service Application Program Interface (GSSAPI)

    B. Kpass.exeD utility

    C. Ksetup.exe utility

    D. AddksetupAPI

4. Your co-worker changed the security requirements for all accounts so that the minimum password length is set at 15 characters. Now Windows 95 users can't log in. Why?

    A. Windows 95 computers require 7 characters or fewer for their passwords.

    B. Windows 95 computers are unable to support Group Policies.

    C. Windows 95 computers must be allowed to support passwords of all lengths and cannot be forced to use a minimum length password.

    D. Windows 95 computers require 14 characters or fewer for their passwords.

5. You have Windows 98, Windows NT 4 Workstation, and Windows 2000 Professional clients. You want the Windows 2000 Professional computers to always use NTLMv2 only, but you still want to be able to support the other computers. What is the highest level that you can set the LAN Manager Authentication Level option in Group Policy to achieve your goals?

A. Send LM & NTLM

B. Send NTLM Response Only

C. Send NTLM Version 2 Response Only

D. Send NTLM Version 2 Response Only\refuse LM

6. Your Unix administrator read that Windows XP Professional can be configured to use the Kerberos v5 implementation that he has for his Unix systems. He uses the `Ksetup.exe` utility to configure the KDCs in his realm and maps a local computer account to a Kerberos account in his realm. However, it doesn't work. What is the most likely reason it is failing?

A. The local computer account is used for more than one Kerberos mapping.

B. Windows XP Professional clients can only use Kerberos in Windows 2000 Active Directory domains.

C. The Unix servers must be running Samba.

D. The Windows XP Professional client is installed as a member of the Windows 2000 Active Directory domain.

7. You have finally finished your migration to 100 percent Windows 2000 Professional client computers and 100 percent Windows 2000 servers and have Active Directory running. Your Windows 2000 Active Directory implementation required using two forests, and you set up a trust relationship between these two forests. You are preparing for a security audit by a third-party company and want to make sure that NTLM is no longer being used. Your network administrator has been capturing packets and analyzing them for you and finds that NTLM is being used, but it is only used between the domain controllers at the forest root between the two forests. How do you force the servers administering the trust relationship to use only Kerberos?

A. Configure the LAN Manager Authentication Level option to refuse LM, NTLMv1, and NTLMv2.

B. Make sure to physically locate a domain controller for each forest in all sites.

C. You cannot force them to use Kerberos. They can only use NTLM for interforest trusts.

D. Configure the routers between the two forests to filter out NTLM traffic.

8. Your public web server is configured to use Anonymous authentication. It has been working for several months. Your co-worker changed the password of the IUSR_*computername* account on the local web server, and now nobody can access the website. What is the most likely cause?

A. The password was not synchronized with the password in the Master Properties for the web server for the IUSR_*computername* account.

B. Somebody must have disabled Anonymous authentication.

C. Another administrator must have added Basic authentication.

D. Another administrator changed the NTFS permissions for the files and folders for the public website.

9. Your co-worker has enabled Basic authentication in order to allow users to access restricted content using their user name and password for the domain. Users are prompted for their user name and password, but it does not seem to work. What is the most likely cause?

    A. Basic authentication does not work unless it is combined with SSL.

    B. The option to set the domain name for Basic authentication was not used, and the logons fail because they need to be formatted with `domainname\username`. Users are not aware of this requirement.

    C. The SSL certificate used on the website is not a trusted certificate.

    D. Digest authentication must also be set, and it is causing a conflict.

10. Your co-worker has configured a website to use Basic authentication and anonymous authentication only, but when testing the site, you are never prompted to enter your logon credentials. What is the most likely cause?

    A. The ACLs for the web content were not configured to restrict access to certain users and are allowing anonymous users to access the content.

    B. Digest authentication must also be set, and it is causing a conflict.

    C. Basic authentication without SSL will cause failures in most browsers.

    D. The site must also be configured with Integrated Windows authentication.

11. Your co-worker configured a website to use Digest authentication. All the users are complaining that they are not able to access the content even though they have the proper permissions. You check the ACLs, and they should be able to access the content. Why is it failing?

    A. IIS 5 can only use local computer accounts for NTFS permissions.

    B. Not all the accounts were configured to enable the Store Password Using Reversible Encryption option.

    C. IIS 5 cannot use Digest authentication for external users; it only works on intranet sites.

    D. Anonymous authentication must also be set on the site, and the two methods cannot be used on the same website.

12. Your co-worker configured a website to use Digest authentication. A few of the users are complaining that they are not able to access the content even though they have the proper permissions. You check the ACLs, and they should be able to access the content; and you have verified that the Store Password Using Reversible Encryption option was set and that the passwords were reset afterward. Why are some users unable to access the content?

    A. Anonymous authentication must also be set on the site, and the two methods cannot be used on the same website unless using Internet Explorer 5 or later.

    B. Users must be using a browser that does not support HTTP 1.1.

    C. The web server is a member of the Active Directory domain, and it needs to be a standalone web server to support Digest authentication.

    D. Their passwords must be too short. Digest authentication requires passwords of more than eight characters.

13. Your co-worker has configured a website to use Integrated Windows authentication. Users are complaining that they are unable to access it from outside the company. What is the most likely reason that they cannot access the site outside the office?

    A. The company firewall is causing Windows Integrated authentication to fail.

    B. The users are not using Internet Explorer 5 or later.

    C. The certificate mapping is not configured properly.

    D. Anonymous authentication must be set and is causing conflicts.

14. Your supervisor has requested that you come up with a solution that will enable all extranet users to access the web data on `Server1.companyname.com` from the Internet. He wants your solution to be as secure as possible but to require the minimal administration for the web administrator when setting up NTFS permissions for the content. He says that all the external users will have the same rights to content. What would you do?

    A. Configure a web-based certificate authority so that all extranet clients can get certificates, and then map all the certificates to a single account in Active Directory and use that account for the NTFS permissions.

    B. Configure the website to use Digest authentication, and make sure that all external users have the proper browsers needed to meet the requirements.

    C. Configure the website to use Integrated Windows authentication and force use of Kerberos.

    D. Configure a web-based certificate authority so that all extranet clients can get certificates, and then map the all the certificates on a one-to-one basis in Active Directory and use all the accounts for the NTFS permissions.

15. Your co-worker configured a Windows 2000 server for Routing and Remote Access Service for dial-up users. Several users are complaining that they are not able to access the service, while others are not having any problems. Investigation shows that Windows 2000 Professional and Windows XP Professional systems are not having any problems, but all other Windows operating systems are unable to access the RRAS server no matter how they configure their dial-up clients. What is the most likely cause of the problems for everyone using older Windows operating systems?

    A. PAP and CHAP are both configured. Windows 9x and Windows NT 4 clients are unable to use PAP and CHAP for dial-up access; they can only use MS-CHAP.

    B. MS-CHAP is the only authentication method configured on the server. Only Windows 2000 Professional and Windows XP Professional can use MS-CHAP for dial-up access.

    C. MS-CHAPv2 is the only authentication method configured on the server. Only Windows 2000 Professional and Windows XP Professional can use MS-CHAPv2 for dial-up access.

    D. EAP has not been configured, and it is needed to properly support older Windows operating systems for dial-up access.

16. Your co-worker configured a Windows 2000 server for Routing and Remote Access Service for dial-up users. Several users are complaining that they are not able to access the service, while others are not having any problems. Investigation shows that Unix, Linux, and Macintosh users are all having problems no matter how they configure their dial-up clients. What should you do to fix the problem?

A. Configure PAP and CHAP.

B. Remove MS-CHAP.

C. Remove MS-CHAPv2.

D. Configure EAP.

17. Your supervisor has requested that you install a two-factor authentication system for remote users. What should you do?

A. Configure thumb-print scanners on all local workstations.

B. Implement VPNs.

C. Remove PAP and CHAP, and use only MS-CHAPv2 and EAP.

D. Configure EAP and implement smart cards.

18. Your supervisor has asked you to implement EAP-TLS for remote network users. Your company has Windows 98, Windows NT Workstation, and Windows 2000 Professional installed for its remote users. What should you do? (Choose all that apply.)

A. Set up a certificate authority.

B. Work with the remote users to acquire certificates.

C. Map the certificates to Active Directory accounts.

D. Tell your supervisor that it is not possible.

19. Your co-worker configured a many-to-one mapping for all partners to access the extranet. One of your partners went out of business. What should you do?

A. Create a new account for access, and map all the certificates to it except for the failed partner.

B. Delete the account in Active Directory.

C. Edit the certificate mapping.

D. Change the password on the Active Directory account.

20. Your co-worker configured Integrated Windows authentication for your company's website. Some external clients are unable to log on even though they are using the correct user name and password. What is the most likely reason for this failure?

A. Integrated Windows authentication does not work for Windows $9x$ clients.

B. Integrated Windows authentication does not work for websites.

C. Integrated Windows authentication does not work with IE 5.5 or later.

D. Integrated Windows authentication does not work if the remote client is behind a proxy server.

Answers to Review Questions

1. B. Installing the Directory Service client and configuring the Registry will allow Windows 98 to use NTLMv2.

2. A. Kerberos requires the KDC in Active Directory. Without a KDC, Windows 2000 and Windows XP clients will fail over to NTLM.

3. A. All systems and applications supporting the GSSAPI will be able to receive tickets from the Windows 2000 KDC.

4. D. Windows *9x* clients support passwords of 14 characters or fewer. Longer passwords can cause logons to fail.

5. C. With this option, clients will use NTLM Version 2 authentication only, but the domain controllers will accept LM, NTLM, and NTLM Version 2 authentication. Remember, only Windows 2000 and Windows XP can apply Group Policy options.

6. D. Windows XP Professional clients must be a member of a workgroup in order to log in to a third-party Kerberos implementation.

7. C. Interforest trusts authenticate using NTLM only.

8. A. It is important to make sure that when changing the password manually that it is also changed in the Master Properties for the web server.

9. B. Setting the default domain name for Basic authentication will allow users to enter just their user name and password.

10. A. In order for Basic authentication to happen, the Anonymous authentication must fail first. Basic authentication will never be used if the content is accessible using anonymous.

11. B. If the Store Password Using Reversible Encryption option is not set and the password is not reset afterward, Digest authentication will fail.

12. B. HTTP 1.1 is required for Digest authentication.

13. A. Many firewalls do not support Integrated Windows authentication.

14. A. Certificates will be required for the highest level of secure authentication because they will support mutual authentication.

15. C. Only Windows 2000 Professional and Windows XP Professional support MS-CHAPv2 for dial-up connections.

16. A. Non-Windows clients will not use MS-CHAP or MS-CHAPv2 in most cases. You will need to allow PAP or CHAP depending on the authentication that they support.

17. D.   Two-factor authentication requires the use of multiple authentication methods such as a smart card and then a PIN.

18. D.   Windows 9*x* and Windows NT do not support EAP-TLS.

19. C.   All that needs to be done is to remove the mapping for the failed partner's certificate to the Active Directory account.

20. A.   Proxy servers and some firewalls can prevent Integrated Windows authentication from working properly.

Chapter

8

Configuring and Troubleshooting Virtual Private Network Protocols

---

THE MICROSOFT EXAM OBJECTIVES COVERED IN THIS CHAPTER:

✓ Configure and troubleshoot virtual private network (VPN) protocols. Considerations include Internet service provider (ISP), client-computer operating system, Network Address Translation (NAT) devices, Routing and Remote Access server, and firewall server.

✓ Manage client-computer Configurations for remote access security. Tools include remote access policy and Connection Manager Administration Kit.

It seems like most organizations are finally starting to utilize remote network connections. Business demands require keeping the field staff up-to-date with e-mail and providing access to applications and data on the intranet. Business demands also require providing proper access to business partners to improve communications and the efficiencies of doing business together.

Previously, we discussed how partners and other remote network users can access data via web interfaces and other technologies. The *virtual private network (VPN)* has made connecting remote users from any place on the planet covered by the Internet to our company network possible and cost effective. VPNs allow us to connect computers securely across shared networks, private and public. The perfect example is a computer on the Internet, connecting to the company network and being able to access all the company network resources as if it were on the office network. Several years ago, VPN technology was rather expensive and required some specialized skills. Today, with Windows 2000, it has become much easier to implement and much more cost effective.

The most popular uses of VPN technology include the following:

1. Connecting remote computers over the Internet to the company intranet

2. Connecting two or more networks over the Internet

3. Creating an extremely secure perimeter network for company network users and partners

In this chapter, we will discuss how to configure VPNs, and we will also discuss how to troubleshoot VPN connections.

VPN troubleshooting is like troubleshooting any WAN problem. The process is usually complex because data has to travel through so many links. For a VPN, the typical flow is from the client to the *Internet service provider (ISP)* router, through the ISP's *firewall*, across the ISP's network, through other ISPs, to the destination company's ISP, to the company router, to the company firewall, and to the VPN server. Then, there is the trip back. In this chapter, we will discuss the VPN technology and the problems you might encounter.

VPNs and Internet Service Providers

The ISP contact at your company will become a familiar person if you ever have problems with your VPN connections. If you receive good help and response, treat them well! You always need to consider the role of the ISP and the potential they have to break your VPNs. Any time you connect to the Internet, you do so through your ISP.

ISPs used to sell packages allowing completely unfiltered TCP/IP connections to everyone. The idea at the time was that people would buy an ISP package so they could send and receive e-mail, browse the web, and download content. Then many ISP clients started getting smarter. They would keep their systems online 24 hours a day if allowed. These computers would run scripts to make it appear that the connection was alive so as not to get disconnected by the ISP. The clients started hosting their own e-mail and web servers, and then peer-to-peer networks started taking off. To combat this unexpected use, ISPs began filtering traffic to allow only basic services and to prevent their clients from hosting web and e-mail sites that were consuming a great deal of bandwidth. A major problem arose when ISPs started cracking down on home users. ISPs often caused problems for their business clients in their attempts to control the usage by their small home clients.

You will need to consider your company needs when contracting with an ISP. Make sure that you will not have any of your ports filtered by the ISP, or at least those ports that you intend to use. However, don't forget the ISP used by the remote computer that you will be troubleshooting.

Of course, if the ISP is not filtering ports, you are susceptible to many attacks from the Internet. Remember to protect yourself with a firewall.

When troubleshooting any connection, you deal with multiple ISPs. After all, your VPN connection will really look something like Figure 8.1.

FIGURE 8.1   ISP connections

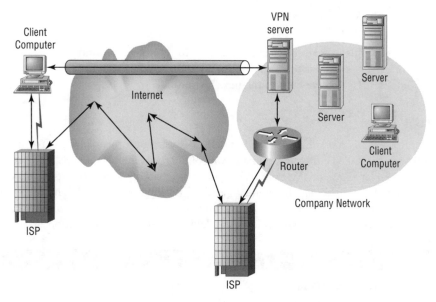

The VPN client computer connects to its ISP, and the company network connects to its ISP. In between the two ISPs are several other higher-level ISPs and the Internet backbones. Logically, the VPN connection travels from the client computer to the VPN server and back using the tunnel. Physically, the route is much different. In between the physical route are at least two ISPs; the company ISP and the remote use ISP, but many more could be involved.

Be aware that some ISPs used by remote users do not support VPNs. Check with these ISPs during your troubleshooting process; doing so might save you pulling out a great deal of hair. If the ISP does not support VPNs, find another ISP for your remote client systems.

 Real World Scenario

Connecting Branch Offices Using VPNs

Your company has three small branch offices and a larger headquarters office. All four offices have direct connections to the Internet. All three branch offices are connected to the headquarters office using leased line connections. The problem is that the cost of the leased lines is going up, and you need some alternatives.

Using VPNs to connect the three branch offices to the headquarters office might be the perfect solution. If you use VPNs, you can drop the leased lines completely and invest the money saved in other areas, including increasing the Internet pipes.

Routing and Remote Access Services (RRAS) Server

Assuming you just got started and selected your ISPs for the company and for your remote network clients, the next step is to configure the VPN server. You will then need to configure the client computers (which we'll do in the next section).

Configuring RRAS

Configuring *Routing and Remote Access Services (RRAS)* is a straightforward process. You need Windows 2000 Server installed either as a domain controller or as a member server. You can use Windows 2000 Server as a standalone server, but you must create separate accounts and passwords on the standalone server. Although the standalone server deployment of RRAS is more secure, it is also more complex to manage. In Exercise 8.1, we will use a member server. Remember, you might need a more secure implementation requiring a standalone server in your production environments.

EXERCISE 8.1

Configuring RRAS for VPN

In this exercise, you will configure RRAS as a VPN server.

1. Choose Start ➤ Programs ➤ Administrative Tools ➤ Routing And Remote Access.

2. Right-click the server name, and choose Configure And Enable Routing And Remote Access from the shortcut menu.

3. Click Next to start the Routing And Remote Access Server Setup Wizard.

4. In the Common Configurations screen, click the Remote Access Server radio button, and then click Next to open the Remote Client Protocols screen. (A number of selections will allow VPN services. We chose Remote Access Server here to allow dial-up connections too. Selecting the Virtual Private Network (VPN) Server enables filtering on the external interface that can cause problems with other services running.)

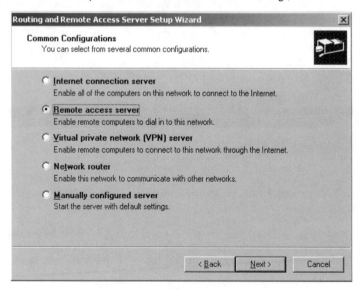

5. Verify that TCP/IP is on the list of protocols, and then click Next.

EXERCISE 8.1 *(continued)*

6. Select the Local Area Connection for the external connection facing the Internet, and click Next (provided you have two or more network cards installed) to open the IP Address Assignment screen.

7. Select the From A Specified Range Or Addresses button, and then click Next.

8. Click New, enter the addresses to be used by VPN clients, click OK, and then click Next to open the Managing Multiple Remote Access Servers screen.

9. Select the No, I Don't Want To Set Up This Server To Use RADIUS Now radio button, and then click Next.

10. Click Finish, and then click OK on the warning message about the issue with needing to install the DHCP Relay Agent.

RRAS is now configured and ready for VPN clients.

You might have noticed that when you installed RRAS, it automatically configured 5 *Point-to-Point Tunneling Protocol (PPTP)* ports and 5 *Layer 2 Tunneling Protocol (L2TP)* ports. RRAS can support 256 connections. However, it is a good idea to create only the number you need to support all your remote network clients. If your company needs only 20 PPTP connections and only 5 L2TP connections, create only those ports.

     If RRAS is configured using the Virtual Private Network option, it will automatically create 128 PPTP ports and 128 L2TP ports. This is often more than a company will need, so make sure you remove some after the configuration is completed.

In Exercise 8.2, you will create and delete VPN ports.

EXERCISE 8.2

Creating and Deleting VPN Ports

In this exercise, we will go through the steps to create and delete VPN ports.

1. Choose Start ➢ Programs ➢ Administrative Tools ➢ Routing And Remote Access to open the RRAS MMC console.

2. Expand the RRAS server if necessary until the Ports icon is exposed in the left pane.

3. Right-click the Ports icon, and choose Properties from the shortcut menu to open the Ports Properties dialog box.

4. Highlight the port type that you want to increase or decrease, and then click Configure.

5. Enter the number of ports in the Maximum Ports box. Click OK.

6. Repeat Steps 4 and 5 for the other port type if needed.

7. Click OK to close the Ports Properties dialog box. Close the Routing And Remote Access window.

Because you must have enough IP addresses to support the VPN clients, you need to configure the server to assign IP addresses. The IP addresses can come from either a static address pool or from DHCP (Dynamic Host Configuration Protocol). When using a static address pool, RRAS clients receive the same DNS (Domain Name System) and WINS (Windows Internet Naming Service) settings that the RRAS server uses. If the RRAS server can browse the network and access resources, clients should also be able to browse the network and access network resources with the same settings. You can also configure RRAS to use DHCP. Options provided by DHCP, such as the DNS and WINS addresses, can be provided to RRAS clients.

Configuring Authentication Protocols

RRAS can use various authentication protocols as discussed in Chapter 7. Configuring authentication protocols for the RRAS server is a straightforward process. Simply open the Routing And Remote Access MMC console, right-click the server, and select the Security tab. In the Security tab, click the Authentication Methods button. Figure 8.2 shows that the default authentication protocols for RRAS are MS-CHAP and MS-CHAPv2.

FIGURE 8.2   Authentication methods

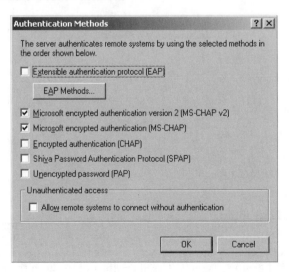

To support devices and systems other than Microsoft operating systems, you will need to use one of the other *authentication methods* as supported by the VPN client that will be used. Also note that EAP (*Extensible Authentication Protocol*) is available for authentication for PPTP and L2TP tunneling. EAP requires either Windows 2000 or Windows XP clients, however.

Troubleshooting RRAS

Once RRAS is properly configured, you will find that VPN connections through RRAS are dependable and secure. However, much can go wrong with RRAS, and you need to be ready to troubleshoot. Some basics steps for troubleshooting VPN connections from the RRAS server include the following:

- Test basic Internet connectivity from the RRAS server.
- Verify that IP addresses are available either through the static pool or through the DHCP server environment. If more IP addresses are needed, you can add them to the static pool by right-clicking the RRAS server in the Routing And Remote Access MMC console and then clicking the IP tab. To add addresses, you can click the Add button; to edit the existing pool, click the Edit button, as in Figure 8.3.

FIGURE 8.3   The static address pool

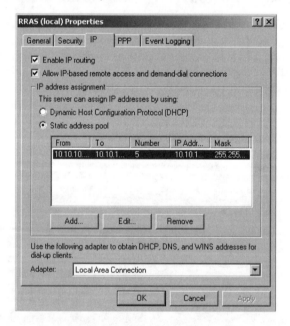

- Verify that VPN Ports are available as in Figure 8.4. If all the ports are active, create more ports.
- Verify that certificate authorities used for EAP authentication are trusted by both the RRAS server and the VPN client systems. Remember, for L2TP tunnels with *IPSec (Internet Protocol Security) protocol*, you will need certificates for both the RRAS server and for each VPN client system.

FIGURE 8.4 VPN port availability

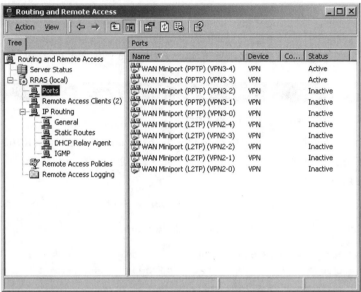

- You can enable or disable *PPTP filtering* in the Routing And Remote Access MMC console. Since PPTP filtering is fairly complex, it is addressed in more depth in the next section. Troubleshooting might require verifying that these filters were set properly or removing them for testing.

- *Authentication protocol* mismatches can be a problem. Make sure that the client operating system and the RRAS server are configured to use the same authentication protocols. If Unix and Macintosh computers are having problems, you might want to check to see if lower-level authentication protocols are enabled for them. Many administrators forget that other operating systems do not support MS-CHAP and MS-CHAPv2. PPTP VPNs require MS-CHAP, MS-CHAPv2, or EAP-TLS (*Extensible Authentication Protocol with Transport Layer Security*). Refer to Chapter 7 for details on authentication protocols.

- TCP/IP (Transmission Control Protocol/Internet Protocol) configuration issues often require troubleshooting.

  - DNS configuration is important at the server level because VPN clients will inherit the DNS server address from the RRAS server.

  - WINS configuration is also important at the server level because VPN clients will inherit the WINS server address from the RRAS server.

  - DHCP configuration can be a problem for many RRAS implementations. It is vital that the DHCP Relay Agent is properly installed on the RRAS server; if it is not, VPN clients will not be able to connect and work on the network.

  - Default gateway configurations should be left blank for the internal LAN interface, and the default gateway should be set with the ISP-provided gateway on the WAN interface.

PPTP Filtering

Configuring *PPTP filtering* requires setting up six filters. You need to configure three filters as input filters and three filters as output filters. PPTP filtering is a fantastic way to lock down the RRAS server that is exposed to the Internet. The RRAS server will not respond to any requests other than VPN connections using PPTP. In Exercise 8.3, you will manually configure PPTP filtering.

EXERCISE 8.3

Manually Configuring PPTP Filtering

In this exercise, you will create six filters so that the external interface of an RRAS server will not allow any packets other than PPTP packets for VPN client connections.

Selecting the External Interface

1. Choose Start ➤ Programs ➤ Administrative Tools ➤ Routing And Remote Access.

2. Expand the RRAS server, and then expand IP Routing.

3. Click General, right-click the external interface, and select Properties from the list in the right pane to open the Local Area Connection Properties dialog box at the General tab.

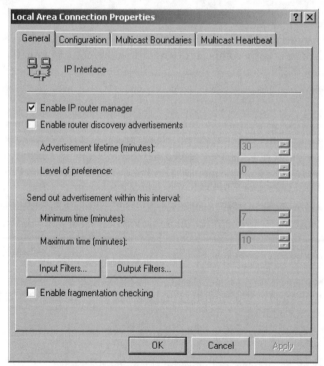

Setting the Three Input Filters

4. Click the Input Filters button, and then click Add to open the Add IP Filter dialog box.

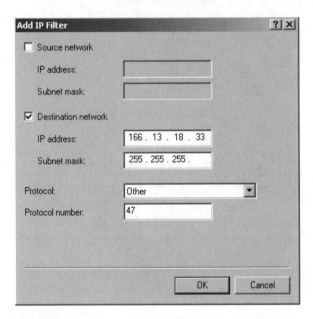

5. Click the Destination Network check box, and then enter the IP address and the subnet mask for the external interface.

6. In the Protocol drop-down list box, select Other. In the Protocol Number box, type **47**, and then click OK to close the Add IP Filter dialog box.

This completes the first filter.

7. In the Input Filters window, click Add.

8. Click the Destination Network check box, and then enter the IP address and the subnet mask for the external interface.

9. In the Protocol drop-down list box, select TCP. In the Source Port box, enter **0**, and in the Destination Port box, enter **1723**. Click OK.

10. This completes the second filter.

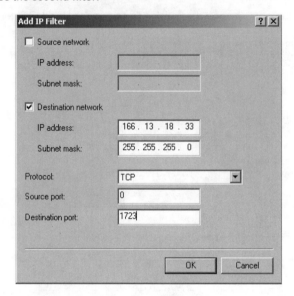

11. In the Input Filters window, click Add.

12. Click the Destination Network check box, and then enter the IP address and the subnet mask for the external interface.

13. In the Protocol drop-down list box, select TCP. In the Source Port box, enter **1723**, and in the Destination Port box, enter **0**. Click OK.

14. Click the Drop All Packets Except Those That Meet The Criteria Below radio button. Click OK.

This completes the third filter. This filter is optional and is only needed if the RRAS server will also be used as an RRAS client to connect to other servers. The best example is an RRAS server that connects external clients and also connects branch offices. Step 10 is required even if the third filter is not configured.

Setting the Three Output Filters

15. In the Local Area Connection Properties dialog box, click Output Filters, and click Add.

16. Click the Destination Network check box, and then enter the IP address and the subnet mask for the external interface.

17. In the Protocol drop-down list box, select Other, type **47**, and click OK.

18. This completes the fourth filter.

19. In the Input Filters window, click Add.

20. Click the Destination Network check box, and then enter the IP address and the subnet mask for the external interface.

21. In the Protocol drop-down list box, select TCP. In the Source Port box, enter **0**, and in the Destination Port box, enter **1723**. Click OK.

22. This completes the fifth filter.

23. In the Input Filters window, click Add.

24. Click the Destination Network check box, and then enter the IP address and the subnet mask for the external interface.

25. In the Protocol drop-down list box, select TCP. In the Source Port box, enter **1723**, and in the Destination Port box, enter 0. Click OK.

26. Click the Drop All Packets Except Those That Meet The Criteria Below radio button. Click OK.

This completes the sixth filter. This filter is optional and is only needed if the RRAS server will also be used as an RRAS client to connect to other servers. The best example is an RRAS server that connects external clients and also connects branch offices. Step 20 is required even if the third filter is not configured.

Troubleshooting PPTP filtering requires verifying that all the filters were set properly. In some cases, it will be necessary to remove one or even all the filters to get VPNs working properly.

Auditing and Event Logs

You can increase auditing to assist with troubleshooting RRAS. To set logging to the maximum level, open the Routing And Remote Access MMC console, right-click the RRAS server, and choose Properties from the shortcut menu to open the RRAS Properties dialog box. Click the Event Logging tab, and select the options shown in Figure 8.5.

You can also turn on account logon and logon events auditing though the Default Domain Controllers Policy. With auditing turned on, you can try the connection again to see if anything shows up in the Security log in Event Viewer. If the username is incorrect, if the password is wrong or is expired, or if there is no valid computer account, you will see this in the Security log. On the other side of the equation, if the user logs on properly, you will also see the success message in the Security log.

FIGURE 8.5 Event logging

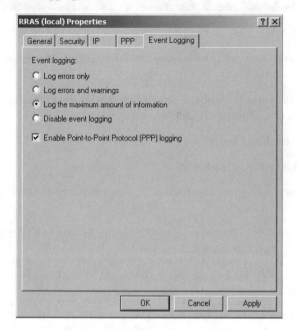

Configuring and Troubleshooting VPN Client Systems

So far, you've checked the ISPs as one of the first steps in troubleshooting your VPNs, especially when coming from the client side. Assuming that you are doing your troubleshooting correctly, you have checked your server and found that many other users are connecting without any problems. So, the next step is to troubleshoot the client system.

Configuring Client Systems for VPNs

Before you can troubleshoot your client connection, you must configure the client, which you'll do in Exercise 8.4.

EXERCISE 8.4

Configuring a Windows XP Professional VPN Client

In this exercise, you'll configure a Windows XP Professional system as a VPN client and connect to an RRAS server.

1. Choose Start ≻ Control Panel ≻ Network And Internet Connections.

2. Click Create A Connection To The Network At Your Workplace.

3. If you have never set up the telephony configuration for your system, you will be prompted
    to enter the information as shown in this graphic. Click OK, and then click OK on Dialing
    Rules screen.

4. Since you want a VPN connection, click the Virtual Private Network Connection radio button,
    and click Next to open the Connection Name screen.

5. Enter the name of your company or some other information that will help you iden-
    tify the connection for later reference. Click Next to open the VPN Server Selection
    screen.

6. Enter the computer name or the IP address of the VPN server. In most cases, enter-
    ing the IP address is preferred because it will eliminate troubleshooting later.
    Click Next.

7. Check the Add A Shortcut To This Connection To My Desktop check box. Click
    Finish.

8. Close the Network And Internet Connections window.

EXERCISE 8.4 *(continued)*

9.   Double-click your new shortcut to open the Connect VPN ServerName dialog box.

10.   Click on Properties to open the Properties dialog box for this connection, and then click the Options tab. Click the Include Windows Logon Domain check box. Click OK.

11.   Enter the logon credentials, including the domain information, and then click Connect.

At this point, you should be connected properly to the VPN server. You can further test the connectivity by pinging devices on the company network and attaching to file and printer shares. You can disconnect by double-clicking the VPN connection icon in the Taskbar and clicking Disconnect. You can also disconnect by choosing Start ➢ Control Panel ➢ Network And Internet Connections ➢ Network Connections and then right-clicking the VPN connection and selecting Disconnect.

Windows XP Professional is the best client operating system to use for VPN connectivity. The built-in features of the VPN client make it easy to configure and easy to change and troubleshoot as needed, and it is extremely secure. After Windows XP Professional, Windows 2000 Professional is probably the next best bet for a VPN client operating system. Both client operating systems make fantastic VPN clients. In Exercise 8.5, you'll configure a Windows 2000 Professional VPN client.

EXERCISE 8.5

Configuring a Windows 2000 Professional VPN client

In this exercise, you will configure a Windows 2000 Professional system as a VPN client and connect to an RRAS server.

1.   Choose Start ➢ Settings ➢ Control Panel, and then click Network And Dial-up Connections.

2. Click Make New Connection.

3. If you have not filled in the telephony information before, you will need to fill it in at this time. Enter the area code and other information as necessary, click OK, and click OK again. If you have already filled this in before, proceed to the next step.

4. Click Next at the Welcome To The Network Connection Wizard screen to open the Network Connection Type screen.

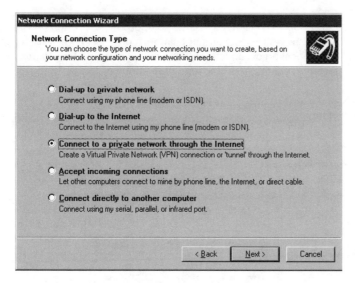

5. Click the Connect To A Private Network Through The Internet radio button and click Next.

6. Enter the host name of the RRAS server or enter the IP address of the RRAS server. Click Next.

7. Click the Only For Myself radio button so that the VPN connection cannot be used by others on the network. Click Next.

8. Name the VPN connection with a user-friendly name that will be easy for the user to recognize. Check the Add A Shortcut To My Desktop check box. Click Finish.

This completes the basic configuration of the VPN client and will immediately open the VPN connection application so you can test it.

VPN clients can use three technologies for the tunnels:

- PPTP
- IPSec
- L2TP

PPTP is popular and has a fairly long history. PPTP supports secure encapsulation of IP, IPX (Internetwork Packet Exchange), and NetBEUI (NetBIOS Enhanced User Interface) traffic sent across private and public IP-based networks. IPSec tunneling allows only IP packets to be encrypted and sent over private and public IP-based networks. L2TP allows IP, IPX, and NetBEUI traffic to be encapsulated and sent over any IP, X.25, Frame Relay, and ATM (asynchronous transfer mode) networks. PPTP and L2TP are both layer 2 tunneling protocols. IPSec is a layer 3 tunneling protocol. IPSec tunneling has several weaknesses, which we will not discuss in this book. However, combining IPSec and L2TP makes a very secure tunneling protocol combination. Microsoft has been recommending this combination for the last couple of years.

L2TP/IPSec is considered a better solution because it supports computer authentication as well as user authentication, it provides for header compression, and authentication occurs after IPSec encryption is in place so that all credentials are encrypted. L2TP/IPSec requires Windows 2000 or Windows XP VPN clients.

Once the VPN client is installed, you can review its configuration and see that it supports both PPTP and L2TP/IPSec as shown in Figure 8.6. Support for IPSec tunneling is not offered by itself.

FIGURE 8.6   VPN types

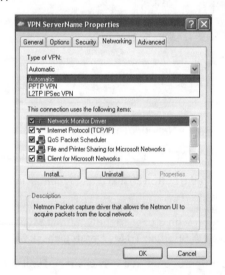

In reality, a VPN client has to maintain two sets of TCP/IP information. One set is maintained for its network connection to the LAN or its connection to the ISP. The second set is maintained for the VPN connection. Because there are two routes for all IP traffic, one to the local network or ISP and the other through the VPN, the routing table must direct packets to the ISP for all Internet traffic and must also be configured to direct the traffic bound for the remote network through the VPN interface. If the default gateway is improperly configured, or if the routing table is not correctly built, ugly things will happen.

Troubleshooting Client Systems

We have found the following steps to be most successful when troubleshooting client systems:

Test basic client Internet connectivity.   Testing helps to verify connectivity to the ISP and the Internet. This basic testing will also tell you whether the client has proper IP configuration information and DNS entries.

Verify that the Allow Access permission is granted for dial-in users.   Using Active Directory Users And Computers, check the properties for the remote user and verify that they have Allow Access permission on the Dial-In tab.

Verify that all utilized CAs are trusted by both the VPN server and the VPN clients when using L2TP with IPSec.   If the CAs are not trusted by both the VPN server and the VPN client, the mutual authentication will fail. Without mutual authentication, the connection will not be established.

You might need to create computer accounts for the VPN client, depending on the operating system they are using.   This is particularly important when it comes to browsing the network. If the client system is not part of the domain, it will be in a workgroup and will be tough to find. Also, because the computer account trust is reset in as little as 7 days (depending on the operating system), deleting and re-creating the computer account may be required.

Make sure that the client operating system and the RRAS server are configured to use the same authentication protocols.   Authentication protocol mismatches can be a problem. Refer to Chapter 7 for details on troubleshooting authentication protocols.

TCP/IP configuration issues often require troubleshooting.   Be sure to consider the following TCP/IP configuration issues:

- DNS configuration is important at the client level because VPN clients will need the proper DNS configurations just to connect to the RRAS server by the server name.

- WINS configuration is also important. The VPN clients will inherit the WINS server address from the RRAS server. It is a good idea to verify that WINS information was properly received.

- DHCP configuration can be a problem for many RRAS implementations. It is vital that the DHCP Relay Agent is properly installed on the RRAS server; if it is not, VPN clients will not be able to connect and work on the network.

- Default gateway configuration can be a problem. When the VPN client connects to the RRAS server, it will start using the default gateway provided by the RRAS server. To prevent this, you need to open the Properties dialog box for the VPN client. Click the Networking tab, select Internet Protocol (TCP/IP), click Properties, then click the Advanced button. On the General tab, clear the Use Default Gateway On Remote Network check box. Click OK, and then close the rest of the configuration windows.

The computer name of the RRAS server can be a problem, especially if it is not properly registered in DNS or if there are client DNS problems.   The best fix is to use the IP address when possible, as in Figure 8.7.

FIGURE 8.7   VPN connection properties

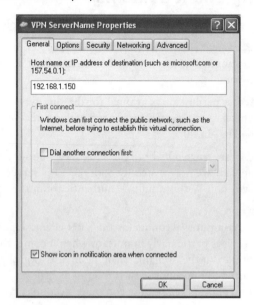

The lists in the "Troubleshooting RRAS" and "Troubleshooting Client Systems" sections are good starting points to troubleshoot these configuration errors.

Network Address Translation (NAT) and VPNs

Network Address Translation (NAT) allows a device that supports NAT to intercept all traffic bound for the Internet from the intranet and replace the source IP in the packet with its own source IP address. When the packet response returns from the destination and reaches the NAT device or service, NAT then replaces the destination IP with the IP address of the internal device. Figure 8.8 illustrates this process.

NAT is a strong solution because it hides the originator's IP address from the Internet. NAT is also nice from the standpoint of ISPs that can now reduce the number of IP addresses leased to most companies since they can use NAT devices or services. Using NAT allows most companies to use private IP address ranges for all internal networks.

The major problem with NAT is that it is not able to properly handle all IP packets going from the internal network out to the Internet. One of the biggest problems with NAT is that it cannot support L2TP/IPSec tunneling because the IPSec *Encapsulating Security Payload (ESP)* packets become corrupted. VPN servers and VPN clients cannot use L2TP/IPSec tunneling if any of them are behind NAT devices or servers using NAT.

FIGURE 8.8 The NAT process

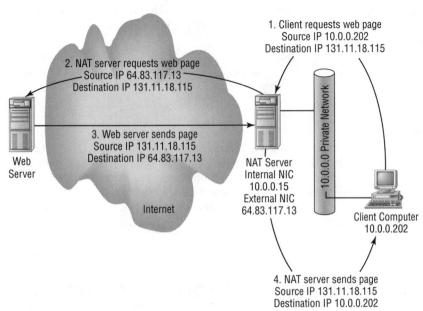

If NAT is used for remote network clients using VPNs or if the VPN server is behind NAT, the solution will require using PPTP tunnels. Although PPTP is not as secure as L2TP/IPSec, it will meet the needs of most organizations.

Firewall Servers with VPNs

Firewalls can be a problem for VPN connections. Almost every company on the Internet uses firewalls to protect their internal networks from Internet attacks. Many individuals also use firewalls on their personal computers; these firewalls are often referred to as personal firewalls. And many ISPs use firewalls to protect their hosted environments, as do many users that have signed up for additional services.

In order for VPNs to work through firewalls, the proper protocol IDs and port numbers must be enabled. The following will be required (L2TP requires IKE [Internet Key Exchange] and ESP too):

Protocol	Protocol ID	Port Number
PPTP (GRE)	47	TCP 1723
L2TP		UDP 1701
IKE		UDP 500
ESP	50	

Generic Routing Encapsulation (GRE) is a problem with some ISPs because they use GRE to manage internal network routers. If the ISP is using GRE, they may filter it out to and from client connections for security reasons. GRE filtering is not common, but if GRE is filtered out, it will prevent a PPTP connection.

The best solution, when it comes to firewalls, is to ask the firewall vendor if they have any compatibility problems with VPN tunneling in or out of their firewall. Some older firewalls may not support L2TP/IPSec or PPTP.

Firewalls that allow VPN clients through will fail to stop VPN clients from accessing all protocols that would normally be filtered by the firewall. Since all other traffic is encapsulated, the firewall cannot filter what it cannot see. For example, an internal user is not allowed to use instant messaging technologies. If they are going through the firewall using VPN to another location, the instant messaging packets will be encapsulated within the VPN packets and will not be visible to the firewall.

Managing Client Computer Configurations for Remote Access Security

Configuring the client side for VPN connectivity can be simple for small-scale deployments. However, properly configuring larger-scale deployments may require the use of other tools. Many organizations also have to be concerned with how VPNs are used by the general population. Resulting VPN policies will often require enforcement as to who can use VPN and under what conditions. These remote access policies can be enforced with the aptly named *Remote Access Policies*.

Remote Access Service Policies

Remote Access Service Policies define and enforce which users and groups can use RAS, when they can use RAS, under what conditions they can use RAS, and what levels of encryption and authentication are required for RAS connections. RAS policies are important, because we want to verify and ensure the following:

- Only authorized users can access RAS and during approved times.
- Users must be using the proper authentication protocols.
- Users must be using the proper encryption levels.
- Idle time and session lengths are properly constrained.
- Only approved media types are used.
- Only approved tunneling protocols are used.

You can place other types of constraints on RAS connections for remote network users, but these are the major constraints and should address most of your needs.

RRAS is configured with a default policy during its initial configuration. The default policy specifies any day of the week and any time of the day. This means that the default policy conditions will always be met. The default policy permission is Deny Remote Access Permission. Most administrators are confused when they see these settings, and then they see that the title for this policy is Allow Access If Dial-In Permission Is Enabled. The logic does not work here. However, the logic does work if you understand that the default policy allows access for all users that have been granted Allow Access permission in the Dial-In tab of their user account properties. The permissions in the policy are overridden by the Dial-In tab permissions. Many organizations use this as the very last policy in a list of policies as a final catch-all policy. Other companies delete this default policy because they want to enforce only a certain number of policies and do not want any others that might affect the environment without their expressed desires.

RRAS policies can best be described as having three sections.

Conditions   Under what conditions will the policy apply. These conditions can include the day and time restrictions, security group restrictions, tunnel type restrictions, and other restrictions regarding phone numbers and IP addresses for remote connections and RADIUS servers if Internet Authentication Service (IAS) is used. Conditions are in Specify The Conditions To Match box. Clicking the Add button displays the conditions that can be used, as shown on the right in Figure 8.9.

FIGURE 8.9   RAS policy conditions

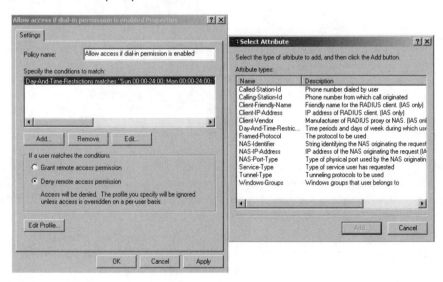

Permissions   After the conditions are reviewed and met, the policy applies the proper permissions. Either the connection is granted or it is denied based on whether the Grant Remote Access Permission or the Deny Remote Access Permission radio button is selected. Notice that in Figure 8.9 that the Deny Remote Access Permission radio button is selected. A note underneath states that "Access will be denied. The profile you specify will be ignored unless access is overridden on a per-user basis." This means that whatever permission is granted here can be overridden in the user account attributes using Active Directory Users And Computers. With the Deny in the policy, the attributes for the Administrator account in Figure 8.10 will override the Deny, and the administrator can use this policy to access the RRAS server.

FIGURE 8.10   The Administrator Properties dialog box in mixed mode

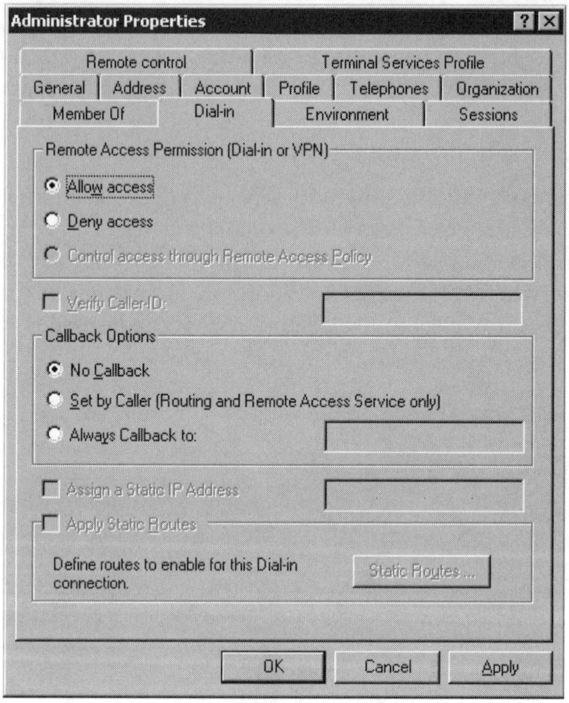

Figure 8.10 shows the properties when Active Directory is in mixed mode. In mixed mode, policies are more difficult to enforce because they can be overridden. When mixed mode is changed to native mode, the Control Access Through Remote Access Policy radio button becomes available, as shown in Figure 8.11.

Profile   The profile provides restrictions on the connection once it is made. In the policy properties, click the Edit Profile button to open the Edit Dial-in Profile dialog box (see Figure 8.12). The profile is basically a user profile for RAS connections whether they are dial-in or VPN connections. The Authentication tab specifies what authentication protocols can be used for the connection, and the Encryption tab specifies what level of encryption can be used (or multiple levels that will be allowed) for the connection.

FIGURE 8.11   The Administrator Properties dialog box in native mode

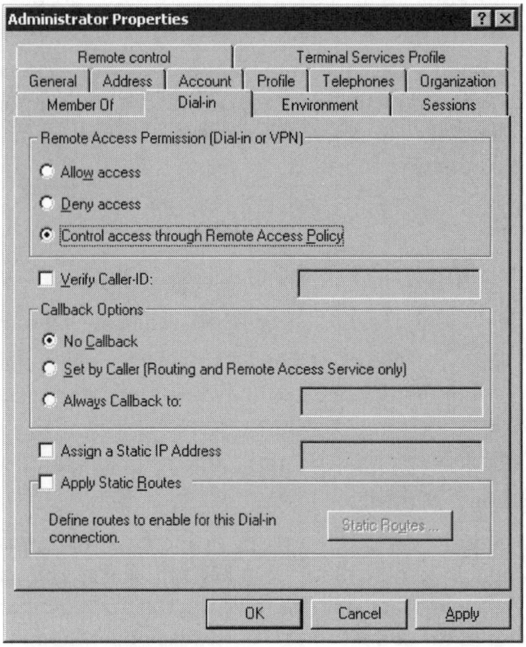

FIGURE 8.12   The RAS profile

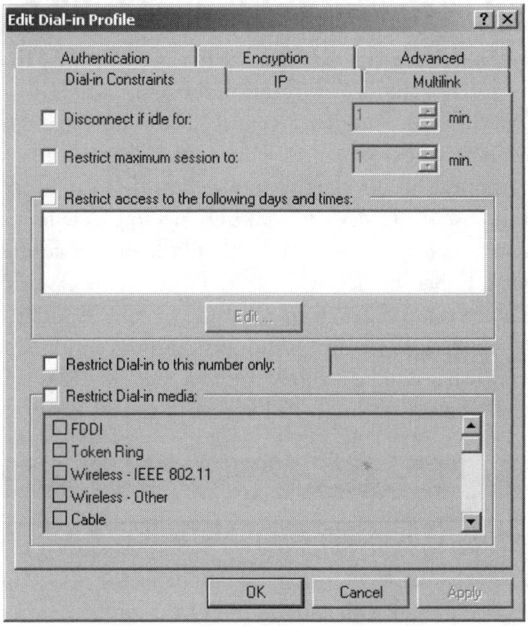

A remote network user trying to connect to the RRAS server will go through several steps that take an extremely short time to happen. The process is well documented in many places, but it deserves some attention here. The high-level steps are as follows:

1. RRAS tries to match a policy with the conditions of the current connection attempt. It starts from the top of the list of policies and goes down. If it finds a policy that matches the conditions, it uses that policy to determine permissions. If no policy is found that matches the conditions, the connection is denied.

2. If a policy is found that matches the conditions, RRAS processes it for permissions. This works as follows:

    a. If the account Dial-In tab is set to Allow Access, the connection can proceed.

    b. If the account Dial-In tab is set to Deny Access, the connection is denied.

    c. If the account Dial-In tab is set to Control Access Through Remote Access Policies, the permissions section of the policy is evaluated and processed according to its Grant or Deny permissions.

3. The profile is applied to the connection. If the connection does not meet a parameter in the profile, the connection is denied.

As you can see, making the connection work properly involves many considerations. Troubleshooting RAS policies can be easy if you keep these steps in mind and remember that RRAS evaluates each policy in order starting from the top and going down. If RRAS finds a match to the conditions and the connection fails because of permissions or profile constraints, RRAS will not attempt to find another policy that might also match farther down the list.

The Connection Manager Administration Kit

You can use the *Connection Manager Administration Kit (CMAK)* to distribute the service profile to remote clients and to provide information for remote clients to find updates. You can, for example, use the CMAK to generate phone books for remote clients so that they can dial up to local ISPs or local branch offices when traveling. In addition, you can use the CMAK to provide VPN server configuration information as well as dial-up information.

Many larger companies use the CMAK to make connecting easy for remote users; however, other companies create images for remote users with all the proper configuration information already input and installed. Either method will work, but using the CMAK method has some other benefits such as the ability to get updates from a web server specified in the service profile created.

You can run the CMAK Wizard on any Windows 2000 server. It is probably best to run the wizard on the RRAS server that will be used. If you run the CMAK Wizard on the RRAS server, the files will automatically be stored on it. In Exercise 8.6, you'll run the CMAK.

EXERCISE 8.6

Running the Connection Manager Administration Kit

In this exercise you will install the CMAK, run it, and then use the resulting executable to install and test the resulting service profile. You can run the CMAK processes on any Windows 2000 Server, Windows 2000 Professional, or even Windows XP Professional machine.

Installing the CMAK Wizard

1.   Choose Start ➢ Settings ➢ Control Panel, and then double-click Add/Remove Programs.

2.   Click Add/Remove Windows Components.

3.   Select Management And Monitoring Tools, then click the Details button.

4.   Click the Connection Manager Components check box, and then click OK.

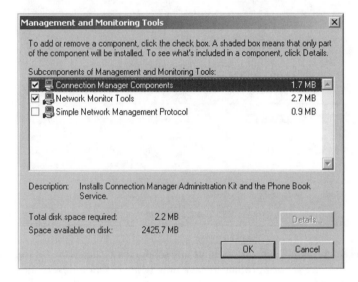

5.   Click Next. If prompted, you may have to respond to the Terminal Services Setup dialog box. Verify that the proper radio button is selected and click Next again.

6.   Windows copies the proper files. Be prepared to provide the latest service pack CD and the location of the Windows 2000 Server installation files. Click Finish when the file copy process is completed. Close the Add/Remove Programs window and any other windows that might still be open.

     At this point, the CMAK Wizard is installed on the RRAS server.

Run the CMAK Wizard

7.   Choose Start ➢ Programs ➢ Administrative Tools ➢ Connection Manager Administration Kit to start the CMAK Wizard.

8.   At the Welcome To The Connection Manager Administration Kit Wizard screen, click Next to open the Service Profile Source screen.

9.   Click the Create A New Service Policy radio button, and then click Next to open the Service And File Names screen. In the future, you can use this wizard to edit this profile as well as other service profiles.

EXERCISE 8.6 *(continued)*

10. In the Service Name box, enter a filename of 8 characters or fewer. This name should be meaningful and self-explanatory. Click Next to open the Merged Service Profiles screen.

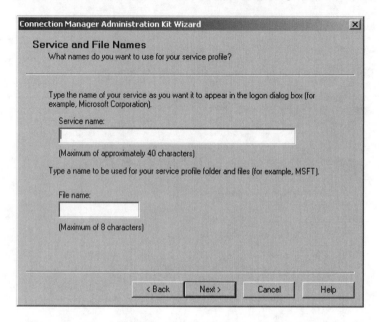

11. Since this is a new profile, we will not have any others to merge. In the future, you can use this screen to merge service profiles to save time when creating new ones. Click Next to open the Support Information screen.

12. Enter support information. This information will appear in the logon dialog box for users so they know where to call or send e-mail if they have problems. Click Next to open the Realm Name screen.

13. Verify that the Do Not Add A Realm Name radio button is selected and click Next. The Realm name is a nice option if you have to provide it as part of the authentication; it is not required in this case.

14. Click the Add button to edit the dial-up networking entries. You can also set each entry with the appropriate IP configuration information and even assign a dial-up script to be run. If you don't have any that you want to add at this time, click Next to open the VPN support screen.

15. Click the This Service Profile check box, and then click Next to open the VPN Connection screen.

16. Enter either the host name or IP address of the RRAS server for VPN access in the Server Address box. Click the Use The Same User Name And Password For A VPN Connection As For A Dial-Up Connection check box. Click Next.

17. Clear the boxes for Connect Actions as you feel appropriate. In this exercise, they are not required, so it is best to clear all the boxes. If you leave any of the boxes checked, you will be asked for additional information about scripts or programs to be run for the action. Click Next to open the Auto-Applications screen.

18. Enter the names of any applications that you want all VPN or dial-up users to run while they are connected to the RRAS server. Click Next to open the Logon BitMap screen.

19. Verify that the Use The Default Bitmap radio button is selected. If you want to customize your clients, you can create a company graphic to replace the default graphic. Click Next to open the Phone Book BitMap screen.

20. Verify that the Use The Default Bitmap radio button is selected. If you want to customize your clients, you can create a company graphic to replace the default graphic. Click Next to open the Phone Book screen.

21. Enter the filename for any phone books that you would like to deploy with the service file in the Phone-book File box. You can leave this box blank if you do not want to distribute any phone books. Click Next to open the Icons screen.

22. Verify that the Use The Default Files For All Icons radio button is selected. If you want to customize your clients, you can create company graphics to replace the default graphics. Click Next to open the Status-Area-Icon-Menu screen.

23. Enter any shortcuts that you would like to make available for the status icon in the notification area on the Taskbar. Any shortcuts added here will be made available for users that right-click the VPN or dial-up connection icon while the connection is available. Click Next to open the Help File screen.

24. Verify that the Use The Default Help File radio button is selected. A custom help file can be deployed if needed. Click Next to open the Connection Manager Software screen.

25. Verify that the Include The Connection Manager 1.2 Software check box is enabled. Click Next to open the License Agreement screen.

26. You can create your own custom license agreement that will be displayed whenever anyone attempts to run the service profile.

27. Click Next at the Additional Files screen. You can deploy other files, if needed, in the service profile.

28. Click Next at the Ready To Build The Service Profile screen. The service profile file will be compiled.

29. Click Finish to complete the wizard. Note the name and location of your service file. This is the file that will be used in the next step to deploy your dial-up and VPN configurations.

The file created in these steps can now be sent out and installed on remote client systems.

EXERCISE 8.6 *(continued)*

Client Deployment and Testing

30. Copy the service profile executable to a remote client system.

31. Double-click the executable on the client system. Click Yes to install the connection.

32. Click the My Use Only radio button and verify that the Add A Shortcut To The Desktop check box is checked. Click OK.

33. The installation will run and automatically create a shortcut to access the RRAS server on the Desktop. The VPN client will automatically run.

34. Enter your user credentials and click Connect.

You will be logged in, and the VPN will be established.

Using the CMAK can really be helpful if you support a large number of remote network clients. Updating one package and sending it to everyone that uses remote network connections via dial-up or VPN can be extremely cost effective.

Summary

Virtual private networks are secure, are cost effective, and can be deployed efficiently. To properly troubleshoot VPN connections, you must understand that the connections can be impacted in several places:

- ISPs
- RRAS servers
- Client systems

- Firewalls
- NAT servers
- Policies
- Permissions

With VPNs becoming more prevalent in network designs, it is vital to understand the basic problems that you might encounter from the server side as well as the client side with issues such as remote access permissions, types of VPN protocols, and authentication protocols.

Deployment of VPN configurations and access control options allow administrators the ability to control who uses VPN connections, when they use VPN connections, and what configurations they must use. With these decisions made, you can also make it easy for remote users to install the VPN client by creating a service profile and sending them an installation package.

The Routing and Remote Access Service provided by Windows 2000 Server is an excellent platform for VPN connections, and it is a much more cost effective solution than the third-party solutions of the past.

Exam Essentials

Understand the details of troubleshooting VPN protocols.   Make sure you understand the basics of VPNs, including which protocols are available.

Make sure you understand that ISPs can impact VPNs through protocol filtering.   Not all ISPs are equal, so it is important to contact the ISP from the client side as well as the server side when troubleshooting VPN problems.

Make sure you know how to configure the RRAS server to support VPN connections.   Know where to set the encryption level and when to use a standalone RRAS server instead of a member server. Understand how to create and delete VPN ports. Understand how to implement a static pool, and understand when to use DHCP. Make sure you understand what PPTP filtering is and how it can impact troubleshooting if it is being utilized.

Make sure you understand the basics of troubleshooting the VPN client.   Make sure you know how to create the client side VPN connection and know how to force it to use L2TP/IPSec instead of PPTP.

Understand how to successfully use NAT with VPNs.   Make sure you know which VPN protocol works through NAT and which does not.

Understand use of firewall servers and VPNs.   Understand which ports and protocol ID are needed to support VPN connections through firewalls. Understand that some firewalls can also use NAT. Understand why GRE might be filtered at an ISP firewall.

Know how to set RAS policies.   Make sure you understand the components of an RAS policy and how the permissions in the policy interact with the permissions in Active Directory. Make sure you understand how policies are applied and in what order policies are evaluated. Make sure you understand which conditions can be set in the policy and which connection requirements can be set through the profile.

Know how to leverage the Connection Manager Administration Kit (CMAK).   Make sure you know what CMAK is and how it can be used to create service profiles for dial-up and VPN connections to the RRAS server. Make sure you know how to create the executable and how to use the executable file to install the VPN client configuration on a client system.

Key Terms

Before you take the exam, be certain you are familiar with the following terms:

authentication methods	L2TP/IPSec
authentication protocol	Layer 2 Tunneling Protocol (L2TP)
Connection Manager Administration Kit (CMAK)	Network Address Translation (NAT)
Encapsulating Security Payload (ESP)	Point-to-Point Tunneling Protocol (PPTP)
firewall	PPTP filtering
Generic Routing Encapsulation (GRE)	Remote Access Policies
Internet service provider (ISP)	Routing and Remote Access Services (RRAS)
IPSec (Internet Protocol Security) protocol	virtual private network (VPN)

Review Questions

1. For which of the following can you use virtual private networks? (Choose all that apply.)

   A. Connect remote client machines to an intranet

   B. Connect multiple offices together over the Internet

   C. Build extremely secure extranets

   D. Provide secure e-mail traffic with the Internet

2. Your company has changed ISPs over the weekend. On Monday, VPN users report that they can no longer access the company network using VPN connections. What is the most likely solution?

   A. Reconfigure VPN clients to use a new IP address.

   B. Change VPN clients from PPTP to L2TP.

   C. Reconfigure VPN clients to use a new host name for the RRAS server.

   D. Disable software compression for VPN clients.

3. Your company just started a new division in another building 20 miles away. The new division uses NetWare and Windows 2000 Server. Many of the division members will be work in the new building, and others will split time between the buildings. Your supervisor is planning to purchase a leased line between the two offices. Both offices will have direct Internet connections. Both offices use private IP addresses, and the RRAS servers providing VPN services are located behind firewalls running NAT. Your supervisor asks you for options. Which of the following options will work?

   A. Build a VPN between the two offices using L2TP tunneling. NWLink and IPX can traverse the VPN. Do not purchase a leased line.

   B. Build a VPN between the two offices using IPSec tunneling. NWLink and IPX can traverse the VPN. Do not purchase a leased line.

   C. Build a VPN between the two offices using L2TP. Purchase a leased line to handle the IPX traffic.

   D. Build a VPN between the two offices using PPTP tunneling. NWLink and IPX can traverse the VPN. Do not purchase a leased line.

4. Your company installed RRAS and intends to use it for VPN access from remote clients. You set up RRAS to use DHCP. VPN clients are not able to connect. What is the most likely reason?

   A. DHCP delivers the wrong DNS address, and the VPN clients can't find the RRAS server by its host name.

   B. It is necessary to install a DHCP Relay Agent on the RRAS server.

   C. RRAS needs a different DHCP scope than for internal addresses.

   D. DHCP is delivering the wrong default gateway address to RRAS clients.

5. Your coworker configured RRAS as a Remote Access Server. It worked during testing with three different VPN users; however, it doesn't seem to be working now that it is in full production. What is the most likely reason?

    A. RRAS creates only 5 PPTP and 5 L2TP ports. All the ports are being consumed.

    B. The test users must have all been using L2TP ports, and all the new users do not have certificates needed for L2TP.

    C. The RRAS server will support only 5 users when configured as a Remote Access Server.

    D. The production users do not have the proper certificates to support IPSec in combination with L2TP.

6. Your company plans to put the RRAS server directly on the Internet and then connect it to the company intranet. What can be done to secure the RRAS server from Internet attacks and still allow it to provide VPN services?

    A. Configure Remote Access Policies.

    B. Disable multicasting on the external interface.

    C. Use PPTP filtering on the external interface.

    D. Configure all ports as L2TP, and use L2TP/IPSec tunneling only.

7. Your company hosts critical data in a protected perimeter network. Users access the data using VPN connections from the Internet. An internal user at the company would also like to connect to this server through the company network instead of having to dial up the Internet through a local ISP. What do you tell him.

    A. He can connect directly to the RRAS server from the LAN using a VPN.

    B. He can only connect via the Internet.

    C. It will require a third-party VPN device; RRAS cannot accept intranet addresses.

    D. He can connect directly to the RRAS server, but he can use L2TP/IPSec tunneling only.

8. Your company runs RRAS to support VPN connections. One of the company VPs is working from a hotel while on vacation. The hotel filters out certain websites, one of which is your company beta site. How can you help him?

    A. Tell him he can use a VPN and connect directly to the website using the URL for the destination host name.

    B. Tell him that he can use his VPN connection to the RRAS server and then access the beta site through the company intranet.

    C. Tell him he can use a VPN and connect directly to the company website using the IP address for the destination address.

    D. Tell him to use the Security tab in the VPN Properties dialog box to set the Require Data Encryption option and then use the VPN to connect directly to the beta site.

9. You just added five more VPN users to the network. You receive a call from a VPN user saying that he cannot connect. This is a VPN user that has never had any problems. You think that you may have run out of VPN ports and need to create more. How do you do this?

   A. Open the Routing And Remote Access MMC console on the RRAS server. Click Remote Access Clients to see how many VPN ports are in use and how many are available.

   B. Open the Routing And Remote Access MMC console on the RRAS server. Click Ports to see how many VPN ports are in use and how many are available.

   C. Open the Routing And Remote Access MMC console on the RRAS server. Click Remote Access Logging to see how many VPN ports are in use and how many are available.

   D. Open the Routing And Remote Access MMC console on the RRAS server. Click Remote Access Policies to see how many VPN ports are in use and how many are available.

10. You received a call from a remote network user. He bought a new computer and has been having trouble using his VPN client ever since he installed it. He installed the client using the service profile that you sent him earlier. Troubleshooting reveals that PPTP works, but L2TP/IPSec does not work. What is the most likely reason?

    A. The Options tab does not have the Include Windows Logon Domain check box enabled.

    B. The advanced settings on the Security tab do not include PAP authentication.

    C. He has Windows XP, and his Internet Connection Firewall is enabled.

    D. He does not have a certificate for his new computer.

11. You received a call from a remote network user. He is having trouble using his VPN client over the last few hours. Troubleshooting reveals that he can access the VPN server using the IP address but not the fully qualified domain name. Other VPN users are not experiencing this problem. What is the most likely reason for this user's problem?

    A. The DNS server he has configured for his ISP is unavailable.

    B. The company DNS server is unavailable.

    C. PPTP filtering has stopped DNS resolution of the RRAS server.

    D. The ISP firewall must be stopping external DNS from resolving.

12. You received a call from a remote network user. She is having trouble using her VPN client ever since she installed it. Troubleshooting reveals that she has configured the advanced settings on the Security tab. She has configured PAP, CHAP, and SPAP for authentication protocols. What can be done to fix the problem?

    A. Change the client to use Extensible Authentication Protocol (EAP).

    B. Configure the client to include the Windows Logon Domain in the Options tab.

    C. Add PAP, CHAP, and SPAP to the RRAS authentication methods.

    D. Remove PAP, CHAP, and SPAP from the client configuration, and add MS-CHAP and MS-CHAPv2.

13. Your company has decided to deploy RRAS to support VPN connections from remote network clients. Your supervisor states that the authentication protocols must support mutual authentication. Which protocols can you configure to meet this requirement? (Choose all that apply.)

    A. CHAP

    B. MS-CHAP

    C. MS-CHAPv2

    D. EAP

14. Your company has decided to deploy RRAS to support VPN connections from remote network clients. Your supervisor states that the EAP must be used. Which client operating systems can you use to meet this requirement? (Choose all that apply.)

    A. Windows 9x with DUN v1.3

    B. Windows NT 4

    C. Windows 2000

    D. Windows XP

15. Your company has decided to deploy RRAS to support VPN connections from remote network clients. Your supervisor states that the L2TP/IPSec must be used. Which client operating systems can you use to meet this requirement? (Choose all that apply.)

    A. Windows 9x with DUN v1.3

    B. Windows NT 4

    C. Windows 2000

    D. Windows XP

16. Your company has decided to deploy RRAS to support VPN connections from remote network clients. Your supervisor states that the L2TP/IPSec must be used. Which steps must you take to meet this requirement? (Choose all that apply.)

    A. Install a computer certificate on the RRAS server.

    B. Install a computer certificate on all VPN clients.

    C. Use only Windows 2000 or Windows XP clients.

    D. Make sure that the RRAS server and the VPN clients are not behind a NAT device.

    E. Configure Remote Access Policies to enforce L2TP/IPSec.

17. You received a call from a remote network user. She is having trouble using her VPN client ever since she installed it. She states that she tried to ping the RRAS server and it didn't respond, so it must be something wrong with the server. You know that many people are connected using VPNs to the RRAS server, so it is not down. What is the most likely reason that ping fails from the client system?

    A. The ISP is filtering ICMP.

    B. The RRAS server has the wrong default gateway.

    C. PPTP filtering is enabled on the external RRAS interface.

    D. The client system has the wrong default gateway.

18. You received a call from a remote network user. He is having trouble using his VPN client ever since he installed it. He states that he is no longer able to access website through his local ISP connection to the Internet. What is the most likely reason?

A. You need to clear the Use Default Gateway On Remote Network check box in the VPN client configuration.

B. You need to check the Enable IP Routing check box on the IP tab in the RRAS Properties dialog box.

C. You need to configure the RRAS server as a router by checking the Router check box on the RRAS General Properties tab.

D. You need to check the Allow IP-Based Remote Access And Demand-Dial Connections check box on the IP tab of the RRAS Properties dialog box.

19. Your just set up a new user in Active Directory Users And Computers. You added the user to the VPN users security group which has a Remote Access Policy. The Remote Access Policy for the VPN Users group has the conditions set for Monday to Friday from 6 A.M. to 8 P.M. You walk the user through setting up the VPN client for PPTP tunneling over the phone, but he is unable to connect. What is the most likely reason?

A. The user is in a different time zone.

B. The user needs a certificate for his computer.

C. You need to configure DNS on the client computer.

D. You forgot to select the Allow Access radio button on the Dial-In tab for the user account.

20. You just configured RRAS to support VPN connections. You configured a new Remote Access Policy for users to access the intranet using VPN connections during work hours. During testing, however, your test user always connects even when the policy is set to Deny Remote Access Permission. You check the Dial-In tab on the test account in Active Directory Users And Computers. You find that the user account is set to Allow Access. You want to set the user to Control Access Through Remote Access Policy, but it is grayed out. How can you make this option available?

A. Join the RRAS server to the Active Directory domain.

B. Configure the RRAS server with a static IP address for both the internal and external network interfaces.

C. Change the Windows 2000 Active Directory to native mode.

D. Configure the Remote Access Policy profile to Server Settings Define Policy.

Answers to Review Questions

1. A, B, C. VPNs can provide secure tunnels to connect remote computers, connect branch offices over public networks, and provide secure access to perimeter network resources such as an extranet.

2. A. Changing ISPs will almost always require changing IP addresses for Internet facing resources such as a web server. Although the host name for the RRAS server might have been updated with the new IP through DNS, it is likely that there are statically configured VPN clients.

3. D. L2TP will not work because of NAT being in place, and IPSec tunneling will not support IPX. PPTP supports NAT and IPX along with TCP/IP.

4. B. Even though the RRAS configuration wizard warns administrators to configure a DHCP relay, they can still forget.

5. A. To support more than 5 PPTP and 5 L2TP ports, RRAS must have additional ports configured when originally configured as a Remote Access Server.

6. C. PPTP filtering configures the external interface so it only responds to VPN connections.

7. A. VPN connections do not have to originate from the Internet.

8. B. The hotel's ISP will not be able to stop the access of the website because it cannot see the information inside the VPN.

9. B. Ports will show all ports that are currently active and all ports that are inactive.

10. D. The client computer must have a computer certificate that is trusted by the RRAS server.

11. A. The local ISP DNS is probably down or unavailable for a short time. He should call his ISP to verify, or he should configure a secondary DNS server to avoid the problem in the future.

12. D. RRAS, by default, uses MS-CHAP and MS-CHAPv2. The client and the server must match with at least one authentication protocol in order to connect.

13. C, D. MS-CHAPv2 and EAP both provide mutual authentication. EAP requires certificates, but there is still mutual authentication.

14. C, D. Only Windows 2000 and Windows XP support EAP authentication.

15. C, D. Only Windows 2000 and Windows XP support L2TP/IPSec tunneling.

16. A, B, C, D. L2TP/IPSec requires certificates and the proper network operating systems to function. Also, L2TP/IPSec does not work through NAT.

17. C. PPTP filtering will cause the RRAS server to drop all packets except VPN packets, making it look as if it is offline to users trying to ping it.

18. A. This check box is enabled by default and will prevent the VPN client from accessing the Internet directly using its Internet connection.

19. D. If the Deny Access radio button is selected, the connection will fail.

20. C. Active Directory must be in native mode to enable the Control Access Through Remote Access Policy.

Chapter 9

Installing, Configuring, and Managing Certificate Authorities

---

THE MICROSOFT EXAM OBJECTIVES COVERED IN THIS CHAPTER INCLUDE:

✓ **Install and configure certificate authority (CA) hierarchies. Considerations include enterprise, stand-alone, and third-party.**

  ▪ Install and configure the root, intermediate, and issuing CA. Considerations include renewals and hierarchy.

  ▪ Configure certificate templates. Considerations include LDAP queries, HTTP queries, and third-party CAs.

  ▪ Configure the publication of Certificate Revocation Lists (CRLs).

  ▪ Configure public key Group Policy.

  ▪ Configure certificate renewal and enrollment.

  ▪ Deploy certificates to users, computers, and CAs.

✓ **Manage certificate authorities (CAs). Considerations include enterprise, stand-alone, and third-party.**

  ▪ Enroll and renew certificates.

  ▪ Revoke certificates.

  ▪ Manage and troubleshoot Certificate Revocation Lists (CRLs). Considerations include publishing the CRL.

  ▪ Back up and restore the CA.

Understanding PKI and the use of certificates to secure networking will be extremely important to network administrators if it isn't already. Certificate-based encryption and authentication provides a much higher level of security and should be used whenever security is extremely important to an organization.

Certificate authorities are key components of a PKI. The CA issues and manages the certificates used by all users and computers involved in secure transactions. The CA has to be trusted by all parties involved in the transactions, and it must be kept as secure as possible to prevent any breaches that could compromise the integrity of the PKI. If all users and computers can not trust the CA, there is no reason to use it. Trust is paramount.

In this chapter, we will install and configure certificate authorities, and we will go through the processes of managing a certificate authority.

Public Key Infrastructure and Certificate Authorities

Public Key Infrastructure (PKI) is the combination of systems and technologies used to provide the foundation of completely trustworthy and secure communications and business transactions. A true PKI will include *certificate authorities (CAs)* that provide *digital certificates* to individuals, computers, and even applications. The certificates used in the PKI will be based on *public-private key pairs* used for signing and sealing communications, data, and transactions.

For a PKI to be acceptable to everyone involved in business communications and transactions, it must provide high levels of the following:

Integrity We know that the transaction has not been changed since it was transmitted.

Confidentiality We know that nobody has read the message since it was transmitted.

Authenticity We know that the message is not a replay or a fake with a spoofed origination address.

Nonrepudiation We know that the sender is who they say they are and that the message is their transaction.

A PKI must also be highly available, meaning that it must be running and must be accessible at all times when business transactions are running that depend on its services. An example of a PKI-enabled application is an e-mail application that can sign and seal messages sent to receivers on the Internet as well as internally within the company. Another example is a fully secured website accessed using SSL-enabled sites and pages so that all content and information sent to the site are fully encrypted. These are only two examples of many in which PKI-enabled applications provide security and confidence to business transactions. Some other major PKI-enabled applications include the following:

- 802.1x authentications

- EFS (Encrypting File System)

- IPSec (Internet Protocol Security) encryption

- Smart card logons

Larger organizations will have a hierarchy of CAs such as that shown in Figure 9.1. The three-tiered structure is considered a best practice for organizations in which security is important.

FIGURE 9.1   A CA hierarchy

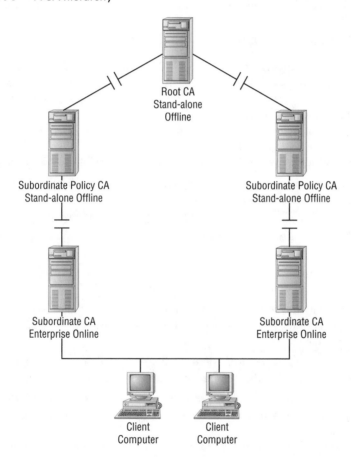

Let's take a look at the three types of CAs shown in Figure 9.1.

Root CA   In larger organizations, a *root CA*, is usually a stand-alone offline CA. The root CA is kept in a secure area and is not put on the network. The root CA provides certificates for intermediate CAs.

Intermediate CAs   *Intermediate CAs* are used to separate classes of certificates. For example, intermediate CA might be used specifically for users and another specifically for computers. Or the structure might be based on geography. Intermediate CAs are usually stand-alone offline CAs just like root CAs.

Issuing CAs   *Issuing CAs* are used to provide certificates to users, computers, and services. In some cases, there will be multiple issuing CAs, and they will be used for separate processes much like intermediate CAs. For example, one issuing CA might be used for all computer certificates and another for all user certificates. Multiple issuing CAs allow multiple CAs to share the load of issuing and managing certificates on the network. Issuing CAs can be used in many ways. For example, an issuing CA might be located at each physical location of a company to service the network segments at the remote sites.

    We will discuss the installation and configuration of these types of CAs in the next sections.

Installing and Configuring the Root CA

The root CA is the most important CA for a PKI. The root CA is the first CA in a PKI. The root CA is used to issue certificates to subordinate CAs that are then used to issue certificates to users, computers, and services on the network. A root CA is self-signed; the root CA issues itself a certificate. This requires a great deal of confidence and trust in the CA and its processes since you must accept that it is vouching for itself and verifying its own identity. All clients on the network must trust the root CAs; otherwise, the PKI will not meet the requirement of integrity. The root CA can be added to the client's list of trusted root certificates in several ways:

- An administrator can add the root CA manually using the Certificates MMC console to add the root CA's certificate to each computer's trusted list.

- A user can add the root CA manually using the Certificates MMC console. Any certificates added to the list of trusted root certificates will apply only to that single user on the computer, however.

- An administrator can use a Group Policy to distribute trusted root certificates for all computers under the control of the Group Policy.

- An administrator can use `certutil.exe` to modify the Configuration container and publish trusted root certificates to the Certification Authorities container under the Public Key Services container.

- An administrator can use *certutil.exe* to modify the Configuration container and publish trusted root certificates to the AIA container under the Public Key Services container.

    No matter which method is used, it will take some testing to verify that the trusted root certificates are properly updated. You will also want to note that the first two methods work with Windows NT 4 and later and that the rest work only with Windows 2000 and later systems.

    The root remains off the network so that if something happens that compromises an issuing CA, the root CA can be brought back online to revoke the certificate for the compromised issuing CA. The root CA can then be used to issue a certificate to a new replacement CA. The company does not have to scrap its entire PKI if it uses an offline stand-alone root server. Smaller organizations may have only one CA, which is the root CA as well as an issuing CA. A single CA is generally not recommended because if it fails, the entire PKI is compromised and must be re-created.

The prerequisites for installing a stand-alone offline root CA are as follows.

The stand-alone offline root CA must be a workgroup member and not a member of any domain. Since the root CA will be offline and secured, it cannot have network connections and cannot be linked to any domain.

The computer name must be unique for the entire forest. Even though the computer is offline, the name is part of the information published in Active Directory.

A *certificate revocation list (CRL)* must be published even though the server is offline. The *CRL distribution point (CDP)* is always included in the certificate. The CDP must be accessible to users on the network. This process is normally completed after the root CA is installed.

The root CA certificate, itself, should also be made available to the network for verification of the root CA and the CA chain. This process is normally completed after the root CA is installed.

The *authority information access (AIA)* distribution point needs to be configured for the intermediate and other CAs farther down the chain so that the CA chain can be properly verified. This process is normally completed after the root CA is installed.

The server for the CA must be running IIS (Internet Information Services). Since the server will not be online on the network, the only way to request and retrieve certificates from the offline CA is to use the web forms.

 VMware is a great piece of software that you can use to create the three-server hierarchy of PKI certificate servers without multiple physical servers in your lab. You can find information about VMware at www.vmware.com.

In Exercise 9.1, you will install a stand-alone root CA.

EXERCISE 9.1

Installing a Stand-Alone Root CA

In this exercise, you will install and configure a stand-alone root certificate authority server.

1. Choose Start ➤ Settings ➤ Control Panel to open Control Panel.

2. Double-click Add/Remove Programs to open the Add/Remove Programs window.

3. Click Add/Remove Windows Components in the left pane to start the Windows Components Wizard.

4. Click the Certificate Services check box. Click Yes when you see the message stating that you cannot change the computer name or its domain membership.

5. Click the Details button, and notice that Certificate Services will install two components, the Certificate Services CA and Certificates Services Web Enrollment Support. Click OK to close the window.

6. Click Next to start the installation. If the Terminal Services Setup window opens, click Next again. The Terminal Services Setup window will always open if Terminal Services is installed on the server. Click Next to open the Certification Authority Type screen.

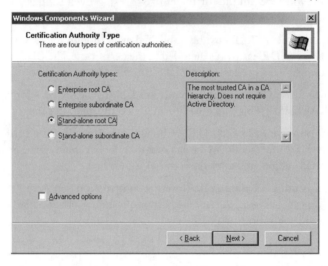

7. Notice that you have two choices for root CAs: the Enterprise Root CA and the Stand-Alone Root CA. Click the Stand-Alone Root CA radio button, and then click Next to open the CA Identifying Information screen.

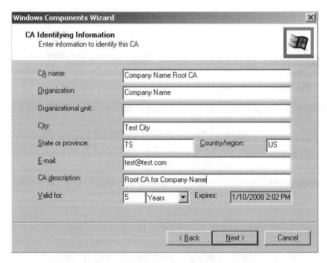

8. Fill in the CA identifying information. By default, the CA expires in two years. For an offline root CA, you might want to consider increasing it to five years as shown here. Click Next to open the Data Storage Location screen.

9. Select the location of the certificate database and its log files. It is a good idea to put the database and the log files on separate hard drives. In the event of a hard-drive failure, you'll have better restore capability. Click Next.

10. Click OK when you see the warning that IIS will be stopped.

11. You may be prompted for the location of the latest service pack and the original Windows 2000 CD. Make sure you have them available. If you are prompted, click OK and point the installation program to these files. Click Finish.

12. Close all the remaining windows.

At this point, you will have a functioning stand-alone root CA. You can now remove it from the network and place it in a secure location.

Installation of a stand-alone root CA is just the first step in building a certificate authority hierarchy as part of the PKI for an organization. The next step is to properly publish information about the stand-alone offline root CA so it can be accessed by systems that need to check for the CRL and install any intermediate CAs that might be needed for the organization.

Configuring the Publication of CRLs

Publishing the CRL is extremely important to the PKI. The users of the network and the network resources need to know when a certificate has been revoked. If a certificate is revoked, and the network users and resources do not know that it has been revoked, it still has the same value as a current certificate. This is not acceptable in most environments.

For offline CAs, publication requires some manual configuration. Exercise 9.2 will walk you through the process of publishing the CRL so that it is accessible to the users of the network. Keep in mind that if you are using a CA for external use, the CRL must be available to external users too.

Creating the CDP for the Stand-Alone Offline Root CA

You can create the CDP using either a file share location, a web URL, or an LDAP (Lightweight Directory Access Protocol) directory location. In this exercise, you will create the CDP using a web URL and the file URL.

Create a Share Point for the CDP

1. Select a server on the network running IIS. This server should be a part of the Active Directory forest.

2. On the selected server, choose Start ➢ Programs ➢ Accessories ➢ Windows Explorer to open Windows Explorer. Navigate to the drive you want to use for the CDP.

3. Click the hard drive, choose File ➢ New ➢ Folder, and enter the folder name. Name it **CDP**.

4. Right-click the folder and choose Sharing from the shortcut menu. Click the CDP Properties-Sharing tab, and then click the Share This Folder radio button. Accept the default name of CDP.

5. Click the Permissions button, and then clear the Full Control and the Change check boxes. Only the Read check box should be enabled. Click OK. Click OK.

Create a Virtual Directory for the CDP

6. Choose Start ≻ Programs ≻ Administrative Tools ≻ Internet Services Manager. Expand the server. Expand the Default Web Site.

7. Right-click the Default Web Site, and then choose New ≻ Virtual Directory to start the Virtual Directory Creation Wizard.

8. Click Next, name the Alias CDP, and click Next.

9. Enter the directory to the new folder created. Click Next.

10. Accept the default virtual directory Access Permissions and click Next. Click Finish.

Copy the CertEnroll Folder Contents from the Root CA to the New Directory

11. Go to the root CA server and copy the files and folders from the %systemroot%\system32\ certsrv\certenroll folder on the stand-alone offline root CA to a floppy disk.

12. Copy the contents of the floppy disk to the new share point created.

13. Write down the URL to access the virtual directory and the universal naming convention path to the file share.

Add the CDP and AIA to the CA Certificate

14. On the root CA, choose Start ≻ Programs ≻ Administrative Tools ≻ Certification Authority.

15. Right-click the CA server, and choose Properties from the shortcut menu to open the CA Server Properties dialog box.

16. Click the Policy Module tab, click Configure, and then click the X.509 Extensions tab.

17. Click the Add CDP button, and enter the URL for the CDP virtual directory configured in Steps 6 through 10. For example, enter **http://*servername*/cdp**. Click OK.

18. Click the Add CDP button again, and enter the URL for the CDP file share configured in Steps 1 through 5. For example, enter **file://*servername*/cdp/%ca_name%%cert_suffix%.crl**. Click OK.

19. Click the Add AIA button, and enter the URL for the CDP virtual directory configured in Steps 6 through 10 pointing to the certificate file. For example, enter **http://*servername*/cdp/%server_dns_name%_%ca_name%%cert_suffix%.crt**. Click OK.

20. Click the Add AIA button, and enter the URL for the CDP file share configured in Steps 1 through 5 for the certificate file. For example, enter **file://*servername*/cdp/%server_dns_name%_%ca_name%%cert_suffix%.crt**. Click OK.

21. Click OK to close the X.509 tab.

22. Click OK when you see the message stating that Certificate Services must be restarted for these changes to take effect.

23. Click OK to close the CA Server Properties dialog box.

The CRL distribution point is now properly published along with the certificate chain information, and the certificate itself is on the network.

Once the stand-alone offline root CA is properly installed, you must configure the publication points and place them where they can be readily found on the network. Publishing updates to the distribution point will require manually copying the `certenroll` folder files to the CDP folder. You need to remember that Certificate Services will publish a new CRL every week regardless of whether an update is needed. You need to copy and move the CRL to the publication point each week. If you fail to manually move these CRLs to the publication point, you will have a broken chain when the CRL expires and the updated CRL is not available.

After you complete this process, you can install the next level of a CA hierarchy, which means installing any intermediate CAs that might be needed for the organization.

Installing and Configuring the Intermediate CA

After an offline root CA is properly installed, you can start on the next layer of the CA hierarchy. The second layer in a three layer-model is the offline subordinate intermediate CA. The intermediate CA is often used to separate classes and types of certificates that can be distinguished by policy. Organizations that use a three-level CA configuration typically use two stand-alone offline intermediate CAs. Many organizations use one intermediate CA to support external use and a second intermediate CA to support internal use.

The prerequisites for installing a stand-alone offline intermediate CA are as follows.

The stand-alone offline intermediate CA must be a workgroup member and not a member of any domain.   Since the intermediate CA will be offline and secured, it cannot have network connections and cannot be linked to any domain.

The computer name must be unique for the entire forest.   Even though the computer is offline, the name is part of the information published in Active Directory.

A CRL must be published even though the server is offline.   The CDP is always included in the certificate. The CDP must be accessible to users on the network. This process is normally completed after the root CA is installed.

The intermediate CA certificate itself should also be made available to the network for verification of the intermediate CA and the CA chain.   This process is normally completed after the root CA is installed.

The AIA distribution point needs to be configured for the intermediate CA so that the CA chain can be properly verified.   This process is normally completed after the root CA is installed.

The root CA must be available, or it must have its CRL and AIA information properly published. Certificate users and services must be able to verify that a certificate is still valid by referring to the CA or by referring to the CRL and AIA publication points.

The server for the CA must be running IIS. Since the server will not be online on the network, the only way to request and retrieve certificates from the offline CA is to use the web forms.

In Exercise 9.3, you will install an intermediate CA.

EXERCISE 9.3

Installing an Intermediate CA

In this exercise, you will install an intermediate CA using the root CA installed in Exercise 9.1 as the basis of your new CA. The intermediate CA will be much like our root CA in that it will be a stand-alone offline CA.

1. Choose Start ➢ Settings ➢ Control Panel to open Control Panel.

2. Double-click Add/Remove Programs to open the Add/Remove Programs window.

3. Click Add/Remove Windows Components in the left pane.

4. Click the Certificate Services check box. Click Yes when you see the message stating that you cannot change the computer name or its domain membership.

5. Click the Details button. Notice that Certificate Services will install two components: the Certificate Services CA and Certificates Services Web Enrollment Support. Click OK to close the window.

6. Click Next to start the installation. If the Terminal Services Setup window open, click Next again. The Terminal Services Setup window will always open if Terminal Services is installed on the server. Click Next to open the Certification Authority Type screen.

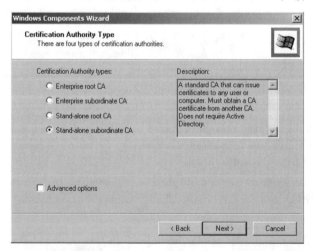

7. Notice that you have two choices for intermediate (subordinate) CAs: the Enterprise Subordinate CA and the Stand-Alone Subordinate CA. Select the Stand-Alone Subordinate CA radio button, and then click Next to open the CA Identifying Information screen.

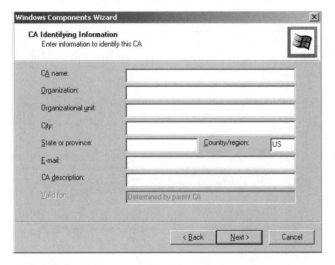

8. Fill in the CA Identifying information. Note that the Valid For field is grayed out. Click Next to open the Data Storage Location screen.

9. Select the location of the certificate database and its log files. It is a very good idea to put the database and the log files on separate hard drives. In the event of a hard-drive failure, you'll have better restore capability. Click Next to open the CA Certificate Request screen.

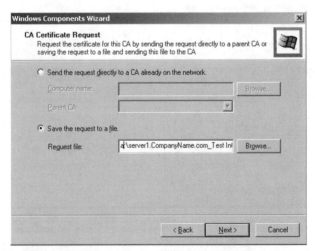

10. Click the Save The Request To A File radio button. You must use this option because the root CA is an offline CA and is not available on the network. Save the file to a floppy disk that you can then take to the root CA for processing. Click Next.

11. Click OK when you see the warning that IIS will be stopped.

12. You may be prompted for the location of the latest service pack and the original Windows 2000 CD. Make sure you have them available. If you are prompted, click OK and point the installation program to these files.

13. During the rest of the processing, you will see a message stating that the Certificate Services installation will not be complete until you get the certificate from the root CA and then manually install it. Click OK.

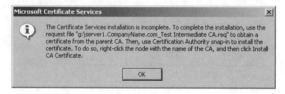

14. Click Finish.

15. Close all the remaining windows. At this point, you will have a nonfunctioning stand-alone intermediate CA. To complete the installation, you need to get a certificate from the root CA.

16. Go to the root CA. Start Internet Explorer, and in the Address bar enter **http://*servername*/ certsrv** to open the Microsoft Certificate Services screen shown here. Verify that the Request A Certificate radio button is selected. Click Next.

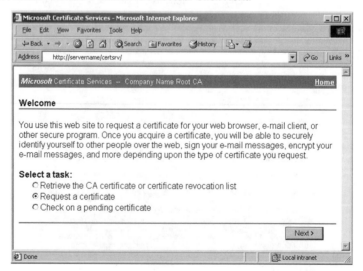

17. Click the Advanced Request radio button, and then click Next.

18. Select the Submit A Certificate Request Using A Base64 Encoded PKCS #10 File or the Renewal Request Using A Base64 Encoded PKCS #7 File option. Click Next.

19. Using Notepad, open the request file saved to the floppy disk. The content of the file is a certificate request like we used in our SSL exercises in Chapter 6. Copy and paste the certificate request into the Saved Request field as shown here. Click Submit.

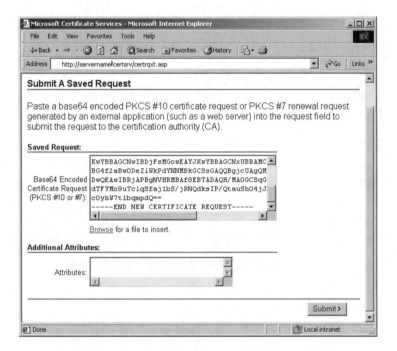

20. The root CA will then respond with a message to the browser stating that the request has been received; however, you must wait for an administrator to approve the request and issue the certificate.

21. Go to the root CA server, and choose Start ➤ Programs ➤ Administrative Tools ➤ Certification Authority to open the Certification Authority MMC console.

22. Expand the root CA server, and click Pending Requests to display the request submitted in Step 19. Right-click the certificate request in the pane on the right, and choose All Tasks ➤ click Issue from the shortcut menu.

EXERCISE 9.3 (continued)

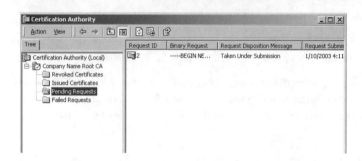

At this point, the certificate for the intermediate CA is now approved and is ready to be picked up and installed on the intermediate CA.

23. Using the web browser on the root CA, go to http://*servername*/certsrv. This time, instead of clicking Request A Certificate, click the Check On A Pending Certificate radio button. Click Next.

24. In the web browser, click the certificate and then click Next to retrieve it.

25. Click the Download CA Certificate and Download CA Certification Path links. Save the files to the floppy disk.

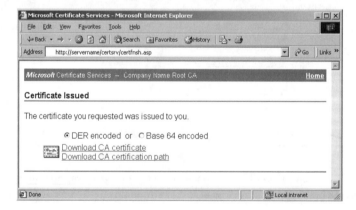

At this point, the root CA has done its part and has provided a certificate for the intermediate CA. Now, you must install it on the intermediate CA so that it will be fully functional.

26. Take the floppy to the intermediate CA and insert it in the floppy drive.

27. On the intermediate CA, choose Start ➢ Programs ➢ Administrative Tools ➢ Certification Authority. A red square indicates that the intermediate CA is not running.

28. In the Certification Authority MMC console, right-click the intermediate CA server name, and then choose All Tasks ➢ Install CA Certificate.

29. Enter the filename and location of the certificate on the floppy disk and click Open to install the certificate needed for the intermediate CA.

At this point the intermediate CA is operational, and you can remove it from the network and place it in a secure location.

Once the stand-alone offline intermediate CA is properly installed, you must configure the publication information and placed it where it can be readily found on the network, as you did earlier for the stand-alone offline root CA. It is vital that the CRL and the AIA information are made available to the network users to verify the certificate, verify that it is not revoked, and verify its chain. The process for the stand-alone offline intermediate CA is exactly the same as it is for the stand-alone offline root CA.

Publishing updates to the distribution point requires manually copying the CertEnroll folder files to the CDP folder. Remember that Certificate Services will publish a new CRL every week regardless of whether an update is needed. You must copy and move the CRL to the publication point each week. If you fail to manually move these CRLs to the publication point, you will have a broken chain when the CRL expires and the updated CRL is not available. You can also choose to extend the length of time between publication periods to make it much longer than a week.

After this process is completed, you can install the next level of a CA hierarchy—any issuing CAs that might be needed for the organization.

Installing and Configuring the Issuing CA

After an offline root CA is properly installed and the appropriate offline intermediate CAs are installed, you can start on the next tier of the CA hierarchy. The third tier in the three-tiered model is the enterprise issuing CA. The issuing CA is usually an enterprise CA because it is used for computers, users, and services that require rapid response for enrollment. Issuing CAs are often configured to provide automatic enrollment for certificates based on permissions. For example, Active Directory domain controllers automatically request certificates when an enterprise CA comes online. Organizations that use a three-level CA configuration typically use two or more issuing CAs for redundancy and for performance reasons.

The prerequisites for installing an issuing CA are as follows.

The server must be a member or domain controller of an Active Directory domain if it is to be an enterprise CA. It must have access to Active Directory domain controllers.

The higher-level CAs in a tiered CA environment must have published their CRL and AIA information to a distribution point that is included in the CA certificate. Certificate users and services must be able to verify that a certificate is still valid by referring to the CA or by referring to the CRL and AIA publication points.

DNS must be installed. Installing an issuing CA requires that DNS be installed in support of the Windows 2000 Active Directory.

IIS must be installed on the same computer as the CA.   The CA needs to authenticate clients to verify that they are requesting only certificates they have permissions to request.

You can approach the placement of servers running enterprise CAs in different ways. One approach is to place an enterprise CA in each production domain. Another is to keep all CAs in a separate domain for CAs only. A third approach is to place CAs in the forest root domain only. Benefits and liabilities are associated with each approach:

- Placing an enterprise CA in each production domain allows for quick certificate enrollment and authentication processes. However, the resources to do this are fairly significant.

- Placing all enterprise CAs in their own domain makes management fairly easy and allows good separation of administrative tasks, but it requires the resources for another domain and all the management tasks associated with another domain.

- Placing CAs in the forest root domain might sound good on the surface, but such an approach means having more administrators with rights to the forest root domain, which is a considerable security risk.

Probably the most common approach is to place an enterprise CA in each physical location to issue and manage certificates for that location without having to worry about certificate enrollment failures or other problems caused by the occasional down WAN link.

Installing and configuring an enterprise issuing CA is similar to configuring an intermediate CA because the process of requesting and retrieving a certificate from an offline CA is the same for both. The main difference is in the way you publish the information about the CA after it is installed and the type of CA you select during the installation process. In Exercise 9.4, you will install an issuing enterprise CA.

EXERCISE 9.4

Installing an Issuing Enterprise CA

In this exercise, you will install an issuing CA using the intermediate CA installed in Exercise 9.3 as the provider of the certificate for your new CA. The intermediate CA will be much like your root CA in that it will be a stand-alone offline CA too.

1. On the new issuing CA, choose Start ➤ Settings ➤ Control Panel to open Control Panel.

2. Double-click Add/Remove Programs.

3. Click Add/Remove Windows Components in the left pane.

4. Click the Certificate Services check box. Click Yes when you see the message stating that you cannot change the computer name or its domain membership.

5. Click the Details button. Notice that Certificate Services will install two components: the Certificate Services CA and the Certificates Services Web Enrollment Support. Click OK to close the window.

6. Click Next to start the installation. If the Terminal Services Setup window opens, click Next again. The Terminal Services Setup window will always open if Terminal Services is installed on the server. Click Next to open the Certification Authority Type screen.

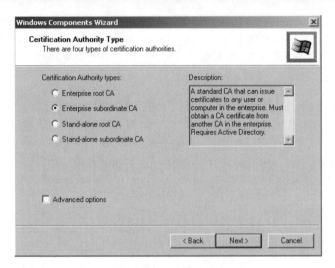

7. Notice that there are two choices for intermediate (subordinate) CAs: Enterprise Subordinate CA and Stand-Alone Subordinate CA. Click the Enterprise Subordinate CA radio button, and then click Next.

8. Fill in the CA identifying information. Note that the Valid For field is grayed out. Click Next to open the Data Storage Location screen.

9. Select the location of the certificate database and its log files. It is a good idea to put the database and the log files on separate hard drives. In the event of a hard-drive failure, you'll have better restore capability. Click Next to open the CA Certificate Request screen.

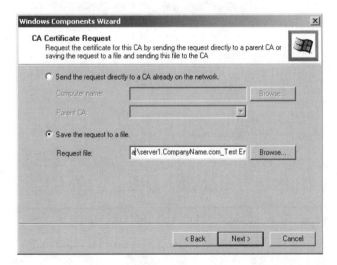

10. Click the Save The Request To A File radio button. You must use this option because the intermediate CA is an offline CA and is not available on the network. Save the file to a floppy disk that you can then take to the root CA for processing. Click Next.

11. Click OK when you see the warning that IIS will be stopped.

12. You may be prompted for the location of the latest service pack and the original Windows 2000 CD. Make sure you have them available. If you are prompted, click OK and point the installation program to these files.

13. During the rest of the processing, you will see a message stating that Certificate Services installation will not be complete until you get the certificate from the root CA and then manually install it. Click OK to acknowledge the statement.

14. Click Finish.

15. Close all the remaining windows.

At this point, you will have a nonfunctioning enterprise issuing CA. To complete the installation, you need to get a certificate from the intermediate CA.

16. Go to the intermediate CA. Start Internet Explorer, and in the Address bar, enter **http://** **servername/certsrv** to display the Microsoft Certificate Services screen. Verify that the Request A Certificate radio button is selected. Click Next.

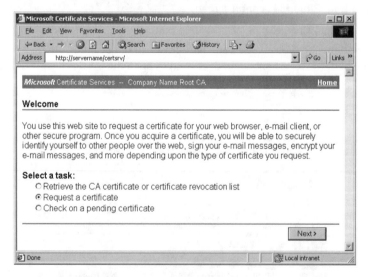

17. Click the Advanced Request radio button, and then click Next.

18. Select the Submit A Certificate Request Using A Base64 Encoded PKCS #10 File or the Renewal Request Using A Base64 Encoded PKCS #7 File option. Click Next.

19. Using Notepad, open the request file saved to the floppy disk. The content of the file is a certificate request like we used in our SSL exercises. Copy and paste the certificate request into the Saved Request field. Click Submit.

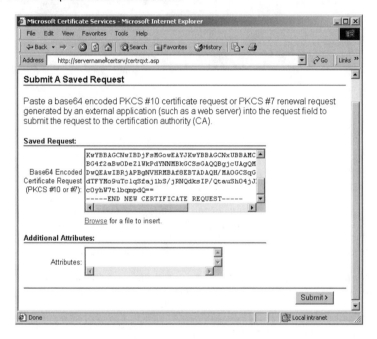

20. The intermediate CA will then respond with a message to the browser stating that the request has been received; however, you must wait for an administrator to approve the request and issue the certificate.

21. Go to the intermediate CA server, and choose Start ➢ Programs ➢ Administrative Tools ➢ Certification Authority to open the Certification Authority MMC console.

22. Expand the intermediate CA server, and click Pending Requests to display the request submitted in Step 19. Right-click the certificate request in the pane on the right, and choose All Tasks ➢ Issue.

At this point, the certificate for the enterprise issuing CA is now approved and is ready to be picked up and then installed on the enterprise issuing CA.

23. Using the web browser on the intermediate CA, go to http://*servername*/certsrv. This time, instead of clicking Request A Certificate, click the Check On A Pending Certificate radio button. Click Next.

24. In the web browser, click the certificate and then click Next to retrieve it.

EXERCISE 9.4 *(continued)*

25. Click the Download CA Certificate and the Download CA Certification Path links. Save the files to the floppy disk.

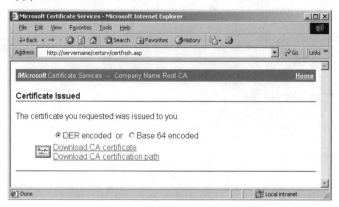

At this point, the intermediate CA has done its part and has provided a certificate for the enterprise issuing CA. Now you must install it on the enterprise issuing CA so that it will be fully functional.

26. Take the floppy to the enterprise issuing CA and insert it in the floppy drive.

27. On the enterprise issuing CA, choose Start ➤ Programs ➤ Administrative Tools ➤ Certification Authority. A red square indicates that the enterprise issuing CA is not running.

28. In the Certification Authority MMC console, right-click the enterprise issuing CA name, and choose All Tasks ➤ Install CA Certificate.

29. Enter the filename and location of the issued certificate on the floppy disk and click Open to install the certificate needed for the enterprise issuing CA.

At this point the enterprise issuing CA is now operational, and you can remove it from the network and place it in a secure location.

Once the enterprise issuing CA is properly installed, you must configure the publication information and place it so that it can be readily found on the network. It is vital that the CRL and the AIA information are made available to the network users to verify the certificate, to verify that it is not revoked, and to verify its chain. To verify that the information has been properly entered into Active Directory, use the Active Directory Sites And Services MMC console. In Exercise 9.5, you will view published certificates and CRLs in Active Directory.

EXERCISE 9.5

Viewing Published Certificates and CRLs in Active Directory

In this exercise, you will go through the steps to properly view the published certificates and CRLs in Active Directory.

EXERCISE 9.5 *(continued)*

1. Choose Start ➢ Programs ➢ Administrative Tools ➢ Active Directory Sites And Services to open the AD Sites And Services window.

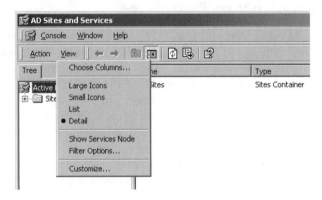

2. Choose View ➢ Show Services Node

3. Expand the Services folder, expand the Public Key Services folder, and then click AIA to view the certificates that have their AIA information in Active Directory: the root CA, the intermediate CA, and the enterprise CA created in earlier exercises.

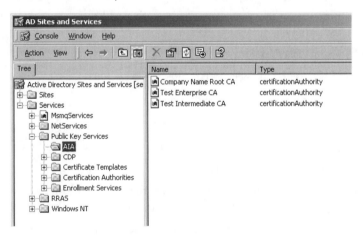

4. Click CDP to display the folders for each server used in the CA hierarchy. Clicking each folder displays which CRLs are on each server.

Not only will the CA information be published in Active Directory, but the certificates it issues can also be published in Active Directory. In the Certification Authority MMC console, right-click the CA server, and choose Properties from the shortcut menu. Click the Exit Module tab, and then click Configure. Notice the little check box that allows all certificates to be automatically published in Active Directory.

Now that all the CAs are installed, it is time to discuss how to work with templates.

Configuring Certificate Templates

Only enterprise CAs can use *certificate templates*. A certificate template is simply a rule or a profile that defines the contents and structure of a certificate based on how the certificate will be used. You can think of a certificate template as a type of certificate that will be used based on the needs of the business. A good example is the certificate used for EFS. The EFS certificate has a particular use, and it meets a specific business need.

Each template is stored in the Configuration container of Active Directory. The entire forest must know about the template and its definition, and the Configuration container is replicated to all domain controllers in the forest, making it available to everyone in the forest. Along with the definitions that include the rules and profiles of the template, a discretionary access control list is attached to each template to identify which users or groups of users have permissions to read the templates and also to identify which users and groups of users have permissions to enroll the certificate template and use its capabilities.

When the enterprise CA is installed, a default set of templates are created. These templates can be categorized according to the intended target: users and computers. Another way to view them is as either single use or multipurpose certificates. The following templates exist as well as others:

Administrator   Used for a variety of purposes, including authentication, secure e-mail, EFS, and certificate trust signing

Authenticated Session   Used to authenticate clients

Basic EFS   Used to encrypt and decrypt data files

Computer   Used to authenticate clients and servers

Code Signing   Used to sign applications and drivers

EFS Recovery Agent   Used to recover encrypted files created and stored by EFS users

IPSec   Used to establish IPSec communications

Smart Card Logon   Allows the user of the certificate to authenticate on the network using the certificate stored on the smart card inserted in a smart card reader

Smart Card User   Used for authentication and for secure e-mail

Subordinate Certification Authority   Used to add a subordinate CA to a CA hierarchy

User   Used for authentication, secure e-mail, and EFS

Web Server   Authenticates the web server to client systems and provides SSL protection of sessions

By default, only Administrator, Domain Controller, Computer, Basic EFS, EFS Recovery Agent, User, and Web Server templates are available on an enterprise CA. To add other templates, you must use the Certification Authority MMC console, as in Exercise 9.6.

EXERCISE 9.6

Adding/Deleting Certificate Templates

In this exercise, you will add and delete certificate templates using the Certification Authority MMC console.

Adding Certificate Templates

1. On your enterprise CA server, choose Start ➢ Programs ➢ Administrative Tools ➢ Certification Authority to open the Certification Authority MMC console.

2. Expand the CA server name, and then click Policy Settings to display all the currently installed certificate templates in the right pane.

3. Choose Action ➢ New ➢ Certificate To Issue.

4. Select the templates that you want to add and click OK.

Deleting Certificate Templates

5. Choose Start ➢ Programs ➢ Administrative Tools ➢ Certification Authority to open the Certification Authority MMC console.

6. Expand the CA name, and then click on Policy Settings to display all the currently installed certificate templates in the right pane.

7. Right-click the certificate template you want to delete, and choose Delete from the shortcut menu.

Add the only certificate templates needed to meet business requirements. Adding templates for rules that you do not want to support can be a potential security problem and can lead to extra administration. For example, if there is no business requirement for EFS, removing the Basic EFS template from all CAs will effectively prevent all users from using EFS within the Active Directory forest. If the template is installed, users have permissions to enroll themselves and to implement EFS even if you do not want them to do so. If users leave the organization and you need their files, you'll run into a major problem if no recovery agent is available. It is better not to have the capability than it is to try to solve problems after the fact without any prior planning and testing.

Configuring Public Key Group Policies

Windows 2000 and Windows XP Professional computers can use Group Policies to assist with the distribution of certificates in an organization. Normally, somebody with administrative privileges on a computer needs to request and install computer certificates. The process can be an administrative nightmare because it requires visiting all the computers in an organization. However, with Group Policies, certificates can be enrolled by all users, and the renewal process can be automated as well.

Prerequisites for Using Group Policies to Distribute Certificates

To use Group Policies to assist with the distribution of certificates in an organization, the following requirements must be met:

- The computers must be members of an Active Directory domain.

- The users must be logged in to the domain.

- You need to know the type of certificates needed by computers.

- You need to know which CA will be used for the process.

Computer certificates include the certificate needed for IPSec, Web Server, and Computer roles. You can install any of these certificate types using Group Policies to automate the enrollment process.

The first step is to install the required certificate template. Exercise 9.6 showed the steps required to install the certificate template. The next step in the process is to configure the Automatic Certificate Request Policy. In this case, we will install the Computer certificate template. Exercise 9.7 will walk you through the steps.

EXERCISE 9.7

Configure the Automatic Certificate Request Group Policy

In this exercise, you will configure the default domain Group Policy to allow the automatic enrollment of Computer certificates.

1. Choose Start ➢ Programs ➢ Administrative Tools ➢ Active Directory Users And Computers to open Active Directory Users And Computers.

2. Right-click your domain, and choose Properties from the shortcut menu.

3. Click the Group Policy tab.

4. Click the Default Domain Policy, and then click the Edit button.

5. Expand the Computer Configuration folder, the Windows Settings folder, the Security Settings folder, and the Public Key Policies folder.

6. Right-click the Automatic Certificate Request Settings folder, and then choose New ➢ Automatic Certificate Request.

7. Click Next to start the Automatic Certificate Request Setup Wizard.

8. In the Certificate Template screen, select Computer in the Certificate Template list and click Next.

9. Select the enterprise CA you want to use from the list and click Next.

10. Click Finish to complete the wizard.

11. Close the Group Policy window and click OK.

Once the Group Policy is configured to automatically enroll for certificates, the certificates will be automatically requested the next time users log on or the next time the Group Policy refreshes. As new computers join the domain, they are automatically enrolled for Computer certificates.

You can verify that certificates are installed on computers by using the Certificates MMC console. This will not be installed on most client computers. To install it, enter MMC in the Open box of the Run dialog box, press Enter, and then use the Add/Remove snap-in to add the Certificates snap-in to the console. Use the Computer Account option with the snap-in installation.

You can use the process shown in Exercise 9.7 to edit the Domain Controllers OU Default Domain Controllers Policy. Except in this case, instead of installing the Computer certificate template, install the Domain Controller certificate template. Once the template is configured for automatic enrollment, do not remove it. Doing so can cause WinLogon errors, in particular, Event ID 1010 errors.

You can also use Group Policies to distribute certificates for offline certification authorities. Using a Group Policy to distribute an offline root or intermediate certificate is good practice. Do not use Group Policies to distribute an enterprise CA certificate since it is automatically published in Active Directory. Whenever possible, manage the Trusted Root Certification Authorities list with Group Policies. Adding a certificate to this list ensures that all Active Directory domain clients receive the certificate automatically. In Exercise 9.8, you'll use Group Policy to configure the Trusted Root Certification Authorities list.

EXERCISE 9.8

Configure the Trusted Root Certification Authorities List Using Group Policy

In this exercise, you will add an offline root CA's certificate to the Trusted Root Certifications Authorities list using Active Directory Group Policies.

1. Choose Start ➤ Programs ➤ Administrative Tools ➤ Active Directory Users And Computers to open Active Directory Users And Computers.

2. Right-click your domain, and choose Properties from the shortcut menu.

3. Click the Group Policy tab.

4. Click the Default Domain Policy, and then click the Edit button.

5. Expand the Computer Configuration folder, the Windows Settings folder, the Security Settings folder, and the Public Key Policies folder.

6. Right-click Trusted Root Certification Authorities, and choose All Tasks ➤ Import to start the Certificate Import Wizard.

7. Click Next to open the File To Import screen.

8. Enter the filename and its location in the File Name field or click the Browse button to find it. Remember, this file was copied to a floppy disk in Exercise 9.2. Click Next.

9. Verify that the Place All Certificates In The Following Store radio button is selected and that the Certificate Store field shows Trusted Root Certification Authorities. Click Next.

10. Click Finish to complete the wizard. Click OK to acknowledge that the import was successful.

11. Close the Group Policy window and click OK.

Once the information is configured in the Group Policy, all affected systems receive the certificate. The root certificate becomes part of the computer policy, and all users inherit the certificate trust.

You can also automate the configuration of the Enterprise Trust list using Group Policies. First, create and install an Enterprise Trust list. You can edit it later using the Group Policy, and all the changes will be pushed out to all the computers in the Active Directory domain. In Exercise 9.9, you'll configure the Enterprise Trust list using Group Policy.

EXERCISE 9.9

Configure the Enterprise Trust List Using Group Policy

In this exercise, you will create an Enterprise Trust list and add it to the Default Domain Group Policy to deploy the settings using Active Directory Group Policies.

Add a Certificate with Trust List Signing Capabilities

To add the Trust List Signing certificate template, follow the steps in Exercise 9.6. Then follow these steps:

1. Choose Start ➢ Run to open the Run dialog box, enter MMC in the Open box, and press Enter.

2. Choose Console ➢ Add/Remove Snap-In.

3. Click the Add button. Select the Certificates snap-in from the list and click Add.

4. Click the My User Account radio button and click Finish.

5. Click Close in the Add Stand-alone Snap-In window. Click OK in the Add/Remove Snap-In window.

6. Expand the Certificates folder, and double-click Personal.

7. Right-click Certificates, and then choose All Tasks ➢ Request New Certificate to start the Certificate Request Wizard.

8. Click Next.

9. Select Trust List Signing from the Certificate Templates list, and then click Next.

10. Enter a friendly name and a description for the certificate, and then click Next.

11. Click Finish to complete the wizard. Click Install Certificate when you see the notice that the certificate request was successful. Click OK in the Certificate Request Was Successful message box.

12. Close the MMC.

Create the Enterprise Trust List

13. Choose Start ➢ Programs ➢ Administrative Tools ➢ Active Directory Users And Computers to open Active Directory Users And Computers.

14. Right-click your domain, and choose Properties from the shortcut menu.

15. Click the Group Policy tab.

16. Click the Default Domain Policy, and then click the Edit button.

17. In the Group Policy window, expand the Computer Configuration folder, the Windows Settings folder, the Security Settings folder, and the Public Key Policies folder.

18. Right-click Enterprise Trust, and choose New ➤ a Certificate Trust List to start the Certificate Trust List Wizard.

19. Click Next to open the Certificate Trust List Purpose screen.

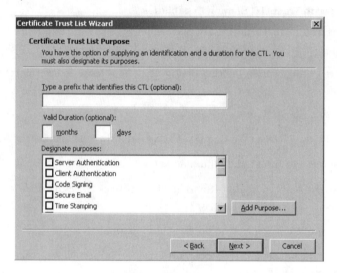

20. Enter the information for the new trust list. Select a prefix for the trust list so you can identify it later. This is optional but recommended. Enter a valid duration, and select all the purposes required from the list. You can add more purposes using the OID of the purpose if you know it. Click Next when complete.

21. Click Add From Store to add the certificates from the CAs that you want to trust. This step allows you to not select CAs that you do not want to trust in your organization. Alternatively, you can add the list from a file if you have it.

22. Select the CAs that you want on the list, click OK, and then click Next.

23. You can select a certificate to sign the newly created list. You will want to use the certificate obtained in Steps 1 through 12 earlier. Click Select From Store. Select the certificate listed with the friendly name you created in Step 10. Click OK.

24. Click Next. Click Next again.

25. Enter a friendly name for the new *certificate trust list (CTL)* in the Friendly Name box. Enter a description. Click Next.

26. Click Finish to complete the wizard. Click OK.

27. Close the Group Policy window and click OK.

You can edit and update this newly created CTL through Group Policy by right-clicking the CTL and choosing All Tasks ➢ Edit. To delete this CTL and remove it from the computers in the domain, right-click the CTL, and choose Delete from the shortcut menu.

Configuring Certificate Enrollment and Renewals

There are basically three processes for certificate enrollment, two manual techniques and auto-enrollment. Each process has some requirements that might prevent it from being used.

Manual Enrollment

Any system can use manual enrollment processes. You can manually enroll a certificate in two ways:

- Using the Certificates MMC snap-in
- Using the Certificates Enrollment web pages

Since Windows NT and Windows 9x do not support auto-enrollment, you have no other option than to use a manual process. However, only Windows 2000 and Windows XP Professional computers can use the Certificates MMC snap-in to enroll certificates. The MMC does not exist for Windows NT and Windows 9x computers. This means that Windows NT and Windows 9x computers will be required to use the Certificates Enrollment web pages.

Microsoft also recommends that you use the manual process for high-value certificates such as Web Server certificates and EFS Recovery Agent certificates. Having those certificates available for auto-enrollment probably is not a good idea and would certainly be a great security risk. Since the entire idea of using certificates is based on the security needs of an organization, it makes sense that manual enrollment will still be used for certain types of certificates. These high-value certificates should be clearly identified and documented.

The process of requesting and installing a certificate using the Web Enrollment pages has been discussed and used in a few exercises in this chapter and in previous chapters. For a Windows NT and Windows 9x user, the process is no different. In Exercise 9.10, you use the Web Enrollment pages to manually request a certificate.

EXERCISE 9.10

Using the Web Enrollment Pages To Manually Request a Certificate

The Standard Method

1. Using the Web browser, connect to the CA at http://*CAServerName*/certsrv.

2. Click the Request A Certificate radio button, and then click Next.

3. Select the User Certificate Request, select the certificate template you want, and click Next to open the Identifying Information screen.

4. Fill in the information, and then click Submit.

5. Click Install This Certificate.

EXERCISE 9.10 *(continued)*

This completes the standard method of using the CA website to enroll a user certificate.

The Advanced Method

6. Using the Web browser, connect to the CA at http://*CAServerName*/certsrv.

7. Click the Request A Certificate radio button, and then click Next.

8. Click the Advanced Request radio button, and then click Next.

9. Select Submit A Certificate Request To This CA Using A Form. The other requests will not apply to a Windows NT or Windows 9*x* user. Click Next and complete the Identifying Information, Intended Purpose Key Options, and Additional Options screen.

10. Select the certificate template you want, select the specific CSP you want, select the key usage and the key size, select any other options you want, and click Submit.

11. Click Install This Certificate.

This completes the advanced method for using the CA website to enroll a user certificate.

Using the advanced method you can select many more options, but only individual with specific needs should use it. Most of the time this will not apply to any Windows NT or Windows 9*x* users. The User certificate received through the standard process can be used for secure e-mail, authentication, and EFS.

The other way to manually enroll a certificate is to use the Certificates MMC snap-in, which is used in Exercise 9.11. Remember, this snap-in can only be used by Windows 2000 and Windows XP Professional computers.

EXERCISE 9.11

Using the Certificates MMC Snap-In to Enroll for User and Computer Certificates and for Renewing Certificates

Configuring an MMC

1. Choose Start ➢ Run to open the Run dialog box, enter **MMC** in the Open box, and press Enter.

2. Choose Console ➢ Add/Remove Snap-In.

3. Click the Add button, select the Certificates snap-in from the list, and click Add.

4. Click the My User Account radio button, and then click Finish.

5. Verify that Certificates is still highlighted in the Add Standalone Snap-In window, and click Add again.

6. Click the Computer Account radio button, and click Finish.

7. Close the Add Standalone Snap-In window. Click OK in the Add/Remove Snap-In window.

Requesting a User Certificate

8. Expand the Certificates folder, and double-click Personal.

9. Right-click Certificates, and then choose All Tasks ➢ Request New Certificate to start the Certificate Request Wizard.

10. Click Next.

11. Select User from the Certificate Templates list, and then click Next.

12. Enter a friendly name and a description for the certificate, and then click Next.

13. Click Finish to complete the wizard. Click Install Certificate when you see the notice that the certificate request was successful. Click OK in the Certificate Request Was Successful message box.

Requesting a Computer Certificate

14. Expand the Certificates folder and double-click Personal.

15. Right-lick Certificates, and then choose All Tasks ➢ Request New Certificate to start the Certificate Request Wizard.

16. Click Next.

17. Select Computer from the Certificate Templates list, and then click Next.

18. Enter a friendly name and a description for the certificate, and then click Next.

19. Click Finish to complete the wizard. Click Install Certificate when you see the notice that the certificate request was successful. Click OK in the Certificate Request Was Successful message box.

Renewing a Certificate

20. Right-click any certificate that you want to renew, and choose All Tasks ➢ Renew Certificate With New Key or choose All Tasks ➢ Renew Certificate With Same Key. It is a good idea to select the New Key option because this will recreate the certificate key. If anyone has been trying to break your certificate key, this would require that they start their attempt over again.

21. Close the MMC. You might want to save the MMC for later use.

When using the Web Enrollment forms, it is important to know that the user requesting a certificate must have administrator or power user rights on their own computer. They need these rights to install the ActiveX controls and to then install the certificate that is received. If the user does not have the proper rights, the enrollment will fail.

Auto-Enrollment

One of the bigger problems with certificate enrollment is that users make mistakes and obtain the wrong kind of certificate or they select the wrong options and the certificate is not as strong as they would like. The process can be confusing and can take considerable time for each user on the network.

Certificate auto-enrollment can be set up using Group Policies as discussed earlier in this chapter in the section on configuring public key Group Policies and as detailed in Exercise 9.7. Windows 2000 and Windows XP Professional computers can automatically receive computer certificates through auto-enrollment. Windows NT and Windows 9x computers cannot participate in auto-enrollment processes since they do not support Group Policies.

Managing Certificate Authorities

Managing CAs involves many day-to-day tasks and some tasks that are done less frequently, such as restoring a CA that you hope you never have to restore. Microsoft has provided some tools to assist us with managing certificates.

Certificates MMC snap-in   Use this tool to manage the local certificate store and to request, delete, and manage certificates issued to a user or computer.

Certification Authority MMC snap-in   Use this tool to manage the CA and the certificates issued by the CA. You can also use this tool to publish CRLs.

certutil.exe   This is an extremely powerful command line tool that you can use in scripts to create CAs, to publish CRLs and certification authority certificates, to revoke certificates, and to recover archived private keys. The online help for **certutil.exe** is several pages.

certreq.exe   You can use this command line tool to request certificates from a CA.

dsstore.exe   You can use this command line tool to publish the CRL and the AIA to Active Directory. Microsoft has clearly stated that the preferred process is to use **certutil.exe** on a Windows XP Professional computer.

You should practice using each of these tools and understand how each of them is used in configuring and managing the CAs in an organization.

Viewing Certificates

You can view certificates if you are running Windows 2000 or Windows XP Professional. Using the Certificates MMC snap-in, you can view certificates issued to you and to your computer. The process of installing the Certificates MMC snap-in was covered in Exercise 9.11 earlier in this chapter.

To view your personal certificates, open the console, expand the Certificates–Current User folder, expand the Personal folder, and then click Certificates to display all your user certificates in the right pane of the window. Double-clicking a certificate opens the Certificate dialog box (see Figure 9.2), which displays information about the certificate.

FIGURE 9.2   The Certificate dialog box

The Certificate dialog box shows all the details of the User certificate, including the following:

- The capabilities of the certificate. For example, it might show that the certificate can be used for secure e-mail.
- The date issued.
- The expiration date.
- The issuing CA.

Clicking the Details tab displays even more information about the certificate, including the following:

- Version
- Serial number
- Length of the key
- Certificate template used
- CRL publication point
- AIA publication point

The Certification Path tab of the Certificate dialog box shows the certificate chain. It will show which CA issued the certificate to the user, which CA issued the certificate to the issuing

CA, which CA issued the intermediate CA's certificate, and so on all the way to the root CA of the certificate chain.

You can also view the certificates issued to the computer. Open the console, expand the Certificates (Local Computer) folder, expand the Personal folder, and then click Certificates to display all certificates for this computer in the right pane of the window. Double-clicking a certificate opens the Certificate dialog box, which displays details about the Computer certificate.

Using the Certification Authorities MMC console, an administrator can click the Issued Certificates folder, as shown in Figure 9.3. The certificates are visible in the right pane of the window. Double-clicking any certificate displays details about it.

FIGURE 9.3   The Certification Authority MMC

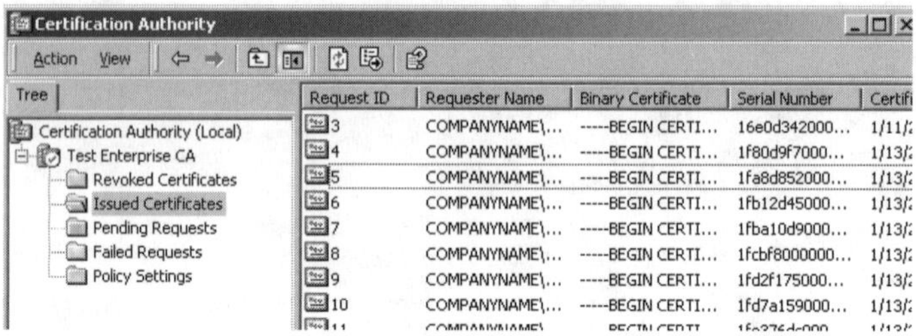

Revoking Certificates

Revoking certificates will be necessary on some occasions. Most of the time, revocation involves an employee leaving the company or a partner that is no longer a partner. In both cases, you cannot allow these certificates to be used on your network, so you must revoke them. If you do not revoke these certificates, they will be valid until they expire. Since many certificates are created for considerable lengths of time, it is important that you not let them continue to exist on the network.

To revoke a certificate, use the Certificate Authority MMC console on the CA, as shown in Exercise 9.12.

EXERCISE 9.12

Revoking a Certificate

1. Choose Start ➢ Programs ➢ Administrative Tools ➢ Certification Authority.

2. Expand the CA server if necessary to display the Issued Certificates folder in the left pane.

3. Click the Issued Certificates folder to display all the certificates issued by the CA.

4. Right-click the certificate that you want to revoke, and choose All Tasks ➢ Revoke Certificate to open the Certificate Revocation dialog box.

EXERCISE 9.12 *(continued)*

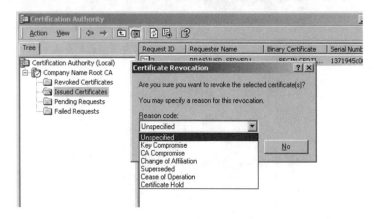

5. In the Reason Code drop-down list box, select the reason for the revocation, and then click Yes.

Following these steps revokes the certificate, and it now appears in the Revoked Certificates folder under the CA.

Editing Certificates

You can edit certificates by using the Certificates MMC snap-in. Open the Certificate dialog box for the certificate, and click the Details tab. Click Edit Properties to open the Certificate Properties dialog box (see Figure 9.2), and edit the friendly name and the description. You can also change the purposes of the certificate. You can choose to disable all the purposes, or you can choose to enable or disable any of the individual purposes for a multipurpose certificate.

Managing CRLs

The CRL is an extremely important piece of the certificate structure and any PKI. Users and computers on the network need to know when a certificate has been revoked; otherwise, they will continue to accept it and use it just like any valid certificate. If you continue to use revoked certificates, you cannot be confident in your PKI. Security will be impaired.

We covered how to manually publish the CRL in Exercise 9.2 for offline certificate authorities. You need to remember to publish all offline CRLs regularly. This should be part of your standard administrative tasks. To reduce the amount of work this takes, you can lengthen the time before a CRL expires by configuring its publication interval to a longer period of time such as every three months or even every year. After all, the only time you revoke a certificate for an offline CA is when an issued certificate has become compromised, and there should not be many issued certificates for an offline CA.

FIGURE 9.4 Editing a certificate

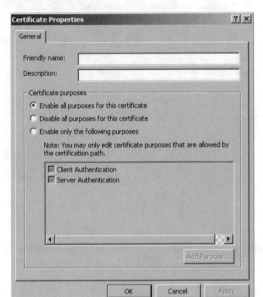

By default, each CA updates and publishes a new CRL based on a time interval. Any certificates revoked between publications of the CRL will still be valid, so it is extremely important that you set the expiration time to minimize these problems. However, you do not want to set this interval to such a small number that your clients have to go to the CA and retrieve updates too often. An alternative to reducing the update time period is to manually publish the CRL after major changes.

In the Certification Authority MMC console, right-click the Revoked Certificates folder and choose Properties from the shortcut menu. In the Properties dialog box, you can set the publication interval and also view the current CRL. Right-click the Revoked Certificates folder, choose All Tasks ➢ Publish to update and publish the CRL immediately. The new CRL is updated in Active Directory, if it is an enterprise CA, and in the %systemroot%\system32\ certsrv\certenroll folder of the certificate authority.

Backing Up and Restoring the CA

As with any resource, it is important that you understand and practice backing up and restoring a certificate authority. You should have documented processes before you actually have to do it, and you should be comfortable with the process. Since you may have to restore a backup that you created, it is important that you know you can trust your backups and that they will work.

CA Backup

The CA maintains information about all certificates it has issued, has revoked, or has pending in its database and its log files. Much of this information is also stored in the Registry, which is another reason to make sure you have the machine physically secured. Since the data for the CA is stored in databases and in the Registry, you need to make sure you back up all the components necessary to properly restore a failed CA. Also, since Windows 2000 uses IIS 5 to issue certificates, you need to make sure that the IIS 5 *metabase* is properly backed up.

Back up the database and log files using `certutil.exe`, which can also be used for many other functions.

- You can back up the CA certificate and the private key using Certutil–backupKey.

- You can back up the database using Certutil–backupDB.

To back up the CA configuration information stored in the Registry, use the NTbackup program that ships with Windows 2000, or use any third-party backup program that will back up the system state data of the server. Because the backups contain valuable information, properly secure and store them in a safe place.

You can use the Certification Authority MMC console to back up the Certificate Services. Open the console, right-click the CA, and choose All Tasks ➢ Backup CA to start a wizard that will complete the backup process. The wizard allows you to back up the private key, the CA certificate, the issued certificate log, and the pending certificate request queue, as shown in Figure 9.5. You must send the backup to an empty folder, however. You will then be prompted for a password and can complete the wizard.

FIGURE 9.5   The Certification Authority Backup Wizard

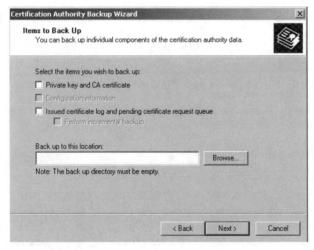

Backing up the IIS 5 metabase requires using the Internet Information Service MMC console. Exercise 9.13 steps you through the process.

EXERCISE 9.13

Backing Up the CA

Backing up the CA requires two steps. First, you must back up the Certificate Services, and then you must back up the IIS 5 metabase.

Back Up the CA

1. Choose Start ➤ Programs ➤ Administrative Tools ➤ Certification Authority.

2. Right-click the CA, and then choose All Tasks ➤ Backup CA to start the Certification Authority Backup Wizard.

3. Click Next to open the Items To Back Up screen.

4. Click the Private Key And CA Certificate check box, and click the Issued Certificate Log And Pending Certificate Request Queue check box.

5. In the Back Up To This Location field, enter the drive and path for the location where the backup will be stored. The wizard will create the folder if needed. The folder must be empty. Click Next to open the Select A Password screen.

6. Enter and confirm the password needed for a restore. Click Next.

7. Click Finish to close the wizard.

8. Close the Certification Authority MMC console.

Back Up the Metabase

9. Choose Start ➤ Programs ➤ Administrative Tools ➤ Internet Information Services.

10. Right-click the server name, and then choose Backup/Restore Configuration to open the Configuration Backup/ Restore window.

11. Click the Create Backup button to open the Configuration Backup Name dialog box.

12. Enter a name for the backup. (It might be a good idea to use a date in the name structure.) Click OK.

13. Click Close when the backup is complete.

14. Close the Internet Information Services MMC console.

Exercise 9.13 is a manual process, and you cannot schedule it. To properly schedule a CA backup, use the `certutil.exe` command line utility and the Task Scheduler. Also use the NTBackup utility or a third-party backup program to schedule the backup of the system state data of the server, which will also properly back up the IIS 5 metabase.

Best practice is to use a high-quality tape drive and a third-party backup program that will capture the system state data and that can be used to schedule backups. Make sure to store the tapes for the CA backup in a secure area.

CA Restoration

The restore process depends on the backup method. Properly restoring the Certificate Services in the event of corruption requires a current copy of the database and the IIS 5 metabase. If the database and certificate were backed up with `certutil.exe`, use `certutil.exe` to restore the information:

- To restore the CA certificate and the private key, use Certutil–restoreKey.
- To restore the database, use Certutil–restoreDB.

To restore the CA configuration information stored in the Registry, use the NTbackup program that ships with Windows 2000 or any third-party backup program that will back up the system state data of the server.

If the backup was done using the Certificate Authority MMC console and the Internet Services Manager MMC console, the restore should use the same tools and the process outlined in Exercise 9.14.

EXERCISE 9.14

Restoring the CA

Restoring the CA requires two steps. First, you must restore the Certificate Services, and then you must restore the IIS 5 metabase.

Restore the CA

1. Choose Start ➤ Programs ➤ Administrative Tools ➤ Certification Authority.

2. Right-click the CA, and choose All Tasks ➤ Restore CA.

3. Click OK when you see the message that Certificate Services must be stopped in order to continue.

4. At the Welcome screen of the wizard, click Next to open the Items To Restore screen.

5. Click the Private Key And CA Certificate check box and the Issued Certificate Log And Pending Certificate Request Queue check box.

6. Enter the drive and path of your backup files. You can click the Browse button to find the folder if needed. Click Next.

7. Enter the password used during the backup. Click Next.

8. Click Finish to close the wizard. Click Yes in the Certificate Authority Restore Wizard notification window. This restarts the Certificate Services as well.

9. Close the Certification Authority MMC console.

Restore the Metabase

10. Choose Start ➤ Programs ➤ Administrative Tools ➤ Internet Information Services.

11. Right-click the server name, and then choose Backup/Restore Configuration from the shortcut menu to open the Configuration Backup Restore dialog box.

12. Select the backup files that you want to restore, and then click the Restore button.

13. Click Yes in the Internet Service window that tells you that restoring is a lengthy process and will require stopping and restarting services.

14. Click OK when the restore is completed. Close the Configuration Backup/Restore dialog box.

15. Close the Internet Information Services MMC console.

You can use the steps in Exercise 9.14 to restore only a corrupted database. If the server itself has failed, you will need to restore the entire server from backups. Hopefully you have recent backups of the server and the system state data. If you have these backups, use the normal restore process for your backup software. Best practice is to use a high-quality tape drive and a third-party backup program that will capture the system state data and that can be used to schedule backups. You can then use this same program to restore the server in the event of a failure.

Summary

With the new focus on security for networking, it is clear that you will have to deploy and support a PKI in the future if not right away. To properly deploy a PKI, you need a trustworthy CA hierarchy and the processes to properly support Certificate Services. To support the PKI and the CA hierarchy, you need to be able to do the following:

- Install and configure three types of CAs
  - Root
  - Intermediate
  - Issuing certificate
- Configure and utilize certificate templates
- Configure publication for the following:
  - CRLs
  - AIA
- Utilize Group Policy Objects to automate certificate processes
- Configure enrollment and renewal of certificates
- Manage CAs

Certificates are an increasingly important part of securing networking today. We need stronger and better methods of authentication, and we need these methods to be standards that will work with many operating systems on both servers and client systems. Not only do you need to know how to use certificates, you need to know how to support the structure to issue and manage certificates.

Exam Essentials

Know how to install and configure the root CA.   Make sure you understand how to install an offline stand-alone root CA. In particular, know how to use the Web Enrollment pages to request and receive certificates and how to publish CRL and AIA information so it is available on the network even if the CA is not available.

Know how to install and configure the intermediate CA.   Make sure you understand how to install an offline stand-alone subordinate CA. In particular, know how to use the Web Enrollment pages to request and receive certificates and how to publish CRL and AIA information so it is available on the network even if the root CA is not available.

Make sure you understand how to apply a certificate to the CA server from the offline stand-alone root CA.

Know how to install and configure the issuing CA.   Make sure you understand the prerequisites for installing an enterprise subordinate CA. Make sure you understand how to publish the CRL and AIA for an enterprise CA.

Understand how to configure certificate templates.   Make sure you understand how to add and delete certificate templates from the list of templates serviced by the enterprise CA. Make sure you understand the difference between a computer and a user certificate template. Make sure you understand how to disable parts of a multifunction template.

Understand how to configure the publication of CRLs.   Make sure you understand how to publish offline and enterprise certificate authority CRLs. Understand how to change the publishing interval and when it is appropriate to manually update a CRL for publication.

Know how to configure public key Group Policies.   Make sure you understand how to use Group Policies to automatically enroll certificates, to provide Trusted Root Certification Authorities lists, and to provide Enterprise Trust lists.

Make sure you can configure certificate renewals and enrollment.   Make sure you understand how to manually enroll certificates and how to manually renew certificates. Make sure you understand how to use both the Certificates MMC snap-in and the Web Enrollment pages to manually enroll certificates. Make sure you understand how to use auto-enrollment for Windows 2000 and Windows XP Professional computers on the network.

Know how to deploy certificates to users, computers, and CAs.   Make sure you understand how to issue certificates as an offline stand-alone CA and as an enterprise CA. Make sure you can issue certificates to users that manually request certificates and that you can use the auto-enrollment capabilities to automatically distribute certificates.

Understand the activities involved in managing CAs.   Make sure you understand how to do the following:

- Enroll and renew certificates
- Revoke certificates
- Manage and troubleshoot CRLs
- Back up and restore the CA

Key Terms

Before you take the exam, be certain you are familiar with the following terms:

authority information access (AIA)	digital certificates
certificate authorities (CAs)	intermediate CA
certificate revocation list (CRL)	issuing CA
certificate templates	metabase
certificate trust list (CTL)	Public Key Infrastructure (PKI)
`certutil.exe`	public-private key pairs
CRL distribution point (CDP)	root CA

Review Questions

1. To which of the following can certificates be issued? (Choose all that apply.)

   A. Computers

   B. Users

   C. Services

   D. Certificate authorities

2. Knowing that the sender is indeed who they say they are is an example of which of the following?

   A. Confidentiality

   B. Nonrepudiation

   C. Availability

   D. Sealing

3. Which services utilize certificates? (Choose all that apply.)

   A. 802.1x

   B. EFS

   C. IPSec

   D. NTLMv2

4. Using a card-sized hardware device with a certificate installed on it to identify the holder of the card is an example of which of the following?

   A. Smart cards

   B. One-time passwords

   C. Biometric device

   D. Scanning devices

5. Which of the following are encrypted protocols? (Choose all that apply.)

   A. Telnet

   B. SMTP

   C. FTP

   D. HTTPS

6. Which of the following are often implemented as stand-alone offline services? (Choose all that apply.)

   A. Root CAs

   B. Intermediate CAs

   C. Enterprise CAs

   D. Issuing CAs

7. Which methods can be used to add a new CA to the list of trusted root certificates on a computer? (Choose all that apply.)

   A. A local administrator can add the CA manually using the Certificates MMC console to add the CA's certificate to each computer's trusted list.

   B. A user can add the CA manually using the Certificates MMC console. Any certificates added to the list of Trusted Root Certificates will only apply to that single user on the computer, however.

   C. An administrator can use a Group Policy to distribute Trusted Root Certificates for all computers under the control of the Group Policy.

   D. An administrator can use the Certification Authorities MMC console to add the CA to all computers in the Active Directory domain.

8. A single level CA hierarchy will contain which of the following? (Choose all that apply.)

   A. An enterprise root CA

   B. An intermediate CA

   C. An enterprise subordinate CA

   D. A stand-alone subordinate CA

9. Stand-alone root CAs often have which of the following? (Choose all that apply.)

   A. Short publication intervals

   B. Large numbers of certificates issued

   C. Long publication intervals

   D. Manual CRL publication processes

10. Stand-alone CAs must have which of the following? (Choose all that apply.)

    A. DNS installed

    B. Unique computer names from the rest of the computers in the forest

    C. IIS 5 running

    D. Self-issued certificates

11. Certificate revocation list distribution points can be published using which of the following? (Choose all that apply.)

    A. HTTP

    B. FTP

    C. LDAP

    D. File shares

12. Which CA requires DNS to be installed in the network?

    A. Enterprise root CA

    B. Enterprise subordinate CA

    C. Stand-alone root CA

    D. Stand-alone subordinate CA

13. Which tool is used to verify that the CRL and the AIA have been properly published in Active Directory?

    A. Certificates MMC console

    B. Certification Authority MMC console

    C. Active Directory Users And Computers

    D. Active Directory Sites And Services

14. Which of the following are default certificate templates? (Choose all that apply.)

    A. Trust List Signing

    B. CEP Encryption

    C. User

    D. Computer

15. You need to back up the CA for your domain. What should you do? (Choose all that apply.)

    A. Back up the system state data

    B. Back up the certificates database

    C. Back up the DNS database

    D. Back up the CDP

16. You need to manually publish the CRL. Which node or folder do you use in the Certification Authority MMC console?

    A. Revoked Certificates

    B. Issued Certificates

    C. Pending Requests

    D. Failed Requests

17. Your company has installed an enterprise CA and has just configured Group Policies to automatically enroll all computers to receive computer certificates. You check your certificates store and do not find a computer certificate. What is the most likely reason?

    A. You need to log out and then log back in to receive the new GPO.

    B. The root CA is an offline CA.

    C. The GPO should be applied to the Domain Controllers OU.

    D. The Enterprise Trust list was not updated with the new CA.

18. You receive a call from a user that wants to enroll for a computer certificate. You try to walk them through the process of using the Certificates MMC snap-in to request a certificate, but they say that they cannot start the MMC. What is the most likely reason?

A. The Enterprise Trust list has not be added to the Group Policy.

B. The computer template is not available on the CA.

C. The user does not have permissions to the Certificates snap-in.

D. The user's computer is running Windows 95 or 98.

19. You receive a call from a user. They are looking at the Certificates MMC snap-in but do not see the computer certificate that they enrolled yesterday. You check the CA and see that it was issued yesterday. What is the most likely problem?

A. The Group Policy permissions stopped the certificate from being applied.

B. The root CA was not online when their request went to the enterprise subordinate CA.

C. They are looking at the Certificates–Current User instead of Certificates (Local Computer) node.

D. They need Service Pack 3 for Windows 2000 to view computer certificates.

20. You are trying to configure a new automatic certificate request for user certificates. The user template is not listed in the Certificate Template screen in the wizard, and you cannot complete your task. What is the most likely reason?

A. You tried to apply the setting to the Domain Controllers OU instead of to the domain.

B. The User certificate template has not been installed, and it needs to be installed first.

C. Windows 2000 does not support distribution of User templates through Group Policies.

D. You need to be an Enterprise Admin in order to deploy User certificates through Group Policies.

Answers to Review Questions

1. A, B, C, D.   Certificates can be issued to computers, users, services, and CAs. Many people forget that a CA must receive a certificate from either another CA or from itself.

2. B.   Nonrepudiation is referred to in authentication as providing proof of the integrity and the origin of the message that can be verified by a third party (the CA).

3. A, B, C.   Certificates are used by 802.1*x* in authentication, in EFS for encryption of files, and in IPSec in encryption of network traffic.

4. A.   A smart card is a plastic card with an integrated chip or embedded integrated circuit that can store information such as a certificate.

5. D.   HTTPS is SSL-enabled HTTP (web traffic) and requires a certificate for encryption.

6. A, B.   Root and intermediate (sometimes called policy) CAs are often implemented as offline CAs and are not connected to the network. Enterprise and issuing CAs are online and need to be online to handle all the transactions necessary.

7. A, B, C.   Certificates can be added using the Certificates MMC Console or using Group Policies. They can also be added using the `certutil.exe` command line tool.

8. A.   A single-level CA hierarchy will always contain an enterprise CA.

9. C, D.   Stand-alone root CAs often have long publication intervals and require a manual CRL publication process because they do not issue many certificates and they cannot automatically update CRL publication points since they are offline.

10. B, C.   The name must be unique because it is used within Active Directory and throughout the forest, and IIS must be installed to manage offline certificate requests. Only the root needs a "self-issued certificate"; offline intermediate CAs will receive a certificate from the root CA.

11. A, C, D.   CDPs can be published using web servers, file shares, and Active Directory (LDAP).

12. A, B.   Enterprise CAs require DNS to support Active Directory which is required for an enterprise CA.

13. D.   ADSS is used with Show Services Node enabled to verify that the CRL and AIA have been properly published.

14. C, D.   By default only the templates for Administrator, Domain Controller, Computer, Basic EFS, EFS Recovery Agent, User, and Web Server are installed.

15. A, B.   Backing up the system state data will get the configuration information in the Registry, including the IIS 5 metabase, and then backing up the database itself will work. You should also back up the CA certificate and its private key.

16. A.   Right-click the Revoked Certificates folder, and then choose All Tasks ➢ Publish.

17. A.   You need to either log out and back in again or wait for the GPO refresh interval to pass.

18. D.   MMC is not available on Windows 95 and 98 clients. To enroll, the user must use the Web Enrollment pages.

19. C.   Only user certificates can be seen using the Certificates–Current User node.

20. C.   Windows 2000 only supports distribution of computer-based certificates though the Automatic Certificate Request Settings in Group Policies.

Chapter 10

Managing Client-Computer and Server Certificates and EFS

THE MICROSOFT EXAM OBJECTIVES COVERED IN THIS CHAPTER:

✓ **Manage client-computer and server certificates. Considerations include SMIME, DFS, exporting, and storage.**

- Publish certificates through Active Directory.
- Issue certificates using MMC, web enrollment, programmatic, or auto enrollment using Windows XP.
- Recover KMS-issued keys

✓ **Manage and troubleshoot EFS. Considerations include domain members, workgroup members, and client-computer operating systems.**

In Chapter 9 we discussed installing, configuring, and managing the certificate authority (CA). In this chapter, we will focus on certificates from the perspective of the client computer and the server. Although it might seem that we are repeating concepts and issues, we are going to explore many new ones in the chapter while we also reinforce some of the previous discussions by looking at them from the client-computer side.

As you saw in Chapter 9, installing and configuring a PKI (Public Key Infrastructure) is vital to properly securing networks. However, we can forget that the whole purpose of a PKI is to properly provide certificates to computers and users on the network.

If we use our driver's license analogy for authentication, it makes a great deal of sense. It does no good to have top-quality driver's licenses with the ability to provide third-party verification if the driver's license office is only open on Friday for three hours. It does no good to have great identity verification tools if nobody can get the identifications and if nobody uses them as proof of identity.

So, we get to put the pieces together in this chapter. We will use certificates for securing data storage and messaging. We will also look at troubleshooting certificate usage from the client side.

Managing Client Certificates

Computer certificates are also known as *machine certificates*. Server certificates are exactly the same thing as client-computer certificates. Computer certificates authenticate computers, whether they are client computers or server computers. Well, it really isn't that simple, but we can use this to get started.

However, client computers generally use different *certificate templates* than servers. For example, a client computer would most likely never need to enroll a web server certificate for *SSL (Secure Sockets Layer)*. So, there is a difference between the two, and it all comes down to the tasks and how certificates are used. In the next sections, we'll take a look at how certificates are used for specific tasks on client computers.

Securing E-mail with Secure MIME

Secure Multipart Internet Mail Extension (S/MIME) has been used for years to sign and seal e-mail across the Internet as well as within organizations. In Chapter 5, we talked about using SSL-enabled SMTP (Simple Mail Transfer Protocol) to send e-mail to an SMTP server out on the Internet and to secure the e-mail during the travel from the client computer to the server. Once the e-mail hits the server and is sent to another SMTP server (the destination) on the

Internet, the e-mail is traveling in the clear. A good analogy is the postal system. The best way to think of these messages is that there are three classes of messages or mail service:

- Totally open and in the clear like a postcard. Standard SMTP is like a postcard.
- Signed with a clear and recognizable signature. Signed SMTP is like a signed postcard.
- Signed with a clear and recognizable signature and sealed in an envelope. Signed and sealed SMTP is like a signed letter in a sealed envelope.

Normally SMTP traffic is all in the clear, like a postcard. You write your message on the back and put a stamp on for postage. While the postcard is being processed by the postal service, every person that handles it can read it. What prevents everyone from reading it? Absolutely nothing other than people have better things to do with their lives. Since postcards are not secure, we generally don't use postcards for sending private information to friends and relatives.

Think about office memos. What is the one item in a memo that really proves who wrote it? It is either a clear *signature* or some initials. If you wanted to ruin somebody's day, write a memo telling them that they will be laid off in four weeks and put in on their desk. The only way to know it is not real is to verify the signature. It is the same with SMTP e-mail. The problem with e-mail is that not everyone uses *digital signatures* to *sign* their messages. Similar to verifying a person's real signature by asking them if it is their signature or comparing it to a previous one, a digital signature can actually be checked with a third party; the certificate authority that issued it. If the e-mail is signed, the signature can be checked, and you can be sure that the e-mail was not replaced in route and that it was not tampered with during the journey.

When we want to send confidential correspondence (private letters), we fold them and put them in envelopes. The receiver can look at an envelope and can verify the letter was not opened and replaced with another letter by verifying the *seal*. This is the same thing as a sealed e-mail. The seal hides the content from prying eyes. Unlike memos lying on desks and postcards, a sealed letter cannot be viewed without some evidence of it being opened.

In standard business correspondence, letters are both signed and sealed. To do the same thing in e-mail is a good practice for messages that need this type of security.

Remember one nice thing about postcards: they are cheaper to send. Security has a cost, and that is the expense of acquiring, maintaining, and managing certificates and the expense of encryption when it comes to CPU time.

S/MIME is based on *public-private key pairs* and requires certificates. As you know from previous chapters, you can use either a private CA or a public CA to get certificates. In the case of e-mail, which will be sent all around the world as well as inside the company, it makes good sense to use a public CA. After all, the receivers are going to want to verify the signature, and a public CA is best suited to handle that task.

The process involves three main steps:

1. Obtain a certificate for e-mail
2. Send a signed e-mail message to everyone that will send you encrypted e-mail messages
3. Receive a signed e-mail message from everyone that you want to send encrypted e-mail

In Exercise 10.1, you'll see how to use S/MIME to sign and seal e-mail.

EXERCISE 10.1

Using S/MIME To Sign and Seal E-mail

In this exercise, we will go through all three steps using Outlook Express.

Acquire the Certificate

1. Go to the web page of your favorite public CA. The process will vary slightly depending on the CA. If you do not have a favorite, you can select one from Microsoft's recommended Digital ID provider list at http://office.microsoft.com/assistance/2000/certpage .aspx?&helplcid=1033&path=outldigid.asp. For this exercise, we will use Comodo Group at www.comodogroup.com.

2. Click the Products link and then click Free Secure Email Certificates. Click Sign Up Now.

3. Enter the information as shown here for the application form. Click Advanced Security Options if you want to choose the *Cryptographic Service Provider (CSP)* and the key size. You can choose a CSP that will work with a smart card if you want. We will use the default options. Click Submit & Continue.

4. You may receive a Potential Scripting Violation warning screen like the one shown here, depending on how your web browser security is configured. Click Yes to request the certificate.

EXERCISE 10.1 *(continued)*

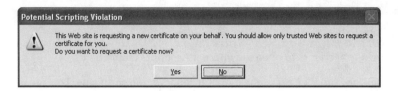

5. Instructions on how to download and install your certificate will then be e-mailed to the address you entered in step 3.

6. Click the link in your e-mail to collect and install your certificate.

7. In the web page that is displayed next, click Collect & Install Certificate.

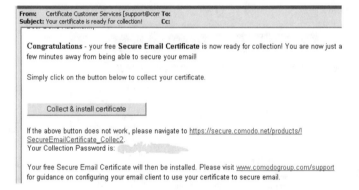

8. Enter the e-mail address and the password provided by Comodo Group in the web form as shown in here. Click Submit & Continue.

9. You may, again, receive a Potential Scripting Violation warning screen. Click Yes, if you receive the warning. You should then receive a message that your certificate is now installed.

Installing the Certificate Using Outlook Express

1. Open Outlook Express.

2. Choose Tools ➢ Accounts to open the Internet Accounts dialog box.

3. Click the Mail tab, and then select the e-mail account for the certificate. The e-mail address for the account must match the e-mail address you used to acquire the certificate.

4. With your account highlighted, click the Properties button to open the Properties dialog box for that account.

5. Click the Security tab.

6. In the Signing Certificate section, click Select, shown here. Select the certificate from the list, and click OK.

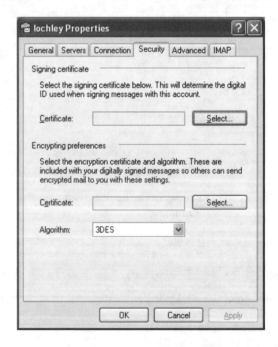

7. In the Encrypting Preferences section, click Select, select the certificate, and click OK.

8. In the Algorithm drop-down list box, select the algorithm you want to be used when people send you encrypted e-mail. *3DES,* or triple DES, is the default and is the strongest algorithm available on the list.

9. Click OK to close the Properties dialog box, and then click Close to close the Internet Accounts dialog box.

Sending Signed E-mail Using Outlook Express

1.   Open Outlook Express.

2.   Click Create Mail

3.   Create an e-mail message as you would normally do.

4.   Click the Sign button.

5.   Click Send.

Adding Received Certificates in Outlook Express

As we discussed, before you can send encrypted e-mail to somebody, you must have their certificate. If they e-mail you a signed message, you can get their certificate from that message. The best way is to configure Outlook Express is to automatically add the certificate.

1.   Open Outlook Express.

2.   Choose Tools ➢ Options to open the Internet Options dialog box.

3.   Click the Security tab.

4.   Click the Advanced button to open the Advanced Security Settings dialog box.

5.   Enable the Add Senders Certificates To My Address Book option.

6.   Click OK to close the Advanced Security Settings dialog box. Click OK to close the Internet Options dialog box.

Sending Encrypted E-mail Using Outlook Express

Again, remember, you cannot send encrypted e-mail unless you already have the receiver's certificate.

1.   Open Outlook Express.

2.   Click Create Mail.

3.   Create an e-mail just as you would normally do.

4.   Click the Encrypt button.

5.   Click Send.

Configuring S/MIME enables improvements in messaging and heightens your confidence that messages are from whom the sender says they are. Knowing that your messages were not altered or even read by others allows for more confidential communications through e-mail. Although these e-mail certificates are actually *personal certificates* and not machine certificates, we cover this topic here because the certificates are stored on the computer. To change computers will require *exporting* the certificates from the current computer and then *importing* them to the new computer.

We'll cover exporting certificates later in this chapter. However, you can use Outlook Express to export certificates. Choose Tools ➤ Options to open the Internet Options dialog box. On the Security tab, click Digital IDs. In the Certificates dialog box, you can select a certificate and then click the Export button to copy the certificate to a file and then store it in a safe place. You can also remove a certificate by selecting it and then clicking the Remove button.

Securing Files and Folders with the Encrypting File System (EFS)

Now that we are confident that our e-mail is not being read by everyone on the Internet and everyone internally in the company, we can move on. You can use the *Encrypting File System (EFS)* to encrypt all the folders and files that you have to protect from prying eyes. You can use EFS to encrypt files stored on Windows 2000 NTFS formatted drives. EFS uses key pairs in combination with a symmetric key to perform *encryption* and *decryption*.

Using EFS is simple from the user perspective. Certificate enrollment and implementation is completely hidden from the network user. In fact, the user doesn't even need a certificate for EFS in order to encrypt files. When the user sets the encryption attribute for a file or folder, EFS attempts to locate a certificate in the user's personal certificate store. If EFS finds a certificate with the EFS template or another template that allows file encryption, it uses that certificate. If the user does not have a certificate for EFS, EFS gets one. It tries to use *auto-enrollment* if it has been set up as we did in Chapter 9. If EFS cannot automatically enroll a certificate, it creates its own self-signed certificate and begins the encryption process. Even though a self-signed certificate will not be trusted, it is still valid for use to encrypt files.

If you are a proactive administrator, you will consider the needs for EFS in your company, and you will set up the automatic enrollment process for your enterprise issuing CA. It is a good idea to do this, because you can also set up and configure *recovery agents* for EFS and have them ready. Without recovery agents, you can run into situations in which you are not able to recover encrypted data because the user's key is lost. You can avoid this problem through some planning and implementation work.

The process of encrypting files using EFS is illustrated in Figure 10.1. The steps are as follows:

1. A network user chooses to encrypt a file. When encryption is required, the user's computer generates a *file encryption key (FEK)*.

2. The computer then uses the FEK and a symmetric encryption algorithm to encrypt the file. At this point it has not used the certificate.

3. The file is now encrypted using the FEK. The computer attempts to retrieve the user's EFS certificate from the personal certificate store. If it finds the certificate, it extracts the public key from the certificate. If it can't find the certificate, it attempts to enroll one. If it can't find an Enterprise CA to enroll the certificate, it creates its own. Once EFS has the certificate, it extracts the public key.

4. The computer use the public key to encrypt the FEK using an asymmetric algorithm. EFS then places the encrypted FEK in the *data decryption field (DDF)* located in the file's

header. In Windows 2000, the DDF can contain only one entry. Windows XP Professional allows multiple entries in the DDF so that EFS files can be shared with other users.

5. The computer retrieves the EFS recovery agent certificate for each recovery agent and extracts its public key. The public key is used to encrypt the FEK, and the encrypted FEK is put into the *data recovery field (DRF)* located in the file's header. This process is repeated for each EFS recovery agent.

6. The encrypted file is stored with the DDF and the DRF entries in its header in the file system.

FIGURE 10.1   The EFS process

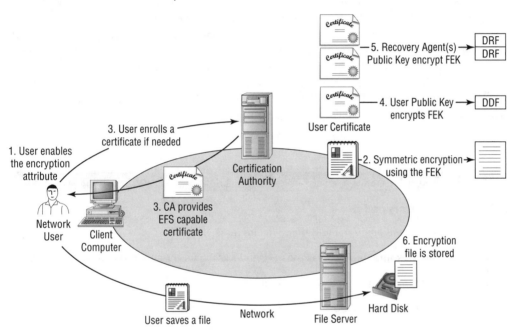

Once the encrypted file is stored on the hard drive, the only user that can open the file and read its contents is the user that stored the file using their public key to encrypt the FEK or an account that has the recovery agent's certificate. In both cases, the private key from the certificate is required to decrypt the file using these steps:

1. The user attempts to open the encrypted file. The computer retrieves the user's certificate and extracts the user's private key from the certificate.

2. The computer uses the private key to decrypt the DDF to get the FEK from the document header.

3. The computer then uses the FEK to decrypt the file.

The process of encrypting the file uses *symmetric* encryption followed by *asymmetric* encryption. The process of decrypting the file uses asymmetric encryption followed by symmetric encryption. While the file is traveling across the network from the client computer to the file server and from the file server to the client computer, it is not encrypted.

We used a couple of terms that can be confusing, so let's address them right now.

Symmetric key   A symmetric key is like a secret password. If you were to send a file encrypted with a special password, the recipient would have to know that special password to decrypt it. Symmetric keys are used in many security products. Symmetric encryption uses the secret key (or password) that is generated to encrypt the contents. The exact same secret key is used to decrypt the contents. Symmetric keys are used for bulk encryption processes because the encryption is between 100 and 1000 times faster than using asymmetric keys.

Public key   A public key (so called because it is available to the general public) is part of an asymmetric key pair. The other half of the pair is the private key. An asymmetric key pair consists of a private key and a public key that are used together. When you send e-mail using the person's public key, the only way to decrypt the e-mail is to use the private key of the key pair. One key can only do half the work. The other key of the pair is required to do the other half of the work. So, if one key encrypts, the other is required to decrypt. The order of use is not important. What is important is that the user or owner of a certificate is the only one that should have the private key. The public key can be given out freely without any worries if the private key is properly maintained.

In Exercise 10.2, you will use EFS to encrypt files.

EXERCISE 10.2

Using EFS to Encrypt Files

In this exercise, you will encrypt a folder and its contents.

1.   Choose Start ➢ Programs ➢ Accessories ➢ Windows Explorer to open Windows Explorer.

2.   Navigate to the folder that you want to encrypt.

3.   Right-click the folder and choose Properties from the shortcut menu to open the Properties dialog box for the folder.

4.   In the Attributes Section, click the Advanced button to open the Advanced Attributes dialog box.

5.   Enable the Encrypt Contents To Secure Data check box. Click OK to close the Advanced Attributes dialog box.

6.   Click OK to close the Properties dialog box.

7.   The Confirm Attribute Change dialog box will appear, asking whether the change (enabling encryption) should be made to the folder only or the folder, its subfolders, and any files underneath the folder and subfolders. Click the Apply Changes To This Folder, Subfolders, And Files radio button. Click OK.

EFS encrypt the folders and files required. It may take a couple of minutes or more depending on how many files are involved and the sizes.

File and folder attributes are applied to each file and folder in the NTFS file system. One of those attributes is the EFS *attribute* showing whether a file has been encrypted. When you copy files and folders, you do not copy their attributes too. They inherit their attributes from their new location.

Think of it as cloning. If you were to clone a human child, the clone would not also get the clothes, the toys, and the pets from his donor. He would have to get new ones from his new parents in his new home. It is the same with files and folders. They gain their attributes (clothes, toys, pets, and NTFS attributes) from their new parents. So, if you copy a file from one location to another, it acquires the attributes of its parent folder. Moving the file or folder is different, though. If you move the child, he will pack up all his attributes and take them with him because he owns them. So, if you move a file from one location to another, it will still have the same attributes (encryption). This rule applies only if it is moved to another location on the same logical hard drive partition. If you move the file to another logical hard drive, it is a different story. NTFS uses a *transactional file system*. This means it has to have the ability to roll back in case of a failure during a transaction such as a copy or a move. To protect itself, NTFS actually copies the folder or file object to the new location (if it is on another drive). After the operating system successfully copies the file, it deletes the original. Since it is really a copy, the object inherits its permissions from the new parent.

Some tips on implementing EFS are probably in order right about here:

Back up and secure EFS certificates.   EFS users should export their keys to a floppy disk (maybe multiple floppies) and store them in a secure place. The private key is required to decrypt the FEK and then decrypt the file. Microsoft support lists this as one of their top 10 phone calls: user calls to report that they cannot decrypt their encrypted files because they lost their private key.

Do not use the administrator account as the default recovery agent account.   Create a special account for the recovery agent. The administrator account's well known SID is a prime target for intruders, and you do not want to expose the recovery agent to intruders that might succeed in damaging the administrator account or compromising it.

Properly back up and restore the EFS recovery agent certificates.   Without the private key from these certificates, you will not be able to save the files for users that have lost their private keys.

Although EFS certificates are actually personal certificates and not machine certificates, we cover this topic here because the certificates are stored on the computer. To change computers will require exporting the certificates from the current computer and then importing them into the new computer.

It is unlikely that you will ever need to move a computer certificate or copy a computer certificate to another machine. After all, that is the whole purpose when it comes to computer certificates; they are used to authenticate a computer. To have the same certificate applied to multiple computers defeats the purpose and actually breaks the PKI. The only reason to export computer certificates is for disaster recovery.

Importing and Exporting Certificates

The main reason to export a certificate is to back it up and store it or to use the exported file to import the certificate on another computer. As you have seen with S/MIME and EFS, the user that the certificate is assigned to actually moves around in the organization, and they need the certificates available wherever they are working.

Exporting Certificates

You will want to export a certificate from a certificate store to a file for the following primary reasons:

- So that you can recover from a disaster. Along with the certificate, also back up its private key.

- So that a user can use another computer to perform tasks that require certificates.

- So that you can install the certificate on a replacement computer.

Part of the export process requires selecting the file format in which to store the certificate information. The file format is important because each format has different features that need to be considered. This is especially true for exporting certificates with their private keys because not all file formats support exporting and storing the private key.

The available formats include the following:

DER Encoded Binary X.509 (.cer)   DER (Distinguished Encoding Rules) is a compatible certificate file format adhering to the X.509 standards. This encoding method is used for encoding objects such as messages and, of course, certificates that need to be transferred to other systems. Many applications use DER encoding because the certification request information has to be DER encoded in order to be signed by a certificate authority. This encoding format is used by many certificate authorities that do not run Windows 2000.

Base64 Encoded X.509 (.cer)   Base64 was developed to be used S/MIME. S/MIME is used in many e-mail systems to encode attachments sent over the Internet. All files that are encoded with Base64 are converted into ASCII format. MIME is covered by RFCs and is an Internet standard for attachments. Its purpose is to reduce the errors and corruption in transferring file attachments, particularly binary attachments, through Internet gateways. Since MIME is a well-established standard, all standard clients can decode Base64 files. It is provided for compatibility with other operating systems.

Cryptographic Message Syntax Standard - PKCS #7 Certificates (.p7b)   PKCS #7 allows the certificate and the certificate chain to be transferred from one computer to another or for the information to be stored in a .p7b file. This file format adheres to the X.509 standard.

Personal Information Exchange - PKCS #12 (.pfx)   This format is another industry standard format. However, this format supports the export of certificates and private keys to a file. The private key can only be exported, though, in certain situations. In particular, the certificate must have been requested using the Windows 2000 certificate authority's advanced method. The key can be marked as exportable when using the advanced method. The private key can also be exported if the certificate is an EFS certificate or an EFS recovery agent certificate. This is the only format supported in Windows XP for exporting a certificate and its associated private key.

Generally, if you plan to import the certificate into a Windows system, the preferred format is PKCS #7. This format is preferred because it will also export the certificate chain information.

It is important to maintain the trust path for the certificate. Other operating systems may not support the PKCS #7 format. If you find that the target system to which you need to restore the certificate does not support PKCS #7, you will want to use DER Encoded Binary or Base64 Encoded formats. These two formats are compatible with many operating systems. In Exercise 10.3, you will export a certificate.

EXERCISE 10.3

Exporting a Certificate

In this exercise, you will export a certificate to a PKCS #7 format, and then you will use this file in Exercise 10.4 to import a certificate.

Create a Certificates MMC Console

1. Choose Start ➢ Run to open the Run dialog box. In the Open box, type **MMC** to open the MMC.

2. Choose Console ➢ Add/Remove Snap-in to open the Add/Remove Snap-in window.

3. Click the Add button.

4. Select Certificates from the list of available snap-ins and click Add.

5. Click the My User Account radio button to manage user account certificates and click Finish.

6. Select Certificates from the list of available snap-ins, again, and click Add.

7. Click the Computer Account radio button this time. Click Next.

8. Click the Local Computer radio button. Click Finish.

9. Click Close in the Add Standalone Snap-in window.

10. Click OK in the Add/Remove Snap-in window.

11. Choose Console ➢ Save. In the File Name field, enter **Certificates.msc** and click the Save button to save this console into the Administrative Tools menu of your computer.

Export a Certificate

Since we used EFS and previously created an Enterprise CA in Chapter 9, there should be a certificate on the computer used for EFS.

1. Open the Certificates MMC you just created. Expand the Certificates - Current User node in the MMC.

2. Expand the Personal folder and then click Certificates. In the right pane of the window, you will see the certificate issued for EFS. You can identify it by looking at the Intended Purposes column.

3. Right-click the certificate and choose All-Tasks ➢ Export to start the Certificate Export Wizard.

4. Click Next.

5. Click the Yes, Export The Private Key radio button. Click Next to open the Export File Format screen.

6. Since we are exporting the private key, the only option for the file format should be the PKCS #12 as shown here. Enable the check boxes for Include All Certificates In The Certification Path If Possible and Enable Strong Protection. Make sure the Delete The Private Key If The Export Is Successful check box is cleared. Click Next to open the Password screen.

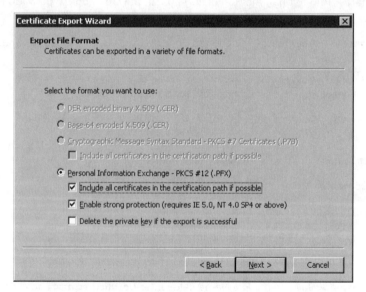

7. Enter a password and then confirm the password using the proper fields. This password will be required when you try to import the certificate in the next exercise. Click Next.

8. Enter the filename and the path for the file in the File Name field, or click Browse to navigate to the location and then enter the filename. The filename needs a .pfx extension. Click Next.

9. Click Finish in the summary screen to complete the wizard.

10. Click OK on the success message.

Importing Certificates

You will need to import a certificate for a few reasons. In particular, you will need to import a certificate:

- When it is delivered or received from the certificate authority in a file format.
- To restore a corrupted or deleted certificate that was previously backed up.
- To install a certificate, its chain, and its private key from a computer previously used by the certificate user.

Importing a certificate is the same as copying the certificate from a file in a standard certificate format to a certificate store on your computer. The certificate store used depends on whether it is a user certificate or a computer certificate.

Using the Certificates MMC snap-in tool is the best way to import a certificate. The import process can also import the private key, if it was originally exported to the file or if the file being imported is the certificate file provided by the certificate authority. You can also import the certificate chain. It is important for the certificate chain to be able to properly follow the certificate to its root certificate authority. If any CA in the chain is compromised, you will likely have to replace the certificate.

Certificates, their chains, and their private keys can be imported from the following file formats:

- PKCS #12
- PKCS #7
- Binary-encoded X.509

In Exercise 10.4, you will import a certificate.

EXERCISE 10.4

Importing a Certificate

A user can obtain a certificate by downloading it from a certificate authority or through some other means. Often you can retrieve the file from the certificate authority through a retrieval program on a website. Once the file is available, you can import it. For this exercise, you will import the file exported in Exercise 10.3.

Import a Certificate

1. Choose Start ➢ Programs ➢ Administrative Tools ➢ Certificates.

2. Expand the Certificates - Current User node of the MMC.

3. Expand the Personal folder. Right-click the Certificates folder, and choose All Tasks ➢ Import to start the Certificate Import Wizard.

4. Click Next.

5. Enter the file path and filename in the File Name field or click the Browse button to navigate to the file location. Click Next to open the Password screen.

6. Enter the password used to export the file in the previous exercise. Enable the Enable Strong Private Key Protection and Mark The Private Key As Exportable check boxes as shown here. Click Next.

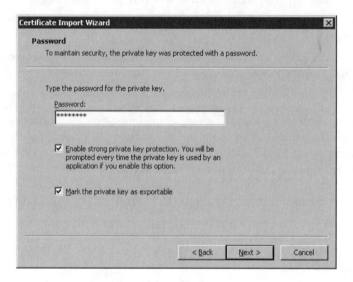

7. Click the Place All Certificates In The Following Store radio button. The Personal store should already be selected. If it is not, click the Browse button to select it. Click Next.

8. Click Finish in the summary screen to complete the wizard.

9. Click OK in the Importing A New Private Exchange Key message box.

10. Click OK on the success message.

The file format makes a difference, as you can see in Exercise 10.4. Properly test and document the recovery of certificates. Also properly document the export of certificates. After all, you can't recover what you have not backed up. It is a really good idea to properly export all the major certificates used in the organization, such as the certificate used to create the CA. You never know when they might be needed. That is the real reason for the many administrative tasks necessary for disaster recovery. You never know when the disaster will hit and what kind of a disaster it will be.

Certificate Storage

When a user acquires a certificate, it is stored in the *certificate store*. This store holds the computer certificates, and it also holds the user certificates that were requested while the user was logged in on the computer. You can view certificates using the Certificates MMC Snap-in as installed in Exercise 10.3. The store has two views, the Certificate Purpose and the Logical Certificate Stores as shown in Figure 10.2. Each view can also display the *Physical Certificate Stores* and the Archived Certificates. The logical view combines all the storage locations into one view. A certificate can appear in the list twice if it is stored in separate physical locations. The logical view combines these separate physical locations into one view.

FIGURE 10.2 The View Options dialog box

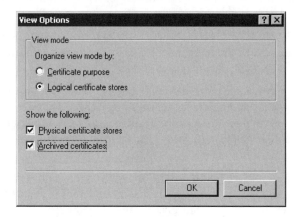

The logical view provides the following locations:

Personal   Certificates associated with personally held private keys. These certificates have been issued to the currently logged on user or the computer that the user is currently logged on to.

Trusted Root Certificate Authorities   Includes self-signed certificates for explicitly trusted CAs. This list includes the prepopulated list of CAs provided by Microsoft, and it also includes root certificates from internal CAs and any other third-party CAs that may have been added.

Enterprise Trust   Includes self-signed root certificates from other organizations and the purposes for which you will trust these certificates.

Intermediate Certificate Authorities   Includes all the certificates issues for intermediate CAs.

Trusted People   Includes all certificates for people that you explicitly trust. These are manually added.

Other People   Includes certificates that are implicitly trusted as part of a trusted certification hierarchy.

Trusted Publishers   Includes certificates from CAs that are trusted according to Software Restriction Policies.

Disallowed Certificates   Includes certificates that are explicitly not trusted. Normally certificates are added through applications such as Outlook.

Third-Party Root Certificate Authorities   Includes certificates for CAs outside the company.

Certificate Enrollment Requests   Certificates that are pending approval.

Active Directory User Object   User certificates published in Active Directory.

Certificate storage is an important issue. Certificates can be stored in three physical locations:

The default store   The profile is the main store for certificates. It is important to keep this in mind when working with roaming profiles or when deciding not to use roaming profiles. With roaming profiles, the same user certificates can be used on multiple computers without having to manually export and import them. Certificates are stored in the user's profile in the `Application Data\Microsoft\SystemCertificates\My\Certificates` folder.

Smart cards   Gemplus and Schlumberger smart cards can store certificates along with other data. Users can then carry their certificates with them.

Active Directory   Enterprise CAs automatically publish certificates to Active Directory by default. To confirm this, open the Certificate Authority MMC, right-click the CA, and choose Properties from the shortcut menu to open the Properties dialog box. Click the Exit Module tab, and then click the Configure button to verify that the Allow Certificates To Be Published In The Active Directory check box is enabled.

If certificates are not properly published in Active Directory and if they are not properly stored using either smart cards or *roaming profiles*, considerable administrative work can be required to maintain certificates. If you store certificates in roaming profiles, you need to maintain high-levels of security on the folders where the profiles are stored since the user's certificates contain the private keys. If the certificates are ever compromised, the files secured using EFS can also be compromised using the private key from the certificate.

Publishing Certificates through Active Directory

As we discussed in the last section, enterprise CAs automatically publish certificates in Active Directory by default. If this configuration is ever disabled, you can reset it in the Certificate Authority MMC. However, there are a couple of issues with using Active Directory to publish certificates. You need to consider how standalone root CAs publish their information in Active Directory. Also, you need to look at the use of child domains. Although the certificates are properly published in Active Directory in the parent domain, they are not properly published in the child domain.

Publishing Certificates from a Standalone Online CA

In Chapter 9, we went through the process of publishing the CRL *(certificate revocation list)* information for a standalone offline root CA. However, this process does not publish the certificates. If you remember, in a couple of exercises you walked through the steps to manually publish the information to the network. If you have a standalone CA that is online, the process is quite different. To publish the certificates, you must take two additional steps. First, you need to properly configure the CA, and then you need to set up the certificate enrollment. Exercise 10.5 takes you through this process.

EXERCISE 10.5

Configuring and Publishing a Certificate from a Standalone CA

In this exercise, you will configure the CA and set up certificate enrollment to properly publish certificate information in Active Directory. This requires that the standalone CA is online and that the server is a member server.

1. On the CA computer, choose Start ➤ Run to open the Run dialog box. In the Open box, enter **cmd** and press Enter to open the command console.

2. At the prompt, enter **certutil -setreg exit\publishcertflags exitpub_activedirectory** and press Enter.

3. Choose Start ➤ Programs ➤ Administrative Tools ➤ Internet Services Manager.

4. Expand the server in Internet Information Services and expand the Default Web Site.

5. Right-click the CertSrv virtual directory, and then choose Properties from the shortcut menu to open the CertSrv Properties dialog box.

6. Click the Directory Security tab.

7. In the Anonymous Access And Authentication Control section, click Edit.

8. Clear the Anonymous Access check box.

9. Enable the Basic Authentication check box.

10. Enable the Integrated Windows Authentication check box. Click OK. Click OK again to close the CertSrv Properties dialog box. Close the Internet Information Services MMC.

The CA can now publish the information properly to Active Directory even though the certificates are enrolled using the Web Enrollment pages. There is one caveat, though. The user must select the Advanced Request type and submit the request using the Submit A Certificate Request To This CA Using A Form as in Figure 10.3.

The requestor must also type **CertificateTemplate:User** in the Attributes field as shown in Figure 10.4.

This is probably a little much to expect for the user population, though, which is why we still recommend using enterprise CAs for all issuing CAs in an organization. The automatic publication capabilities of the enterprise CA is just one of the many benefits.

FIGURE 10.3   Using a form option

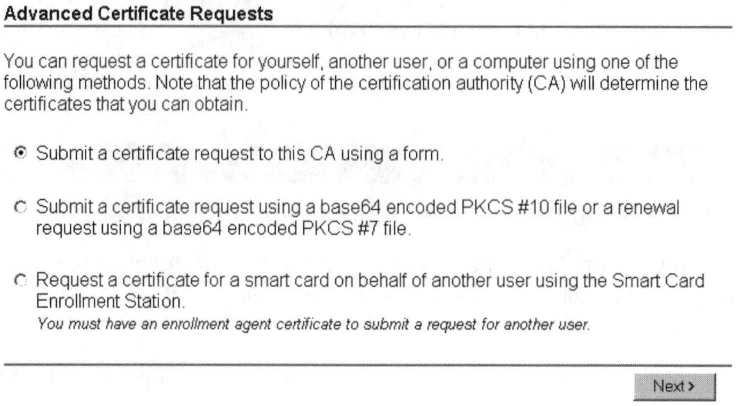

Advanced Certificate Requests

You can request a certificate for yourself, another user, or a computer using one of the
following methods. Note that the policy of the certification authority (CA) will determine the
certificates that you can obtain.

- ⦿ Submit a certificate request to this CA using a form.

- ○ Submit a certificate request using a base64 encoded PKCS #10 file or a renewal
  request using a base64 encoded PKCS #7 file.

- ○ Request a certificate for a smart card on behalf of another user using the Smart Card
  Enrollment Station.
  You must have an enrollment agent certificate to submit a request for another user.

`Next >`

FIGURE 10.4   The Attributes field

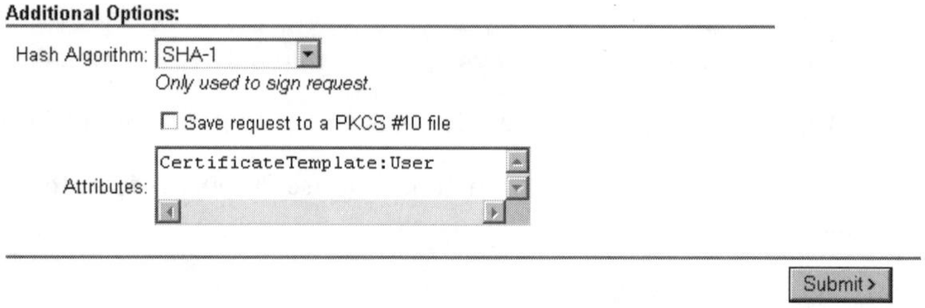

Additional Options:

Hash Algorithm: `SHA-1  ▼`
Only used to sign request.

☐ Save request to a PKCS #10 file

Attributes: `CertificateTemplate:User`

`Submit >`

Using Certificates in a Child Domain

If you have a parent and a child domain in your Active Directory structure, and the enterprise
CA is in the parent domain, you may have problems publishing certificates so that they are visible
in the child domain. The difficulty arises because of the permissions on the CA. Generally,
the CA allows read and write permissions for users in its domain. This does not included trusted
domains such as a child domain, though. To fix this problem, you need to allow child domain
members to enroll certificates, and then you must configure the publication of the certificates
to Active Directory, as in Exercise 10.6.

EXERCISE 10.6

Enable Child Domain Users to Enroll Certificates and Configure Publication to Active Directory

Configure CA Permissions

1.   On the CA, choose Start ➢ Programs ➢ Administrative Tools ➢ Certification Authority.

2. Right-click the CA, and then choose Properties from the shortcut menu to open the Test Eneterprise Root CA Properties dialog box.

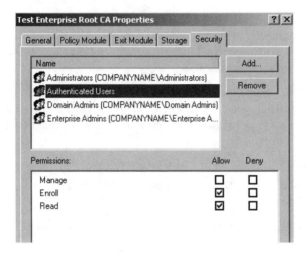

3. Click the Security tab and verify that Authenticated Users are allowed to enroll certificates.

Configure Active Directory Sites and Services

1. Choose Start ➢ Programs ➢ Administrative Tools ➢ Active Directory Sites And Services to open the AD Sites And Services window.

2.   Choose View ➢ Show Services Node.

3.   Expand the Services node, expand Public Key Services, and then expand Certificate Templates.

4.   In the right pane, right-click the certificate template that you want to be used for automatic enrollment and choose Properties. Most organizations will configure auto-enrollment for EFS, Machine, and User certificates.

5.   Click the Security tab. Grant Enroll permissions to Authenticated Users. Verify that the same group also has Read permission. Click OK to close the Properties dialog box for the certificate template, and then repeat this step for all certificate templates that you want to configure for auto-enrollment.

Configure the Exit Module to Publish to Active Directory

1.   On the CA computer, choose Start ➢ Programs ➢ Administrative Tools ➢ Certification Authority.

2.   Right-click the CA and then choose Properties from the shortcut menu.

3.   Click the Exit Module tab.

4.   Click the Configure button.

5.   Verify that the Allow Certificates To Be Published In Active Directory check box is enabled. If it isn't, check it. Click OK to close the Certificate Publication Properties dialog box, and click OK again to close the CA Properties dialog box.

Configure the Child Domain

1.   On a domain controller in the child domain, choose Start ➢ Programs ➢ Administrative Tools ➢ Active Directory Users And Computers.

2.   Right-click the domain name and choose Delegate Control from the shortcut menu to start the Delegation Control Wizard.

3.   Click Next to open the Users Or Groups screen.

4.   Click Add. Select Cert Publishers From The Parent Domain. Click OK. Click Next.

5.   Click the Create A Custom Task To Delegate radio button. Click Next.

6.   Click the Only The Following Objects In The Folder radio button. Enable the check boxes for User Objects. Click Next to open the Permissions screen.

7. Enable the Property-Specific check box. Enable the Read UserCertificate and Write UserCertificate check boxes as shown here. Click Next.

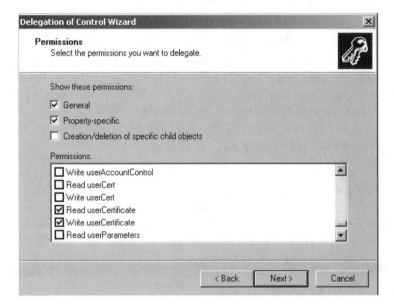

8. Click Finish on the summary screen. Close Active Directory Users And Computers.

9. Choose Start ➢ Run to open the Run dialog box. In the Open box, enter **cmd** and press Enter.

10. At the command prompt type **dsacls "cn=adminsdholder,cn=system,dc=*child*,dc=*domain*, dc=*com*" /G "*CADomain*\Cert Publishers:WP;userCertificate"** and press Enter.

11. At the command prompt type **dsacls "cn=adminsdholder,cn=system,dc=*child*,dc=*domain*, dc=*com*" /G "*CADomain*\Cert Publishers:RP;userCertificate"** and press Enter. *CADomain* is the domain name where the CA is installed, and *dc=child,dc=domain,dc=com* is the domain name of the child domain.

After you configure all the permissions in the parent domain and in the child domain, users in the child domain can enroll certificates using the parent domain's CA, and the CA can automatically publish the certificates in Active Directory for the child domain.

Enrolling Certificates

As we discussed in Chapter 9, you can enroll certificates in three ways:

- By using the Certificates MMC snap-in on the client computer
- By using the *Web Enrollment* pages on the CA
- By configuring auto-enrollment on the CA and in Active Directory

Obviously, the preferred method is to use auto-enrollment, which requires the least amount of day-to-day administration. It is also really nice to be able to set the permissions up to allow only certain security groups to auto-enroll. Using auto-enrollment, you can also exclude certain groups of users through the Deny permission for the Enroll right.

The Certificates MMC Snap-In

Using the Certificates MMC snap-in to enroll certificates is covered in previous chapters. The process is basic and straightforward. You use the Certificates MMC snap-in when auto-enrollment is not configured. You can only use the Certificates MMC snap-in to request certificates from online enterprise CAs. In Exercise 10.7, you'll use the Certificates MMC snap-in.

EXERCISE 10.7

Using the Certificates MMC Snap-in

Configure the MMC

1. Choose Start ➢ Run to open the Run dialog box. In the Open box, enter **mmc** and press Enter to open the MMC.

2. Choose Console ➢ Add/Remove Snap-In.

3. Click the Add button.

4. Select Certificates from the list of available snap-ins and click Add.

5. Click the My User Account radio button to manage user account certificates and click Finish.

6. Select Certificates from the list of available snap-ins, again, and click Add.

7. Click the Computer Account radio button, and then click Next.

8. Click the Local Computer radio button. Click Finish.

9. Click Close to close the Add Standalone Snap-In window.

10. Click OK in the Add/Remove Snap-In window.

11. Choose Console ➢ Save, and in the File Name field, type **Certificates.msc**. Click the Save button to save this console into the Administrative Tools menu of your computer.

Not all users will have permissions to request computer certificates or to manage computer certificates.

Requesting a User Certificate

1. Choose Start ➤ Programs ➤ Administrative Tools ➤ Certificates.

2. Expand the Certificates - Current Owner node. Expand the Personal node.

3. Right-click Certificates, and choose All-Tasks ➤ Request New Certificate to start the Certificate Request Wizard.

4. Click Next.

5. Select the certificate template you want from the list of available templates. Click Next.

6. Enter a friendly name and a description for the certificate. For example, if the certificate is an EFS certificate for a user, enter **EFS** in the Friendly Name field, and in the Description field, enter **For encrypting and decrypting personal files**. This will make it easier to identify the certificate later.

7. Click Finish to complete the wizard. Click Install Certificate to install the requested certificate. Click OK to close the success message window.

Requesting a Computer Certificate

1. Expand the Certificates (Local Computer) folder and double-click Personal.

2. Right-click Certificates, and choose All Tasks ➤ Request New Certificate to start the Certificate Request Wizard.

3. Click Next.

4. Select Computer from the certificate templates listed and then click Next.

5. Enter a friendly name and a description for the certificate, and then click Next.

6. Click Finish to complete the wizard. Click Install Certificate when you see the notice that the certificate request was successful. Click OK when you see the Certificate Request Was Successful message.

The Certificates MMC snap-in is easy to use with a little practice. However, it is not necessarily the best tool for acquiring certificates.

Web Enrollment Pages

Many CAs are not enterprise CAs, and they are not integrated with Active Directory. These CAs will require a Web Enrollment page to request and receive a certificate. The Web enrollment process can also be used for enterprise CAs, but it is not the simplest method available.

Since Windows 95, Windows 98, and Windows NT 4 Workstation clients do not support the Certificates MMC snap-in or the auto-enrollment process, these systems will have to use the Web enrollment process, as outlined in Exercise 10.8.

EXERCISE 10.8

Using Web Enrollment

Standard User Certificate

1. Open your web browser, and in the Address bar, enter **http://*servername*/certsrv**, using the name of your CA server.

2. On the Welcome screen, click the Request A Certificate radio button and click Next.

3. To request a user certificate, click the User Certificate Request radio button and click Next to open the User Certificate - Identifying Information screen.

4. Click Submit. You can click the More Options button if you want to select the Cryptographic Service Provider or if you want to enable strong private key protection.

Depending on your browser security configuration, you may receive a Potential Scripting Violation warning. If you receive the warning, click Yes to proceed.

5. Click the Install This Certificate link to download the certificate and install it on your computer.

Advanced Certificate Request

1. Open your web browser, and in the Address bar, enter **http://*servername*/certsrv** using the name of your CA server.

2. At the Welcome screen, click the Request A Certificate radio button and click Next.

3. Click the Advanced Request radio button and click Next.

You have three choices on this screen. You can either submit the request using a form or you can submit a request using a PKCS file. Normally, you use the PKCS file when a program of some kind generates a Certificate Signing Request. You use the third option only if you are requesting a certificate for a smart card on behalf of another user and you need special permissions to perform this task. So, this leaves the form option as the best selection for the majority of requests.

4. Click the Submit A Certificate Request To This Ca Using A Form radio button. Click Next to open the Advanced Certificate Request screen.

5. From here, you can select the certificate template to be used, the Cryptographic Service Provider, the key length, and several other options. Using the Advanced form, you can select the Mark The Keys As Exportable option. After selecting all the options, click Submit.

Depending on your browser security configuration, you may receive a Potential Scripting Violation warning. If you receive the warning, click Yes to proceed.

6. Click the Install This Certificate link to download the certificate and install it on your computer.

The Web Enrollment form is flexible and supports all operating systems that use certificates. However, we do not recommend its use unless it is required. Users tend to make many mistakes and request certificates that they cannot properly use.

Auto-Enrollment

One of the bigger problems with manual certificate enrollment processes like the Certificates MMC snap-in and Web enrollment is that users make mistakes. They obtain the wrong kind of certificate, or they select the wrong options and the certificate is not as strong as you would like. The process can be confusing, and it takes considerable time for each user on the network to enroll certificates.

You can set up certificate auto-enrollment using Group Policies, as discussed in Chapter 9. Windows Server 2003 will provide even greater support for auto-enrollment with Windows XP Professional client computers. For now, in Windows 2000, we are limited in the number and type of certificates that can be issued through automatic enrollment. Exercise 10.9 will walk you through the steps of configuring Group Policies to support auto-enrollment.

EXERCISE 10.9

Configuring Group Policies to Support Auto-Enrollment

In this exercise, you will configure the default domain Group Policy to allow the automatic enrollment of computer certificates.

1. Choose Start ≻ Programs ≻ Administrative Tools ≻ Active Directory Users And Computers to open Active Directory Users And Computers.

2. Right-click your domain, and choose Properties from the shortcut menu.

3. Click the Group Policy tab.

4. Click Default Domain Policy, and then click the Edit button.

5. Expand the Computer Configuration folder, expand the Windows Settings folder, expand the Security Settings folder, and then expand the Public Key Policies folder.

6. Right-click the Automatic Certificate Request Settings folder, and choose New ≻ Automatic Certificate Request to start the Automatic Certificate Request Setup Wizard.

7. Click Next to open the Certificate Template screen.

8. Select Computer and click Next.

9. Select the enterprise certificate authority you want to use from the list and click Next.

10. Click Finish to complete the wizard.

Windows 2000 and Windows XP Professional computers can automatically receive computer certificates through auto-enrollment. Windows NT and Windows 9*x* computers cannot participate in auto-enrollment processes. Windows NT and Windows 9*x* systems must use the manual Web enrollment forms process.

Recovering KMS-Issued Certificates

Key management server (KMS) is used in Exchange to provide secure e-mail to and from an Exchange server environment. For KMS to work with Windows 2000 CAs, Exchange 5.5 must be installed on a Windows 2000 server. If Exchange 5.5 is installed on Windows NT 4, KMS can only use Windows NT 4 CAs. The policy module installed for Exchange 5.5 is exclusive and forces all certificates issued to be marked for e-mail or S/MIME use only. The Windows 2000 CA will no longer be able to issue any other certificate types if it is being used for Exchange 5.5. Make sure that you have other CAs available to support the other needs of your organization. Exchange 2000 is different from Exchange 5.5 in that the policy module for Exchange 2000 is not exclusive. The CA can be used to provide certificates for Exchange 2000 clients as well as other certificate types for other needs in the company.

Exchange 5.5 KMS provides a unique key recovery capability for users that have forgotten or lost their passwords. If a user loses or forgets their password, they can generate a new key pair with a new certificate. The new key is placed in the same location as the previous key, and then the user can use both keys to decrypt mail because the fields in the Exchange folder are multivalued. Exchange 5.5 does not allow the exporting or recovering of keys as a means of preventing Exchange administrators from impersonating a user. Exchange 2000 is completely different in this aspect. An Exchange 2000 KMS administrator can export, import, and revoke keys. One of the new features in Exchange 2000 is the ability to recover users. This ability allows recovery of lost keys.

In Exchange 2000, a Key Manager object is created in each administrative group that contains an Exchange KMS. You can configure the Key Manager object so that it requires multiple passwords in order to recover a key. The Key Manager requires a password that is separate from the administrator password. It is important that the KMS administrator maintain this information in a secure fashion. If there are multiple KMS administrators, you might need multiple administrators to provide their password in order to recover a key.

If a user needs their key recovered because of a local hard drive crash or because they password-enabled their certificate and forgot the password, the KMS administrator can use the Recover Users feature. Right-click the Key Manager object, and choose All Tasks ➢ Recover Users. Add the user to the Selected Users list and click Recover. The KMS administrator can then have the server provide the temporary password, also called a token, or e-mail it directly to the user. The user can then recover their keys and decrypt their old e-mail as well as encrypt new e-mail.

Managing and Troubleshooting EFS

Security is really the topic of this entire book. Security is the focus of the associated Microsoft exam. So, it makes sense that after looking at the security around authentication, looking at the security around network traffic, providing secure access to remote network users, and securing services, we will have to address storage. EFS is extremely useful when security is extremely important. Although we addressed EFS earlier in this chapter, there is more to know about managing and troubleshooting EFS.

Implementing EFS

EFS is another layer of security. If an intruder does manage to work through all the other defenses, their next step is to defeat EFS. Mobile computers also benefit greatly from EFS. If they are lost or stolen, the data is not easily compromised. Because EFS is tightly integrated with NTFS, the process of encrypting and decrypting files is all done in the background and is transparent to the user.

The user can implement EFS in three ways :

- By setting the advanced properties for existing files and folders

- By adding new files and folders to an existing EFS-enabled folder

- By using the *cipher.exe* command line tool

You can also configure the computer so that the shortcut menu includes the ability to encrypt or decrypt files and folders, which you'll do in Exercise 10.10.

EXERCISE 10.10

Configure the Shortcut Menu

In this exercise, you will edit the Registry. Good practice is to back up the Registy before you start. Be careful, and follow the steps exactly. There is no undo function in the Registry Editor.

1.   Choose Start ➢ Run to open the Run dialog box. In the Open box, type **regedit** and press Enter to open the Registry Editor.

2.   Expand HKEY_LOCAL_MACHINE.

3.   Expand Software, expand Microsoft Windows, expand CurrentVersion, expand Explorer, and then select Advanced.

4.   Choose Edit ➢ New ➢ DWORD Value, and then enter **EncryptionContextMenu** for the value name.

5.   Double-click the new value and then enter **1** in the Value Data field. Click OK.

6.   The change will be effective the next time that Windows Explorer is opened.

Windows XP Professional includes several new features for EFS:

- More than one user can access EFS encrypted files and folders. After a file is encrypted, additional users can be given permission to access it. You specify this setting on a per file basis, but not on a folder. To add another user, right-click the file, choose Properties from the shortcut menu to open the Properties dialog box, click the General tab, and then click Advanced. Click the Details button, and then click Add. You can then search for a user by name and then add them to the file.

- *Offline files* can be encrypted. Configuring this support for offline folders is an extremely good idea. Any data in the offline folders will be encrypted and cannot be recovered by just anyone that happens to find or steal a laptop computer. To enable this feature, in Windows Explorer choose Tools ➢ Folder Options to open the Folder Options dialog box. Click the Offline Folders tab, click the Enable The Offline Files and Encrypt Offline Files To Secure Data check boxes, and then click OK. This will secure all offline files on portable computers.

- Encrypted files can be stored in *web folders*. Web folders are actually more secure than files shares when used with SSL. Traffic to and from the SSL-protected web folder is protected twice. SSL encryption is available, and EFS encryption and decryption take place on the client computer. Normally, files stored on a remote drive, such as a file share, are encrypted and decrypted at the file share and travel across the network without any protection. Of course, the files are protected while stored in the web folder using EFS. Web folders can be used over the Internet as well as on LANs and WANs, which gives web folders an added advantage.

- 3DES is available. Windows 2000 clients use DES-X, which is not as heavily encrypted as Windows XP Professional's 3DES.

The difference between EFS in Windows 2000 and Windows XP Professional clients may lead many organizations to expedite their Windows XP Professional deployments. The value is hard to ignore, and in security-conscious organizations, it makes good sense to deploy the most secure client operating system available.

EFS Encryption for Domain Members

EFS encryption is the same for file shares on a domain member server as it is for local resources with one major difference. Instead of the client computer doing the encryption, the file server actually does the encryption on behalf of the client computer. For this to work, the file server must *impersonate* the client computer by using Kerberos delegation.

If *Kerberos delegation* works like it is supposed to (which requires that the client be logged on to a Windows 2000 domain controller and authenticated using Kerberos), the file server will work with EFS on the client computer to determine if the profile is local or roaming. If the profile is a roaming profile, EFS loads it and retrieves the EFS certificate. If the profile is a local profile, EFS loads it and retrieves the EFS certificate from the local profile. If for some reason EFS cannot locate the profile, it creates a new one.

Once EFS either locates or creates a profile, EFS searches for an EFS certificate. If no EFS certificate is available, EFS attempts to enroll a certificate with a trusted enterprise CA on the network. If EFS is unable to find a trusted CA on the network to enroll a certificate, EFS create its own self-signed certificate. If EFS has to create its own self-signed certificate, it stores the certificate in the user's profile with both the private and public keys. Once EFS has the profile and the certificate, it verifies the existence of a private key (thus verifying that it can later be decrypted) and then it extracts the public key from the certificate.

Once EFS has the public key from the EFS certificate, the FEK is created and is used to encrypt the file's data. After the file is encrypted using the FEK, the FEK is encrypted using the user's public key, and the encrypted FEK is stored in the file header. EFS recovery agent public certificates are also used to encrypt the FEK, and the recovery agent encrypted FEK is stored in the file header as well.

Decryption involves a similar process. Again, of course, EFS on the remote file server must impersonate the client computer using Kerberos delegation. Once impersonation takes place, EFS can obtain the user's private key from the certificate. However, before it can do that, it must find the profile and then find the certificate stored in the profile. Once the private key is retrieved, it is compared to the public key to verify that they have the same thumbprint value associated with the key pair. Public-private key pairs share a common *thumbprint* value to show that they belong together. This is an important step because some users may actually have more than one EFS certificate.

Once EFS has verified that the private key is the correct one, EFS uses the private key to decrypt the FEK. Once EFS has the unencrypted FEK, it uses the FEK to decrypt the file data. The file data is then transmitted across the LAN to the client computer.

EFS and Workgroup Members

In a workgroup environment, there is no enterprise CA, so EFS automatically creates its own certificates any time a user attempts to encrypt a file for the first time. After the certificate has been created and stored in the profile, that same certificate is used for later encryption and decryption. There is one major drawback to EFS in a workgroup environment: the lack of a recovery agent. It is possible to configure a recovery agent for standalone computers, though. In Exercise 10.11, you will configure a recovery policy on a local Windows 2000 computer.

EXERCISE 10.11

Configuring a Recovery Policy on a Local Windows 2000 Computer

1. Choose Start ➢ Run to open the Run dialog box. In the Open box, type **mmc,** and press Enter.

2. Choose Console ➢ Add/Remove Snap-In. Click Add to open the Add Standalone Snap-In dialog box.

3. Click Group Policy and then click Add.

4. Verify that Local Computer is displayed in the Group Policy Object field, and then click Finish.

5. Close the Add Standalone Snap-In dialog box. Click OK to close the Add/Remove Snap-In dialog box.

6. Expand Local Computer Policy, expand the Computer Configuration node, expand Windows Settings, expand Security Settings, expand Public Key Policies, and then expand Encrypting File System.

7. Right-click the Encrypted Data Recovery Agents node and click Add. Click Next to start the Add Recovery Agent Wizard.

8. Click Browse Directory and find the account that you want to add as a data recovery agent. Click OK, and then click Next.

9. Click Finish on the summary page of the wizard.

The process is similar for a Windows XP Professional computer. In all cases, you need to verify that you are logged on as a local administrator.

If a standalone server or client is later joined to a domain, you can replace the self-signed EFS certificates with CA-issued certificates. Run the `cipher.exe` utility with the /k argument to archive the computer's existing EFS certificate and request a new EFS certificate from an available CA. It is a good idea to leave the archived EFS certificate alone. If you delete the archived certificate, it will be impossible to decrypt any files that were encrypted with the old certificate unless than is a valid recovery agent. As old encrypted files are opened, the archived certificate will decrypt them, and the new certificate will be used to encrypt the files as they are re-saved.

Disabling EFS

You can disable EFS for individual files a couple of ways:

- Enable the System attribute on the file or move the file into the system root folder or any of its subfolders. System files cannot be encrypted.

- Remove write permissions. Users cannot encrypt files when they do not have write permission.

You can disable EFS on an entire folder by creating a `desktop.ini` file and placing it in the folder. The *desktop.ini* file must have two lines in it:

```
[Encryption]
Disable=1
```

With those two lines in the `desktop.ini` file, no file in the folder can be encrypted. Any attempts to encrypt the file will result in an error message stating that the folder has been disabled for encryption.

You can disable EFS on a standalone computer in two ways:

- Delete all recovery agents from the computer local policy.

- Create a DWORD Value in the HKEY_LOCAL_MACHINE\Software\Microsoft\ Windows NT\CurrentVersion\EFS subkey. The DWORD Value to create is EfsConfiguration, and the value is 1. If you enter 0, EFS will work again.

Troubleshooting EFS

EFS, like many new technologies, requires that administrators get some experience with it so they can fix problems. Here are some guidelines:

- Using copy and xcopy commands to copy EFS files to a non–EFS-capable volume, local or network, will fail with a message stating that the files cannot be copied or moved without losing their encryption. You do have the option of continuing the copy, though. Windows XP Professional, however, has some new switches for copy and xcopy that allow files to be copied to non–EFS-capable locations. Copy /d works with Windows XP Professional to decrypt the file during the copy to the new location, and xcopy /g works in the same way in Windows XP Professional.

- Antivirus programs will fail to scan encrypted files. If possible, scan all files before encrypting them.

- When users report that they are unable to encrypt files, the most common errors are that the location of the files is not an NTFS partition or that they do not have write permissions.

- When users report that they are unable to decrypt files, the most common error is that the user's profile is not available on the computer they are using. To solve this problem, you may need to export and then import the EFS certificate to the computer, making sure that you also get the private key during the process. Another solution is to convert the user to a roaming profile. It is also fairly common that the computer account or the user account is not trusted for delegation. Check the trust for delegation rights on the object properties.

- Archive keys have been deleted. This does happen when older keys have been used to encrypt files and folders, but the user has deleted the archived certificate. Without the private key from the certificate, EFS will be unable to open files and folders encrypted using the older key.

If a user receives an error message stating that there is no valid key set, that error would seem to map closely to a problem with the archived certificates. If a user receives an error message saying the directory has been disabled for encryption, it is likely that the `desktop.ini` file is in place. An error message stating that the disk partition does not support file encryption sounds much like a FAT partition is being used. The infamous "Access Is Denied" message is a little tougher to troubleshoot since it could be a permissions issue (remember, the user needs write permissions); it could also be an attempt to encrypt a system file or a file with the system attribute enabled on it. It could also be that the private key is not available, or it could be that it is not a file that you have encrypted and the file has not been configured for sharing with another user.

Troubleshooting takes lots of experience with the technology, and it really is an art form. EFS is difficult to troubleshoot because so much of its processes happen behind the scenes and are transparent to users.

Summary

Managing certificates is a little more cumbersome that most administrators would like. However, with Active Directory and the upcoming improvements with auto-enrollment, it is getting much better. Microsoft has worked hard over the last several years to improve on Windows NT 4 and take the extremely large leap to Windows 2000. Along the way, Microsoft has greatly increased the security of network computing. Many security improvements have centered on encryption capabilities that use certificate keys. In this chapter, we looked at how to manage and use certificates. We covered several topics, including the following:

- Securing e-mail using digital signatures to provide proof of identity and using certificates to encrypt e-mail

- Securing data files using EFS to encrypt and decrypt files and folders

- Changes in capabilities with the Windows XP Professional clients that improve on Windows 2000 clients

- Using export and import to provide disaster recovery for vital certificates

- Understanding certificate storage

- Understanding common problems and issues and some solutions to potential problems

The exercises in this chapter gave you an opportunity to practice enrolling certificates and using them to secure both data and messaging. You practiced backing up certificates using the export feature and then recovering certificates using the import feature as well as the KMS recovery features of Exchange 2000.

In this chapter, we also discussed the business needs involving file security and messaging concerns and describe some ways to provide protection.

Exam Essentials

Know how to manage certificates.   Make sure you understand how to use certificates to provide security for messaging.

Understand the steps involved in using EFS and how it uses certificates.   Be able to properly export certificates, including private keys. Make sure you understand how to properly back up important certificates and how to safeguard them.

Be able to import certificates, including private keys. Make sure you understand how to move certificates from one computer to another.

Understand how and where certificates are stored. Make sure you know how to store certificates so they are available to network clients.

Understand how to publish certificates with Active Directory.   Understand how to publish certificates issued by standalone certification authorities and how to make the CA available to multiple domains at the same time.

Make sure you understand the ways that certificates can be issued and which methods need to be used by different operating systems.   Make sure you understand how to use the different processes to enroll certificates for clients.

Know how to recover certificates.   Make sure you understand how to recover certificates for standard CAs as well as for Exchange key management servers.

Make sure you understand EFS and know how to fully leverage its capabilities.   Understand the improvements in Windows XP Professional. Make sure you know how EFS works in domain and workgroup environments. Make sure you understand the basics of troubleshooting EFS.

Key Terms

Before you take the exam, be certain you are familiar with the following terms:

3DES	data decryption field (DDF)
asymmetric	data recovery field (DRF)
attribute	decryption
auto-enrollment	DER Encoded Binary X.509 (.cer)
Base64 Encoded X.509 (.cer)	`desktop.ini`
certificate store	digital signatures
certificate templates	Encrypting File System (EFS)
cipher.exe	encryption
Cryptographic Message Syntax Standard—PKCS #7 Certificates (.p7b)	exporting
Cryptographic Service Provider (CSP)	file encryption key (FEK)

impersonate

importing

Kerberos delegation

key management server (KMS)

machine certificates

offline files

personal certificates

Personal Information Exchange—
PKCS #12 (.pfx)

Physical Certificate Stores

public-private key pairs

recovery agents

roaming profiles

seal

Secure Multipart Internet Mail Extension
(S/MIME)

sign

signature

SSL (Secure Sockets Layer)

symmetric

thumbprint

transactional file system

Web Enrollment

web folders

Review Questions

1. You receive a phone call from a friend asking you to test his new e-mail system by sending him an encrypted e-mail message. You create the message and attempt to send it using encryption. When you click the Send button, you receive an error message stating that the message can't be sent encrypted because of a missing or an invalid certificate. What is the most likely reason?

   A. His e-mail system does not support S/MIME.

   B. You do not have a copy of his public key.

   C. His certificate authority is offline.

   D. Your e-mail system does not support S/MIME.

2. Your coworker is configuring a standalone Microsoft CA to issue certificates for secure e-mail. She says she is doing it to save money for the company so they will not have to get public CA certificates for everyone. What is wrong with her plan?

   A. She will need to configure auto-enrollment.

   B. She needs to use an enterprise CA so that certificates are published in Active Directory.

   C. A private CA will not be trusted by other organizations.

   D. She needs to configure the Exchange certificate templates.

3. You want to get a secure e-mail certificate so you can start digitally signing e-mail. Which CAs can supply these certificates?

   A. Only private CAs can provide secure e-mail certificates.

   B. Only public CAs on Microsoft's recommended list.

   C. Only public CAs that use Microsoft certificate authorities.

   D. Almost any public CA can supply secure e-mail certificates.

4. You have been signing your e-mail for several months after installing a secure e-mail certificate. While preparing for a security audit, you notice that your e-mail can be read using a packet sniffer. What is the most likely cause?

   A. Signed e-mail is not encrypted. This is expected behavior.

   B. Your e-mail system does not support digital IDs.

   C. The CA you used for the certificate is not supported by Microsoft.

   D. Your certificate has expired.

5. One of your coworkers recently left the company. While going through his files, you find that many of them are encrypted. Your company does not have a CA installed. What is the most likely explanation?

   A. EFS can be used regardless of whether there is a CA.

   B. Your coworker used a third-party application.

   C. Your coworker installed a temporary CA to issue an EFS certificate.

   D. Your coworker used a public CA for the EFS certificate.

6. One of your coworkers recently left the company. While going through her files, you find that many of them cannot be opened. The error message states that you do not have access privileges. You take ownership of the files and reset the NTFS permissions to allow you full control. You still receive the error. What is the most likely cause?

   A. You need to reconfigure the share permissions.

   B. The files are encrypted using EFS.

   C. The files are corrupted.

   D. You need to remove the expired account from the NTFS privileges.

7. One of your coworkers recently left the company. While going through his files, you find that many of them cannot be opened. You know that they are encrypted with EFS. Your company does not have a CA installed. How can you access the files?

   A. Use a domain recovery agent.

   B. Use the domain administrator account.

   C. Use the local recovery agent account.

   D. You can't access the files.

8. You receive a call from a network user that is trying to configure an EFS encrypted file to be shared with a coworker. You walk her through the process, but there is no Details button. What is the most likely reason for the missing button?

   A. She needs to install the latest service pack.

   B. The CA is offline.

   C. The person that she wants to share the file with does not have an EFS certificate.

   D. The client computer must be a Windows XP Professional client

9. You receive a call from a network user who is trying to configure an EFS-encrypted file to be shared with a coworker. You walk him through the process and click Add to add a user. The Find User button is grayed out, and there is no way to add another user. What is the most likely cause of this problem?

   A. Nobody else in the company has an EFS certificate.

   B. Nobody else has NTFS permissions to read the file.

   C. The domain controllers are offline.

   D. Your coworker's computer is not a member of the domain and is in a workgroup.

10. You need to encrypt all files for a special project you are working on at work. You don't want to encrypt any other files. All the files have been named with the project code with the first four letters of the filename, `trvt`. You need to encrypt the files as quickly as possible. What should you do?

   A. From a command line, run `cipher.exe /d trvt*.*`.

   B. From a command line, run `cipher.exe /k trvt*.*`.

   C. From a command line, run `cipher.exe trvt*.*`.

   D. From a command line, run `cipher.exe /e trvt*.*`.

11. You receive a call from a user. She moved a bunch of her files from her local hard drive to her home folder on the file server as you requested. She is upset, though, because she was told that moving encrypted files would not be a problem and that they would still be encrypted after they were moved. She says that all the files are now unencrypted. What should you tell her?

   A. Moving files between drives will cause them to inherit the encryption status of the new folder.

   B. The files should have stayed encrypted. The home folder must be on a FAT drive that does not support EFS.

   C. Moving EFS encrypted files to a remote file server is not possible because the file server does not have the user EFS certificate.

   D. Windows 2000 file servers do not support EFS-encrypted files for multiple users. Somebody else must be using EFS encryption already.

12. You receive a call from a user. He regularly uses two different computers. He can encrypt and decrypt files on one computer, but he cannot decrypt the files on the other computer. What should you do? (Choose all that apply.)

   A. Decrypt and re-encrypt all files from both computers.

   B. Export his EFS certificate and the private key from his working computer and then import the certificate and the private key on the other computer.

   C. Change his user profile to a roaming profile.

   D. Obtain an EFS certificate from a different CA.

13. You receive a call from a user. She regularly uses two different computers. She exported her certificate and the private key from her main computer and then imported the certificate and the private key on the second computer. Now, she can encrypt files from either computer, but she can only decrypt files from the second computer. What should you do?

   A. Use `cipher.exe` with the /K switch on the main computer that will not decrypt.

   B. Use the EFS file-sharing capability in Windows XP Professional to share the EFS files between both computers.

   C. Re-export the EFS certificate from the main computer and then re-import it on the second computer.

   D. Export her EFS certificate and the private key from the second computer and then import the certificate and the private key on the main computer.

14. You purchased a new computer for the company's production web server that is used on the Internet for receiving web orders for company products. The old server will be retired. You do not want to purchase a new SSL certificate for this server if it is not required. What should you do?

   A. Export the SSL certificate and import it on the new server.

   B. Replacing servers requires purchasing a new SSL certificate.

   C. Back up the entire web server, take it offline, and then restore it to the new computer.

   D. Back up the system state data from the web server and restore it on the new server.

15. You need to export an SSL certificate with its private key from a web server for disaster recovery. What file format should you use?

   A. DER Encoded Binary X.509 (.cer)

   B. Base-64 Encoded X.509 (.cer)

   C. Cryptographic Message Syntax Standard - PKCS #7 Certificates (.p7b)

   D. Personal Information Exchange - PKCS #12 (.pfx)

16. Where will you find the S/MIME and the EFS certificates when looking in the Certificates MMC snap-in when organized by the Logical Certificate Stores option? (Choose all that apply.)

   A. Certificates - Current User node under the Personal folder

   B. Certificates (Local Computer) node under the Personal folder

   C. Certificates - Current User node under the Active Directory User Object folder

   D. Certificate (Local Computer) under the SPC folder

17. One of the web server administrators needs to renew an SSL certificate for an intranet server. Which tools can he use to renew a certificate?

   A. The Certificates MMC snap-in

   B. Web Enrollment

   C. Auto-enrollment

   D. Internet Services Manager

18. You receive a call from a user who wants to know how to use EFS to encrypt files. Which of the following methods will work? (Choose all that apply.)

   A. Use the Advanced Properties dialog box to enable encryption for individual files.

   B. Use the Advanced Properties dialog box to enable encryption for folders.

   C. Copy files into a folder already configured for encryption.

   D. Run the `cipher.exe` command with the /e switch.

19. You receive a call from a user. He has been using EFS for several months and has heard that the company is now running its own enterprise CA to support EFS encryption. He wants to know if he can get a new EFS certificate and still decrypt all his old files. What should you tell him?

    A. Use the `cipher.exe /k` command to get a new EFS certificate. Remind him not to delete the previous key that will be archived. He will be able to open all newly encrypted files and as well as previous files.

    B. He needs to decrypt all his files that are currently encrypted and then delete their EFS certificate. He should then get a new EFS certificate and re-encrypt all his files.

    C. He can get a new EFS certificate and EFS.

    D. If he requests a new certificate, he can use the new certificate to access his old files as well as his new files.

20. You receive a call from your supervisor. She is extremely concerned that many of the network users are using EFS to encrypt files in their home folders. She does not want them to have this ability. What should you do?

    A. Delete all recovery agents from the home folders local policy.

    B. Remove write permissions on all home folders.

    C. Run the `cipher.exe /d` command on all home folders.

    D. Create a `desktop.ini` file with the appropriate information in it. Set NTFS permissions on the file so users cannot delete it. Copy it to all home folders.

Answers to Review Questions

1.   B.   In order to send encrypted e-mail to anyone, you must first have their public key, which you can get from an e-mail message that they have previously sent with a digital signature.

2.   C.   Every external person that wants to use the certificate to send encrypted e-mail will have to manually trust the certificate if it is issued by a private CA. This is too much to expect from nonemployees and nontechnical users.

3.   D.   The only limiting factor in choosing a CA will be the compatibility of their certificates with others.

4.   A.   Signed e-mail is not the same as sealed e-mail. If you need e-mail encrypted so that it cannot be read, you must send it encrypted, not just signed.

5.   A.   EFS will issue a self-signed certificate if it cannot find a CA.

6.   B.   EFS encryption will generate an access privilege error message that almost sounds like an access denied error. Having NTFS permissions will not allow access.

7.   C.   D might be correct if there is no local recovery agent account; however, if there is a local recovery agent, it can be used. OK, this is not a fair question. You need to remember that, without a CA, there will be no domain EFS recovery agent by default or by intended creation.

8.   D.   Only Windows XP Professional can support sharing EFS encrypted files.

9.   D.   Workgroup computers cannot search for and find others to add to share the file.

10.   D.   The /e switch is used to encrypt files.

11.   A.   Moving files between drives is similar to copying files. The files inherit their encryption status from the new folder.

12.   B, C.   Exporting and importing the certificate will make it available on both computers, and the user will be able to use EFS from either one. Giving him a roaming profile will move his EFS certificate to the server, where it can be used by any computer that he logs on to in the future.

13.   D.   Exporting the private key can cause it to be removed if the Delete The Private Key If The Export Is Successful option is chosen when using the Certificate Export Wizard. The private key is required to decrypt, and the public key is used to encrypt. Without the private key, the computer will not be able to decrypt.

14.   A.   Since the server will have the same name (such as WWW) on the Internet, it can use the same certificate without any problems.

15.   D.   Personal Information Exchange - PKCS #12 (.pfx) supports the export of private keys.

16.   A, C.   The S/MIME and EFS certificates can be found under both folders in the Certificates - Current User node.

17. A.   Only the Certificates MMC snap-in can renew a certificate.

18. A, B, C, D.   You can encrypt files in all these ways.

19. A.   The `cipher.exe /k` command archives the old EFS certificate and gets a new one from the CA. It is important that the user not delete the archived certificate since it will be used to decrypt all the old files. However, opening and resaving encrypted files will cause the new certificate to be used.

20. D.   Although answer B might work, users who can't save to their home folders will be upset. The correct answer in this case is D. With the proper information in the `desktop.ini` file, users will not be able to encrypt files in their folder.

Chapter

11

Configuring and Managing Auditing

THE MICROSOFT EXAM OBJECTIVES COVERED IN THIS CHAPTER:

✓ **Configure and manage auditing. Considerations include Windows Events, Internet Information Services (IIS), firewall log files, Network Monitor Log, and RAS log files.**

✓ **Analyze security events. Considerations include reviewing logs and events.**

   ▪ Manage audit log retention.

   ▪ Manage distributed audit logs by using EventComb.

In any secure environment, you should monitor and record significant events. It is a bit foolish to deploy a system that is supposed to be secure and yet not attempt to monitor and understand significant events that occur on that system.

In this chapter, we will look at how to configure and manage auditing. We'll discuss how to read and understand the various log files in Windows 2000, and we will also dive into using a nifty utility, EventComb. There's much to learn here, so let's get going.

Understanding Windows Events

When Windows 2000 boots up, logging begins automatically in several logs. A *log* is a file that holds event information for later review. *Auditing* is the process of extrapolating events from a log file to ascertain what has happened on the network. An *event* is a significant occurrence in the system or in an application that should be recorded for later review. Events can be recorded in the following logs:

Application   This log is the location where applications record their events. For example, a database program might record a file error in the programs log. Program developers decide which events to monitor.

System   Operating system components are coded to record their event messages in the system log. Events such as services failing to start or disk quota limits exceeded appear in this log.

Security   Failed or successful logon attempts are a prominent type of entry that appears in this log. In addition, the events that you specify in your audit policy also appear in this log.

DNS Server   Events from the Domain Name Service (DNS) server are recorded in this log.

File Replication   This log records events from the File Replication Service (FRS) on computers running Windows 2000 and later.

Directory Service   This log records events related to the functioning of Active Directory (AD). Messages are generated only by domain controllers.

In addition to events that are recorded in logs we've just described, other events are also recorded by some applications in their own text log files. These applications include Internet Information Services (IIS), the World Wide Web Service, the File Transfer Protocol Service, the Internet Locator Service, and Microsoft SQL Server trace logs.

Some events are considered *missing events*, meaning that an event was supposed to occur but did not. You can use the filtering reporting options in Event Viewer to see whether the event occurred. For instance, if you have an automated backup procedure that is supposed to run at a certain time, you can check the logs to see if the procedure ran. If the event is not recorded, you can safely assume that the procedure did not run as scheduled and is a missing event.

In this section, we'll cover the event types that appear in a Windows 2000 event log and discuss how to enable auditing and the information that auditing yields after it is implemented.

Event Messages in Event Viewer

Figure 11.1 shows a typical message in an event log. The point of this particular illustration is not the specifics of the message, but rather the structure of how the information is presented. Regardless of the logs, certain characteristics are always present if the event is viewed in Event Viewer. Understanding how to read an event is important to understanding the event's message.

FIGURE 11.1   An event messages displayed in Event Viewer

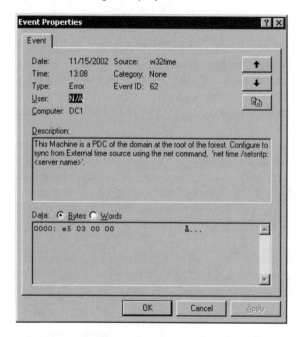

A typical message in an event log displays the following information:

The date and time stamp   The date and time that the message was generated is in the upper portion of the Event tab in the Event Properties dialog box. You might notice that the message details the time of the event only to the minute, whereas Event Viewer details the message time to the second.

The message type   Messages can be of five types:

Information   This type of message is meant to simply inform you that an important event took place. Usually, no action is required because there is no problem to fix. An example is a print job message that merely informs you that a document was printed.

Warning A warning message means that a serious event has taken place and that it is considered critical enough to warn you about it. For example, a warning message might tell you that a driver has disabled a write cache on a hard disk. You might not want the cache disabled, so Windows 2000 informs you of this event even though it is not necessarily an error.

Error An error message means that something has gone wrong—an unexpected event took place that Windows 2000 considers an error. A common example of this is shown in Figure 11.1, in which the Win32 time system is not synchronizing with an external time clock. Other types of error messages from SQL to Exchange to IIS to Windows 2000 will all appear and should not be ignored. Every once in a great while, you'll receive an error message that, after being researched, is found to be benign and can be safely ignored. But these scenarios are few and far between. Never ignore error messages. Research and correct them as soon as possible.

Success Audit You will see this type of message only in the Security Log. This message means that a request to access a secured resource was granted. A common example of this is a message that tells you a user has successfully logged on to the network.

Failure Audit You will see this type of message only in the Security Log. This message means that a request to access a secured resource was not granted. A common example of this is a message that tells you that a user has entered the wrong password when logging on to the network. A failure audit message is entered into the Security Log for later review.

Coded for a summary view, event log entries in the application and system log include the blue i for informational messages, a yellow exclamation mark to designate warnings, and the red x sign for error messages. In the Security Log, you'll find entries that include either a locked or unlocked padlock to indicate failure or success of security events.

The user This is the user account under whose security context the event took place. System-generated messages may not be applicable, so in some cases, as in the example in Figure 11.1, you will see the N/A designation.

The computer This is the computer at which the event occurred.

The source The source is the actual service on the computer that generated the message. When performing a search in TechNet or the MSDN (Microsoft Developer Network) library, it is often helpful to include the source name along with the event ID. Doing so helps refine the initial search so that the result set is more manageable and meaningful.

Another useful resource when researching events in the event logs is the website www.EventID.net.

The category This is the category for the event message.

The Event ID   This is a numeric ID that is associated with the message. It is not uncommon in the Microsoft literature to find tables of event ID messages and their associated numbers. Each message has its own number, and the ID helps identify the message. The Event ID can also be used by Microsoft's Product Support Services (PSS) to help diagnose a particular error message.

Description and Data fields   These fields contain the messages and any associated data. This is really the heart of the message. Often, you can use the phrases in the description field as search strings in TechNet and MSDN. Doing so helps find Knowledge Base articles that will help you think about how to solve a problem.

Messages in an event log are presented in a one-line per message format, meaning that each line in the event log indicates a different message (see Figure 11.2). As you can see, each event begins with an icon indicating the type of message, the date, the time, the source, the category, the event, and user information for the message. If you want to view the entire message, simply double-click it to open it.

FIGURE 11.2   The System Log file viewed through Event Viewer and showing an event on each line in the log file

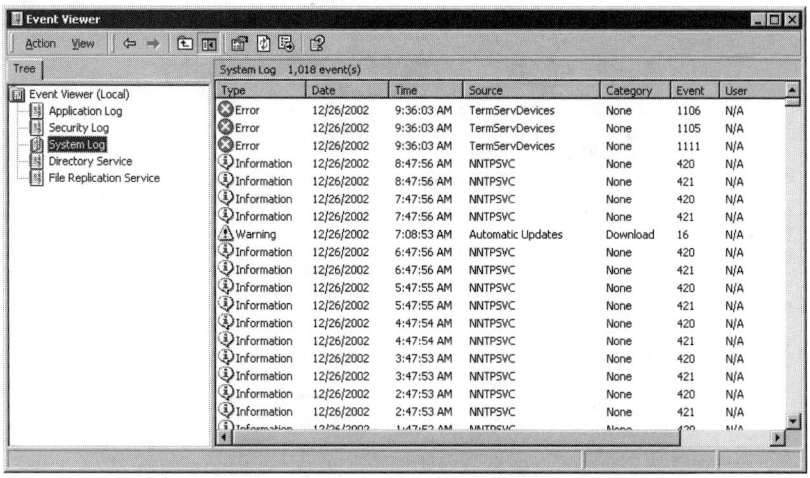

Pay particular attention to Failure Audit, Warning, and Error message types. If you ignore these messages, small problems can snowball into large ones, and possible attacks against your network will continue without a response from you. Investigate and resolve each of these message types in all event logs.

You can manage event logs through the shortcut menu when you right-click a log in the left pane of Event Viewer. From the shortcut menu, you can do the following:

- Open the log file
- Save the log file for later review
- Create a new log file view
- Clear all the events in the log file

There is no way to recover when you choose to clear the events in a log file. Use this option only when you have no need to recover any of the events in the log file.

- Rename the log file
- Refresh your view of the log file to include new events
- Export the log file to a `.csv` or a `.txt` file format
- Open the Properties dialog box for the log file
- Open online Help for Event Viewer

The Properties dialog box for a log file contains two tabs: General and Filter. On the General tab (see Figure 11.3), you can make several configuration changes, including the display name for the log file, the maximum log file size, and the method for overwriting events. Generally speaking, the more actions and activities you plan to audit, the larger your Security Log will be. Hence, you'll need to come to this General tab to increase the log file size and select how you want old events to be overwritten (if at all).

FIGURE 11.3 The Security Log Properties dialog box, open at the General tab

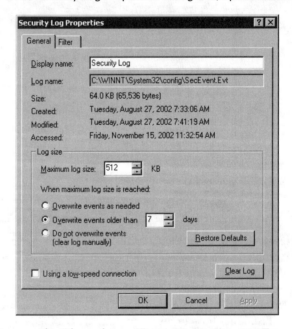

You use the options on the Filter tab (see Figure 11.4) to instruct Event Viewer to display only those events that you want to view. Notice that you can filter the events based on any combination of the following criteria:

- Event type
- Event source
- Category

- Event ID
- User
- Computer
- Date and time

Hence, if you are looking for a specific event that you know is supposed to run at midnight with a certain event ID number, you can filter the event log to display this single event.

FIGURE 11.4   The Security Log Properties dialog box, open at the Filter tab

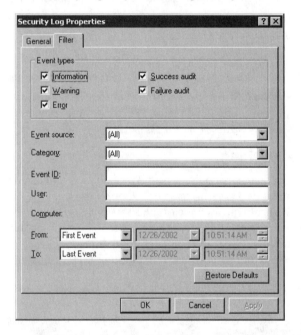

Filtering options available with Event Viewer affect only the log of collected events and the displayed results; filtering options do not affect the actual events that are collected.

Implementing and Configuring Auditing

A part of any security strategy is determining the events to be audited on your network. Auditing should identify successful and unsuccessful attacks. Moreover, auditing should identify events that pose a threat to your network or sensitive resources.

When you implement auditing in Windows 2000, those events are recorded in the Security Log. The more events you select to audit, the more event messages will be generated, and the more difficult it can be to spot the messages that are of greatest benefit to you. Fortunately, you can use event filtering to yield only the most important messages in the Security Log.

Audit events can be categorized as success or failure events. A successful event indicates that the action was committed successfully, such as logging on to a network or gaining access to a resource. A failed event indicates that the action was not successful, such as when a person is denied access to a resource or is unable to print to a particular printer.

If auditing is enabled, attacks that fail on your network indicate that an attempted attack occurred but was unsuccessful. This information can be useful in understanding when the attack occurred, the source location, and so on. Successful attacks can be more difficult to track than failed attacks for any number of reasons:

- Perhaps you are not auditing for successful events on the selected vector.

- The attacker used impersonation to gain entrance, so the successful audit event message will look normal and expected.

- The successful event message fits the user's normal pattern of activity.

- The successful event message is not connected to a series of preceding failed messages.

Audit messages provide information about important events, but always interpret these messages in light of a larger context and picture. Combine audit events with other information you have to properly interpret these event messages.

How to Enable Auditing

You enable auditing through Group Policies in AD. You can enable auditing on the site, the domain, organizational unit (OU) objects and AD, or on the local machine. The audit policy settings are inside the Local Policies node of the Security Settings node.

Unless you have a specific reason to do otherwise, enable auditing at the highest levels in AD to ensure consistency across servers and workstations. For machines that are not members of any domain, you can enable auditing in the machines' local policies or by using the command-line utility, auditpol.exe, which is in the Resource Kit.

In Exercise 11.1, you will enable auditing using a Group Policy.

EXERCISE 11.1

Enabling Auditing Using a Group Policy

1. Choose Start ➤ Programs ➤ Administrative Tools ➤ Active Directory Users And Computers to open the Active Directory Users And Computers (ADUC) MMC.

2. Right-click the domain object in the left pane, and choose Properties from the shortcut menu to open the Properties dialog box.

3. Click the Group Policy tab.

4. Select the Group Policy you want to use to enforce auditing in your domain.

5. Click Edit to open the Group Policy.

6. Under Computer Configuration, expand Windows Settings, expand Security Settings, expand Local Policies, and then select the Audit Policy node. The right pane should now be populated with the individual audit policies that you can configure.

EXERCISE 11.1 *(continued)*

7. In the right pane, double-click Audit Logon Events to open the Security Policy Setting dialog box.

8. Click the Define These Policy Settings check box.

9. Click the Success and Failure check boxes.

10. Click OK button to close the Security Policy Setting dialog box.

11. In the right pane, you should now see that the computer setting for Audit Logon Events is Success, Failure.

12. Close the Group Policy window.

13. Click OK to close Properties dialog box for the domain.

14. Choose Console ➢ Exit to close the ADUC MMC.

You have now implemented auditing for logon events that are both successful and unsuccessful.

To enable auditing on a resource, such as a file, a folder, or printer, you use the Properties dialog box for the resource. By way of example, we have created a mock Payroll folder as an illustration. Let's suppose you want to audit everyone who attempts to access this folder, both successfully and unsuccessfully. Follow these steps:

1. Right-click the Payroll folder and choose Properties from the shortcut menu to open the Payroll Properties dialog box:

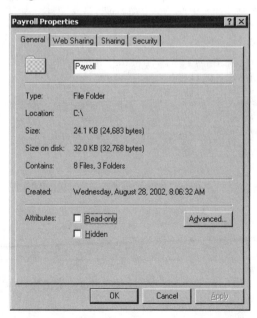

2. Click the Security tab, click Advanced to open the Access Control Settings For Payroll dialog box, and then click the Auditing tab.

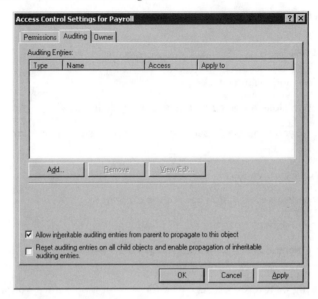

Now, this is where things can get a bit complicated. Let's assume that you want to ensure that you're tracking all failed attempts to access the Payroll folder. What this means is that you'll want to know about *any* attempt to connect to this folder, regardless of which share is used on the payroll server. You'll want to throw a broad net over auditing for failed attempts. The broadest group that is available in Windows 2000 is the Everyone security group. This group could easily be renamed to *Anyone* because that's who it includes: anyone who connects to the server is automatically made a member of the Everyone group. Hence, auditing for the Everyone group is the best practice here for failed attempts.

3. In the Access Control Settings For Payroll dialog box, click Add to open the Select User, Computer, Or Group dialog box:

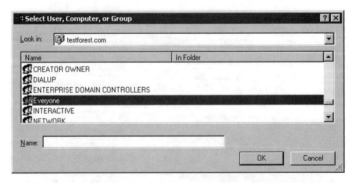

4. Select Everyone in the Name list, and then click OK to open the Auditing Entry For Payroll dialog box.

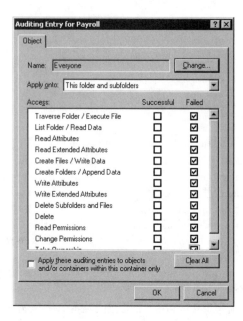

Notice that the Auditing Entry For Payroll dialog box lets you audit access to the Payroll folder at two granular levels. First, in the Apply Onto drop-down list box, you have the following choices as to how pervasive you want to apply this auditing policy:

- The folder only
- The folder, subfolders, and files
- This folder and subfolders
- This folder and files
- Subfolders and files only
- Subfolders only
- Files only

You can apply this auditing policy only to folders, only to files, or to both. And you can bypass the folder upon which you are working and work with only subfolders and files. Very flexible and very nice.

The other granular level is what type of access you can audit. In the Access section, you can select either the Successful or Failed check boxes (or both) for the following actions:

- Traverse Folder/Execute File
- List Folder/Read Data
- Read Attributes
- Read Extended Attributes
- Create Files/Write Data
- Create Folders/Append Data
- Write Attributes

- Write Extended Attributes
- Delete Subfolders and Files
- Delete
- Read Permissions
- Change Permissions
- Take Ownership

The idea here, of course, is flexibility and granularity: you can audit for individual actions or for a plethora of actions. Whatever your audit needs, you can accomplish them here. In our illustration we are setting up an audit policy to record the Everyone security group for failed attempts, so we select all the Failed check boxes, because we want to know whenever anyone attempts any of these actions that failed.

Now, we also want to know who has successfully accessed this folder. To successfully implement this portion of the audit policy, we must first block permissions inheritance on the Security tab in the Payroll Properties dialog box. Blocking inheritance means that we explicitly assign permissions to this object and don't want the object's parent's permissions inherited. To block inheritance, follow these steps:

1. In the Payroll Properties dialog box, click the Security tab, and then clear the Allow Inheritable Permissions From Parent To Propagate To This Object check box to open the Security dialog box:

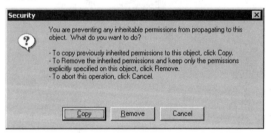

Notice that you can either copy or remove inherited permissions. The Copy function lets you block inheritance but retain the inherited permissions as explicit permissions. This is best selected when you want to block inheritance but want to simply add more security configurations to the existing configurations. The Remove function lets you clear all security assignments and configurations so that you can start with a clean slate and configure your own permissions. This is best used when the explicit permissions that you want to assign is so different from the inherited permissions that it is either (or both) easier and cleaner to simply start over.

2. Click Remove to remove all permissions from this item.

Back in the Payroll Properties dialog box, clicking OK locks everyone out of the object (see Figure 11.5).

Depending on your company's security policies, it is recommended that you enable Allow for the Administrators group Full Control permission before leaving the Security dialog box for administrative purposes.

FIGURE 11.5   The Payroll folder's security configurations after removing all inherited permissions.

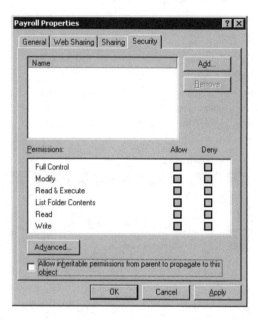

3. To add the Payroll Users security group, click Add to open the Select Users, Computer, Or Groups dialog box and select this group.

4. Click OK to close the Select Users, Computer, Or Groups dialog box and return to the Security tab in the Payroll Properties dialog box:

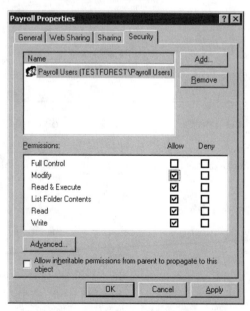

5. To audit the Payroll Users security group's access to the Payroll folder, click Advanced to open the Advanced Properties dialog box, and then click the Audit tab.

6. Click Add to open the Select User, Computer, Or Group dialog box, and select the Payroll Users security group.

7. In the Auditing Entry For Payroll dialog box, select to apply this auditing policy to This Folder, Subfolders, And Files.

8. In the Access selection box, select all the Success check boxes to ensure that you have a complete record of which members of the Payroll Users security groups have successfully accessed the Payroll folder and what actions they exercised successfully, as shown in Figure 11.6.

FIGURE 11.6   Auditing the Payroll Users security group for successful access to the folder

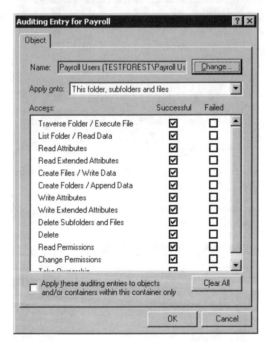

9. Click OK to close the Access Control Settings For Payroll dialog box.

10. Click OK again to close the Payroll Properties dialog box.

Now, whenever anyone attempts to access the Payroll folder, you will see events to this effect recorded in the Security Log.

Types of Events to Audit

You can audit the following categories of events on a system-wide basis.

Logon Events

When you audit for logon events, you capture the timing of when a user logged on and off an individual computer. These events are always logged in the logs of the local computer. At a technical level, an event is logged in the Security Log whenever an access token (AT) is either generated or destroyed.

Tracking such events is useful when an attacker attempts to connect to a particular server from a particular location. You can use the logs to investigate attacks that originated at a specific location. Successful attempts result in a successful event being entered in the event log. Failed attempts result in the opposite: a failed event is entered in the event log.

When auditing logon events, you will see messages from both user and computer accounts. This is by design. Only Windows NT and later operating systems will generate logon events for the computer. Windows 9x machines will not generate such events.

You will often see events 529 ("The logon attempt was made with an unknown username or a known username with a bad password") and 534 ("The user attempted to log on with a logon type that is not allowed, such as network, interactive, batch, service, or remote interactive") when an attacker attempts to log on to your network by guessing either (or both) the username or password. However, these events do not distinguish between a valid user who forgets their password and an attacker who is guessing at a password. The point of the messages is to inform you that the attempted logon failed and the reason that it failed.

Other events, such as 530 through 533 indicate a misuse of a user's account. The user was able to enter a valid username and password, but other restrictions prevented the user from successfully being authenticated in the domain. These event numbers indicate a potential compromise of at least one user account, so don't ignore them. Always investigate failed logon events with these event ID numbers.

Event 539 indicates that an account was locked out for logon purposes. Depending on your account policies, this can indicate that a logon attack failed. Use event ID 539 along with event 529 to establish the timing, pattern, and location from which the attack occurred.

Account Logon Events

Account logon events record when a user attempts to log on or off using a domain account and the request is serviced by a domain controller. Such activity is recorded in the domain controller, not on the local computer. Because account logon events can be recorded at any domain controller, you will need to consolidate the server's logs before analyzing possible attack activities. This activity applies to logon attempts at domain controllers, member servers, and member workstations.

As with logon events, account logon events record both computer and user account activities.

Event IDs 675 and 677 indicate failed domain logon attempts. Also, if a client's computer is off by more than 5 minutes from the domain controller that services the logon request, a 675 message will be generated.

Account Management Events

Account management auditing is used to discern when users or groups are created or modified. Who performed the task is also tracked as part of the event message.

Event IDs 624 and 626 report that a user account was created or enabled. If only certain people are allowed to create user accounts in your domain, you can use these events to determine if unauthorized personnel have created user accounts.

Event IDs 627 and 628 indicate that a user's account password was successfully changed by someone other than the individual user. You can review the event detail to ensure that the account which changed the password is an approved account, such as being a member of the Help Desk or Administrator team.

Event IDs 629 and 630 indicate that an account was successfully deleted. An attacker can use these event IDs to cover their tracks after performing malicious activities under a certain account. Look also for Event ID 626 followed shortly by a 629 event. This succession indicates that a disabled account was enabled, used, and then disabled again.

The lockout of an account is recorded at the PDC Emulator domain controller.

Object Access Events

Nearly every object in Windows 2000 can be audited for object access. Audit events on object access are created when a handle to the object is opened. For instance, when a user attempts to open a file, a message is passed to the system kernel requesting a handle to the file along with the type of access requested, such as Read or Write. The system then compares the user's token to the entries in the DACL (discretionary access control list), and if there is a match, the system compares the user's token to the entries in the SACL (system access control list), which will generate messages based on whether the user was granted access or denied access. Of course, the entries in the SACL tell the system what kind of message to generate. If auditing is turned on only for success events, the SACL will contain no entry for requests that are denied, and, thus, no failure event messages will be generated.

When an event message is generated in this category, nothing has happened to the object at the time the message is generated. The system merely generates the requested audit failure or success message. Hence, write audit messages are generated *before the write operation is performed*, and read audits are generated before the object is exposed for reading.

When attempting to audit for nontrusted accounts, use the Everyone group. This group is broad and includes everyone who can connect to your system, regardless of their method.

Member server and domain controller installations are preconfigured to audit for success and failed object access. Use Group Policies to configure objects that need to be audited that exist on multiple computers. You can configure auditing for a single object on a single computer using either a Group Policy or the Properties dialog box for the object itself.

Event ID 560 indicates that access was granted to an existing object. If you are looking to see who has access to which objects, you'll be looking primarily for 560 event messages. Event ID 562 reports that a handle to an object was closed. Event ID 563 indicates that an attempt to open an object with the intent of deleting that object was recorded. Event ID 564 indicates that a protected object was deleted, and event ID 565 records access to existing object types.

If you want to see who has accessed a particular file, look for 560 events, and in the details, look for the full path to the file. If you want to see what a specific user has accessed, filter for both 560 events as well as the user's account name. Finally, if you want to find out which actions have been performed at a specific computer, filter for that computer and look for 560 events associated with that computer.

Directory Service Access Events

This message type is used to audit access to objects that don't exist in the domain partition. For instance, if you want to audit access to objects in the configuration or schema naming contexts, you'll want to enable Directory Service access auditing. For the configuration partition, you'll enable auditing using the Active Directory Service Interface Edit (ADSIEdit) program from the Windows 2000 Resource Kit.

Because the configuration partition is constantly accessed, you are advised to use failure audit configurations. Success audits will result in large log files that may or may not be useful, even when filtered. Failed access messages to naming contexts other than the domain naming context will result in Event ID 565. You'll need to read and filter these events before they will yield much useful information.

Privilege Use Events

Some users will be given special rights or privileges on your network. You can track exercise of these rights for future reference. Not all uses of privileges are tracked using this method. The following list of user rights are excluded from this category type:

- Bypass traverse checking
- Debug programs
- Create a token object
- Replace process-level token
- Generate security audits
- Back up files and folders
- Restore files and folders

You can override the default behavior of not recording backup and restore user rights by enabling the Audit Use Of Backup And Restore Privilege security policy setting in the Security Options node, which is inside the Security Settings/Local Policies node in a Group Policy (see Figure 11.7).

FIGURE 11.7   The Audit Use Of Backup And Restore Privilege policy setting

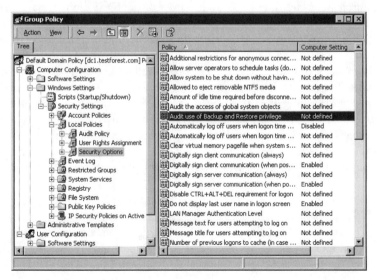

When you choose to audit successful message types on privilege use, you create a large number of messages in the Security Log. Ensure that you have increased the log file size significantly to accommodate these messages.

Event ID 576 indicates that specific privileges were added to a user's access token. This event is only generated at the time a user logs on to the system. Event 577 indicates that a user attempted to perform a privileged system service operation. This does not necessarily indicate whether the user was successful.

Here are some examples of how these event IDs are recorded:

- If a user changes the system time on a server, look for event ID 577 or 578 with the SeSystemtimePrivilege privilege indicated. This event can indicate a user's attempt to change the system time to hide the true time that another event took place.

- When a device drive is loaded or unloaded, look for event ID 577 or 578 with the user right SeRemoteShutdownPrivilege. Such an event can indicate that a malicious drive has been loaded that is intended to cause harm to your server or system.

- When the ownership of files or objects is changed, look for event ID 577 or 578 with the SeTakeOwnershipPrivilege user right indicated. Knowing who has taken ownership of critical files may indicate a (perhaps successful) attempt to copy or modify these files. Other privileges to look for associated with the 577 or 578 IDs include SeShutdownPrivilege, which indicates a successful shutdown of a server, or SeTcbPrivilege, which can indicate an attempt to elevate the user account's privileges to act as part of the operating system.

Process Tracking Events

Event messages for process tracking indicate when a process was created and ended on a Windows 2000 Server machine. It will also record when a process attempts to generate a handle to an object or obtain indirect access to an object.

If you choose to enable process tracking, be sure to increase the size of your log considerably. Process tracking creates a large number of audit entries. Event ID 592 indicates that a new process was created. Event ID 593 indicates that a process exited. Event 594 indicates that a handle to an object was duplicated, and event ID 595 indicates that indirect access to an object was obtained.

You can keep track of every program and process that is run on your network by using process tracking. For instance, if you want to know how often your users are running Free-Cell, enable process tracking on your users' desktops. From there, you can filter the logs and see how often your users are opening FreeCell. From a security standpoint, you can discern every process that runs on your network and pinpoint when a malicious program was started and when it was stopped. However, the amount of material to wade through to pinpoint such a program might be voluminous; therefore, implement process tracking only when necessary.

System Events

When aspects of a computer's environment are altered, system events are generated. These include such activities as shutting down the computer or changing the system time. Auditing system events also audits when the Security Log entries are cleared. This is important to know because good hackers (if there is such a thing) will attempt to cover their tracks after making an environmental change. Member servers and domain controllers are set to audit for system events automatically.

Several event IDs are associated with system events. ID 512 indicates that the Windows operating system is starting, and ID 513 indicates that it is shutting down. Event 517 indicates that the Security Log was cleared. If you feel your system has been compromised, be sure to check the Security Log for event 517. This may indicate that the attacker cleared the Security Log to cover their activities.

Policy Change Events

Your audit policy defines which changes to your environment will be recorded for later review. The more you audit, the more information you'll have on hand to understand the nature and timing of an attack on your system. However, you'll also have more information through which to wade to glean the necessary information.

If you audit for policy change, you will record attempts to change your audit policy. By default, member servers and domain controllers audit policy change for both success and failure.

Event ID 608 records when a user right was assigned, whereas ID 609 records when a user right was removed from the user account. Event ID 610 records when a trust relationship with another domain was created, and ID 611 records when a trust relationship was removed. Event ID 612 indicates when your audit policy was changed.

The two most important events to note are IDs 608 and 609. Most attacks will need elevated privileges, and it is important to note when a user account is given a new right and when it is taken away. In addition to privilege use, you will find that an account that was given the Act as part of the operating system privilege will have Event ID 608 recorded too. When the attack is finished, the attacker may remove this privilege and return the user account to a "normal" state. The removal of this privilege will generate a 609 ID. Table 11.1 lists and describes assigned right names. This table is a handy reference for 608 and 609 IDs.

TABLE 11.1   Assigned Right Names for Events 608 and 609

Assigned Right Name	Description
SeTcbPrivilege	Act as part of the operating system
SeMachineAccountPrivilege	Add workstations to the domain
SeBackupPrivilege	Back up files and folders
SeChangeNotifyPrivilege	Bypass traverse checking

TABLE 11.1 Assigned Right Names for Events 608 and 609 *(continued)*

Assigned Right Name	Description
SeSystemtimePrivilege	Change the system time
SeCreatePermanentPrivilege	Create permanent shared objects
SeDebugPrivilege	Debug programs
SeRemoteShutdownPrivilege	Force shutdown from a remote system
SeIncreaseBasePriorityPrivilege	Increase scheduling priority
SeSecurityPrivilege	Manage auditing and Security Log
SeAssignPrimaryTokenPrivilege	Replace a process-level token
SeRestorePrivilege	Restore files and folders
SeShutdownPrivilege	Shut down the system
SeTakOwnershipPrivilege	Take ownership of files or other objects

Using Event Logs

In the next sections, we'll take a look at the particular logs available to you, how they work, and how to interpret the information they provide.

IIS Logs

IIS writes its events to a text file in the `%systemroot%/system32/logfiles` folder. Each website that is run by IIS will have its own folder under which the log files are generated. The default website's folder name is `W3SVC1`. If you installed a second website, its folder name is `W3SVC2`. The default log format is the W3C Extended Log File Format.

These log files generate the following necessary information:

- Software version
- Date and time of the entry
- Client IP address
- Client username

- Port number
- Method
- URI (Uniform Resource Identifier) stem and query
- Any status messages returned to the user

Windows 2000 Server does not include any user interface (UI) to these logs. They are best opened in Notepad and read manually (see Figure 11.8). Otherwise, you can purchase third-party tools such as WebTrends® to read and present the information in these files in a more intuitive and helpful format.

FIGURE 11.8   IIS logs in Notepad

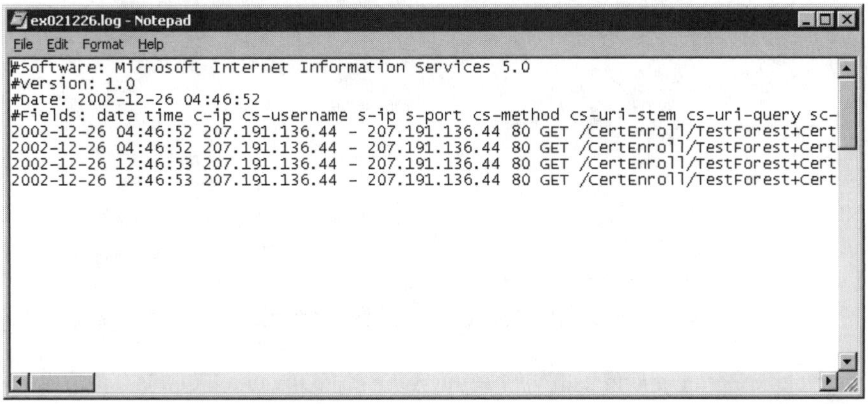

From a security standpoint, it is imperative that you understand these logs even though they can be difficult and boring to read. Port 80 is the most often attacked port, and IIS is one of the most often attacked software packages on the Internet today. Knowing who has attacked and from which IP address might help pinpoint the attacker and stop future attacks.

If you don't want to store the logs in a text file, you can configure IIS to store the logs in a SQL Server database. In Exercise 11.2, you'll configure IIS for this task.

EXERCISE 11.2

Changing the Logging Option for a Website to Log Its Events to a SQL Database

1. Choose Start ➢ Programs ➢ Administrative Tools ➢ Internet Services Manager.

2. Expand the Server object in the left pane to reveal the websites and services offered by this IIS server.

3. In the left pane, right-click the website, and then choose Properties from the shortcut menu to open the *<Name_of_Website>* Web Site Properties dialog box:

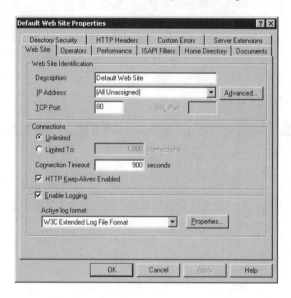

In our example, we are working with the default website, so the name of this dialog box is Default Web Site Properties.

4. Click the Enable Logging check box.

5. In the Active Log Format drop-down list, select ODBC Logging.

6. Click the Properties button to open the ODBC Logging Properties dialog box:

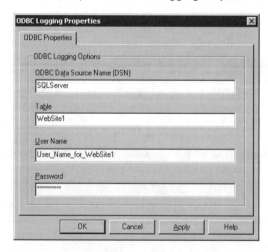

7. Enter the correct information, and click OK to close the ODBC Logging Properties dialog box and return to the Web Site Properties dialog box.

8. Click OK again to close the Web Site Properties dialog box.

9. Close the IIS window.

Once the information is stored in a SQL database, you can have a SQL developer write a UI to the information so that you can more easily view and interpret it.

Firewall Log Files

Internet Security & Acceleration (ISA) Server provides logs for packet filters, the ISA Server Firewall Service, and the ISA Server Web Proxy Service. By default, logs are stored in the W3C Extended Log File Format but can be stored in a SQL Server as well. By default, these logs are stored in the %systemroot%\program files\microsoft isa server\isalogs folder.

Firewall logs are important to monitor because they can tell you when your router or firewall is under attack. Moreover, they can help you figure out who is doing the attacking. Because most firewalls are the first point of entry into a network, it is important to record the packets that flow in and out. Moreover, you can use log file retention to track trends. For example, we know of hackers who send a single ping to potential targets and then wait for several months before sending another ping packet. Patient hackers can often infiltrate a network through the firewall over many months by stealth, most often because the log files are not read with a long-term view and because many organizations don't retain them for any length of time.

Reading and understanding the firewall logs will give you up-to-date information on who is performing port scanning, who is sending suspicious packets to your network, and who is sending information out of your network.

Network Monitor Logs

Network Monitor is a nifty tool that captures and displays all the packets that have run between two devices. The version that ships with Windows 2000 can capture (sometimes called *trace*) packets between itself and a remote machine. The version of Network Monitor that ships with Systems Management Server can capture packets between two remote hosts.

When using this tool, you can view each packet that comes in and goes out of a specific device, such as a router or a Windows 2000 server. The value of this tool is that you can use it to track *exactly* what has happened on your network and servers. For example, you can use Network Monitor (sometimes referred to as NetMon) to capture all the packets from your firewall and then filter the list to view the exact packets you want to view.

Packet traces can reveal immense amounts of information, such as the originating IP address of the attacker, the exact methodologies the attacker used, the servers and workstations the attacker connected to, and the information downloaded or compromised.

In Figure 11.9, you can see that each line in Network Monitor is a distinct packet that includes the source and destination MAC (Media Access Control) address, the protocol used, and a description of what the packet was intended to accomplish. This is where it is good to know the Server Message Block (SMB) commands discussed in Chapter 2. Once you know the SMB commands and other commands for HTTP or SMTP, you can read these packets and have a pretty good idea as to what exactly happened on your network.

FIGURE 11.9   A Network Monitor packet trace

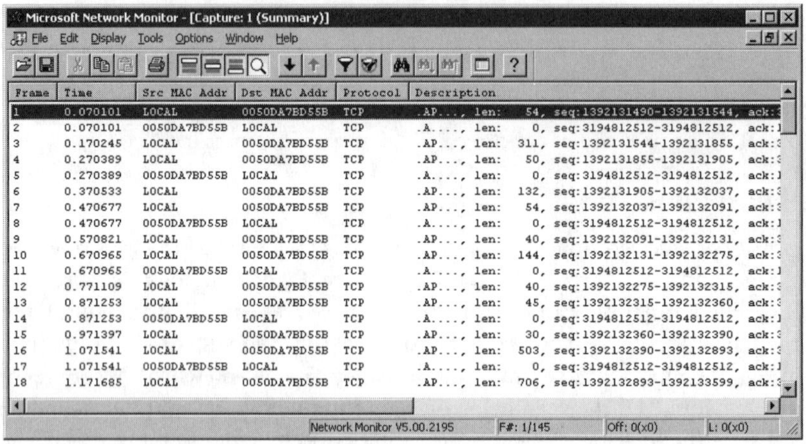

Learning to use Network Monitor is not easy, and it takes some time. But once you get this tool down, you will find it indispensable in learning what information and commands have passed between two devices on your network.

In Exercise 11.3, you will run a packet trace on your computer.

EXERCISE 11.3

Running a Packet Trace on Your Windows 2000 Server Machine

1. Choose Start ➤ Programs ➤ Accessories ➤ Command Prompt to open the Command Prompt window.

2. At the prompt, type **ipconfig /all**, and press Enter.

3. Find the physical address of your network card, and write it down.

4. Choose Command Prompt ➤ Close to close the Command Prompt window.

5. Choose Start ➤ Programs ➤ Administrative Tools ➤ Network Monitor to open Network Monitor. (If Network Monitor does not appear under Administrative Tools, you'll need to add this service inside the Windows Components section of the Add/Remove Programs utility in Control Panel.)

6. If this is the first time that you have run Network Monitor, you'll be prompted to select the network you want to monitor. Select the network that corresponds to the address of your network card, and then click OK to start Network Monitor.

7. Choose Capture ➢ Start to begin capturing packets. You will be able to see this activity.

8. Wait a short period of time, and then choose Capture ➢ Stop and View to stop the capture of packets and automatically display all the packets.

9. Look through the description of each packet. What does the description tell you?

10. Look through the Src MAC Addr, Dst MAC Addr, and Protocol columns. Between which two machines were these packets flowing?

11. To close this view, choose File ➢ Close.

12. To close Network Monitor, choose File ➢ Exit.

13. If prompted to save the capture, click No.

RAS Logs

Remote Access Service (RAS) events are recorded in the System Log and can be viewed in Event Viewer. You can enable event logging on the Event Logging tab in the Properties dialog box of the remote access server (see Figure 11.10). On this tab, you can select which level of logging you want to employ and ensure that Point-to-Point (PPP) packets are logged as well.

FIGURE 11.10   The Event Logging tab in the RAS Properties dialog box

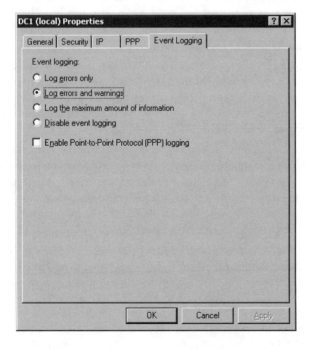

Event logging isn't the only type of logging available for RAS servers. As we just mentioned, you can enable PPP logging, which allows you to record the series of programming functions and control messages that pass between two devices during a PPP session.

You can also use Network Monitor to trace packets between a dial-up connection and an RAS server. Not only can such a packet trace be useful for troubleshooting, but it can also yield information about the attacker and what the attacker did to your server and/or network.

From a security standpoint, it would be a best practice to ensure that Network Monitor is used to trace packets when a dial-up connection is established between your network and a remote computer or network. Obviously, you must do this with some forethought because such a trace could become large rather quickly. But in certain, specific situations, such as when your network is directly exposed via a dial-up connection, it might be a good idea to trace all the packets that flow over that dial-up connection.

Managing Log Retention

In addition to ensuring that you have set each log's properties in Event Viewer correctly, you should be aware of some other best practices for auditing.

- Be sure to schedule regular review of your event logs. This is the most often missed part of using the audit logs. It is one thing to set up the audit policy and enforce it. But if the logs are never read, they are really of little value to you.

- Obviously, the more often you review logs, the faster you can detect vulnerabilities and patch them. If your policy is to regularly review logs your company will be forced to include the review of these logs in at least one person's job description. This is good thing, since it will define who is responsible for reading and understanding these logs.

- Configure log retention to dove-tail with the reading and understanding of the logs in question. For example, if logs are only read once each week, your log retention policy should be such that events are held for longer than seven days. If logs are exported and then retained, there is no industry standard for how long these .csv or .txt files should be retained. Best practice is to consult with your manager and your company's legal advisors on what logs should be retained and for how long.

- As a rule of thumb, once the information becomes unimportant, the files and events should not be retained. For example, logs that contain no remarkable events might be retained for only 14 days, but those that contain evidence of an attack might be retained for years, especially if a legal action is involved. Your log retention policy should account for these scenarios and then specify how long each log file should be retained.

- Associated with this is your event overwriting policies. Remember that some logs can be configured to overwrite events as needed. This may not be the best policy to enforce since there is the potential for critical events to be overwritten simply because the log file is too full. If you need to ensure that you always have every event generated by the system, do not configure the logs in Event Viewer to overwrite older events.

Managing Distributed Audit Logs by Using EventComb

EventComb is a multithreaded tool that will parse event logs from multiple servers simultaneously so that you can find event messages across a range of servers. This tool has tremendous value in that you can aggregate your log data and then analyze it from an enterprise perspective.

Using EventComb, you can perform the following administrative acts:

- Define single or multiple event IDs as search criteria
- Define a range of event IDs as a single search criteria
- Limit the search to specific event logs
- Limit the search to specific event message types
- Limit the search to specific event sources
- Search for specific text within an event description
- Define time intervals to scan back from the current date and time

The EventComb tool is available as part of the overall scripts download from TechNet for the Security Operations Guide for Windows 2000 Server.

You can download EventComb free of charge from Microsoft's website. Simply go to www.microsoft.com/technet, enter **"Security Operations Guide for Windows 2000 Server"** in the search box, and then click Search. On the home page for this guide, click the Downloads link and then download all the scripts associated with this guide. You'll then need to extract the downloaded file. Once extracted, you'll find the EventComb tool inside the EventComb folder. There is no installation per se for this tool. It is merely an executable that runs when invoked.

To run EventComb, double-click the `evencombmt.exe` file to start the tool. Figure 11.11 shows the opening screen.

After starting this tool, the first step is to add the computers you want to include in the event log search. To add computers to the search, follow these steps:

1. In the EventComb utility, ensure that the correct domain appears in the domain box. If it does not, enter the correct domain name.

2. Right-click in the Select To Search/Right Click to Add box to open a shortcut menu that will give you the choices shown in Figure 11.12. Notice that you can select from a variety of servers based on their role, name, domain affiliation, or a list derived from a file. You can also select servers that appear in this box and remove them from the target list.

FIGURE 11.11   The opening screen for the EventComb Tool

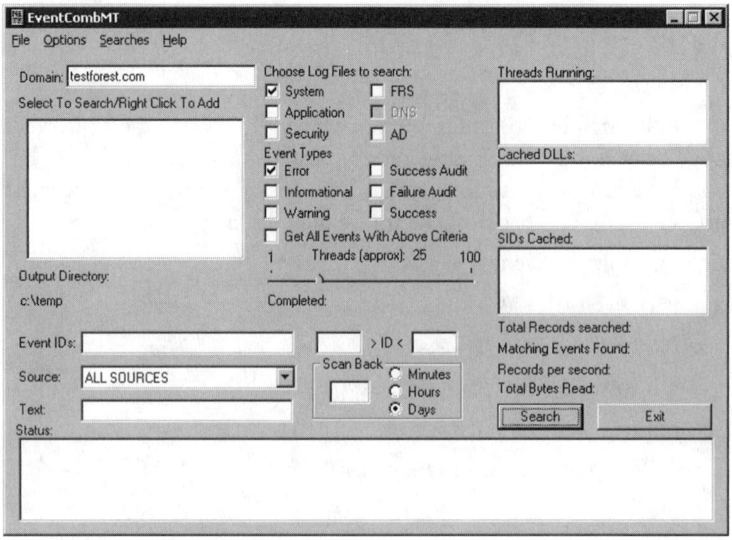

FIGURE 11.12   The shortcut menu for adding servers to the inclusion list for an event log search

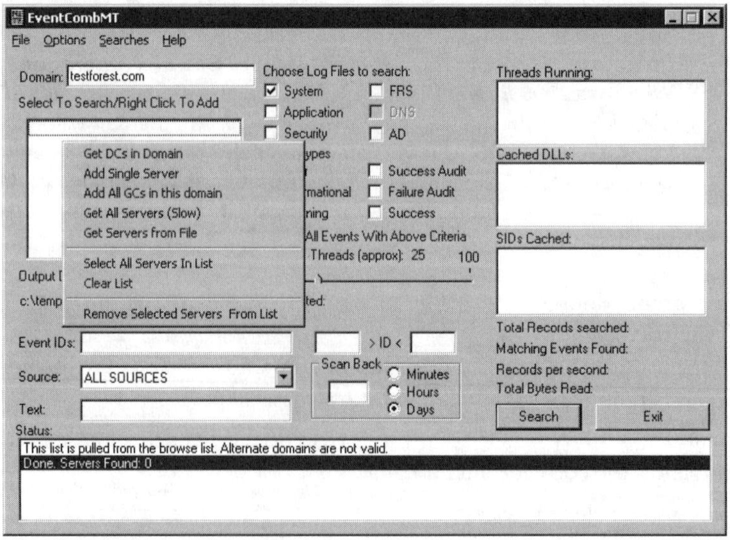

Once the desired servers are added, you must select the servers in the list against which to perform your search. Hence, servers can appear in the list but not be searched for a particular query. What this means is that when the tool is initially run, you need to select the servers you wish to mine two times: once to get them into the list and a second time to include them in the search query. To select multiple servers, use the Ctrl+click combination.

After you select the servers to be included in your search, you are ready to specify the search criteria, which includes the following:

- Log files to search
- Event ID numbers
- Source of the message
- Specific text
- Scope of time

By combining these elements, you can pinpoint your search to yield the best and most helpful information possible. While the search is running (see Figure 11.13), you'll see the number of threads that are being employed to conduct the search. Moreover, you'll see the cached DLLs (dynamic link libraries), which means that the DLL has been cached and is being accessed in the cache instead of being called numerous times to execute the search. Finally, the SIDs cached will also be displayed. Looking up a SID (security identifier) is a rather expensive process, so once a SID has been extracted from the security database, it is cached to improve performance of the EventComb tool.

FIGURE 11.13   The EventComb tool while running.

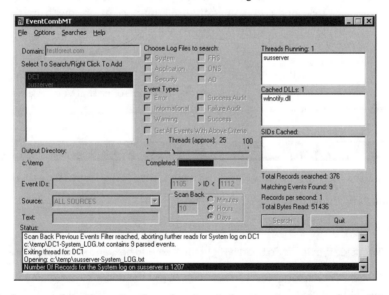

Near the bottom of the EventComb tool main window is a Status box that will indicate the start and end times of the search and how many records matched the search criteria. The actual listing of these records is in the default folder in a simple text file.

When the EventComb tool runs, it places its findings in a set of result files that have a `.txt` extension. There is a summary file named `EventCombMTMT.txt`, and for each computer included in the search query, there is a separate text file named *computername*-`eventlogname_LOG.txt`. A sample text file is shown in Figure 11.14.

FIGURE 11.14 A sample text file generated by EventComb

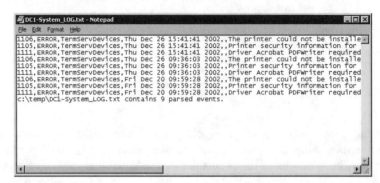

Some built-in searches ship with the EventComb utility. You can find these searches in the Searches menu. There are built-in searches for the File Replication Service (FRS Health), Account Lockouts, Active Directory, Hardware, and DNS Interface Errors. You can also create a customized search and then save that search by choosing Searches ➢ Save This Search.

Finally, you might want to take advantage of a couple of options. First, from the File menu, you can change the output location from the default c:\temp to some other location (choose File ➢ Set Output Directory). Second, you can configure a number of options from the Options menu. One in particular that may interest you is the ability to save the text files as .csv files, which will allow you to open these files in Excel without having to manually change their extension first.

In Exercise 11.4, you will use EventComb to search for restarts of a domain controller. Before you run this exercise, be sure to reboot a domain controller that you can search using the EventComb utility.

EXERCISE 11.4

Searching for Domain Controller Restarts Using the EventComb Utility

1. Open the EventComb tool.

2. Ensure that the correct domain name appears in the Domain box.

3. Right-click inside the Select To Search/Right Click To Add box, and select Get DCs In Domain.

4. In the Select to Search/Right Click To Add box, select the domain controller you rebooted before starting this exercise.

5. In the Choose Log Files To Search section, select the System check box only. Ensure that all other check boxes are cleared.

6. In the Event Types section, select both the Error and Information check boxes. Ensure that all other check boxes are cleared.

7. In the Event IDs box, type the following Event IDs: **1001 6005 6006 6008**. (Type these ID numbers without commas (,) or other symbols between them.)

EXERCISE 11.4 *(continued)*

8. Leave the rest of the tool at default settings.

9. Click the Search button.

10. After the tool finishes its search, a folder list box focused on `c:\temp` will automatically appear.

11. Right-click a file and choose Open from the shortcut menu to open the text file(s) that are named after the servers in your list.

12. Find and read the messages in the text file.

13. Close the text file by selecting Exit from the File menu.

14. Choose File ➢ Close to close the folder list box.

15. Click Exit to close the EventComb utility.

 Real World Scenario

Using EventComb to Understand a Recent Attack Vector

Let's assume that you are managing 14 Windows 2000 Server machines, 3 of which are domain controllers and 11 of which are member servers. Let's further assume that all your servers were operating as expected on Monday morning when you came to work and when you went home.

On Tuesday morning, you start to receive a steady stream of calls from your users indicating Internet access is slow. Moreover, when you check your real-time firewall logs, you find an immense number of files being copied to the Internet—all to the same IP address.

You immediately suspect that you have been compromised. As an emergency measure, you shut down the firewall to kill all inbound and outbound traffic. Then you decide to figure out just exactly what happened on your servers during the night so that you can block future attempts to exploit this vulnerability.

What you would do, among other things, is use the EventComb utility to read the event logs of all your servers to determine which server was first compromised and how the attacker was able to log on to your network. By using this utility, you find that the attacker, after authenticating in your domain, was able to create a new user account, give that account pervasive permissions and privileges, run a program to copy sensitive data to their hard drive, and then delete the user account that was created. The only mistake the attacker made was in *not* clearing the logs before logging off.

Now, you will obviously need to take other actions as part of a larger incident response, but using EventComb will play a key role in understanding how an attacker worked on your network to achieve malicious ends.

Summary

In this chapter, you learned about event logs and the meanings of the different message types. You learned that security messages will not appear in the Security Log unless you audit activities and resources. We briefly covered the Network Monitor tool, IIS logs, and RAS logs, how to read them, and how to configure them. You learned that logging is a vital part to any successful security implementation on a network. And you also learned that event logs on multiple Windows 2000 computers can be aggregated through the use of the EventComb utility.

Logging is an essential part of any security implementation. Learning how to read and interpret logs from an enterprise perspective will help ensure that you are able to respond to a security incident faster and better informed.

Exam Essentials

Understand the difference between an informational, warning, and error message.   Remember that you cannot safely ignore warning and error messages.

Understand that missing events can indicate a security breach.   Missing events are those events that never occurred. As part of your overall security plan, decide which events should occur on a regular basis, such as a weekly, full backup of your server or daily downloads of the latest virus definitions, and then use EventComb to check and ensure that those events actually happened. Missing events can create vulnerabilities on your network that hackers can exploit. You will use EventComb to query multiple servers and see if the event occurred. If it did not, then you have a missing event.

Know why and when to use EventComb.   The big value in using this tool is its ability to aggregate event logs across multiple servers in a single search query so that you can quickly discern a sequence of events that has occurred on multiple servers.

Key Terms

Before you take the exam, be certain you are familiar with the following terms:

auditing	log
event	missing events
EventComb	

Review Questions

1. You have installed a new, customized, web-based application on your Windows 2000 Server machines. You want to view messages that this application generates. In which log should you look for messages from this application?

   A. System Log

   B. IIS Log

   C. Application Log

   D. RAS Log

2. You have installed a new, customized application on your Windows 2000 Server machine that also has installed its own set of services. You want to view messages that this application and its services will generate. In which two logs should you look for messages from this application?

   A. Application Log

   B. System Log

   C. Security Log

   D. DNS Server Log

3. You created an audit policy for both success and failure messages to ensure that all print jobs sent to the payroll printer are recorded in the Security Log. After the next batch of payroll checks printed, you discover that there are no success or failure messages for the payroll printer. You verify that the audit policy has been correctly implemented. What should you do?

   A. Verify that the printer is online.

   B. Verify that the printer has printed the checks.

   C. Verify that auditing has been enabled on the printer.

   D. Verify that the audit policy has been correctly implemented.

4. You enabled the Distributed File System feature on your network. You find that some files are not being automatically synchronized between your domain controllers. You want to diagnose the problem. Where should you look to find DFS error messages?

   A. Directory Service Log

   B. File Replication Log

   C. System Log

   D. Application Log

5. Of the following, which log will only accept messages from Windows 2000 domain controllers?

   A. System Log

   B. Security Log

   C. File Replication Log

   D. Directory Service Log

6.   You are the system administrator for a Windows 2000 Active Directory network. You have three domain controllers on your network: DC1, DC2, and DC3. You enabled auditing for both success and failure events for logon events on DC1 (Domain Controller 1). Later, you discover that no logon events are recorded in the Security Log for DC2 and DC3. What should you do?

   A.   Configure the audit policy to audit account logon events.

   B.   Check the Directory Service Log instead of the Security Log for success and failure account logon messages.

   C.   Enable auditing on each user account.

   D.   Configure a new Group Policy. Have that Group Policy configure the Registry of each workstation to logon at DC1.

7.   You notice in your Security Log are a number of Event ID 529 error messages from the same workstation between the hours of 8:30 P.M. and 10:30 P.M. Your users do not work in the office during this time period. What should you suspect is happening?

   A.   The workstation is attempting to reset its trust relationship password with the domain controller.

   B.   The workstation is repeatedly shutting down.

   C.   Someone is trying to log on to your network and is unable to do so.

   D.   The domain controllers are detecting an IP address confict.

8.   You enabled a success and failure audit policy for account logon events on your network. You have 500 Windows 2000 workstations and 50 Windows 98 workstations. You notice that the Windows 98 workstations are not recording their workstation logon events in the Security Log. What should you do?

   A.   Reset the trust relationship password for each Windows 98 workstation.

   B.   Enable Bypass Traverse Checking on the Syslog folder.

   C.   Move the Windows 98 workstation accounts in Active Directory to their own organizational unit. Reapply the auditing Group Policy to the new OU.

   D.   Do nothing. This is expected behavior because Windows 98 workstations do not have workstation accounts in Active Directory.

9.   You want to audit access to a sensitive research folder on your network. You want to know who has attempted to access this folder, both from trusted and untrusted domains. Which account should you use for auditing purposes?

   A.   Authenticated Users group

   B.   Everyone group

   C.   Domain Users group

   D.   Domain Administrators group

10. You have a sensitive folder named Payroll that only three accountants are supposed to access. You have correctly enabled auditing on this folder. Upon reviewing the Security Log for this folder, you find that a user in the Engineering department has been opening the files in the Payroll folder. What should you do to ensure that this user does not access these file again?

A. Verify that you have secured the folder and file correctly.

B. Remove the Bypass Traverse Checking right from the Engineering user's account.

C. Enable auditing on the files in the Payroll folder.

D. Use the Loopback process mode of the auditing Group Policy to reapply the policy to the Payroll folder.

11. You suspect one of your users is engaging in malicious behavior on the network. You want to isolate that user's activities in the Security Log to help confirm your suspicions. For which two elements should you filter in the Security Log?

A. Event ID 564

B. Event ID 560

C. The user's account name

D. The user's workstation account name

12. You suspect that one of your network administration team members is maliciously changing configurations on objects in the configuration partition. You know this person is leaving your company soon, but this has not become public knowledge yet. You want to provide evidence to your superiors that the current network problems you are experiencing are a direct result of this person's actions. What should you do?

A. Use ADSIEdit from the Windows 2000 Resource Kit to enable auditing on the configuration partition in Active Directory.

B. Create a new Group Policy object. Enable object access for the configuration partition in this new Group Policy object. Create a new organizational unit and link the new Group Policy object to the new OU. Move your team member's user account into the new OU.

C. Use Schema Manager to create a new object in the folder and enable auditing in the object's Properties dialog box.

D. Enable Bypass Traverse Checking and Generate Security Audits for the local system account.

13. You want to audit the backup and restore activities on your network. Before you can begin to audit these activities, there is something you must do. What is it?

A. Enable privilege use auditing on the domain object.

B. Create a new Group Policy. Enable audit use of the backup and restore privilege security policy.

C. Create a new Group Policy. Enable audit use of the backup and restore privilege security policy. Then, enable privilege use auditing on the domain object.

D. Enable Generate Security Audits on the organizational unit that hosts the user's accounts in Active Directory.

14. You have four websites running on your Windows 2000 Server machine. You have correctly enabled logging for all four websites. You then delete the second website, install a new website, and correctly enable logging. After this new website has been running for a few days, you want to view its logs. Under which folder will these logs be located?

A. W3SVC1

B. W3SVC4

C. W3SVC2

D. W3SVC5

E. W3SVC3

15. You want to record all the packets that flow in and out of your network via your TCP (Transmission Control Protocol) filter. What tool could you use to perform this function?

A. ADSIEdit

B. Performance Monitor

C. Event Viewer

D. Network Monitor

16. Remote Access Service events are different from Remote Access Logs. Which of the following statements are true? (Choose two.)

A. Remote Access Service events are recorded in the System Log.

B. Remote Access Service events are recorded in the RAS text-based log files.

C. You can use Network Monitor to trace packets over a dial-up connection.

D. You cannot use Network Monitor to trace packets over a dial-up connection.

17. You are the administrator for a Windows 2000 Active Directory network. You have 14 domain controllers and 47 member servers. You want to filter for Event ID 560 events executed from a single workstation. What is the best way to read the event logs on all your servers?

A. Use Computer Management, connect to each server, and then export each log to a common Excel worksheet.

B. Use Network Monitor to capture the packets on each server. Export the results to a common Excel worksheet.

C. Use EventComb to search and filter all the log files. Export each log file for each server to a common Excel worksheet.

D. Use Event Viewer to view the pertinent log entries and export each log as needed to a common Excel worksheet.

18. You can use the EventComb tool to perform which of the following? (Choose all that apply.)

A. Search by single or multiple Event ID numbers.

B. Focus a search on specific log files.

C. Specify the event source(s).

D. Specify specific text in the event message.

19. Results from the EventComb utility can be output in which two of the following forms?

    A. .doc

    B. .xls

    C. .txt

    D. .csv

20. What is a common problem with regard to auditing?

    A. It is difficult to implement correctly.

    B. Audit logs are not read regularly, and, thus, the auditing process loses its value.

    C. Auditing is resource intensive and can "eat up" server resources.

    D. Auditing is only necessary in high-security environments.

Answers to Review Questions

1. C. Even though this application is web-based, its messages appear in the Application Log. Messages generated by IIS appear in the IIS Log.

2. A, B. The application itself will generate messages and place them in the Application Log. Services associated with the application will generate messages and place them in the System Log. The Security Log will host messages generated by the auditing policy, and the DNS Server Log will host messages generated by the DNS service.

3. C. When auditing a resource, such as a file, a folder, or a printer, not only do you need to create and apply an audit policy, but you also need to go to the resource and enable auditing on the resource. Remember that auditing resources always involves two administrative acts: creating the audit policy and enabling auditing on the resource.

4. B. The File Replication Log records events generated by the File Replication Service. The Directory Service Log records events related to the functioning of Active Directory. Only domain controllers can place messages in the Directory Service Log.

5. D. Because the Directory Service Log records events about Active Directory, it stands to reason that only Windows 2000 domain controllers can actually generate messages for this log. Hence, if you find something wrong with your Active Directory, the place to start troubleshooting this issue is not in the System Log, but in the Directory Service Log.

6. A. The Logon Events audit policy captures events only for local accounts that are created on the local computer. The Account Logon Events audit policy captures logon events for domain accounts. When applied to the domain controllers OU, this enables auditing of all domain logon events across all the domain controllers, and thus you will see logon events in the Security Log from all your domain controllers.

7. C. Event ID 529 indicates that a logon attempt was made with an unknown username or a bad password. A host of these events from a single workstation in a defined time period outside your normal business hours means that a malicious user was attempting to log on but failed to do so.

8. D. Windows 98 workstations cannot participate in workstation account security. This is why it is best to use only Windows 2000 workstations in those environments that require high security.

9. B. You want to use the Everyone security group because this group has the widest reach. Think of it this way: anyone who can connect to your network is automatically made a part of the Everyone security group. Hence, if you want to audit any type of access to sensitive information, audit the Everyone security group.

10. A. All that auditing can tell you is *what* has happened. Now that you've learned that the user in the Engineering department has accessed the payroll files, you'll need to verify (and perhaps reapply) the security settings on the Payroll folder and its files. For example, it could be that the right security settings were configured on the folder, but never applied to the files. Or it could be that the Engineering user's account was inadvertently included in the list of accounts on the Security tab in the Payroll folder's Properties dialog box. In any event, the solution here is not more auditing or a removal of user rights, but a reconfiguration of the permissions themselves.

11. B, D.   Event ID 560 indicates that access to an object was granted. If you want to determine actions that have been performed at a specific computer, filter for that computer and look for 560 events associated with the computer. Of course, this will mean that object access auditing needs to be configured on your servers before this method will yield any meaningful data.

12. A.   To enable auditing on either the schema or configuration partition, you must use ADSIEdit and configure auditing the properties of the root naming context for the configuration partition. What this means is to open up the root object in the configuration partition and then enable auditing in that object's properties.

13. B.   Of the answers given, this is the most correct. Answer C is not correct because privilege use auditing does not include tracking the backup and restore activities. After you create the Group Policy in answer B, you'll want to apply it to the OU(s) that host the backup and restore servers on your network.

14. D.   Even though you deleted a website, its contents, and its logs, that one will be numbered sequentially after the last website when you create a new website, which was number 4. In this case, this website will be number 5. You will look inside the W3SVC5 folder to find the logs for this new site.

15. D.   Network Monitor is the tool to use when you want to record the packets that flow through your network. In this scenario, since you want to record all the packets that are flowing in and out of your firewall—which is sometimes called a TCP filter on Microsoft exams—you'll want to use Network Monitor. Other, third-party products are available to do this, but Network Monitor will work too.

16. A, C.   RAS events are recorded in the System Log and can be viewed by anyone who has access to the logs. There are no separate RAS logs as there are for IIS. Network Monitor is a great tool for recording the packets that flow between a dial-up connection and a server. You can use this method to find out if a dial-up connection was the vector used by an attacker to compromise your network.

17. C.   Using EventComb is the fastest way to read and filter so many log files. Although each server's results is placed in a different file, these files can be easily exported to a common worksheet for further analysis. The other methods mentioned will work, but they are not the best nor the fastest way to accomplish this task.

18. A, B, C, D.   You can use EventComb to filter event logs based on all four of these criteria, plus several others, including time intervals, message types, and a range of Event ID numbers.

19. C, D.   The .doc and .xls formats are not supported by the EventComb utility, but the .txt and .csv formats are supported. From the Options menu in the utility, you can select the output file type. Using the .csv option makes the file readily importable into an Excel worksheet.

20. B.   One of the most common problems with auditing is that the logs are rarely read. Without the regular reading of the logs, there really is little sense in performing logging in the first place. Although these logs can be of help immediately after an attack, they are of equal value in understanding normal behavior on a network. Learning to spot abnormal behavior and what might constitute an attack depends on knowing what normal behavior looks like from a logging perspective. Regular reading of the logs will also help you detect problems that are brewing and give you an opportunity to fix them before they become a big problem that hurts user productivity.

Chapter

12

Responding to Security Incidents

THE MICROSOFT EXAM OBJECTIVES COVERED IN THIS CHAPTER:

✓ **Respond to security incidents. Incidents include hackers, viruses, denial of service (DoS) attacks, natural disasters, and maintaining chains of evidence.**

- Isolate and contain the incident. Considerations include preserving the chain of evidence.
- Implement countermeasures.
- Restore services.

After you discover that a vulnerability on your network has been exploited, you will need to respond. The actions you take in response to a security incident are important. This portion of the exam—and thus, this portion of this book—is dedicated to ensuring that you know how to respond appropriately to security incidents.

Knowing what to do when a security event occurs is essential to good security management. Most organizations learn how to handle a security incident only after an event has occurred. To mitigate risk, think through *in advance* how to handle various events and train yourself and others in the IT department on the correct procedures to follow should an event occur. This chapter will help you do that.

Now, you might be wondering just how you'll know if a security incident has occurred on your network. Well, here are some common indications that your network has been compromised or is under attack.

Network irregularities   If your network performance is decreasing for (seemingly) no reason or if accounts are being used at irregular times, you could be under attack or be compromised. Another sign is the inability to connect to one or more servers while being able to connect to other servers without difficulty.

System irregularities   System irregularities include a marked increase in audited events, system performance degradation, and computers crashing or rebooting without explanation.

Direct reporting of events   You might be tipped off that a security event is happening if user reports these events directly to you. Of, if you have good intrusion detection software, you might be alerted to an intrusion by this software.

Physical indications   Obvious signs of an intrusion include missing servers, broken locks, and video tape of people taking disks and hardware from the premises.

Business indicators   Confidential information on the Internet or in a public location, such as a magazine or television, can indicate that your information has been compromised.

Although many abnormal events on a network are harmless, some will indicate a security event. You'll probably find that, using your detection tools, determining when a real security breach has occurred is still as much art as it is science. However, investigate all events to find their causes and to determine whether the events represent a security incident.

This chapter's outline provides a roadmap for you to use when planning responses to security events, but you also need to bear some other items in mind.

First, there is a strong need for clearly established security policies that are written, understood by all in the organization, and enforced without bias. Some security events are created by those of us—the technology people—who have not followed or understood change management procedures or security configurations. These policies should be clear, practical and tested.

Second, it really does no good to have a well-written set of security policies if upper management routinely ignores and violates them for their own convenience. Gaining management support for security policies and incident handling is necessary to implement any good security program.

Third, ensure that you routinely monitor and analyze the following:

- Event logs
- Network traffic
- System performance
- Intrusion detection logs
- Security training for end users
- Releases of updated patches for all your software
- Backup processes to ensure they are successful

To ensure that you "stay on top" of the security game, give regular attention to each of these areas. A lapse in any one of them can potentially create an attack vector that a hacker can exploit.

Fourth, ensure that at least once each quarter you take the time to run a trial backup and restore of your more important data. Why? Because the time to learn restore skills is not when the battle is raging after a system compromise. You don't learn how to throw a football in the fourth quarter, you don't learn how to drive a car during the Indianapolis 500, and you don't learn how to do system state and other restore procedures after a disaster has occurred. Best practice is to perform these activities once each quarter so that you are assured of two things:

- Your backup hardware is working properly.
- You get regular practice in how to perform restore operations.

Fifth, create a Computer Security Incident Response Team (CSIRT). Train and use this team to handle responses to all security events. Using a team approach will ensure that no area is left unattended during the response phase.

Last, place all emergency and contact information in a central, offline location. This information includes passwords, IP addresses, router configuration information, firewall rule sets, copies of certificate authority keys, contact names and phone numbers, escalation procedures, and so forth. Obviously, this information must be kept in a physically secure location, but it must also be readily available.

The CSIRT should develop an Incident Response Plan so that everyone in the organization is aware of what to do in the event of an incident. This plan should include methods of reporting new events from users and lower-level IT staff. Moreover, regularly review this plan to ensure it meets the ever-changing environment of your business and network. At a minimum, this plan should cover the following areas:

- How to detect a security event
- How to communicate this event to the CSIRT
- How to contain and minimize the damage
- How to identify the type of attack and the severity of the damage
- How to protect and keep evidence of the attack

- When and whom to notify regarding external agencies
- How to recover each system
- How to compile incident documentation
- How to assess the cost of the damage
- When and how to review and update the response policies

Having such a plan in place will give all IT staff and the CSIRT members a working blueprint with which to guide their actions during an incident response. Having a well-defined, well-rehearsed set of responses that you can put in place if a successful attack does occur will enable you to close unknown vulnerabilities and perhaps apprehend the attacker for criminal and civil prosecution.

Creating the First CSIRT in Your Company

After reading the rest of this chapter, you decide to create a new CSIRT in your company. What should you do to be successful? The tips that follow should help you get started. You might also want to check out www.cert.org, a great website that has excellent information on security management.

1. Discuss your plan with your manager and get them to buy into this idea. Outline why it is a good idea and a good use of some people's time to get involved with this team.

2. Ask you manager to obtain upper management approval for a CSIRT.

3. After receiving approval, try to get the following positions placed on this team:

   - Yourself as system administrator
   - Your firewall person
   - Help desk representative
   - Desktop support representative
   - Other IT department members as needed

4. Develop a plan for responding to the following:

   - Worms, viruses, and Trojan horses
   - Intrusions
   - Physical compromise
   - DoS attacks
   - Web services attacks
   - Internal violations of security policies
   - Internal attempts to hack confidential information

5. Practice your responses with the team members. Don't wait for a real attack to teach each team member how to do their job.

6. Enlist legal advice to ensure you are complying with all federal and state laws.

7. Develop lines of communications and procedures for how you will communicate with upper management during a response cycle.

8. Evaluate the plan every six months to ensure the plan is up-to-date and to ensure that new team members know what their responsibilities are and how to act during a response.

Understanding Types of Attacks

Viruses vs. denial of service vs. natural disasters vs. Trojans vs. worms? Although this is a bit like splitting hairs, it is important to understand what motivates hackers and the differences between these types of attacks.

In this section, we'll discuss each of these types of attacks, and you'll find questions about all these on the exam.

Natural Disasters

Natural disasters include such common occurrences as earthquakes, hurricanes, floods, lightning, and fire. Disasters that humans instigate fall into this category too, including riots, wars, and terrorism. All these events can cause severe damage to computer systems. Information can be lost, downtime or loss of productivity can occur, and hardware can be damaged, and other essential services can be disrupted.

Few safeguards can be implemented against natural disasters. The best course of action is to have disaster-recovery and contingency plans in place. These will help an organization restore itself to normal business operations.

Hacker Attacks

It has been suggested that if you don't know your enemy, you are doomed to be defeated by your enemy. Although there is much literature on the technical aspects of securing a resource, a firewall, or even a network, not much has been written about who your enemies are and what motivates a hacker. If you understand who would want to do you harm and what they would gain from such harm, you can better protect yourself and your organization.

Hackers are often motivated, in part, by their invisibleness. Have you ever wondered what it would be like to be invisible? Being able to go wherever you want and do anything you'd like without fear of detection or apprehension is something that all of us would like now and then. Well, on the Internet, you can "peek" into someone else's private world—their network—and learn many things about them while you remain anonymous. This, in and of itself, is a strong motivation—just the pure thrill of being invisible.

However, attackers often have other motivations. For example, some are just curious individuals who commit violations in the process of learning or exploring a system. Mostly without malicious intent, they are unaware that their actions violate security policy or criminal code.

Others are simply trying to help: in their zeal to be helpful, they bypass security policies to fix problems or accomplish their assignments. Often, they believe that their efforts are more efficient than following established guidelines and policies.

Finally, some act with malicious intent, engaging in acts of sabotage, espionage, or other forms of criminal activities. They steal information, sabotage a competitor, or cause outages to facilities to achieve their own ends. *Why* they do this can be as varied as the individuals themselves. It may be to further their own company's ends, it may be the result of a strongly held belief system, or it may be even an antisocial personality who simply enjoys destroying others and their work.

Within all these groups, you might also find certain other personality traits. For instance, they might have a sense of entitlement: they should be treated differently because they perceive themselves as being "special" and "above the rules." You might also find that some act out of revenge for a real or perceived wrong that was committed against them. Others are more methodical and hardened and turn hacking into a career: they might even take employment just to commit theft, fraud, or other illegal acts against a certain company. Some might even become moles, stealing information from the inside and selling that information to competitors or foreign groups.

But in almost all hackers, you will find certain characteristics. For instance, you will likely find a personality whose curiosity sometimes consumes them. In addition, they are usually bright, intelligent people who can "out-think" most others in their field and in technology. More often than not, these folks are individualistic and anticonformist, preferring to carve out their own path instead of following the prescribed path that was given to them. You'll also find that these individuals are stimulated by an array of vast and diverse subjects and that they enjoy the challenge of breaking into a system. A few will even enjoy the public attention and social recognition that comes with hacking a website or starting a new virus or worm that "brings down" the Internet.

The primary targets of most hackers are either e-mail lists or websites. Internal hackers can be interested in financial databases or spreadsheets, marketing plans, research and development information, and the reputation of individuals or companies.

So who is your enemy? Well, the answer is anyone who wants to do you or your organization harm *and* who has the ability and will to carry out their plans against you. And on this point, you must think worldwide. It is not enough to think about your own locale. You must think worldwide because the Internet bypasses nearly all national and international boundaries. Your enemies might be people living half-way around the globe.

Virus Attacks

A *virus* is a piece of code that replicates itself by attaching itself to other programs or files. When these files run, the code is invoked and begins replicating itself. Some of the first computer viruses were found in 1981 on an Apple II computer. Nearly every platform now has viruses that can exploit its vulnerabilities.

Some viruses reside in memory after the original program is shut down. Then when other programs are executed, they become infected with the virus until the computer is shut down or turned off. Some viruses have a dormant phase and will appear only at certain times or when certain actions are performed.

Variants can be produced by modifying a known virus. Examples are modifications that add functionality or evade detection. Usually, the modifications are minor, such as changing the trigger date.

There are many types of viruses. Some viruses overwrite existing code or data. Others recognize whether an executable file is already infected. Self-recognition is required if the virus is to avoid multiple infections of a single executable, which can cause excessive growth in size of infected executables and corresponding excessive storage space, contributing to the detection of the virus.

Resident viruses install themselves as part of the operating system upon execution of an infected host program. The virus remains resident until the system is shut down. Once installed in memory, a resident virus is available to infect all suitable hosts that are accessed.

A stealth virus is a resident virus that attempts to evade detection by concealing its presence in infected files. For example, a stealth virus might remove the virus code from an executable when it is read (rather than executed) so that an antivirus software package will only see the noncompromised form of the executable.

Some viruses are encrypted, rendering them difficult to disassemble and study since the researcher must decrypt the code. Along the same lines, a polymorphic virus creates copies of itself during replication that are functionally the same but have distinctly different byte streams. This variable quality makes the virus difficult to locate, identify, or remove.

Computer viruses spread mainly through e-mail. In earlier days, some viruses spread by writing themselves to the boot sector of diskettes and transferred themselves to new computers when the diskettes where inserted into the floppy drive. These days, it is not uncommon to find viruses in programs that are downloaded from the Internet. Usually, e-mail and the Internet are the two primary methods for distributing a virus.

The damage that viruses can cause ranges from nominal to critical. Some viruses cause little or no damage. Others destroy the file system tables. In all cases, do not ignore viruses, and treat them as a major, potential threat to the server, workstation, and/or the network.

Denial of Service Attacks

A *denial of service (DoS)* attack overloads an individual service on a target server to the point where the service is either totally consumed by the attack or actually stops responding. The purpose of a DoS is to prevent legitimate use of a service and to prevent the server or hosts on a network from communicating over the network. A DoS exploits the fact that services exist and that they must be up and running to be of any value to an organization.

Attackers achieve a DoS by flooding a network or server with more traffic that it can handle. Routers and servers eventually become overloaded by attempting to service each packet or request. The attacker's system is usually masqueraded because the sender's IP address is spoofed in the sending packet. This makes it difficult to trace who the attacker really is. Often, the IP address that is spoofed is the address of another victim on the network, creating congestion between two targets that use each other to self-destruct.

A variation of the DoS is a Distributed DoS (DDoS), which is an attack that involves breaking in to hundreds or thousands of computers across the Internet, installing DDoS software on each one that allows the attacker to control all these computers, and launching coordinated attacks on victim sites. Usually, bandwidth is completely saturated, router processing capacity is exhausted, and network connectivity is broken.

DoS attacks are a growing trend on the Internet because websites in general are open doors ready for abuse. People can easily flood the web server with communications in order to keep it busy. Therefore, companies connected to the Internet should prepare for DoS attacks. They also are difficult to trace and allow other types of attacks to be conducted simultaneously.

Trojan Horse Attacks

Also known as a *Trojan horse*, a *Trojan* is a malicious program embedded inside a normal, safe-looking program. When the normal program is run, the malicious code is run as well and can cause damage, steal critical information, or both. An example of a Trojan is a birthday executable that, when executed, pops up with an animated figure that wishes the reader "Happy Birthday," while, in the background, malicious code is running that deletes files or destroys other programs.

The term *Trojan horse* comes from a myth in which the Greeks gave a giant wooden horse to their foes, the Trojans, seemingly as a peace offering. After the Trojans dragged the horse inside the city walls of Troy, Greek soldiers sneaked out of the horse's hollow belly and opened the city gates, allowing their compatriots to pour in and capture Troy.

Trojans generally are spread through e-mail or worms. The damage that these programs can cause is similar to that of a virus: from nominal to critical. The part that is the most frightening is that in most cases, users are unaware of the damage the Trojan is causing because the malicious work is being masked by the Trojan effect of the program.

Worm Attacks

A *worm* is a program that runs independently and travels from computer to computer across network connections. Worms may have portions of themselves running on many computers, or the entire program can run on a single computer. Worms do not change other programs, although they can carry code that does. In addition, some worms take on the virus aspect of self-replication.

Believe it or not, worms were first used as a legitimate mechanism for performing tasks in a distributed environment. Network worms were considered promising for managing network tasks in a series of experiments at the Xerox Palo Alto Research Center in 1982. However, that all changed when worms were used to perform unwanted and unapproved tasks on multiple computers.

The main difference between a virus and worm is that a worm is self-contained code and does not require a host file to which it must attach. In addition, most worms require a multitasking system and can replicate themselves across network links, unlike a virus.

Both worms and viruses are designed to self-replicate, and both perform a variety of additional tasks. The first network worms took advantage of system properties to perform useful actions. However, a malicious worm takes advantage of the same system properties for malicious ends. The facilities that allow such programs to replicate do not discriminate between malicious and good code. Worms exploit vulnerabilities in the operating system and use a variety of methods to replicate. Release of a worm usually results in brief outbreaks, shutting down entire networks.

The damage that worms can cause, like Trojans and viruses, range from the nominal to the critical. You must assess the type and extent of damage individually for each worm. However, worms can install viruses and Trojans that then run their own code. An attack that combines a worm, a Trojan, and/or a virus can be a difficult attack to survive without significant damage being inflicted.

Isolating and Containing the Incident

Most organizations are not adequately prepared to deal with intrusions. They are likely to address the need to prepare and respond only after a breach occurs. The result is that when an intrusion is detected, many decisions are made in haste and can reduce an organization's ability to engage in critical activities necessary to ensuring that the chain of evidence is preserved, the source of the intrusion is understood and resolved, and future plans are created to reduce the likelihood that an intrusion will occur again.

Even if you have sophisticated prevention measures in place, intrusions can happen. When they do, implement certain practices independent of the size, type, or severity of an intrusion or the methods used to gain access to your sensitive data. You need a strategy for handling intrusions that covers three broad areas: preparation, detection, and response. And you will not know what to do when an intrusion occurs if you have not defined your procedures and then practiced your responses in advance.

Flying at a very high level, here are the actions your plan should include:

- Establish policies and procedures for responding to intrusions
- Maintain the tools necessary to respond to an intrusion
- Analyze the information to best characterize the intrusion
- Communicate with all parties the nature of the intrusion and provide them with regular updates
- Collect and protect information associated with the intrusion
- Eliminate the methods the intruder used to gain access
- Return your systems to normal operations
- Review lessons learned and implement new policies and procedures if necessary

Having the plan won't be enough. You'll also need to ensure that you have trained your team members on the plan, that *you have practiced the plan in advance of an intrusion.* As we've said, you don't learn to shoot a basketball in the fourth quarter of a championship game, you don't learn to swim while trying to save another person, and you can't learn how to use your response tools during a crisis.

Preserving the Chain of Evidence

If you intend to pursue criminal prosecution, the evidence an investigator may want might reside in a Word document, on spreadsheet, or in some other file. Evidence may also reside on erased files, file slack (that area of a sector that is hosting a file but is not filled with any data), or even a Windows swap file, all of which are volatile and easily changeable if not properly accessed. Sometimes, simply booting up a computer can alter and even destroy data fragments that can potentially make an investigation a success or failure. In addition, it is also possible to activate a Trojan program a user left on the computer on purpose, which potentially could modify or destroy the file structure.

To ensure that this does not happen, create a mirror image of the drive in question. A mirror image is a byte-by-byte, sector-by-sector duplicate of a hard drive, which should be authenticated by a cyclic redundancy check (CRC) at the initial image and restore process.

To support this type of activity, you'll need to develop a firm policy and a set of procedures to ensure that no action is taken that can potentially damage the chain of evidence and cause an otherwise good examination to be inadmissible in a civil or criminal court proceeding.

Here are some steps you can take to ensure you have adequately preserved your chain of evidence.

Collect all information associated with the intrusion.   This information will include the following:

- The name of the system
- The date/time of the intrusion
- What was compromised
- What actions were taken
- What you said
- What you did
- Who was notified
- Who had access
- What data was collected
- What information was disseminated to whom, for what purpose, by whom, and when
- What was submitted to legal counsel, by whom, when, and for what purpose

Collect and preserve the evidence.   Develop your collection procedures in conjunction with your legal advisors so that you know you are following all laws and regulations that will affect the strength of your case against the intruder. Also, be sure to get a replica of the server as fast as possible so as to preserve the state of the server at the time of the compromise. In all actions, document meticulously all actions performed by all participant from detection through analysis, response, and recovery that preserve the chain of evidence.

Ensure that evidence is captured and preserved securely.   Ensure that all log files containing information regarding an intrusion are retained for at least as long as normal business records are kept and even longer if your legal counsel advises you to do so. Furthermore, ensure that all critical information is duplicated and preserved both onsite and offsite.

Preserve the chain of custody of the evidence.   Document who handled the evidence and in what sequence, for what purpose, and for how long. In other words, the evidence must be accounted for at all times, the passage of evidence from one person to another must be fully documented, and the passage of evidence from one location to another must be fully documented.

WARNING

Be sure to contact law enforcement immediately if you decide to pursue and prosecute an intruder. Be aware, however, that if you decide to keep your systems up and running to gather more information about the intruder, you and your organization can be held liable if the intruder is successful in using your servers as a launch point for attacking another site. Be sure to consult with your legal counsel about this.

Implementing Countermeasures

When you first hear the term *countermeasure*, you might initially associate it with "revenge" or "getting back" at the intruder. Actually, this is not the case. In most instances, if you try to hurt the intruder, most of your actions will probably be illegal, and you could be held liable for them.

When considering countermeasures, think about pro-active actions you can implement to make it more difficult for the intruder to attack your network or use your servers in a malicious manner. Another way of conceptualizing a countermeasure is to say that a countermeasure is a method of mitigating risk. For example, the e-mail program Sendmail has a feature called "tarpitting" (you won't need to know this term for the Microsoft exam), which is a process that slows down connection response times between e-mails. The theory is this: if a junk mail sender wants to send you many e-mails, the longer it takes for the sender to send each e-mail, the more likely it is that the sender will remove you from their junk mail list because it is too "expensive" for them to spend time trying to send you one e-mail when they could be sending that e-mail to 10 or 50 or even 100 other recipients. Hence, tarpitting is a type of countermeasure.

Throughout this book, we have discussed some administrative activities that you could rightly term countermeasures. For instance, in the section on hardening the TCP/IP stack

(Chapter 2), we discussed ways to make a DoS attack more difficult to execute against a Windows 2000 server. Hardening the TCP/IP stack against DoS attacks is a countermeasure that minimizes the risk of exposure to such an attack.

What other types of countermeasures can you implement to mitigate intrusion and risk on your network? Well, although not exhaustive, the following table lists some common attacks and possible countermeasures that you might want to implement:

Type of Attack	Possible Countermeasures
Physical access to the server	Locked doors Biotech authentication
E-mail flooding	Tarpitting Content filters Spam filters
Virus, Trojan, and worm	Antivirus software Regular scanning
Loss of data	Regular backups
Use of user accounts	User training Network security policies
DoS	TCP/IP hardening Router hardening
Operating system vulnerabilities	Installing all software patches Service offering minimization
Web service attacks	Require authentication Isolate server in demilitarized zone Use SSL Use unique port number
General intrusion	Install a honeypot Use a network-wide intrusion detection software product

This table contains one item—honeypots—that we've not discussed yet. A *honeypot* comes from the analogy of a plate of sugar that attracts bees. If you put out something sweet on a plate or in a bowl, such as sugar water, you'll find it has attracted bees after a while.

By the same token, a honeypot is a server that is designed to look like a real production server, but it is not. It is basically a decoy, something that you make available to intruders that they will think is a real production server and that you allow them to intrude and compromise.

Why do this? Well, for two reasons. First, it attracts intruders to a decoy server, thus ensuring that your real production servers are left alone. But the second reason is even more instructive: if you can analyze the server, you can figure out how the intrusion took place and patch those holes *before* the attacker attacks your real production servers. In larger or more secure environments, a honeypot server is a good way to trap attackers before they get at your more important production servers.

Developing and installing countermeasures is an ongoing process. As your network and information changes over time, so will your need to update countermeasures that protect your information.

Restoring Services

Restoring services means bringing the server(s) back online so that they can return to normal service. Don't attempt this step until you have finished analyzing and patching the vulnerabilities in your system(s), preserving the evidence, and ensuring that any changes in policy and procedures have been implemented.

Now, our comments here reflect a bit of idealism: in many environments, the longer a compromised server is down, the more money is lost to the organization. In these environments, it is still best to at least understand the full nature of the attack and close the avenues the attacker used to access the information before bringing the server(s) back online.

The timing of all these actions—analysis, vulnerability patching, preserving evidence, and updating policies and procedures—takes time, and if you are pressed for time because your servers need to be up and running, it really does make sense to use a team of people to respond to security incidents. It really makes no sense at all to try and do this by yourself.

Upper management needs to be informed and consulted on a realistic response time to a network disaster. Their input into the balancing act between running an appropriate response to an intrusion vs. the need to have servers up and running so that the economic impact is minimized is essential to using intrusions as an opportunity to improve security rather than playing a game of "duck and blame" between your team members and managers. In other words, the planning process for a solid response to an intrusion should be a collaborative effort.

Summary

In this chapter, you learned the differences between a worm, a Trojan, and a virus. Worms are independent programs that cause damage and use the underlying network to replicate themselves. Trojans are pieces of malicious code that embed themselves inside legitimate programs and execute when the host code is executed. Viruses are malicious code that attach themselves to other code and replicate themselves when the code is run. In all three cases, these code bits can cause serious damage and loss of productivity to an organization.

484 Chapter 12 · Responding to Security Incidents

You also learned about the motivations of a hacker and how different elements motivate hackers for different reasons. We took a brief look at the personality types and at what hackers hope to accomplish. Understanding your enemy is paramount in being able to defend yourself.

In this chapter, we also discussed the need to isolate an intrusion, understand the nature of the attack, close the methods or avenues the intruder used to gain access, and preserve the chain and custody of the evidence during this entire time. Preserving the evidence is crucial if you want to press legal or civil charges against the intruder.

Finally, we briefly discussed what countermeasures are and why they should be implemented. We also noted that trying to get revenge on an intruder will probably expose you legally, something you really don't want.

Exam Essentials

Be sure that you understand the different between a Trojan, a virus, and a worm. Some questions on the exam will reference these terms and knowing what each one means, how it replicates, and its general characteristics will help you understand the thrust and point of the question.

Understand the importance of preserving the chain of evidence. Some questions may reference this concept or even test it directly. Knowing that the evidence of the intrusion must be preserved as well as the custody of who held that information and at what time may help you correctly answer some questions.

Understand that hackers are motivated by different elements. Not all these elements will need to make sense to you, only to the hacker. Therefore, be sure to note some of the underlying personality characteristics, what tends to interest a hacker, and how a honeypot might interest them as much as a production server—provided they don't know that the honeypot is a decoy!

Key Terms

Before you take the exam, be certain you are familiar with the following terms:

countermeasure	Trojan horse
denial of service (DoS)	virus
honeypot	worm
Trojan	

Review Questions

1. Which of the following is in the correct order?

    A. Respond ➤ Intrusion ➤ Develop Policy ➤ Restore Services

    B. Develop Policy ➤ Intrusion ➤ Restore Services ➤ Respond

    C. Develop Policy ➤ Intrusion ➤ Respond ➤ Restore Services

    D. Intrusion ➤ Respond ➤ Develop Policy ➤ Restore Services

2. You have 12 Windows 2000 Server machines on your network. You find that you cannot connect to the DNS and the Exchange server over the network. You run your own DNS server and forward Internet requests to an Internet-based DNS server. In addition, the receptionist's workstation appears to be running slowly. All other servers and workstations are able to communicate on their own subnet without difficulty, but all are experiencing problems opening e-mail with their Outlook client. In addition, when users try to connect to the Internet using Internet Explorer, they report that sometimes the connection to websites is timing out. They can, however, connect to the internal intranet web server without difficulty. You suspect a DoS attack, but your network-wide intrusion detection software is not reporting anything significant. What are some of the common indicators in this scenario that you can identify?

    A. Network irregularities

    B. System irregularities

    C. Direct reporting of events

    D. Physical indicators

    E. Business indicators

3. Which of the following is the first step in responding to a security event?

    A. Develop a strong set of security policies that are enforced for everyone.

    B. Ensure that upper management follows all the security policies.

    C. Train the security incident response team to respond to an event.

    D. Develop a strong set of response procedures that are used by your security incident response team.

4. Which of the following are reasons for creating a CSIRT? (Choose all that apply.)

    A. No area of a response is left unattended.

    B. A response can happen more quickly with a team.

    C. The chain of evidence can be preserved better.

    D. The chain of custody can be better preserved.

5. Your UPS catches on fire and destroys your servers. What kind of disaster is this?

   A. Trojan

   B. Virus

   C. Worm

   D. Natural disaster

6. The best protection against a natural disaster is to do which of the following? (Choose two.)

   A. Use offsite storage for backup tapes.

   B. Maintain a list of hardware and software vendor contacts.

   C. Use offsite storage for all program CDs and disks.

   D. Maintain a list of emergency numbers near the servers.

7. You are the system administrator for a Windows 2000 Active Directory network. You are working on a user's workstation to resolve an issue and find that you cannot log in as that user. Your network security policies require passwords that are 8 characters in length. Security policies are not enforced by Group Policies. You decide to use the Terminal Services client from your user's workstation to unlock the user's account and reset their password to blank. You then log in as the user and resolve their issue. After returning to your server, you set up the user's account to change their password at next logon. You manager finds out what you have done. What should your manager say to you?

   A. Good job! You solved the problem quickly.

   B. You solved the problem, but you also violated our security policy.

   C. You should have unlocked the user's account and then had the user log in.

   D. You should have changed the user's password before leaving their workstation.

8. One of your users in the Engineering department is exceptionally bright and talented. This person can figure out complex problems that puzzle the other engineers. This person also enjoys learning about a wide range of topics. You now hear that this individual is taking night classes to learn basic networking concepts to build his own home network. Yet, everything you've seen and heard about this individual is that they are trustworthy and above reproach. Should you be concerned?

   A. Yes. Several personality traits indicate that this individual might become an internal hacker. Even though he is trustworthy right now, he could compromise your information if he ever becomes disgruntled.

   B. No. This individual is trustworthy, and even if he becomes disgruntled, he would never think to compromise information for malicious purposes.

9. You learn that one of your employees has been running an Internet-based used-car business from their workstation without your knowledge and without approval from any manager in your organization. Your manager fires this individual. Your company is considering legal action against this individual. What is the first thing you should do to preserve the chain of evidence?

A. Boot up the computer and copy all the files to a network location for further study.

B. Boot up the computer and format the hard drive.

C. Ask the individual to come back and remove all their personal files before giving the workstation to their replacement person.

D. Pull the hard drive and install it into another machine. Boot that machine and create an image of the hard drive for later analysis.

10. You are the system administrator for your Windows 2000 Active Directory network. The manager for the research and development area comes to you very excited. She has just hired a top research scientist who voluntarily left a direct competitor over a year ago. She immediately wants this individual to have access to your company's most sensitive research information. You ask your manager about this, and your manager okays your actions. What should you do?

A. Comply with the manager's requests.

B. Comply with the manager's requests but audit the actions of this new scientist closely.

C. Refuse the manager's requests on the grounds that your information may be compromised.

D. Refuse the manager's requests on the grounds that you suspect this individual is a spy working for their old employer.

11. You find that there is malicious code embedded inside the `word.exe` file on your user's workstations. Of what is this an example?

A. Trojan

B. Virus

C. Worm

D. DoS

12. You find suspicious code attached to an e-mail. One of your users has opened this e-mail, and now new e-mails with this code attached are appearing in other users' inboxes. You also are receiving e-mails from vendors and customers that they are being infected too. Those who have not opened their e-mail are not reporting any problems. Of what is this an example?

A. Trojan

B. Virus

C. Worm

D. DoS

13. What is the difference between a denial of service attack and a distributed denial of service attack?

   A. A DoS is implemented from a single source.

   B. A DDoS uses DCOM to distribute its attack.

   C. A DDoS uses multicasting to distribute its attack.

   D. A DoS is implemented from either a single source or multiple sources.

14. You discover a file called `root.exe` in the `temp` folder on your server. You've not seen this file before. You also are noticing a degradation in server and network performance. What should you do? (Choose all that apply.)

   A. Disconnect the server from the network.

   B. Update the virus definitions on the server.

   C. Scan the server for viruses and ensure that the server is virus free.

   D. Delete the `root.exe` file.

   E. Gather the CSIRT team and conduct a response.

15. You are the system administrator for a Windows 2000 Active Directory network. You discover that your servers are infected with the Nimda virus. Network and server performance has degraded to the point where no one in the company can perform any work on their computers. You take down the servers and call your antivirus software vendor for assistance. After discussing your situation with them, you inform upper management that all computers will be inoperable for at least 48 hours while you fix the problem. Your manager tells you to solve this problem in 24 hours or find another job. What could you have done to prevent this scenario?

   A. Assemble and train a CSIRT team.

   B. Gain upper management buy-in on response procedures.

   C. Obtain better training for yourself on antivirus methods.

   D. Ensure that all routers are updated with the latest firmware.

16. What is a countermeasure?

   A. A way to retaliate against an attacker

   B. Similar to a counter weight

   C. A way to mitigate risk

   D. A way to analyze an attack

17. Which of the following is an effective countermeasure against your servers being stolen?

   A. Bioidentity of those who enter the server room

   B. TCP/IP hardening

   C. Service offer minimization

   D. Using SSL on your websites

18. Which of the following is an effective countermeasure against known exploits for Windows 2000 Server?

A. TCP/IP hardening

B. Using SSL on your websites

C. Performing regular backups

D. Installing all software patches and hotfixes

19. Which of the following is an effective countermeasure against a DoS?

A. TCP/IP hardening

B. Using SSL on your websites

C. Performing regular backups

D. Installing antivirus software

20. Which of the following is a decoy designed to attract an intruder to keep the intruder away from your real production servers?

A. Decoy

B. Honeypot

C. Blackhole

D. Spidernet

Answers to Review Questions

1. **C.**   The point of this question is to ensure that you have some idea as to the big picture of developing and implementing network security in your environment. The correct answer is C because, in the big picture, you first write your security policies. Then, if there is an intrusion, you first respond and then restore services. Answer A is incorrect because you can't respond before an intrusion has occurred, and answer B is incorrect because you shouldn't restore services without some type of response first.

2. **A, B, C.**   Even though the intrusion detection software (IDS) is not reporting any unusual activity, there are significant indicators that your DNS and Exchange servers are under a DoS attack. This would account for slow Outlook experiences and the inability to resolve DNS website names with IP addresses. Moreover, one or more of your routers may be saturated with traffic, which would account for users being able to connect to each other without much difficulty. Finally, if this scenario were real, we would strongly advise you to either reconfigure your intrusion detection software or purchase something better. Most IDS software should be able to detect a DoS rather quickly.

3. **A.**   Some security events are created by information technology people who have not followed or who do not understand the security policies. The development of such policies also defines the boundaries of accepted and unaccepted behavior on your network and provides the background for what a security event is.

4. **A, B, C, D.**   All four answers are reasons for creating a CSIRT. When an incident happens, each team member can focus on a given area for analysis and evidence preservation. The combined efforts will mean a faster response time, a faster restore time, and a better chance of catching the intruder.

5. **D.**   Obviously, a UPS catching on fire is very rare (though one author of this book had it happen in real life…), but of the answers given, answer D most closely describes this type of a disaster.

6. **A, C.**   Offsite storage of your data is really the only way to best protect your data from a natural disaster. If a riot, fire, tornado, or some other disaster occurs, the best place for your data is *not* where the disaster is. Offsite storage in a secure building is your best bet.

7. **B, C.**   While the problem was resolved, the IT professional also violated the company's security policy, something that should never happen. If the user needed their account unlocked, it would be appropriate to use Terminal Services to perform this action, but to change the password for ease of logging in by the administrator to an insecure password is a clear violation of the security policy. Had the administrator not violated security policy, the password would not need to be changed after the issue was resolved.

8. **A.**   This person, while trustworthy, has several personality traits that indicate he is a potential hacker. Especially since he is learning basic networking concepts, you should be auditing his actions on the network and reviewing his hard drive from time to time. You might also want to run packet traces from time to time from his computer to see what he is up to. Also, in most states, you can read his e-mail to ensure that he is not engaged in any illegal activity.

9. D. Sometimes, booting a machine can change the evidence of wrongful activity. In this scenario, since this is a single hard drive, you should pull the drive and place it in another workstation that is already configured to run an imaging software package that can pull an image of the entire hard drive for future analysis. Of course, you'll also want to meticulously record who handled the drive and computer once the individual was fired.

10. B. There is nothing in the scenario to indicate that this individual is coming into your company with malicious intent. Clearly, there is a small risk here, but you should discuss that risk with your manager and then comply with their requests. However, if this individual did take employment for the sole purpose of stealing information, auditing and monitoring this individual's activities will reveal this.

11. A. Trojans embed themselves inside normal and legitimate programs. This code only runs when the program itself is invoked. Often, the program is also coded to replicate itself in some form or fashion.

12. B. Viruses attach themselves to other programs or files. When these files are executed, the code in the virus is invoked and begins replicating itself. Most viruses spread through the use of e-mail and should be closely monitored since their presence can result in significant damage to your most sensitive data.

13. A. The only difference, conceptually, between a DoS and a DDoS is that the DoS is executed from a single source whereas a DDoS is executed from multiple sources, usually in nearly simultaneous fashion.

14. A, B, C, D, E. This is an example of a worm that has landed on your server. Worms are independent files that travel from computer to computer across network connections. Chances are good that more than just this server is infected. In all likelihood, you will probably want to gather your CSIRT team and immediately start a response to this event. Other actions that you would want to take include the other steps listed in the question.

15. A, B. Notice that in this question there is an assumption that you are solving this entire event by yourself. It is also obvious that 48 hours is way too long for servers and workstations to be down while a virus is fixed. A team effort here, coupled with training and upper management buy-in, will ensure that a response to such a virus attack will be fast and effective.

16. C. A countermeasure is a way to mitigate risk by ensuring that all necessary precautions have been implemented to impede an intrusion. Tarpitting is an example of a countermeasure.

17. A. Requiring either a fingerprint or retina scan for entry into the server room is a good way to authenticate a person based on their unique biological makeup.

18. D. Known exploits for Windows 2000 are run against known vulnerabilities in the operating system. Installing all the latest patches and hotfixes will ensure that these exploits won't work when run against your servers.

19. A. The TCP/IP stack on a Windows 2000 server can be hardened so that it quits responding to a DoS attack more quickly than default standards.

20. B. A decoy designed to attract an intruder to keep the intruder away from your real production servers is called a honeypot.

Glossary

A

3DES   A more secure variant of DES, Triple DES encrypts each message using three different 56-bit keys in succession. 3DES extends the DES key to 168 bits.

802.11a   IEEE wireless networking standard using the 5GHz radio frequency band. Covers up to approximately 165 feet in distance under ideal conditions. Capable of up to 54Mbps data transfer.

802.11b   IEEE wireless networking standard using the 2.4GHz radio frequency band. Capable of up to 11Mbps data transfer. Covers up to approximately 300 feet in distance under ideal conditions. It is often referred to as Wi-Fi.

802.1x   IEEE wireless security protocol using EAP to send messages to authentication servers such as RADIUS.

Access Control Entry   An entry in the Access Control List of an object that specifies one or more user, group, or computer account(s) and their level of access to an object, such as Read, Write, or Full Control.

Access Control List (ACL)   The Access Control List contains the Discretionary Access Control List and the Security Access Control List for each object and resource on a Windows 2000 network. Each list comprises one or more Access Control Entries.

access point (AP)   Also known as a WAP, or wireless access point. All wireless clients connect to wireless access points, and the wireless access point either relays signals to another wireless access point or puts the packets onto the wired network.

access token   An object that is used to describe the security context of user-spawned processes. A token will contain the SID of the user account and all group accounts for the user.

Active Directory   A proprietary name given to Microsoft's X.500-compliant directory structure hosted by domain controllers. Active Directory is composed of three partitions: schema, configuration, and domain. Active Directory is a distributed, yet hierarchical database used to host user, computer, and group accounts as well as domain, application, and object configuration information.

Active Directory Sites and Services   The Microsoft Management Console snap-in that is used to manage the configuration partition in Active Directory.

Active Directory Users and Computers   The Microsoft Management Console snap-in that is used to manage the domain partition in Active Directory.

Anonymous authentication   Authentication as an anonymous user. Anonymous authentication is often used for web servers on the Internet when individual users do not have accounts on the server.

asymmetric   The opposite of symmetric. Asymmetric operations do not use the same processes in both directions.

asymmetric keys   Asymmetric keys are two keys that are used to perform opposite processes. For example, one key might be used to lock a lock, but it cannot be used to unlock it. The unlock process requires a different key. Asymmetric keys are used in private/public key pairs using for encryption and decryption.

attribute   A descriptor of an object. For example, an attribute of an object such as a user account includes the full name of the user. Another attribute is a permission or right associated with the object.

auditing   The process of recording a sequence of events on servers, workstations, and other networking devices. Audited events are recorded in one or more logs. The audit policy is configured in a Group Policy in Active Directory.

authentication   The process of verifying the identity of a user. For example, a user might be authenticated by providing the user name and password combination.

Authentication Header (AH)   An AH does not encrypt the data, but instead provides integrity and authentication for the packet. The AH contains several items: a Payload Length field, a Security Parameters Index (SPI) field that identifies a specific IP Security (IPSec) security association (SA), a Sequence Number field that provides anti-replay protection, and an Authentication Data field that contains an integrity check value (ICV). The ICV provides data authentication and integrity. AH can be used with Encapsulating Security Payload, which provides data encryption.

authentication methods   Processes used to authenticate a user. For RRAS, the methods include the following:

- Extensible Authentication Protocol (EAP)

- Microsoft Encrypted Authentication Version 2 (MS-CHAPv2)

- Microsoft Encrypted Authentication (MS-CHAP)

- Encrypted Authentication (CHAP)

- Shiva Password Authentication Protocol (SPAP)

- Unencrypted Password (PAP)

- Unauthenticated Access

authentication protocol   See *authentication methods*.

authenticator   A system or a device capable of receiving authentication requests and either responding with an allowed or denied message or passing on the request to another system or device.

authority information access (AIA)   Specifies locations where a user can obtain information about a certificate. The information can be found in LDAP directories, on web servers, and on file servers in many configurations. AIA needs to be specified for a certificate so users of the certificate can check information for the certificate.

auto-enrollment   The process of obtaining a certificate from a certification authority without having to specifically request the certificate. For example, all computers can be configured to receive computer certificates from a CA without having to use any specific interfaces to make the request.

B

Base64 Encoded X.509 (.cer)   Base64 was developed for encoding attachments sent over the Internet. All files that are encoded with Base64 are converted into ASCII format. Its purpose is to reduce the errors and corruption in transferring file attachments, particularly binary attachments through Internet gateways. All standard clients can decode Base64 files. It is provided for compatibility with other operating systems.

beacon   A broadcast of information. Wireless access points can beacon their configuration information to potential wireless clients.

C

canonicalization   Canonicalization is the process of making something conform to a specification. To canonicalize is to ensure that data conforms to canonical rules and is in an approved format. Canonicalization may also mean generating canonical data from noncanonical data.

certificate   An electronic piece of identification received from a certificate authority. The certificate contains information about the certificate holder, including the public keys used for signatures and encryption.

certificate authority (CA)   A certificate authority is a certificate server that has authority to issue certificates for security purposes. Some CAs are considered root CAs, while others, called subordinate, derive their authority from a root CA.

certificate revocation list (CRL)   A list of all certificates that have been revoked by the certificate authority.

Certificate Signing Request (CSR)   A file generated and submitted to a certificate authority. The file contains information about the requestor and is used to create the certificate.

certificate store   A location where certificates, certificate revocation lists, and certificate trust lists are permanently stored.

certificate templates   Templates used to define the role and capabilities or purposes of a certificate. For example, a user certificate contains the ability to encrypt data using EFS, to use secure e-mail, and to authenticate a user. Certificate templates save the certificate requestor from having to make multiple low-level decisions when requesting a certificate.

certificate trust list (CTL)   A list of certificates that have been signed by trusted certificate authorities.

certutil.exe   A command-line utility used to display information about certificates, to install and configure certificate authorities, and to manage certificate authorities.

Challenge Handshake Authentication Protocol (CHAP)   A challenge-response authentication protocol. The protocol uses Message Digest 5 (MD5) hashing to authenticate user identities. CHAP is an industry-wide standard used to authenticate non-Windows clients.

child server   Servers that have downstream or subordinate roles to another server are sometimes referred to as child servers. Upstream or root servers can be referred to as parent servers.

cipher.exe   A command-line utility used to display the current encryption status of files and folders and to alter the encryption status of files and folders.

client certificate mapping   A process used to map a certificate to an account in Active Directory. When a certificate is presented to a resource, the resource can use the mapping in Active Directory to identify the proper account to test for permissions and rights.

Common Internet File System (CIFS)   CIFS is a method for implementing a common file-sharing system across multiple servers. CIFS is a remote file system access protocol that enables users to share documents over a network.

condition   In remote access policies, a section that specifies states such as day, time of day, and security group membership that are evaluated to decide if the policy should be applied to the remote client.

Connection Manager Administration Kit (CMAK)   A tool used to build a service profile for remote access. The service profile contains all the files needed to create and install the remote access software on the remote access client and to configure the settings for the remote access user.

countermeasure   Anything that makes it more difficult for a would-be attacker to compromise the physical or logical security of a network. Examples include locks on doors, firewalls, security policies, the use of passwords, and shutting down unnecessary services.

CRL distribution point (CDP)   The CDP is a place or places on a Windows 2000 network where users and resources can check to see if certificates have been revoked. Every time a new CRL is published, it is placed in the CDP specified in the certificate.

Cryptographic Message Syntax Standard - PKCS #7 Certificates (.p7b)   A file format used to export and import certificates and the certificate chain. The file uses a .p7b file extension. This file format adheres to the X.509 standard.

Cryptographic Service Provider (CSP)   The algorithm used to generate keys and use the keys to authenticate, encode, and decode. Some providers offer stronger algorithms than other providers.

D

data decryption field (DDF)   Used in EFS encryption to store the symmetric key used to encrypt and decrypt a file stored with the encryption attribute enabled. The DDF contains the file encryption key used to encrypt a file and is encrypted using the user's public key. Only the user that encrypted the file can then decrypt the DDF and retrieve the file encryption key and decrypt the file.

Data Encryption Standard (DES)   Adopted in 1977, the DES is the official encryption standard for the U.S. Department of Defense. DES is based on a 56-bit key, and the chosen key is applied in 16 rounds of permutations and substitutions to each 64-bit block of data in the message. DES was cracked in 1997 by using the ideal processing cycles of 14,000 computers cooperating on the Internet.

data recovery field (DRF)   Used in EFS encryption to store the symmetric key used to encrypt and decrypt a file stored with the encryption attribute enabled. The DRF contains the file encryption key used to encrypt a file and is encrypted using the recovery agent's public key. Only the recovery agent can then decrypt the DRF and retrieve the file encryption key and decrypt the file.

decryption   The process of taking an encrypted file and decoding the encryption so that it can be read in its original format.

Delegated authentication   Delegated authentication occurs when a Windows service impersonates clients to access resources on the clients' behalf. The Kerberos protocol has a proxy mechanism that allows a service to impersonate its client when connecting to other services.

Demilitarized Zone (DMZ)   Usually existing between (logically) two firewalls, a DMZ is considered a neutral area that is not part of the local network nor is it part of the Internet. Servers are placed in the DMZ that should be accessed from the Internet but still need to be managed from locations on the local network. The DMZ prevents outside users from getting direct access to a server that has company data on the local network. The term comes from the geographic buffer zone that was set up between North Korea and South Korea following the United Nations "police action" in the early 1950s.

Denial of Service (DoS)   A form of attack conducted against a system or a network that occurs when a malicious user consumes so many resources on a server that few or none are left to service legitimate requests.

DER Encoded Binary X.509 (.cer)   A highly compatible certificate file format adhering to the X.509 standards. This encoding method is used for encoding certificate information and can be used to import certificates or export certificates. This encoding format is used by many certificate authorities that do not run Windows 2000.

desktop.ini   This file is used to customize a folder. You can customize folders to provide different views of their data and to apply special properties to the data in the folder.

Diffie-Hellman Algorithm   A method for passing information between two parties. The key agreement is not based on encryption and decryption, but instead relies on mathematical functions to generate a shared secret key for exchanging information in a confidential manner online. Diffie-Hellman works by having each party agree on a public value g and a large prime number p. Next, one party chooses a secret value x, and the other party chooses a different secret value y. Both parties use their secret values to derive new public values that are different from g. They exchange their new public values. Each party then uses the other party's public value to calculate the shared secret key that is used by both parties for confidential communications. A third party cannot derive the shared secret key because they do not know either of the secret values, x or y.

Digest authentication   An authentication protocol used to overcome many of the weaknesses in Basic authentication. It requires using reversible encryption for account passwords in Active Directory. Digest authentication is used to send cryptographic hashes of the password for the user account that are extremely difficult to break.

digital certificate   See *certificate*.

digital signature   Certificates used to prove the identity of the user or company. Often used for signing email or for code signing. Provides non-repudiation.

Directory Services   An application installed on Windows 95 and Windows 98 computers to allow the older operating systems to provide Active Directory awareness to the client computers. With the Directory Services installed, Windows 9*x* computers become aware of Active Directory sites, can use any Windows 2000 domain controller to change their passwords, and can select domain controllers within their site to identify DFS locations. This application also allows Windows 9*x* clients to use NTLMv2.

Discretionary Access Control List (DACL)   That part of the Access Control List (ACL) that can be modified using the Security tab in the resource's Properties dialog box. The DACL lists user and group SIDs that have access to the resource along with each SID's level of access. Each entry is called an Access Control Entry (ACE). The Deny Access permission is also listed at the top of the DACL. Together with the Security Access Control List (SACL), the DACL forms the overall ACL.

dynamic rekeying   A method used by IPSec to determine how often a new key pair is generated during a communication. IPSec sends communications in blocks, and each block can be encrypted using a different, new key pair. Even if an attacker obtains the whole communication, each block's key pair will need to be cracked in order to obtain the message of the communication. The exchange of these key pairs is made possible by the Internet Key Exchange.

E

Encapsulating Security Payload (ESP)   Encrypts the data of a packet and can be used alone or in conjunction with Authentication Headers (AH). In an IP packet, ESP is inserted after the IP header and before an upper layer protocol, such as TCP, before any other IPSec headers that have already been inserted. Everything following the ESP header, including the data, is signed. When ESP is used, the IP header is not signed and therefore is not protected from modification.

Encrypting File System (EFS)   The EFS is unique to Windows products and is a core technology of Windows 2000. It is used to store files in an encrypted format on an NTFS file system.

encryption   Encryption is the process of changing data from its native format to a ciphered format that cannot be read by unauthorized users.

event   An occurrence or lack of an occurrence that is noteworthy.

EventComb   A utility provided by Microsoft that will filter and search multiple event logs and coalesce the results for faster analysis and response.

Exchange Installable File System (ExIFS)   A method for exposing data held in an Extensible Storage Engine or Web Storage System database as a virtual file system.

exporting   The process of taking data from its native format and storing it in another format that can be used by other systems or applications.

Extensible Authentication Protocol Message Digest 5 (EAP-MD5)   An authentication protocol that uses a challenge-handshake authentication process that sends message digests through EAP messages to authenticate passwords. Typically used for RRAS authentication.

Extensible Authentication Protocol Over LANs (EAPOL)   A method for encapsulating EAP messages so they can be sent over Ethernet or wireless networks.

Extensible Authentication Protocol Transport Layer Security (EAP-TLS)   An authentication protocol used with certificate-based authentication. Smart cards use EAP-TLS to authenticate the user. EAP-TLS provides mutual authentication and is the strongest authentication and key exchange method in use for remote access clients.

extranet   An extension of the internal network or intranet that allows access for remote clients or partner networks. Usually involves connections over the Internet.

F

file encryption key (FEK)   A random symmetric key generated by the computer for bulk encryption of files and folders for EFS.

firewall   A system with special security configurations used to protect the company network from untrusted networks such as the Internet. A firewall is used to filter out undesirable network traffic.

G

Generic Routing Encapsulation (GRE)   A protocol used to embed a network protocol in another network protocol. It is often used in tunneling applications.

Generic Security Service Application Program Interface (GSSAPI)   An application program interface that is used for client-server authentication. It is included with most Kerberos 5 distributions, including the MIT Kerberos 5 distribution.

Group Policy container (GPC)   That portion of a Group Policy that contains computer and user configuration information.

Group Policy template (GPT)   The container in which administrative template–based policy settings, security settings, applications available for software installation, and script files are stored.

Group Policy/Group Policy Object (GPO)   In Active Directory, a method for grouping Registry configurations into a single policy that can then be applied to one or more objects to control user settings, computer behavior, and audit events on your network.

H

honeypot   A honeypot is a decoy designed to look like a production server but one that is really a server that can be compromised without any loss to the organization. Honeypots are designed to be attractive to hackers and keep them away from the real, production servers.

hotfix   Usually a small executable file that is distributed by Microsoft to fix a specific security vulnerability. The file will expand and then overwrite certain .dll and .exe files to fix the vulnerability.

I

IIS metabase   Registry configurations for Internet Information Service that are held in RAM for faster access and better response times.

impersonation   A process in which one computer or user pretends or acts as another through Kerberos delegation of the permissions. For example, a user might connect to a server such as an RRAS server and then connect from there to other systems using impersonation.

importing   Transferring information from a file or other storage into a different program or application or even a different computer.

Initialization Vector (IV)   The IV is a part of the encryption used in WEP. The IV is a 24-bit value transmitted in the clear.

Integrated Windows authentication   An authentication method using cryptographic exchanges of challenges and responses using Internet Explorer.

Internet Authentication Service   Microsoft's implementation of RADIUS in Windows 2000.

Internet Key Exchange (IKE)   Dynamic rekeying is made possible by the Internet Key Exchange. This service provides on-demand security negotiation and automatic key management between two computers. IKE provides a standard method for creating a Security Association between two computers and the exchange of keys so that each block in an IPSec stream can be encrypted with different key pairs.

Internet Protocol Security (IPSec)   A method for exchanging information between two computers such that different portions of the overall communication are encrypted using different key pairs. Packets are encapsulated or tunneled between the two computers using Layer 2 Tunneling Protocol.

Internet service provider (ISP)   An organization that provides connections to the Internet for its clients.

issuing CA   A certificate authority that issues certificates to users and computers on the network.

K

Kerberos delegation   Allows use of the same user credentials across multiple layers of systems or physical layers of an application.

Kerberos Key Distribution Center (KDC)   Only found on an Active Directory domain controller in a Windows 2000 environment, the KDC is a service that installs with Active Directory to generate session keys between domain members for authentication purposes. You do not need to install Certificate Services in order for the KDC to operate correctly.

Kerberos V5   An authentication protocol developed for use with multiple operating systems.

key management server (KMS)   Used by Exchange to provide keys for secure e-mail.

L

L2TP/IPSec   A tunneling protocol combined with IPSec to provide encryption.

LAN Manager (LM)   An authentication protocol used for older Microsoft operating systems such as Windows 3.11.

Layer 2 Tunneling Protocol (L2TP)   An extension of the Point-to-Point Protocol used for VPNs.

Lightweight Directory Access Protocol (LDAP)   An Internet standard for accessing directory information based on X.500 standards, but simpler.

Local Security Authority (LSA)   A protected Windows subsystem used to authenticate users onto the local computer.

log   A file that holds records of noteworthy events.

M

MAC filtering   Using media access control addresses that are assigned to hardware devices to control which computers may or may not access the wireless network.

machine certificates   A certificate assigned to a specific computer. See *certificate*.

Media Access Control (MAC)   An address encoded on most network devices that consists of an assigned number that identifies the manufacturer and a serial number assigned by the manufacturer.

Message Digest 5 (MD5)   An algorithm used to verify data integrity through the creation of a 128-bit message digest from the data itself. Because the message digest is derived from the contents, each MD is thought to be unique. MD5 is used with digital signatures. MD5 is the fifth iteration of the Message Digest algorithm.

metabase   A database that holds information about other data and other databases.

Microsoft Challenge Handshake Authentication Protocol version 2 (MS-CHAPv2)   An authentication protocol that provides mutual authentication through the exchange of encrypted challenge and response strings.

Microsoft Challenge Handshake Authentication Protocol (MS-CHAP)   An authentication protocol that provides authentication through the exchange of encrypted challenge and response strings. Considerably weaker than MS-CHAPv2.

Microsoft Graphical Identification and Authentication (MSGINA)   A dynamic link library that provides the logon prompt for Windows 2000 and then collects the user name, password, and domain name from the user logging on to the network.

missing event   An event that was to have occurred but did not. Sometimes, missing events indicate a security event or a security vulnerability.

N

Network Address Translation (NAT)   An Internet standard process that allows the user of one set of IP addresses internally for a company and completely different IP addresses for the perimeter devices exposed to the Internet. All internal addresses are converted to an external address before any information or requests are sent out of the network.

NT LAN Manager (NTLM)   An authentication protocol used primarily with Windows NT 4 and earlier operating systems.

NTLM Version 2   An authentication protocol used primarily with Windows NT 4 with the release of Service Pack 4.

O

offline files   Allow users to have local copies of network resources on their hard drives. While offline, off the network, users can open, modify, delete, and create new files that can then be synchronized with the network resource once the client computer is reconnected to the network.

Outlook Web Access (OWA)   Microsoft's web-based interface to the public and private stores on an Exchange server.

P

parent server   An upstream or root server. Parent servers usually have some type of root or authoritative relationship to other servers, termed child servers.

Password Authentication Protocol (PAP) A plain-text authentication method. The user name and password are transmitted in the clear without any encryption.

Perfect Forward Secrecy (PFS) When used with IPSec, Perfect Forward Secrecy determines how a new key pair is generated, not when a new key pair is generated. PFS ensures that a key used to encrypt a data block cannot be used to generate a new key pair. If a master PFS key is used for dynamic rekeying, the Internet Key Exchange will need to re-authenticate identities in order to generate a new key pair. This will add noticeable overhead on computers that use PFS to communicate.

personal certificate A certificate issued to the user and stored in the user's profile. See *digital certificate* and *certificate*.

Personal Information Exchange - PKCS #12 (.pfx) A file format used for importing and exporting certificates. This format supports the export of certificates and the private keys to a file. The private key can only be exported when the key is marked as exportable. The private key can be exported if the certificate is an EFS certificate or an EFS recovery agent certificate. This is the only format supported in Windows XP for exporting a certificate and its associated private key.

Point-to-Point Tunneling Protocol (PPTP) A tunneling protocol used in VPNs that encapsulates Point-to-Point Protocol (PPP) in IP traffic.

PPTP filtering A process used by RRAS servers to prevent the server from receiving and processing any IP traffic that is not related to VPN communications.

private certificate authorities Certificate authorities that are not available to the general public to request or verify certificates.

private key Half of the public-private key pair issued with most certificates. The private key is held and protected by the user of the key. It is not published or made available to others.

profile A storage location for many configuration settings for a user account. It contains many folders and files specifying how the computer desktop should be configured on a client computer.

Protected Extensible Authentication Protocol (PEAP) A protocol used for securely transferring authentication data over 802.11 networks.

public certificate authorities Certificate authorities available to the general public. Anyone can purchase a certificate provided they meet the requirements of the certificate authority when proving their identity.

public key Half of the public-private key pair issued with most certificates. The public key is made available to everyone to verify the user or computer.

public key cryptography The use of private-public key pairs to provide encryption and decryption as well as authentication by breaking the key into two pieces that work together. The public key is published and made available to everyone while the private key is held and kept secret. Actions taken with the public key require other actions to be taken with the private key.

Public Key Infrastructure (PKI)   Consists of protocols, services, and standards that support public key cryptography. A PKI consists of applications and services that use public-private key pairs provided by certificates issued by either public or private certificate authorities.

public-private key pairs   Asymmetric key pairs issued to the holder of a certificate. The private key is held and secured from others while the public key is published and made available to everyone.

R

recovery agent   Used to recover EFS-encrypted files when the user is not available to decrypt the files.

Remote Access Policies   Conditions, permissions, and profiles for remote users that control who can access the resources remotely, when they can access them, and what changes will be made to their profile while they are connected to the remote access server.

Remote Authentication Dial-In User Service (RADIUS)   Defines a standard used for maintaining and managing remote user authentication and validation. The new Routing and Remote Access Service (RRAS) in Windows 2000 can operate as a RADIUS client. This allows RAS clients and dial-up routers to be authenticated against a RADIUS server instead of being authenticated by a Windows 2000 domain controller.

replay   The process of capturing a session between systems and then retransmitting the session in an attempt to break in to another computer or trick it into believing the intruder is another person or computer.

roaming profile   A profile stored in a central location that can be accessed from any computer on the network.

root CA   The initial certificate authority that issues its own certificate. Other certificate authorities and certificates will be issued by the root certificate authority to support the rest of the certificate authority hierarchy.

Routing and Remote Access Services (RRAS)   A Windows service that provides access to LAN resources to remote users through dial-up or VPN connections.

RP-TNC   Reverse polarity threaded naval connector. A connector type used for external antennas on some higher-end wireless access points to improve their range.

S

seal   The process of encrypting data and data flows so that others cannot open the packets and view the contents.

Secure Multipurpose Internet Mail Extension (S/MIME)   A security standard for e-mail messages using public key encryption.

Secure Sockets Layer (SSL)   Also called Transport Layer Security, SSL is used to encrypt data at the Transport layer when that data flows between a web server and a web client.

Security Account Delegation (SAD)   The ability to pass security credentials from one computer to another. With each hop between computers, the user's security credentials are preserved. Kerberos uses SAD to provide better security. SQL Server 2000 fully supports Kerberos, including the ability to accept delegated Kerberos tickets and to delegate these tickets further (when running on the Windows 2000 operating system) with Windows 2000 domain controllers and Active Directory.

Security Accounts Manager (SAM)   A protected Windows subsystem used to manage user and group account information. Found in local resources such as domain member servers and network clients as well as NT 4 and earlier domain controllers.

Security Association (SA)   A Security Association is the end result of a negotiation between two computers wherein they agree on a key pair to encrypt their data, determine how the data will be tunneled between the two computers, and specify other session information. An SA must be established before two computers using IPSec can begin to send messages.

Security Configuration and Analysis tool   Provides a graphical interface that allows you to edit security configuration files. This tool allows you to import security templates and either apply them to the local computer or use them to analyze the current computer's security settings against those in the template.

security principle   A user, computer or group account that can engage in authentication and access resources in a Windows 2000 Active Directory.

Security Support Provider Interface (SSPI)   A security services API used for user authentication. Applications can use this API to tie to the Windows security model and use security services.

security template   A predefined set of security configurations that can be used to create a new Group Policy Object. Windows 2000 installs with a set of security templates, but you can use the Security Configuration and Analysis tool to create your own security templates as well.

Server Message Block (SMB)   The series of commands that are passed between two computers to execute file, folder, and directory commands.

Service Set Identifier (SSID)   The network name of a wireless network. All wireless access points have defined SSIDs to help distinguish them as belonging to a specific wireless network and to distinguish them from other wireless networks.

sign   Applying a digital signature to data or data transfers to verify the point of origination and that the content has not been altered.

signature   See *sign*.

single sign-on   The process of logging on one time and being able to access resources throughout the network, including resources on different operating systems.

slipstreaming   The process of upgrading a Windows 2000 operating system package of original installation files with updated versions of those files so that after the installation of Windows 2000 (or later), you do not need to install the latest service pack.

SMB signing   The process of inserting digital signatures into the SMB packets as they are passed back and forth between two computers. SMB signing verifies packet integrity and authentication.

Software Update Services (SUS)   Free software from Microsoft that is designed to download updates and hotfixes from Microsoft and then internally distribute these updates to all your Windows 2000–based (and later) servers and workstations. There is an SUS client that interacts with the SUS server.

symmetric   Processes that utilize a single key. Unlike asymmetric processes that require two different keys, a symmetric process requires only a single key to encrypt and decrypt a file. Many symmetric keys are simple passwords.

System Access Control List (SACL)   That portion of the Access Control List that contains entries specifying what actions and user, group, or computers accounts will be audited.

T

thumbprint   A hash used to identify a particular certificate.

Ticket-Granting Ticket (TGT)   A ticket issued to a user by the Kerberos Key Distribution Center (KDC). The user presents the TGT to the KDC to request session tickets for services on other servers in a network.

transactional file system   A file system that treats all processes as transactions that must be completed. If they are not completed, they are undone or rolled back.

Transport Layer Security (TLS)   A protocol used for secure communications over IP networks. The protocol is used to authenticate servers and even client computers.

Transport mode   As opposed to Tunnel mode, Transport mode ensures security from end to end. Since the encryption occurs at the Transport layer, routers can pass encrypted packets without needing to decrypt the entire packet.

Trojan/Trojan Horse   A malicious program or software code hidden inside what looks like a normal program. When a user runs the normal program, the hidden code runs as well. Trojans are normally spread by e-mail attachments.

trust relationship   A relationship between domains that allows user and computer authentication in a multidomain environment. Accounts can potentially be used from one domain while a resource may physically exist in another domain. User accounts and global groups created in a trusted domain can be given access to resources in a trusting domain.

Tunnel mode   As opposed to Transport mode, Tunnel mode provides security to a predefined point in the traversal path, but not necessarily to the endpoint of this path. For instance, Tunnel mode can provide security of a packet to the next router, but not between that router and the packet's final destination. Tunnel mode is normally used when security is provided by a device that did not originally generate the packets.

U

URL normalization   See *canonicalization*.

V

virtual private network (VPN)   A connection to an existing network from a remote location through private or public IP networks using encapsulated packets that are encrypted and difficult to decrypt by unauthorized users.

virtual server   A resource or resources that exists on a server that may have a different name or logical structure than the physical server.

virus   A piece of self-replicating code attached to some other piece of code. This code can be harmless or harmful, depending on what the developer wrote the code to do. The virus code searches users' files for an uninfected executable program for which the user has security write privileges. The virus infects the file by putting a piece of code in the selected program file. When a program that is infected with a virus is executed, the virus immediately takes command, finding and infecting other programs and files. Unlike Trojans, viruses spread either through program invocation or by e-mail.

W

war driving   Using a wireless network sniffer while driving around a neighborhood and capturing all wireless traffic and analyzing it for security failures. Building a database of insecure wireless networks.

web enrollment   The process used to obtain certificates from a certificate authority through the use of a web browser connecting to a web server.

web folders   A file system that can be accessed using a web browser.

Windows Update Synchronization Service   A service installed on each Windows 2000 and later operating system that can be configured to automatically download security and operating system updates and install those updates. As an alternative, there is server-based software, Software Update Services, that will internally distribute these updates.

Wired Equivalent Privacy (WEP)　The encryption specification that provides the same security to a wireless network that is provided on a wired network. In wireless networks, because the data is broadcast using an antenna, the signals can be intercepted, and, if not encrypted, viewed by an intruder to the system. WEP provides encryption services to protect authorized users of a wireless LAN from eavesdroppers by encrypting a data frame and its contents.

Wireless Access Point　A physical device much like a hub or switch used to connect multiple wireless systems together using radio transmissions.

Wireless Equivalent Privacy (WEP)　An encryption process used to secure wireless network traffic and provide similar security available on wired networks that do not use radio transmissions.

wireless LANs　Networks and network devices using radio devices to communicate with each other and pass network traffic between each other in place of network cables.

worm　A program that runs independently and travels from computer to computer across network connections. Worms can be distributed programs that have portions of themselves running on many different computers. Worms do not change other programs and do not attach themselves to other programs, nor do they rely on code invocation to spread.

Index

Note to the Reader: Throughout this index **boldfaced** page numbers indicate primary discussions of a topic. *Italicized* page numbers indicate illustrations.

F

T

X

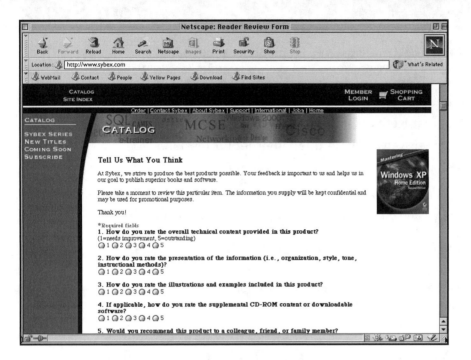

The Official
Juniper™ Networks Certification Study Guides
From Sybex

The Juniper Networks Technical Certification Program offers a four-tiered certification program that validates knowledge and skills related to Juniper Networks technologies:

- JNCIA (Juniper Networks Certified Internet Associate)
- JNCIS (Juniper Networks Certified Internet Specialist)
- JNCIP (Juniper Networks Certified Internet Professional)
- JNCIE (Juniper Networks Certified Internet Expert)

The JNCIA and JNCIS certifications require candidates to pass written exams, while the JNCIP and JNCIE certifications require candidates to pass one-day hands-on laboratory exams.

The Only OFFICIAL Juniper Networks Study Guides Are From Sybex

Written and reviewed by Juniper employees, the Juniper Networks Study Guides are the only official Study Guides for the Juniper Networks Technical Certification Program. Each book provides in-depth coverage of all exam objectives and detailed perspectives and insights into working with Juniper Networks technologies in the real world.

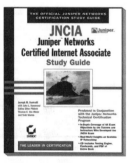

JNCIA: Juniper Networks Certified Internet Associate Study Guide
ISBN: 0-7821-4071-8

JNCIS: Juniper Networks Certified Internet Specialist Study Guide
ISBN: 0-7821-4072-6

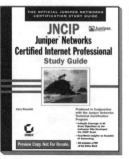

JNCIP: Juniper Networks Certified Internet Professional Study Guide
ISBN: 0-7821-4073-4

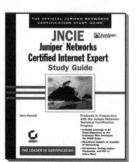

JNCIE: Juniper Networks Certified Internet Expert Study Guide
ISBN: 0-7821-4069-6

Sybex Offers the Complete Solution

The Microsoft® Certified Systems Administrator (MCSA) is a new certification from Microsoft developed to address demands from the IT industry for a mid-level Microsoft certification. No matter what combination of exams you decide to take, Sybex has the study tools you need so you can approach the exams with confidence.

MCSA Virtual Lab software
by James Chellis
ISBN: 0-7821-3030-5
US $199.99

**MCSA/MCSE: Windows® 2000
Network Management Study Guide**
*by Michael Chacon, James Chellis,
Anil Desai, and Matthew Sheltz*
ISBN: 0-7821-4105-6 • US $49.99

MCSA: Microsoft Certified Systems Associate Exam Requirements	
Pass ONE Client OS Exam	
70-210	Installing, Configuring and Administering Microsoft Windows 2000 Professional
	—OR—
70-270	Installing, Configuring and Administering Microsoft Windows XP Professional
Pass TWO Networking System Exams	
70-215	Installing, Configuring and Administering Microsoft Windows 2000 Server
70-218	Managing a Microsoft Windows 2000 Network Environment
Pass ONE Elective Exam	
70-216	Implementing and Administering a Microsoft Windows 2000 Network Infrastructure
70-028	Installing, Configuring, and Administering Microsoft SQL Server 2000
70-224	Installing, Configuring, and Administering Microsoft Exchange 2000 Server
70-227	Installing, Configuring, and Administering Microsoft ISA Server 2000
70-244	Supporting and Maintaining a Microsoft Windows NT Server 4.0 Network
220-201	CompTIA's A+ and Network+ Combination
220-202	
N10-002	
220-201	CompTIA's A+ and Server+ Combination
220-202	
SK0-001	

For a list of all Sybex products that will help prepare you for any of the MCSA exams, visit www.sybex.com.